the last mouthpiece

The man
who dared to defend
the mob

Robert F. Simone

Camino Books, Inc.
Philadelphia

Manufactured in the United States of America

1 2 3 4 5 03 02 01

Library of Congress Cataloging-in-Publication Data

Simone, Robert F., 1933-
    The last mouthpiece : the man who dared to defend the mob / Robert F. Simone.
        p. cm.
Includes index.
    ISBN 0-940159-69-4 (hardcover : alk. paper)
    1. Simone, Robert F., 1933- 2. Lawyers—Pennsylvania—Biography. 3. Mafia—Pennsylvania—Philadelphia Metropolitan Area. I. Title.
    KF373.S568 A3 2001
    340'.92—dc21   2001001333

Cover and interior design: Jerilyn Kauffman

This book is available at a special discount on bulk purchases for promotional, business, and educational use. For information write to:

Camino Books, Inc.
P.O. Box 59026
Philadelphia, PA 19102

www.caminobooks.com

This book is dedicated to the memory of my dear friends: Gus Braccia, John McCullough, Stanley Branche, Bobby Stone, Saul Kane, and Vince Pileggi, all gone but none forgotten.

ACKNOWLEDGMENTS

I started writing this true account of my trials and tribulations in the late 1980s as I walked and sometimes ran through so many minefields. I relied on my memory, conversations with several criminal lawyers and former clients, interviews with family members, trial transcripts, an occasional newspaper story, and several other reliable sources that I just can't identify. The large number of individuals makes it impossible for me to list them but I am grateful to all of the above.

I particularly want to thank Bob Hester and Bob Hauge for their much-needed encouragement and valuable early proofreading and edits. Jeffrey Merrick, a competent lawyer and a writer who will be heard from soon, did a masterful job in helping to prepare an outline and, more importantly, in guiding me through some much-needed rewrites. Also, thanks to all the guys at Nellis for taking their time, no pun intended, to read the manuscript and offer their suggestions.

I thank my buddy Matt for taking the time and effort to type the original manuscript. Barbara "B.J." Futty Shustock, my loyal former secretary and office manager, retyped and edited the original manuscript without remuneration. I am eternally grateful to her.

Jennifer Ellis stuck with me, often prodding me not to give up on this time-consuming project. Her moral and financial support got me through some tough times. Jack Scovil, my literary agent, stayed on board while many others abandoned ship.

The publisher, Edward Jutkowitz, was the only one who had the guts to legitimize this work and make my dream come true. I always did admire a gambler. I also thank the editors at Camino Books, Joan Bingham, Brad Fisher, and Michelle Scolnick, for performing the tedious task in such a professional manner. Special thanks to Michelle for that last extra read and edit as well as her help with the book's title.

Finally, I thank my brothers, Joe and Ron, and my children, Scott and Kim, for their love, loyalty, and support.

CONTENTS

PART 3

PART 4

Mouthpiece

1. *Oxford American Dictionary and Language Guide*: (A) A person who speaks for another or others; (B) A lawyer (colloquial, used in familiar conversation).

2. *Encarta World English Dictionary*: (3) Lawyer, criminal lawyer. Slang: a spokesperson.

3. *Webster's New World College Dictionary:* A person used by another person to express their views and ideas, etc. Slang: a lawyer who defends criminals.

PROLOGUE

I was a criminal lawyer for over 35 years. The question most often asked of me is this—"How can you represent someone you know to be guilty?" The simple answer—the presumption of innocence owed every criminal defendant and the proposition that no one is guilty until and unless a jury, or in some cases a judge, says so after a fair trial.

Every defendant has a right to competent counsel who has a sworn duty to zealously defend, rather than prejudge, his or her own client. Many dedicated criminal defense lawyers have paid an expensive price for protecting the constitutional rights of their clients.

Oftentimes they are deemed by the public to be as undesirable and unpopular as their clients.

A lawyer who represents an alleged drug dealer is called a "drug lawyer." One who represents an accused murderer is often referred to as "that greedy lawyer willing to accept blood money."

If you represent someone whose name ends with a vowel, you are more than likely going to be labeled a "mob lawyer." That tag has followed me around for years like some dime store perfume. I have paid a hefty price for my long-ago decision to take on the causes of the most undesirable and unpopular among us. I have not only represented but also in many cases befriended men and women with rap sheets, alleged dangerous propensities, and associates in deep shadow. This is especially the case when you consider that several of the clients you will meet here were reputed members and associates of the powerful Philadelphia La Cosa Nostra.

Allegedly, reputedly, purportedly.

You will hear these words often from me. Not because I am trafficking in rumors and innuendo here but because I've always viewed hearsay with great suspicion, always taken my clients' confidences seriously, and I will take them to my grave. I will not pretend that my clients were all altar boys or in the cement business, that every allegation made by the prosecution was fabricated.

You will read a lot about Nicodemo Scarfo, reputed to have been the boss of the Philadelphia–South Jersey La Cosa Nostra family, and how our association over the years played out in court and for a time on every front page. Like the thousands of jurors I've addressed in my time, I leave it to you to make your own decisions. Not just as to the guilt or innocence of clients ranging from the glamorous Lillian Reis to the infamous Scarfo, but whether yours truly at some point crossed some irreversible line.

The government does not like to lose. Most prosecutors win over 90 percent of their cases. Defense lawyers who do win often receive a motion to disqualify, barring them from continuing to represent their client. Should these lawyers refuse to withdraw voluntarily, they soon find a subpoena has been slipped under their door. They will be asked to testify against the client who has already confided in them. "How much money did you receive as a fee in this case?" is a question frequently asked.

Next, the authorities investigate the lawyer. Oftentimes a wiretap or other electronic bugging device has been placed in his office. Some of the clients are sent in wired to the gills to entrap their lawyer into saying or doing something illegal or unethical. The government promises to drop the more serious charges against the real criminal in exchange for cooperation. The end result is that the accused criminal no longer has need for the services of the lawyer.

To make matters worse, law enforcement people, including prosecutors, who are supposed to put people in prison, actually free them instead. Just about anyone charged with a serious crime can gain freedom and often a substantial cash reward by giving the authorities incriminating information, true or false, about a more notorious criminal or his lawyer. Government prosecutors free more criminals than all the best defense lawyers in the country.

It might strike you as odd that I'm still somewhat surprised and offended by all the assumptions that go with defending those accused of unspeakable acts of violence, racketeering, and all those impossibly convoluted conspiracies. Then there are the bodies to consider, found sometimes daily in vacant warehouses, floating in dank harbors or else stuffed in car trunks. I know that there are those of you who won't believe most of my clients deserved a defense, let alone the best one I could provide. The thing to keep in mind is my strong belief that every defendant deserves the best defense. And while some of my former clients currently sit in jail or have met ends as untimely as they were grisly, I can tell you that many of them were, and still are, my close friends.

My successes and failures in the courtroom, many of which are detailed here, play out against our government's war on organized crime, and crime in general, escalating every bit as quickly and illicitly as Scarfo's alleged spoils are said to have grown. At the peak of my career I became the prime target—four separate prosecutions leave no doubt as to this—with my own reputation, freedom, and livelihood very much at stake.

Of more concern, I believe, is the chilling effect my story might have on another person's right to counsel of choice. This has indeed been a dangerous walk through minefields, and the line I've walked has not always been an easy one. It is my hope that you will consider the basic questions of fairness raised by the many cases and dealings presented here, not just in terms of the accused, the mob client, and ultimately myself. As with my signature trial strategy, our government will find itself on trial here, and when I have finished I hope that no reader's sense of fair play will be left unchallenged.

Robert F. "Bobby" Simone

PART ONE

"Anyone can rat, but it takes a certain
amount of ingenuity to re-rat."

Winston Churchill

CHAPTER ONE

And You Get Paid for Doing This?

When I first walked through the front doors of Temple University's School of Law in September 1955, little did I know that I was taking the first step toward what I now know to be a dangerous profession. For as long as I could then remember, growing up in the predominantly Jewish neighborhood of Logan in the City of Brotherly Love, I desperately wanted to be a lawyer. Whenever I saw a courtroom scene in the movies and later on television, I always imagined myself to be the lawyer representing the underdog. From the time I attended Birney Elementary School through Jay Cooke Junior High and Olney High there was no other profession or business that interested me. If I had to make that choice now, knowing about the minefields that lay ahead, I would still walk through those doors. I might even run. I harbored those feelings during my first two college years at Penn State's Ogontz Center and my final two years after I transferred to Temple University. I guess I was just a city boy at heart.

While studying at Temple Law I had two major concerns. I needed to earn that law degree and a living wage at the same time. Even though I had worked every summer during my college days in Atlantic City and Wildwood, New Jersey, and one year in the Catskill Mountains in New York as both a waiter and bartender, the funds were just not there. Most of the money I earned, waiting on tables and tending bar, had already been invested and lost on a hot tip at the racetrack, or a sure thing, like the New York Yankees. It seemed like they only lost a game when I bet on them.

I was enrolled as a daytime student, but I soon learned that I could work during the day and take most of my courses at night. During the first year I worked as a substitute teacher, usually a couple days a week, and I drove a cab on a part-time basis for several months. I even sold ice cream off the back of a small, white Jack and Jill truck. I still remember how crowds of young kids would run to me when they heard the melodious sound of jingling bells. The street was empty just a few minutes before. Where did they all come from? When some of them did not have the money to pay for a cone of ice cream or a Popsicle there was no way I could leave the area without flinging a few free frozen treats their way. Once I lost my change bag filled with approximately $50 in silver. No, I did not misplace it, and it was not stolen. I lost it in a friendly, neighborhood poker game. Between the give-aways, my own sweet tooth, and the card game, I soon realized this was a job I needed like a hole in the head.

On many of those weekend nights I would tend bar at whichever drinking and eating establishment my father, Joseph F. Simone, owned and operated at the time. He was born in the town of Santo Stefano in the province of Cosenzo, in the region of Calabria, located on the toe of Southern Italy, and he immigrated to the United States in 1901 at the age of seven with his mother, Madalien, and older brother, Gaetano. His father, Dominick, had arrived in the States a few years earlier in order to find a job as a stonemason and a place for his family to live. Dad's early years in America were spent with his two brothers, his sister, and his parents in an Italian section in Northeast Philadelphia known as Frankford. He was only five feet seven inches tall, but he was a tough hombre. Although Joseph had to leave school in order to work and help support his family, he was an intelligent man who knew the value of an education and was mainly responsible for instilling that thought in the minds of his three sons—Joseph Jr., the first-born; Ronald, the youngest; and me in the middle. All of us graduated college and nothing made Dad prouder, not even being an injured World War I veteran.

Mom was born and raised in South Philadelphia. Angelina Amoroso was the oldest of three sisters. There were seven brothers as well. Mom's parents, Gaetano and Maria, were born in the northeastern part of Sicily just a few miles from Calabria across the Strait of Messina. Maria Campo and Gaetano Amoroso were born in two different towns in Messina Province but did not meet until after their families moved to Strasbourg, France. Several years later they immigrated to America with their two oldest, French-born sons. Mom left school at an early age so that she might help her parents operate their meat market. She also spent many hours daily looking after her nine younger siblings.

The freshman class at Temple Law started with approximately 100 students. By the end of the first year, 50 students either flunked out or quit.

The "A" in Criminal Law saved me from such a fate. Barely ending up with a 1.0 average, I looked forward to my sophomore year.

The second year was much the same — work during the day, classes at night. Betting on a horse or a sporting event made it all a lot more exciting. The craving for action and excitement played a big part in my gravitation to the courtroom. I discovered that it wasn't really necessary to attend all the classroom hours. I became a crammer. I managed to pass all of my courses by studying and reading just hours before the exams. I continued to earn enough money for tuition and books by working at various jobs which by now included acting as a recreation assistant at a city playground. During the summers I continued tending bar and waiting on tables in Wildwood and Atlantic City on the South Jersey coast.

My parents, Angelina and Joseph, seemed content to have me live with them in the two-bedroom apartment in Logan, a middle-class neighborhood in North Philadelphia. My brothers, Joe Jr. and Ronny, had already married and were securely living on their own. Outside of law school my living expenses were nil, excluding what drinking and gambling cost me. I did have a long winning streak betting horses and baseball games, and I was well on my way to becoming a compulsive gambler.

By the end of the second year of law school ten more students had dropped out, leaving only 40 of the original 100. I breezed by with a 1.04 average, right at the bottom of the class. Thanks to an "A" in Criminal Procedure and some exhaustive cramming, I was still eligible for the third and final year.

Just before that last year, I started a decent job as a claims adjuster at Allstate Insurance Company. The "good hands" people provided me with a new company car, a substantial salary, and an expense account. I was taught quite a bit about the law of negligence and torts while working on the job settling and denying claims. Actually, I cannot recall denying a single claim. The job and experience helped me get through law school and eventually pass the bar examination.

The last year sped by without any casualties. About 40 of us graduated. No honors came my way, but I did have a law degree. All that remained was the bar exam.

The exam was much tougher in those days. It was a two-day essay test with no chance for a lucky correct multiple-choice answer. Preparation for the bar exam required a six-week cram course. My experience in cramming came in handy. I spent the night before the test with my friends at the neighborhood bar. What started out as a cocktail and dinner ended up as an all-night load. We drank and partied until about 5:00 in the morning. None of the others who took the exam that morning was as loose and stress-free as I. This was not recommended procedure, but it worked for me.

I know in my heart that I received an "A" in both the criminal law and torts questions. I well remember the letter I received from the State Board of

Law Examiners. I ripped open the envelope, and to the surprise of everyone but myself, the letter stated that I passed the Pennsylvania bar examination. Approximately 20 of my classmates failed. Only 20 percent of the original freshman class passed the bar on the first try. I felt real good. I was ready to start my career as a lawyer.

Future events would provide me with many opportunities to apply my acquired legal knowledge and skills in the defense of scores of high-profile accused criminals. Unfortunately, Robert F. Simone would rise to the top of the dubious list. But before I could move to the next level there was a matter of required military service. Brother Joe had already completed his two-year hitch in the U.S. Army. Ron was exempted because of two severely banged-up knees he suffered from experiencing too many sacks while quarterbacking Temple U's varsity football team. My draft deferments were terminated and I received notice to leave for Fort Dix, New Jersey. Three years earlier I had passed my first physical. I could think of no reason to keep me off that bus.

The night before I was scheduled to leave, my buddies — Perry, Reds, Gus, Louie, Bones, Turk, Foxy, Jay, and the Goniff — threw me a bash in the same local bar in which I prepared for the bar exam. O'Donnell's was certainly a good-luck saloon for me. We were all surprised when I was rejected by another examining doctor and sent home because of a scar on my right leg caused by a third-degree burn I suffered when I was four years old. That was the first time I got too close to the flames — too close to the edge. It would not be the last.

I had quit my job at Allstate Insurance within days of learning that I had passed the bar. Returning the company car hurt more than the loss of the paycheck. Allstate gladly accepted my resignation. My first position in law was with Maximillian J. Klinger, who was an active sole practitioner with offices in the Robinson Building in Center City Philadelphia. He was engaged in the general practice of law. Most of his clients were injured plaintiffs, accused criminals, and bar and restaurant owners.

Max had represented my father in the purchase and sale of a few bars and restaurants, and he agreed to let me serve my clerkship with him mainly as a favor to my dad. I was paid $35 a week, no more or less than anyone else was paying for an inexperienced law clerk, and I was able to learn a great deal while working on many diversified and interesting cases. In addition, Max let me keep my own cases and build my own practice. In May 1959, I was admitted to the bar after clerking for six months.

In one of the first legal cases I remember, Max was representing an Indian wrestler who owned a bar. The man was accused of killing his wife in a jealous rage. I watched a smiling Max leave for court in the morning, impeccably dressed. After court adjourned, he would return to the office resonantly. His elevated mood made him appear and act as "high as a kite."

The few days that he let me accompany him explained the look, the feeling, and the high. It was the cross-examination that Max enjoyed so much.

He was great. He told me it was mostly a matter of preparation. I learned later that it is just as much a matter of being born with the talent. It is something that cannot be taught. You either have it or you don't.

Watching him set up and then destroy a prosecution witness made me wonder, *You get paid for doing this? I can't wait.*

When the jury retired to deliberate in the wrestler's case, I waited in the hallway outside the courtroom. I kept watching Max walking up and down, chain-smoking. His dark blue, double-breasted silk suit, light blue shirt, red and blue tie, along with his perfectly shined dark shoes, were in sharp contrast with the dimly lit hallway and the shabbily dressed courtroom observers, who also waited for the verdict.

The jury delivered a gift to both the defendant and the prosecution — guilty of third-degree murder, not guilty of first-degree murder. The dapper Max Klinger had performed well. The defendant was spared the death penalty or life imprisonment. Instead he would later be sentenced to ten years in prison. Not too shabby a result, considering the alternatives. The prosecution was saved from an embarrassing total loss, but they were not satisfied. They never are.

Within days of the verdict, the District Attorney's Office commenced their investigation of the sharp defense lawyer. They got lucky. In the haste and excitement of seeing his bar-owner client become a high-profile, criminal defendant, Max overlooked the Slayer's Act. The law prohibited anyone convicted of murder from inheriting any assets from the victim's estate. Since the Bombay-born defendant owned his bar jointly with his wife, he was precluded from using the proceeds of sale of the bar for his own benefit. It seemed that Max Klinger was paid his fee and costs out of those proceeds. The prosecutors, still pissed that they had not won a first-degree murder conviction, were now trying to get even with the lawyer who stymied them.

Fortunately, Max Klinger was able to prove that he had no criminal intent, and therefore he was not charged with any crime. He did, however, have to sweat it out for several months and return his entire fee to the victim's estate. He had saved his client's life and received no financial remuneration. In addition, he and his family had to worry about whether he would be prosecuted and perhaps sent to jail.

I couldn't help but think how exciting it all was, the trial and its aftermath. It still didn't dawn on me how easy it was for even a smart and ethical lawyer to get in trouble if he did his job too well. I would learn soon enough.

No matter, I now knew why I went to law school and did so well in criminal law courses. This was to be the major part of my life and just about everything else would have to play second fiddle. This was where the action was.

CHAPTER TWO

Lillian Reis—
Don't Call Her
"Tiger Lil"

The first two years or so as a lawyer found me working mostly on civil cases, both Max Klinger's and my own. Not very exciting, but I was learning and eating. I went to court whenever Max had a hearing or trial. I listened and watched and later asked questions. Max was patient with me, and he always answered and explained. He was an excellent mentor, the first of two.

I didn't realize I had so many aunts, uncles, and cousins, most of whom seemed to be accident-prone. Fortunately for them and me, it was usually the other person's fault. Within a few months I had a backlog of negligence cases. With the knowledge and experience I had from Allstate and working for Max, I was soon able to settle my first case.

The fee was around $3,000. Before the ink was dry on the release form, I was in a Plymouth showroom using my entire fee as a down payment on my first new car, a two-tone blue Fury convertible. Peter Gunn, the TV detective, had been driving the same model and color for a while.

My friends began to call me Peter Gunn. That didn't last too long. I soon totaled the car, fortunately without injury to myself or anyone else. It was the first of many cars to meet the same fate.

During those early years of practice, my friends and I used to frequent the Celebrity Room, a nightclub in the downtown section of Philadelphia near Locust Street that was brimming with bars and strip joints. The place was always crowded with everyone from small-time racketeers to well-dressed businessmen, each of them buying cocktails for equally well-dressed call girls, gold diggers, and secretaries with their glasses off and their hair down. It was also a hangout for undercover cops and entertainers; thrill-seeking, jewelry-drenched society types snapping silver cigarette lighters and trying to look bored, and the high-profile gangsters of the day, flanked by the usual wannabes trying a little too hard. Never a dull moment—you could people-watch there for hours at the odd mix.

The Celebrity Room featured top nightclub acts, mostly comedians like Dick Shawn, Don Rickles, and Joey Bishop. I found hanging out there not only entertaining but a good source of business. New people, new clients. I was enjoying being part of the nightlife of Philadelphia.

Lillian Reis was a tall, lean, raven-haired beauty. And while she moved around a lot in those days, she could usually be found at the Celebrity Room. A dead ringer for Ava Gardner through the Vaseline lens. Dark-eyed with high cheekbones, she was always dressed to the nines, always standing in the right light. The kind of woman who'd stare you down and make a grown man blush if he looked at her the wrong way. She was hands down the prettiest of at least five chorus girls dancing there every night, and there was no question that it was Lillian drawing the crowd. Her legs were indescribable, they went on and on and made me think of the velvet ropes cordoning off masterpieces in museums—not just their smoothness, but she seemed that unapproachable. There was also a certain danger to Lillian. Trouble followed her like a schoolboy with a crush. Exhibit A was Lillian's boyfriend, Ralph Staino, Jr., or "Junior" as he was known.

It was the beginning of the sixties and Lillian had purchased the Celebrity Room. She was now the owner-manager, leaving her place in the chorus line. Junior was in the club just about every night with several of his friends. They called him Clark Kent, and he was the spitting image even without the glasses. Junior helped Lillian manage the club, and was the reason many customers traveled from South Philadelphia to what had become the favorite watering hole in Center City.

Soon after the purchase of the Celebrity Room, in August 1960, Lillian and Junior were arrested and charged with a high-profile burglary and theft that took place in Pottsville, Schuylkill County, Pennsylvania, a haven for coal miners and gambling degenerates. The victim was John Rich, a local coal baron whose house was burglarized in the evening hours in August 1959 when the perpetrators cracked the large safe in his den. The cash inside was stuffed in pillowcases and carefully taken from the home late at night, while Rich and his wife were vacationing in Florida. The next morning Rich's son reported the burglary and theft to the local police. The original police report stated that approximately $3,000 was stolen from the safe. Months later, Captain Clarence Ferguson of the Philadelphia Police Department, working with the Pottsville law enforcement authorities, obtained warrants for Lillian, Junior, John Berkery, and Robert Poulson. Two brothers, Vincent and Richard Blaney, were known to have been cooperating with the police. The affidavits supporting the arrest warrants stated that approximately $500,000 had been stolen from John Rich's safe, far in excess of the $3,000 originally reported. Both Captain Ferguson and the IRS surmised that Rich only reported the loss of $3,000 since the other $497,000 had never been declared as income. The evidence, garnered mostly by Ferguson, consisted of statements by Poulson and the Blaney brothers directly implicating Lillian, Junior, and John Berkery. In addition, Clyde "Bing" Miller, a big spender at the Celebrity Room who lived in the Pottsville area, told the police that he set up John Rich by passing on the information about the cash in the safe to Lillian. Miller had a certain weakness for Lillian, it seemed, spending much of his fortune on expensive gifts for her. Like Rich, he had made his fortune in coal, strip-mining vast stretches of land, the earth left looking eerily like a war zone, barren and full of holes.

After being beaten and stabbed and left for dead in the front seat of his car, Poulson found some new religion, recanting his statement and going to trial alone in March 1961. Berkery and Staino were tried together in May 1961, even though the Blaney brothers never came to court to reaffirm their statements. The three were convicted despite the lack of substantial evidence and sent to prison soon after they lost their first round of appeals before the trial judge.

Lillian had retained John LaVelle, an experienced trial lawyer from Pottsville who was able to get her a separate trial. Her trial started in September 1961. The local and national media had a field day with the case. Due to a combination of Lillian's glamour and her wild sense of humor, the press couldn't get enough of her. At times it seemed they were more interested in what she was wearing than the facts of the case. Maybe it was that certain strut of hers, that bravado that brought to mind Mae West and occasionally Bacall, and beyond this it was not difficult to imagine that band of Irish thugs burglarizing at her whim. Then there were the bizarre facts surrounding the case, the conflicting "proof" about the safe's contents for instance, the victim swearing only a few thousand dollars were stolen while the state argued close to half a million.

Prior to the Staino-Berkery-Poulson trials, Vincent Blaney's bloated body washed up on a beach, and it was no accident, weighted down as he was with heavy chains. His death caused his brother, Richard, to testify for the state. It made no difference. He was blown up soon after, a bomb igniting when he started his car in front of his house. The newspapers and television newscasts were full of prejudicial pretrial publicity. The finger was pointed at Lillian time and time again, always referred to as a "showgirl" with one eyebrow raised. And yes, it was the strangest of coincidences, the timing of the Blaney brothers' deaths was as convenient for Lillian as it was grisly.

Despite all of this, Lillian's first trial ended with a hung jury, and she was free to return to the softer lighting of the Celebrity Room. The prosecution vowed to retry her. Meanwhile, Junior, Berkery, and even Poulson were cooling their heels in separate Pennsylvania prisons, where they continued to appeal their convictions and sentences. It was shortly after this that Lillian approached me at the bar of the Celebrity Room for some advice. She knew I was a novice, without much experience in criminal law, but she seemed to trust me and we would become fast friends.

Sometime between Lillian's first trial and the scheduled second trial, I represented her successfully in a routine personal injury claim. I couldn't settle the case, mainly because of all her adverse publicity, but I won a verdict for her, and she did collect a couple thousand dollars. She was satisfied with the way I tried the case.

Lillian couldn't afford to pay John LaVelle his substantial fee to retry the criminal case, so she asked me if I would represent her in the retrial in Pottsville. She said she would pay my expenses. I jumped at the opportunity. By then Lillian, Junior (who I visited in prison), and I had become good friends. It was a chance to help them both out and also build myself a reputation as a criminal lawyer. Then there were those legs to consider and the disappointment on her face if I declined. I've always had a hard time saying no to women like Lillian, which strikes me as terribly unfair—they've never had a problem saying no to me.

Lillian and I were both taking a risk. She was more or less putting her life in the hands of a young and inexperienced lawyer, and I was agreeing to represent her in what I knew would be a lengthy and hard-fought trial. And for no fee. I also knew that if we lost, I might very well get the blame and be relegated to handling accident cases for the rest of my career.

The fact that Lillian was willing to gamble with her life and freedom increased my commitment to doing all I could do on her behalf. I was determined to put everything else aside and concentrate solely on her case. I put my pending accident cases on hold. The few criminal clients I had were happy to have their cases postponed for several more weeks while I was busy in Pottsville. After all, if they don't try you, they can't convict you.

Shortly after I entered my appearance as Lillian's counsel, I filed a motion to suppress her alleged tacit admission. I had learned that the prosecution had read the contents of the incriminating statements of Robert Poulson and the Blaney brothers to the juries in all of the preceding trials. This was allowed under the pretext of the failure of each defendant to deny the statement when it was read to him or her. The trial judge denied the motion but the record was protected on Lillian's behalf.

Pottsville was about two hours away from Philadelphia by car. I had to stay there for the duration of the trial that commenced in March 1964. Commuting would just be too much. My wife of less than two years, Arlene, understood. She would come up for a weekend or two during the trial. On one such weekend our son, Scott, was conceived. At the time of this trial, I had tried only one previous criminal jury trial, a statutory rape case in Philadelphia. My client was acquitted. I was hungry for another win and couldn't wait to get to Pottsville.

Jury selection was scheduled to start at 9:00 on Monday morning. I picked up Lillian at about 7:00 on Sunday evening at her South Philadelphia row house. She lived only two blocks away from where Veterans Stadium was built a few years later.

I drove us out of the city, along the narrow, winding roads, past several rural farming towns and into the anthracite coal regions of Schuylkill County. We discussed trial strategy during the two-hour ride, finally reaching the Necho Allen Hotel in Pottsville. We checked into our rooms and agreed to meet downstairs in the bar and restaurant designed to look like a coal mine. The atmosphere was dark, and the walls were covered with a material resembling shiny black coal. I thought absent-mindedly of coal miners, collapsing shafts, black lung, and a constant craving for sunlight. Not at all unlike the doubts that must be overcome by every young lawyer on the eve of his first big trial.

We had just ordered sandwiches and some coffee when a stranger approached our table. He introduced himself to us as Bill Malone, a reporter for the *Philadelphia Daily News*. We motioned him to sit down. He told us he would be at the same hotel for the duration of the trial while he was covering it for his paper. As Bill waited for his beer, Lillian excused herself to go to the ladies' room.

The next morning's *Daily News* included a story citing the arrival of Lillian Reis and her new, young, and unknown defense counsel. Malone wrote that Lillian went to the ladies' room to fix her lipstick, suggesting that it had become smeared somewhere between Philadelphia and Pottsville. The implication was clear enough.

After reading the article, Lillian said, "It's not bad enough I have to face these phony charges in court, but now the newspapers are trying to get me in trouble with Junior." She also told me, "Bobby, don't worry about it. Just concentrate on the case."

When I saw Malone, I blasted him. Even back then my temper was pretty fiery. Lillian seemed to take it lightly. She had loads of experience with the press from her first trial. She knew that they'd write anything they wanted about her without regard to the truth, as long as it sold newspapers.

Strangely enough, Bill Malone—many people called him "Wally"—later apologized to both of us, and the three of us became good friends. We remained so for many years. Wally recently left us to become the ace reporter for that great newspaper in the sky. The handsome and muscular Junior laughed at the *Daily News* article even though he was still behind bars. He knew it was bullshit. His concern, like Lillian's, was the case. He was hoping that eventually they both would be exonerated.

The jury selection process stretched out for the better part of a full week. The state would start presenting witnesses and other evidence on the second Monday of the trial.

Given the death of the Blaney brothers and Robert Poulson's recanting of his statement, the proof against Lillian consisted mainly of the state's so-called tacit admission evidence. It seemed that after Lillian was arrested and confronted with the incriminating statements made by the Blaney brothers and Poulson, she refused to make a statement denying the accusations. Her silence, the prosecutor argued, amounted to a "tacit admission" of her guilt. The trial judge overruled my strenuous objection to this evidence.

The state also relied on the testimony of Clyde "Bing" Miller, who said he told Lillian about the huge sums of money Rich kept in his safe. He testified to many incriminating conversations he claimed to have had with Lillian prior to the heist. Miller received a no-jail sentence in exchange for his testimony, still the quid pro quo for the purchase of testimony by many prosecutors. The prosecution also sought to establish that Lillian purchased the Celebrity Room with $40,000 in "unexplained" cash shortly after the burglary. Lillian contended she saved the cash from generous tips and gifts given to her by her many admirers. Miller was probably the most generous of the group.

Probably the most potent weapon the prosecution had was the extensive prejudicial news coverage. The murders of the Blaney brothers were constantly referred to in the daily news reports. Again there were the press reports accusing Lillian of causing these murders to eliminate potential witnesses against her. While there was no evidence confirming these accounts, there was likewise no way to defend her against the power of the press and the prejudicial effect of the story they persisted in printing. The wide dissemination of these news articles could not help but contaminate the jurors' minds.

As with the first trial, every day Lillian's wardrobe was described in detail by most of the newspapers and television anchors. "The beautiful showgirl never wore the same outfit twice." Almost as an afterthought, my name and photo were appended. Little did I know then that the press would be a constant presence throughout my career, often tainting the process and my clients' chances for a fair trial, but sometimes to my surprise remarkably accurate and supportive. This would be the first of many cases to be tried in a fishbowl, something I'd have to get used to and learn to use to my client's advantage.

Every morning as we left the Necho Allen Hotel for court, several residents of the apartments across the street would be leaning out their windows, straining to catch a glimpse of Lillian. I also remember the scores of notes Lillian scribbled excitedly throughout the trial, passing them to me in plain sight of the jurors. The more I tried to stop her from doing this, the more she'd scribble and the more notes were coming my way. God, what a pain in the ass that was. And it had to be interpreted by the jury as evidence of her street smarts, her familiarity with criminal proceedings and yes, another indication of guilt. Beyond this it wouldn't be hard to buy the hard-boiled picture the state and the press kept painting of Lillian, one ear pressed hungrily to a millionaire's safe, pulling off one diamond earring first the way some women answer the phone.

The safe was gigantic, about ten feet tall, five feet wide, and two feet deep. It was rolled into the courtroom on a dolly by two uniformed court officers, an unexpected stunt. So this was John Rich's cracked safe, the door swung wide open and conspicuously empty. All eyes were glued to it, the jurors and even for a moment the judge, all those spectators in the courtroom and the reporters taking notes. Lillian looked at me as if to say, "What now, Bobby?"

I leaned over and whispered to her, "We'll bring in a stack of newspapers and cut them into the size of bills. You know, fives, tens, twenties. We'll put them in the safe and prove that $500,000 in small bills couldn't fit in there."

She leaned back, considering this for a few moments. Finally she turned to me and whispered with a smile, "It fits." I looked at her, incredulous. And with a grin she said softly, "Only kidding." Like I said, she had a wild sense of humor.

I'll never forget the elderly, white-haired woman sitting in the front row of the jury. She kept winking at me throughout the whole trial. Lillian and I took this as a good sign for us, commenting on it all the time. With every wink from that woman, we'd steal a quick glance at each other, our spirits that much higher.

While the jury was deliberating, Captain Clarence Ferguson came up to me. Ferguson, a Philadelphia cop for over 20 years, also had roots in Pottsville. It seemed he had two families, one in Philadelphia, the other in Pottsville, a possible advantage with the jury. He was a local J. Edgar Hoover, refusing to resign after reaching retirement age; no police commissioner or mayor dared to fire him. "You did a fine job, son," he said in a slightly condescending manner. "And it looks like you have that one juror. But you can't win. We have at least two jurors who'll never change their guilty vote."

As we left the courtroom, the coal-smothered sun squatting low on the horizon, I wondered which two jurors Ferguson had in mind. There was that winking elderly woman, I reminded myself, and one holdout vote for Lillian was at least enough to hang the jury.

As the writer John O'Hara once observed, Pottsville was a town as well known for its gambling as its mining. Illegal crap games, numbers, betting parlors, and slot machines guzzling silver in every dimly lit bar. I remember someone telling me that the local banks would call the bars when they ran out of change, and cigar boxes full of nickels, dimes, and quarters would arrive when the slots were drained. So in the middle of a gambling town with the stakes so high, it's odd how gradually it occurred to me that this case had been one hell of a gamble, a long shot. And if the courtroom was the green felt, then my career and credibility were the chips, Lillian's freedom the cash with which they were bought.

The winking juror was encouraging, sure, but there was also the matter of the incriminating statements and Lillian's refusal to deny them. And what to make of the disappearance of the witnesses, the Blaney brothers remembered daily in the local rags, one washing up on some beach lousy with fog, the other blasted with more dynamite than the local mines used in a week?

Who stood to gain more than Lillian, the jurors' exchange of glances could've meant, and how cold-blooded was this vixen after all? It was in the way the jurors kept sizing her up, that unrepentant showgirl over there appraising her manicured nails, her rumored conspiracies and knack for grand larceny, her silence in the face of such accusations, all of it flashed before them repeatedly as the lights on a marquee. And then there was the massive safe itself to consider, gaping open-mouthed at the gallery as Lillian entered the courtroom.

One thing was for sure. They didn't wear clothes like hers in Pottsville, and their hips sure as hell didn't swing like that either. If this was a drive-in, some of those jurors' faces seemed to be daydreaming, then Lillian had to be the black-and-white starlet, the silhouette viewed through the private detective's door. Complete with a one-way ticket to Buenos Aires and a loaded derringer in her purse, and all the while she's thinking double indemnity, that unsuspecting husband of hers, what a sap.

Maybe I should've taken it as a bad sign when the prosecutor asked Lillian to dance with him at the tavern one evening before the verdict came in, and to my surprise she'd actually said yes, extending one arm as though it was gloved. The music was sexy and low; it could have been something crooned by Sarah Vaughan, Lillian swaying on the tiny dance floor and the prosecutor, slightly inebriated, grinning hard. A little too hard, I remember thinking.

The next memory I have, the jury was back, my tie feeling a little too tight. The courtroom was packed, more reporters than usual. The jury convicted Lillian, a unanimous verdict. I remember being more surprised, and if possible, more disappointed than Lillian herself. There she was, facing God knows how much time behind bars and she was consoling me. We learned after the verdict that the elderly woman wasn't winking at me after all. She had some sort of nervous affliction.

Lillian and I considered it a partial victory when the trial judge set bail, enabling her to remain free pending appeal. The same trial judge had earlier disallowed bail on appeal for Berkery and Junior and they were sent to prison. Their lawyers mainly attacked the conflicting versions of how much money was stolen from the safe. Even though we'd lost the battle in Pottsville, Lillian still wanted me to represent her in the appellate court.

I felt strongly that the trial court was wrong in permitting her silence to be used against her, a violation of her Fifth Amendment right to remain silent, as unconstitutional as commenting on an accused's failure to take the stand. Equally unconstitutional in my opinion were the incriminating statements themselves. Recall that she was confronted with the recanted statements of Poulson and the Blaney brothers, men of shady credibility with rap sheets to prove it. And what of their motivations at the time? No doubt each man was desperate to cut a deal in that interrogation room. There was no opportunity to face her accusers in open court, never a possibility of cross-examining them.

I had several conversations along these lines with Junior, Berkery, and their lawyers, and I remained convinced that the tacit admission evidence was illegal and should not have been used against Lillian, Junior, or Berkery. None of us made any attempt to work with Poulson; none of us could trust him after he cooperated with the prosecution. After a long and exhaustive legal battle, stacks and stacks of briefs later, I had my chance for oral argument. The exchange in the trial court was heated, often louder than I'd expected. And longer—it went on for hours. I convinced the court that we were right. It was a complete turnaround. The judge who allowed the prosecution to use the tainted statements at trial reversed his own order and Lillian was granted a new trial. In 1965, he held it was an error for him to have admitted the tacit admission into evidence, a violation of Lillian's Fifth Amendment right to remain silent. Two years later, Junior and Berkery also won new trials on the same basis and were released from prison. They were never retried.

In 1969, ten years after the "Pottsville Burglary," the District Attorney of Schuylkill County decided not to oppose my motion to dismiss the case against Lillian. No retrial. Without the use of Lillian's silence and the incriminating statements, the evidence was deemed insufficient to proceed to trial. The cases against Staino and Berkery were also dismissed for basically the same reasons. They didn't have to go through another trial either.

My name had been highly publicized in the press during the entire trial, and more importantly, throughout the appeal and reversal process which took over five years. The original unfavorable publicity had come full circle. Often winning an appeal can create more new clients for a lawyer than winning a trial. In this instance, with Lillian Reis as a client, the publicity resulted in a deluge of phone calls from new prospective clients, most of whom were in serious trouble with the law. Overnight, it seemed, my practice had changed drastically. I was well on my way to becoming a criminal lawyer, and for the time being I was known as "Lillian Reis' lawyer."

▼ ▼ ▼

Before the retrial, the conviction, and the reversal granting a new trial in Pottsville, an enraged but still beautiful Lillian would resurface, this time pacing back and forth in my office like something caged. Tucked under one arm was a copy of the most recent *Saturday Evening Post* dated October 26, 1963. It contained an article entitled "They Call Me Tiger Lil." Freelance writer Al Aronowitz wrote the story of her life, naturally highlighting the Pottsville burglary. He'd interviewed several people, including Lillian and Captain Clarence Ferguson. By the time the story was edited and published there was no question that it was slanted to make Lillian out to be a vulgar woman in every respect. Ferguson was quoted as saying, "She cursed like a truck driver and drank like a fish." He also reputedly said she was guilty of looting Rich's safe. Imagine being branded a criminal with charges still pending, after a hung jury and only months before the jury trial was to begin. Most upsetting for Lillian was the title of the article itself, the derogatory label of Tiger Lil. It was never her nickname as Aronowitz had claimed, and the label was hardly a flattering one, conjuring up as it did some streetwise cupcake on a mobster's arm, chewing gum and reeking vice, something straight out of Sam Spade. Behind this there was the sense of betrayal, all along Aronowitz giving Lillian the impression she'd be portrayed in a positive light. I filed a lawsuit against the *Post* on behalf of Lillian and her two daughters, claiming libel and invasion of privacy. A lengthy, hard-fought trial would follow.

By the time the civil trial against the *Saturday Evening Post* commenced in 1966, the Pottsville court had reversed Lillian's criminal conviction. Lillian and I still wonder whether or not the prejudicial *Post* article influenced the jury that convicted her.

When my chance to cross-examine Captain Ferguson finally arrived, I was ready. I remembered how he'd rambled on and on in Pottsville, volunteering all sorts of statements helpful to the prosecution, an obvious effort to bury Lillian. Not this time, I said to myself. I was determined to box him in, to tear him apart if he started playing games with me. But to my surprise the cross-examination of Ferguson, star witness for the *Post*, was anything but confrontational. He continually denied that he'd made the disparaging remarks about Lillian to the writer Aronowitz. He was a cop merely doing his job, he explained, just investigating the Pottsville heist, that's right, everything by the book. Her guilt or innocence was a matter to be decided by the courts, not by him—just the facts, ma'am. He also denied ever making any comments about her personal life, never suggesting she was foul-mouthed or a drunkard. It seemed he had no interest in civil matters like this, especially after the satisfaction of Lillian's guilty verdict in Pottsville.

So Ferguson, the primary source of Aronowitz's information, went south on the *Post*. He couldn't or wouldn't confirm that he'd supplied the defamatory statements. When Ferguson left the stand, it was clear that Aronowitz and the *Post* had been hung out to dry, and it was poetic in a way, since they had done much the same to Lillian. Inasmuch as Ferguson's performance must have been a disappointment to the defense, I knew as soon as I started my direct examination that Lillian was going to make a sensational witness. Through her tears she decried the disparaging descriptions of her, explaining convincingly to the jury that she was too busy being a good mother to live the tawdry lifestyle the article attributed to her. How she loathed the name Tiger Lil and every filthy implication that went along with it. She especially resented the photos of her daughters in the article, she said, and how it had affected them in their school and home lives.

On cross-examination, the lawyer for the *Post* wasted no time getting to the Pottsville heist, truth as a defense his only hope at this point, and in memory it went like this:

Q. Ms. Reis, you just testified that you weren't involved in the Pottsville burglary and heist?
A. Yes.
Q. You were convicted of that crime?
A. Yes, but the conviction was overturned on appeal.
Q. And the charges are still pending and you're facing a new trial?

A. Yes, and presumed innocent like all other citizens of this
country.

"No further questions, Your Honor," the visibly shaken lawyer said
weakly, looking deflated, no doubt regretting the last confrontation. Lillian,
the picture of confidence, left the stand with her usual grace, the jurors' eyes
tracking her in a way that said, baby, we're yours.

While the case was eventually settled for considerably less, approximately five years later, the verdict in Lillian's favor was quite a victory, the
largest award to that date for a libel case in Pennsylvania: $1,850,000, the
foreman read to our delight.

▼ ▼ ▼

A year or two later, another well-known Philadelphia cop, Inspector Frank
Rizzo, sought and made headlines by harassing Lillian Reis and her nightclub,
the Celebrity Room. During one six-month period, he had police under his
command raid the club at least once a week. Several times, newspaper and
television reporters were on hand, their cameras capturing shot after shot of
Lillian, dragged out of the club in handcuffs and always dressed to kill.

I found myself in police court standing at her side, arguing successfully
that she'd broken no law. The phony claims that she served alcohol to minors
or overcharged her customers were continually dismissed. After several
attempts by Rizzo to get Lillian held over for trial in the criminal court, he
finally succeeded. She was indicted for stealing money from an undercover
cop who posed as a customer. He claimed he saw her take a $20 bill from his
pile of money on the bar. The bill was marked, and the officer said he found
it in her garter belt, calling Inspector Rizzo in to arrest her. Jesus, I thought
when she told me about it, was this a set-up or what?

The trial lasted eight days. One of Philadelphia's toughest judges, Leo
Weinrott, presided. He was a real law and order judge, and clearly a fan of
Rizzo. Fortunately, Lillian exercised her right to have a jury decide her fate.
Nine of the twelve jurors ultimately seated were African Americans. This was
encouraging since Rizzo, future mayor of the City of Brotherly Love, was not
well liked by Philadelphia's black community. Several months before the trial,
he'd forced eight black males to strip naked while they were being arrested and
frisked on a well-lit neighborhood street. A freelance photographer happened
on the scene. His photo of these naked men, standing with their hands on their
heads, appeared on the front page of both Philadelphia newspapers. Next to
them was the towering figure of Rizzo and several of his uniformed officers.
The photograph created quite a furor in black neighborhoods, another example
of Rizzo in action. No wonder he was nicknamed "The Cisco Kid." Of course I
had this incident in mind during jury selection. I must say that, to his credit,
Rizzo overcame this reputation later in his career.

As the trial proceeded, Rizzo testified that Lillian was drunk and disorderly when he placed her under arrest. He said he had a tough time controlling her, but that he still treated her with kid gloves despite her cursing.

Lillian took the stand in her own defense, taking her time, by now more savvy before a jury than many lawyers. I asked her if she'd just heard the testimony of Rizzo concerning her arrest and alleged use of foul language. "Frank Rizzo lied," she said, visibly upset. "He pushed me out of the club and shoved me in the wagon. I cried, 'Why are you treating me like this? I'm a woman.' He looked at me and said, 'Shut up, you black Jew. I'm going to treat you like I treat the rest of the niggers in this town.'"

I didn't have to look at the jurors to register their reaction. You could feel the standstill she'd brought to the courtroom, the accusing glares of the jurors, all eyes turning toward Rizzo.

The silence was reminiscent of a scuba dive at the bottom of the Caribbean; all you could hear was the breathing. This and the determined sound Lillian's heels made as she crossed the well, returning to her seat.

Shortly after closing arguments and Judge Weinrott's charge on the law, the jury was ushered out of the courtroom to begin their deliberations. The judge motioned to the DA and me to approach the bench.

"Mr. Simone," he began in an angry tone I hadn't at all expected, though all along it was obvious he was siding with the prosecution, "I was going to give your client probation. But since you and she wasted eight days of my calendar time, you can bet I'm going to send her beautiful ass to jail now."

Before he could finish, and he was clearly just getting started, the court crier walked over to the bench and said the jury was back.

"They have a question already?" the judge said, as surprised as I was.

"No, Your Honor, they've reached a verdict."

A verdict reached in five minutes is extraordinary in any trial, especially so after an eight-day trial. The foreman rose and announced in a clear, loud voice, "Not guilty." We'd hear these words another twelve times as the jury acquitted her of all charges. All of the jurors, mostly male, seemed to relish the opportunity to say these words directly to Lillian.

The courtroom was suddenly loud, a blur of spectators and reporters, policemen and courtroom personnel, all of them on their feet. Rather than leaving as I'd expected, each juror came over to embrace and congratulate Lillian and me. Frank Rizzo and his squad left the courtroom, shaking their heads in disbelief.

The feeling a lawyer has when he hears the words "not guilty" is tough to describe. The high is short-lived, but you never forget it. Especially in a case like this where your client is actually innocent. And there's no question in my mind about it—it's a hell of a lot harder representing an innocent client than a guilty one. While there are many who shudder at the prospect of a guilty person walking the streets, and understandably so, the thought of an innocent client being dragged off to prison has always been for me far worse.

CHAPTER THREE

▼

Hung Jury

My civil practice had grown to the point where I could no longer be of much service to Max Klinger, so a short time before Lillian's trial began in Pottsville, I left his employ. I stayed on at his suite and started to pay my own expenses. Every once in a while I referred him a serious accident case, which, if won or settled, would result in a referral fee for me.

Soon after, my good friend Ed Reif and I formed a partnership. He was a former assistant district attorney, an experienced trial lawyer, and a confirmed bachelor. The original plan was for Eddy to represent all of our criminal case clients because of his experience as a prosecutor. I was going to handle the civil cases. That's the way it started, but when the Pottsville trial ended I found my office filled with clients needing a criminal lawyer. It became necessary for me to refer most of the civil clients to Max Klinger in order for me to effectively represent the growing number of accused criminals I was now handling. There was just too much criminal work for Eddy alone.

People were flocking to my office mainly as a result of the vast amount of publicity I received from the Pottsville trial. Many of them were happy to tell their friends they were being represented by "Lillian Reis' lawyer." It was just like the old saying, "It doesn't matter what they write about you, good or bad, so long as they spell your name right." The fact that the jury convicted Lillian seemed to make no difference.

Every time I went to court, I found I was a smarter and better lawyer by day's end. I spent hours watching and learning from several excellent criminal lawyers as I sat and waited for my cases to be called. I made mistakes, but usually immediately after asking the wrong question, or one question too many, or making a confusing or illogical argument, a bell would go off in my head. I rarely, if ever, made the same mistake twice.

When you are representing someone whose life or freedom is on the line, you better not make too many mistakes and never the same one more than once. Money and property rights seem inconsequential compared to the stakes in a criminal proceeding.

The nature of the cases soon changed from the ordinary misdemeanor such as illegal lottery and drunken driving to more serious cases involving felonies like burglary, robbery, rape, and murder. The stakes were getting higher, much higher.

I also found myself defending some clients in federal court. There the atmosphere was totally different. It was much more formal and staid. The judges demanded respect. Most of them deserved it. A lawyer had to be well prepared, more concise and to the point in his cross-examination and legal arguments. Those who were not soon felt the wrath of the federal district court judges which often resulted in embarrassment and humiliation for the lawyer and worse for his client. For the most part, I was spared the degradation since I came to court prepared thanks to the teachings of Max Klinger.

In my first trial in the United States District Court for the Eastern District of Pennsylvania, I represented a former neighbor charged with possession with intent to sell stolen property in interstate commerce. I told the jurors the defense was stupidity, which in effect meant a lack of criminal intent. I argued, "This defendant shouldn't have to go to the state pen, rather he should be compelled to go to Penn State for an education." The jury was unable to agree on a verdict. A mistrial was declared. The judge called the prosecutor and myself to sidebar and managed to instigate a guilty plea agreement and a subsequent sentence of probation rather than prison for my misguided client.

One of my clients had recently been released from prison after serving a long sentence for a couple of bank robberies. He was on parole when he was arrested and charged with a recent bank robbery. The trial was held in state court. Two tellers had positively identified him as the sole perpetrator. I sent an investigator out to interview the witnesses.

In their statements to Bill Christine, my investigator at that time, one said, "He looks like the guy," and the other said, "He resembles the guy."

Christine was a retired police captain. He was a highly qualified and experienced investigator. The words "looks like" and "resembles" were in contrast to "That's the man," or "He is the guy that robbed the bank." These discrepancies, together with the fact that the accused was arrested the day after the robbery with only two dollars in his pocket, when the bank had been robbed of in excess of $30,000, were the basis of a "reasonable doubt" defense.

After several hours of deliberations, the jury reported they were dead-locked. To my surprise and delight, the judge immediately declared a mistrial. Some of the jurors were quoted as saying they had a reasonable doubt due to the statements the witnesses made to Bill Christine, and further, as a result of the defendant having such a small amount of money on him at the time of his arrest. The result of this trial was a good indication of just how important it is to conduct a thorough investigation before you walk into the courtroom.

The District Attorney's Office was understandably upset with the hung jury. In this instance there was a second trial. The prosecutor was prepared this time for the defense strategy, and unfortunately for the defendant, the retrial resulted in a conviction and a stiff sentence. You can't win them all. I once heard Evel Knievel say, "If you're going to drive a motorcycle often enough, you got to expect to fall once in a while."

The criminal cases kept coming and coming. I found myself in court just about every day. I continued work on Lillian's appeal. I was retained by an older ex-con to represent him in a guilty plea in New York, my first out-of-state case. By now I was earning enough to afford a house so that my wife Arlene, our son Scott, and I could live more comfortably.

My friend and partner Eddy represented most of the bar owners in the red-light district and just about all of the madams and hookers in town. He and I spent many nights together in the Locust Street bars and strip joints in the name of business and PR. The bar owners constantly raided by Philadelphia's finest were always in need of legal services. One such bar owner, Sidney Brooks, an acquaintance of Lillian Reis, had more than his share of grief with the police. He was soon to be my next headline client.

Just as my career and reputation seemed to be blossoming, I found myself under personal attack from an unlikely source. There had been some publicity about an ongoing probe of a group of personal injury lawyers being conducted by the Disciplinary Board of the Philadelphia Bar Association. Accusations had been made against 18 or 19 active plaintiff's lawyers. These charges dealt with alleged inflated and fraudulent medical bills and bogus lost-wage claims that were submitted to insurance companies to increase the value of personal injury lawsuits.

A retired Army lawyer, Colonel Jaffe, was retained by the Disciplinary Board to investigate and move to suspend or disbar the lawyers in question. He was highly recommended by the insurance companies and many of the blue-blood civil defense litigation law firms. He had previously succeeded in his endeavors in at least one other state.

The investigation was pending for several months when Colonel Jaffe and his staff had a meeting to discuss the status and procedures of their probe. Several of the staff attorneys commented on the fact that all of the lawyers who had received subpoenas notifying them that they were targets just happened to be Jewish. They were concerned about talk of unfairness and prejudice. It was suggested that they should add another lawyer to the list, one who was not Jewish. This would put to rest any claim of prejudice and anti-Semitism on the part of the inquisitors. They kicked around the names and legal backgrounds of quite a few non-Jewish lawyers who had been engaged in representing plaintiffs in accident cases.

When the name Robert F. Simone surfaced, it was easy for these overzealous investigators to add it to the list. The publicity and notoriety I had received from my criminal cases made them believe I would be an easy target. This group, looking to clear themselves of accusations of prejudice against the Jewish members of the bar, thought they now had a patsy. Most of the lawyers and much of the public had heard my name. It was the best way to advertise the impartiality of this legal inquisition, and at the same time camouflage their obvious anti-Semitic views.

All of the others being charged retained counsel to represent them in the proceedings. An older, experienced judge, Kendall Shoyer, who had a reputation for being both tough and fair, was assigned to listen to the evidence. The Board subpoenaed doctors' records, the clients of the lawyers, and the lawyers charged with the improprieties.

By the time I received a written complaint, many of the others had already chosen to plead the Fifth Amendment, and they refused to testify at their hearings before the judge. I could not figure out how or why I became a target. It wasn't until months later that I learned from a reliable source, a Philadelphia detective, about the meeting and the manner in which my name surfaced.

I decided not to hire a lawyer. I would go against the axiom that any lawyer who represents himself has a fool for a client. I also decided not to plead the Fifth Amendment and to answer all the questions. The lawyer assigned to prosecute my case was visibly surprised and shaken when I started answering the questions in open court before Judge Kendall Shoyer.

I fully and adequately answered every question. My answers and the total lack of evidence resulted in my being exonerated. It seemed that the doctor who treated my mother, Dr. Raymond Silk, had treated approximately 20 of my clients. I had referred most of them to him because he was not only a good doctor, but also he was willing to wait for the patient's case to be settled or won before collecting his fee. Most of my clients who were his patients would not have been able to afford medical treatment otherwise. The investigators assumed that I was referring people to Dr. Silk so that he would submit excessive fraudulent bills and that I would send them on to the insurance companies in furtherance of some illegal scheme to defraud them. It was an insult to Ray Silk, who treated scores of patients without compensation.

Judge Shoyer seemed pleased to see me answer the witch-hunting questions. I was the first and only targeted lawyer to do so. In a few months I received notice that I was cleared of any wrongdoing.

The probe fizzled out shortly after the ruling in my case. However, a few lawyers were suspended for varying periods of time. I still think of how easy it was to be formally accused of doing something illegal without any valid factual or legal basis. It was the first of many threatening experiences I would have with the "authorities." Fortunately for me, I had successfully walked through the first minefield without tripping an explosion.

The incident reminded me of something that occurred many years earlier while I was living in Logan. My brothers, Joe and Ronny, and I were just about the only gentiles living east of Broad Street, the Jewish section of the neighborhood.

Before high school, Joe and I played on the same neighborhood football team as our Jewish friends. There were about 15 of us, all Jews except for Joe and me. We had a game in Stenton Park, west of Broad Street, an area inhabited only by Christians. We were winning the game pretty convincingly. The further into the game we got, the larger the crowd grew. By game's end, just about the entire field was surrounded by fans and buddies of the losing team. The gun went off. We won. Within seconds, the now unruly crowd ran onto the field. They started jumping on us and beating us. Two of them grabbed my arms. Others came up and started punching me in the face. "Take that, you dirty Jew," is all I can remember them saying.

I was one of the smallest on our team. My brother Joe and several of his friends were bigger and stronger. They helped free me from the strong grasp of the sore losers. We all fought our way out of the park and returned to our own neighborhood east of Broad Street with a win and our pride intact. My buddies of the Jewish faith were not only much better at football than those other guys thought—they were a hell of a lot tougher.

When I was being hit and called "a dirty Jew," I couldn't very well yell, "Why are you hitting me? I'm not Jewish." I am glad I didn't even think to do that. Years later, when these older anti-Semites attacked me in court along with all the Jewish lawyers, I understood what was happening. Only this time I was better prepared.

CHAPTER FOUR

Invasion of
the Rats

Sidney Brooks was a handsome man, despite the large scar on the left side of his face. He wore it as a result of a vicious fight with another bar owner who was a fierce competitor, both in his business and as a womanizer.

Sidney, in his early forties, was about six feet tall, well built, and had the smooth voice of a radio announcer. He owned numerous bars on Locust Street in the red-light section of downtown Philadelphia.

No matter how much business these bars did, Sidney soon saw them close due to an unexplained fire that left nothing standing but the bare four walls. Brooks collected large settlements from insurance companies after the fires. There were so many claims that Sidney had to put his newly purchased bars in other people's names.

As Brooks' bankroll grew, so did his reputation as the premier arsonist in the area. Other bar and restaurant owners sought Brooks' advice. Many of them hired him to do the job they didn't have the balls to do themselves. He always obliged.

The money he made from his successful bars and prosperous arson was not enough for the greedy Sidney. He dabbled in stolen credit cards and then moved on to burglaries. When he was arrested, the newspapers called him "The Master Criminal."

Sidney sought me out for legal representation. He was facing a criminal trial in which his partner in a burglary flipped and agreed to testify for the state. The miserly Brooks went shopping for a lawyer as soon as he made bail. He wanted the best lawyer for the best price. He knew Lillian Reis. At one time he, Lillian, and Junior Staino owned and operated a bar in Atlantic City during the pre-casino era. She had recommended me highly.

I remember going to the Harlem Club on Kentucky Avenue with Arlene, Lillian, and Junior to see the 5:00 a.m. breakfast show featuring a young Sammy Davis, Jr. and his uncle and father. They were called The Will Mastrian Trio and they were hot. Everybody who was able to stay awake in Atlantic City till early Sunday morning would stand in line hoping to get in to see Sammy. No problem if you happened to be with Lillian and Junior. Arlene and I managed to be on the scene every weekend. It struck me as funny how Lillian, Ava Gardner's lookalike, used to tell me that Arlene reminded her of the beautiful actress Arlene Dahl. They were both named Arlene, both redheads, and both had remarkable, almost perfect facial features.

Sidney Brooks never went to the Harlem Club. He did not want to risk getting stuck with a check. He was one cheap son of a bitch.

Sidney's burglary trial was reported on the front pages of the Philadelphia newspapers every day. It was easy to discredit the informant on cross-examination. He admitted to committing at least 100 burglaries and thefts in the past. The District Attorney and the police had granted him immunity, and in exchange for his testimony against Brooks, he would be released from prison.

The jurors were unable to reach a verdict. A mistrial was granted. I personally thought it was a great result, but Sidney was not totally satisfied.

When Brooks was first arrested on the burglary charge, the police found and seized several keys from his pocket. One of them was for a safe deposit box in a bank in Northeast Philadelphia. Armed with a court order, the police opened the box and found exactly $100,000 in cash. The Internal Revenue Service was immediately notified. They sent an agent to the bank. Unbelievably, after counting the cash hoard, he merely put it back in the box and placed a red paper official seal over the lock. No one knows how many other safe deposit boxes Sidney had at the time.

Some months had passed when a well-dressed gentleman walked into the bank with a spare safe deposit box key supplied by Brooks. As he entered the bank, one of his confederates threw a brick that smashed the bank's large plate glass front window. Simultaneously, another conspirator drove a car onto the sidewalk, crashing through another of the bank's windows around the corner. The only two security guards left their posts and ran outside. "What the hell is going on?" the older one yelled.

The man with the key nonchalantly walked over to the unguarded counter and quietly reached down, grabbing the passkey from the hook on which it was hanging. He quickly moved through the bank, descending the one flight of stairs leading to the safe deposit boxes. He opened the gate and bars, which separated the boxes from the public, with the passkey. He inserted the passkey into the one large lock on the box, and at the same time he pulled the smaller key from his pocket and easily put it through the red IRS label.

It was like stealing candy from a baby. He emptied the contents of the safe deposit box into a plastic bag, closed and re-locked the box, turned, walked up the steps and out the front door of the bank unnoticed. All of the bank employees, including the two guards, were preoccupied with the broken windows. One act of vandalism and a reckless driver were more than enough diversion.

The bold entry into the vault and safe deposit box was not discovered until later in the day when the bank was about to close. It was almost the perfect crime. Things changed when the well-dressed perpetrator was arrested for other crimes and spilled his guts to the police. He ratted on Brooks and his fat, cunning friend, Sylvan Scolnick. Together they had planned the heist.

I shall never forget that early morning visit sometime in 1965. Sidney Brooks rang my doorbell continuously and loudly enough to awaken Scott, less than a year old at the time. Sidney could not wait to tell me how someone had stolen his money from the bank. He was pissed. Well, that was the impression he was trying to convey. What an actor. Scott, deprived of his sleep, was crying. Sidney took him in his arms, swaying him back and forth so he could silence the crying, giving him an opportunity to cry himself about his stolen $100,000. "What can we do about this?" he moaned. Before I could answer he said, "I want to sue the bank for negligence." Months later he did, but not with me representing him. What chutzpah!

On the eve of the retrial, Sidney and his 700-pound partner in crime, Sylvan Scolnick, came to my suburban home in Cheltenham. They claimed to have located the man who actually committed the burglary with the informant. They tried to convince me that this man was the guilty party and that Sidney was really innocent.

Sidney Brooks was one of those few clients I represented who wanted to control his own defense. I thought the case was tried the right way the first time. I also believed that the District Attorney would have a hell of a time convincing twelve jurors that Sidney was guilty. Another hung jury and the case would probably be dismissed.

Against my advice, Sidney and Sylvan insisted I put their new witness on the stand to testify he was the second burglar. Up to this point the retrial seemed to be going well, but once this obvious liar took the stand to tell his story, the jury was suddenly turned off.

I did question the witness several times before putting him on the witness stand and he swore to me that he was the guilty one, not Sidney. Whether or not I believed him was irrelevant. My client was protesting his innocence as he always did with me. Brooks continued to insist I use this witness.

He paid the price. The jury found him guilty, not because they believed the informant, but mainly because they disbelieved Brooks' new-found witness. The judge sentenced Brooks to ten to twenty years in prison.

The wealthy Brooks was permitted to remain free on bail pending his appeal and he did not waste his time. After personally researching the law on extradition he vanished from the Philadelphia area. He became a fugitive. With all of his millions intact, he arrived in Rhodesia in southern Africa, a country with no extradition treaty with the United States. The country has since been renamed Zimbabwe.

As smart as he was, Sidney couldn't help but continually telephone his few friends and associates in Philadelphia. Soon everyone knew he had taken up residence in Rhodesia.

The Philadelphia District Attorney's Office took every measure to have him returned. Sidney hired the top criminal lawyer in Salisbury, the Rhodesian capital. The counselor guaranteed he would be able to prevent the American authorities from throwing him out of the country. He asked for a fee of $20,000 to keep Sidney Brooks in Africa and out of prison. Brooks just couldn't or wouldn't part with that much money.

He was soon expelled from Rhodesia and put on an airplane bound for the States. Two county detectives from Philadelphia met the plane at the Johannesburg airport in South Africa when it made its first stop. On the long flight home, Sidney cut his deal with the pursuing authorities. He would give up all his criminal confederates in exchange for freedom and the right to keep his money.

The many bar and restaurant owners who hired Brooks to torch their establishments had reason for concern, and those who participated in the numerous burglaries with Sidney were now about to pay for their crimes.

Shortly after his return to Philadelphia, Sidney was brought from prison every day to the District Attorney's Office in City Hall. He was wined and dined in exchange for his cooperation. He admitted his guilt in the case I handled for him. He also admitted suborning perjury in getting someone to swear in court that he, not Sidney, committed the burglary in question.

He made the most out of his new alliance with the police and the District Attorney's Office. Sidney had full access to the office telephones on a daily basis. Brooks had the temerity to use those phones to extort large sums of money from his criminal associates. "Pay or be arrested" is what he told them. Many paid, many were arrested. Becoming a rat had its financial rewards.

He never threatened to extort me, but after about a month of debriefings, Sidney called and asked me to visit him in the District Attorney's Office. I had visited him several times before the call when he told me of his plan to bargain for his freedom. I walked in and saw him sitting comfortably behind a desk. He looked like he was running the DA's office, obviously enjoying a feeling of power. He looked at me and smiled, his white caps gleaming, and he cavalierly said, "Bob, I'm sorry but I can't make my deal unless I tell them it was your idea to call Mooney as a witness."

Mooney was the creep who testified falsely at the burglary retrial. I couldn't believe it at first. I said nothing, just turned around and walked out of the office.

In a couple of days, my name and picture were plastered on the front page of the *Philadelphia Inquirer* and the *Daily News*. I surrendered on a warrant charging me with subornation of perjury and obstruction of justice. I learned from the affidavit of probable cause that Brooks, his fat friend Sylvan Scolnick, and Mooney were going to testify against me.

Mooney was a small-time parasite who had a few burglary and theft charges pending in addition to the perjury case. He was immunized and granted freedom in anticipation of his future testimony against me.

Scolnick, on the other hand, was a career criminal. He had masterminded and set up scores of burglaries and robberies with and for Sidney Brooks. He also made millions of dollars in at least a dozen bankruptcy frauds. He set up companies, fraudulently obtained credit, and then purchased millions of dollars' worth of diverse goods. No sooner were they delivered at the front door than the goods were sold out the back door.

He, like Brooks, was facing a lifetime in jail. The local and federal authorities were more than glad to give him a pass to get me out of their hair. Brooks and Scolnick were not only promised freedom, but they were permitted to keep most of their ill-gotten gains. And they say crime doesn't pay.

Brooks, Scolnick, and Mooney concocted this absurd story that I solicited and then paid Mooney $50 for his false testimony. The police and the prosecutors must have known that only Sidney Brooks would be so cheap as to believe that anyone would accept such a meager sum in exchange for committing perjury.

I didn't have time to be frightened by the potential dire consequences of these most serious accusations. I was looking at years in prison and certain disbarment. I surrendered without the benefit of counsel. I knew that any decent criminal lawyer would have advised me not to make a statement to the press. And yet I believed it was imperative for me to do so. I had to say something to offset all the bad press I was receiving. So again I would act as my own lawyer—at least until I told my side of the story to the press and the public.

When I left the Police Administration Building, I was met by more than the usual number of newspaper reporters and photographers, along with numerous representatives of every television station. I proceeded to verbally blast the witnesses, the police, and the DA's office. I pointed out the criminal records of the so-called witnesses. I asked, "How can they use admitted perjurers to nail me?" I told them about how Brooks was using the DA's office to extort money from his criminal confederates. All of the news reports carried my side of the story. My relationship with the press corps remained on solid ground.

As I drove to my suburban home that early evening, I had the strangest thought. I actually felt relief that my father was dead so he wouldn't have to live through this disgraceful situation. I thought to myself, *this would kill him*. A few years earlier, when my dad was alive and well, he made no secret of how proud he was of his son, the lawyer.

Arlen Specter was the District Attorney of Philadelphia at the time. He assigned his top gun, Richard Sprague, to prosecute me. Choosing a lawyer for myself was no easy task. After speaking with several of the top defense lawyers in town, I retained Raymond Bradley. He was short, thin, soft-spoken, and extremely intelligent. He taught law at the University of Pennsylvania while he maintained an active criminal practice as a partner in Wolf, Block and Schorr, one of Philadelphia's largest and most prestigious law firms. I made the right choice.

At that time there was a criminal statute in Pennsylvania which prohibited anyone who had been convicted of perjury or subornation of perjury from testifying as a witness, except for and on behalf of himself. Mooney had admitted his own perjury, and Brooks and Scolnick had admitted their roles in suborning that perjury. If they were to plead guilty before my trial, they would be disqualified as witnesses. A guilty plea is the same as a conviction.

The DA's office, the police, and the FBI were too busy interviewing and debriefing Brooks and Scolnick on other matters to realize that my case was sitting idle for an unusually long period of time. After about a year, Ray Bradley filed a motion to dismiss my case on the grounds that I was denied a speedy trial. In addition, he alleged that the state had failed to move in a timely fashion to convict or accept guilty pleas from their three lying informers. Bradley also accused the state of purposely avoiding and stalling in proceeding against the three witnesses so that they would remain legally qualified to testify against me.

On the first day of my scheduled trial, Judge Emanuel Beloff heard legal arguments from Bradley and Sprague. He took the matter under advisement. Several months later our motion was granted, and the case against me was dismissed.

Specter and Sprague decided not to appeal Judge Beloff's order. I believe they felt that justice was served, and it really was not proper to use the likes of Brooks, Scolnick, and Mooney to convict, imprison, and disbar a lawyer whose only prior contact with the criminal courts had been as an advocate, not as a criminal.

Shortly after this Arlen Specter, later to be elected to the United States Senate, and Richard Sprague, who became a lawyer of national repute, played prominent roles in my escape from another very dangerous legal situation.

Brooks violated his plea agreement and went to prison for a few years. Scolnick had too much of a health problem for prison authorities due to his 700-plus pounds. He ate himself to death within a few years while enjoying his freedom. Mooney disappeared into obscurity.

At the time this matter was pending before Judge Emmanuel Beloff, I was a mere acquaintance of Leland Beloff, his son. Later, Lee became a client and one of my best friends.

I know that I was lucky to survive this harrowing experience. From that time forward there was instilled in me a genuine empathy for those unfortunate souls who found themselves sitting in the dock before judge and jury because of the word of some lowlife career criminal and the ambition of some overzealous prosecutor.

During this stressful time, I had the full support of my wife, Arlene, and my two brothers, Joe and Ron. But the incident that stuck in my mind is the time my toddling son, Scott, lying in bed with me, asked, "What happens to someone when he goes to jail?" Tears welled in his eyes.

Holding back my own tears, I told him not to worry. "Nobody around here is going to jail." I touched the top of his head, rubbing his straight, black hair, and added, "They don't put people in jail if they don't do anything wrong." You see, I still had not learned how the justice system really works.

On a lighter note, dear old Mom would call the office often, and whenever she was informed, "Bobby is in court," she invariably answered, "What did he do now?" What a sense of humor!

CHAPTER FIVE

▼

Usual
Suspects

At about the time of the Brooks episode, I became one of the busiest criminal lawyers in Philadelphia. The stigma of my arrest did little to deter the growth of my practice. No lawyer can win all of his cases, but I was on a roll, winning more than my share.

I represented Luther Fleck, a bartender, in the first loansharking case to be tried under a new federal statute in the United States District Court in Philadelphia. The two victims who testified for the government borrowed $20,000 from Luther to use in a new business. One was a waspish lawyer and the other a fast-talking, well-dressed businessman. Both were bad pay.

Fleck testified that he did lend them the money, his life savings. He admitted making verbal threats, but claimed he did not mean the violent things he said. He never intended to harm the debtors. He told the jurors he had served as a marine in the Pacific during World War II. He also testified he was now a bartender and had worked hard and for a long time to save the money he had loaned to these educated con men.

In my closing argument, I coined the word "borrowshark" and argued that people who borrow money without intending to pay are worse than loansharks.

The jury believed Luther and accepted my argument. In effect, I put the witnesses on trial. The government attempted to tie Luther to organized crime in Philadelphia. He was tending bar at the Friendly Lounge in South

Philadelphia. The owner was Felix DiTullio, known as "Skinny Razor," alleged to be a high-ranking member of the Philadelphia La Cosa Nostra family. The prosecutor and the assigned FBI agents insinuated that Fleck was lending mob money, not his own. They were wrong.

The trial judge, the Honorable John Hannum III, instructed the jury that they were not to judge credibility on the basis of the education and appearance of a witness. He further stated, "Just because the government's witnesses went to college does not mean they are telling the truth. And just because the defendant is a bartender, who looks and talks tough, doesn't mean he is lying."

The jury got the message and their verdict of not guilty was rendered in less than two hours. A few weeks later I learned that Judge Hannum was a former marine and that he highly regarded all of his "fraternity brothers."

One night, shortly after the surprise verdict, I was at the Friendly Lounge to visit Luther, probably to borrow money to help fuel my gambling addiction. I was sitting there drinking scotch, eating ribs, and talking to Luther and Skinny when in walked Angelo Bruno and Phil Testa. Everyone stopped talking, and all eyes turned to the two well-dressed men wearing dark suits, white shirts, rather ordinary ties, and of course both with shoes so shiny you could see your face even in the dim lighting of the bar. Bruno was reputed to be the boss and Testa the underboss of Philadelphia's La Cosa Nostra family. They came to speak with DiTullio. He immediately left Luther and me and walked with the two men down to the other end of the bar.

They huddled for a few minutes, whispering into each other's ears. To my surprise, Skinny brought them over to where I was sitting in front of Luther. I had heard and read a lot about these two men. Skinny merely said, "Ange, Phil, this is Bobby Simone, the kid who won the case for Luther."

Both Angelo Bruno and Phil Testa smiled and extended their hands. "It's nice to meet you and nice job," they said.

I said, "Pleasure to meet you and thank you." *Not at all like I expected. What gentlemen.*

That was it. They turned and disappeared out the door as quickly and quietly as they entered.

A couple of months later, a young Italian man came to see me. He said he was referred by "people from downtown." It wasn't hard to figure out what he meant.

He was one of ten men indicted by the "feds" and charged with running an illegal lottery business. My client's nine co-defendants all took their lawyers' advice and pled guilty. My guy opted for a jury trial. He was found not guilty despite the existence of hundreds of damaging wiretaps.

The electronic surveillance evidence consisted mostly of conversations between the co-defendants, some of which mentioned my client's name. He himself was not picked up on tape talking to anyone. The argument on his behalf was that the government failed to prove my client actually accepted or laid off any number bets.

After the trial, some of the other defendants complained to their lawyers that the evidence was identical in their cases. But for them it was too late.

During this period, I was going from one courtroom to another, one jury to the next. Most of my clients exercised their right to a jury trial. There were few guilty pleas, and fewer guilty verdicts. There was little or no rest and no time to celebrate a win or agonize about a loss. I found myself trying a series of murder cases in a short period of time.

First there was the young black woman whose baby had been scalded to death in the bathtub. The judge and the assistant district attorney refused to believe that she was an epileptic. They were both hoping to see the defendant convicted of at least voluntary manslaughter for causing her three-year-old daughter's painful death.

Her medical records were sparse and unconvincing. No one seemed to believe her husband's testimony concerning her previous epileptic seizures that rendered her unconscious. She was in serious trouble as I called her to the witness stand in a last-ditch effort to gain some sympathy. Her testimony might just sway one or two jurors her way.

Then it happened. Just as she was being sworn in, her left hand on the Bible, as she was raising her right hand, she suffered an epileptic fit. She fell from the witness stand, her whole body shaking and convulsing. Her own strange sounds were drowned out by the screams of the jurors and spectators. She appeared to be dying. After about ten minutes of her rolling on the floor, a doctor came into the courtroom to tend to her needs. No one, including Bette Davis, could have faked that scene.

The case was over. The prosecutor asked the judge to dismiss the case. He obliged with apologies to the poor woman and her frightened but loyal husband.

Alexander Hempill was the City Controller and a private lawyer as well. He was not permitted to try criminal cases because of his position with the city. Alex referred one of his clients to me. He was a well-to-do businessman who was charged with killing his wife.

One evening, as my client approached his house after a short walk from the neighborhood bar, he saw several police cars and an emergency ambulance outside his home. The client asked one of the cops why they were there. The officer replied, "I have bad news for you. Your wife is dead. She suffered carbon monoxide poisoning from the car's gas fumes in the closed garage."

He volunteered, "I know that. I helped her kill herself."

Earlier that night the police arrived at the scene in answer to an anonymous telephone tip. They found the man's car, with its motor running, in the garage, the door closed and a hose attached to the tailpipe extending into the car's front window. The victim, a woman, was slumped over in the front passenger seat. She was already dead from toxic fumes.

Soon after my client offered his rather foolish verbal admission, homicide detectives took him into custody and obtained a more formal and lengthy written statement, a confession, from him.

In summary, the man stated that for the past ten years his wife had complained to him that she was unhappy with life, her marriage, and her husband's drinking and absences from home. He went on to say that she asked him to help her kill herself every day. He continued to refuse her requests until this day. It wasn't that he couldn't take the nagging anymore, but rather, "I spoke to Jesus Christ and he told me to do it." He added that "I am Bishop Neumann and Christ told me what to do."

He admitted he put his wife in the front seat of the car, hooked the hose to the tailpipe, and strung it out into the front window. He started the motor and left through the garage, closing the door behind him. He went down to the corner bar for a few drinks and finished with "that's all I know."

On the basis of the evidence found at the scene and the defendant's verbal and written statements, the police charged him with first-degree murder. Now that they had a signed confession, there was little if anything else to do. The case was already solved, or so they thought.

I filed a motion to suppress the defendant's statements, claiming he was not legally competent to give a statement at the time. I argued that someone who says he is Bishop Neumann and had spoken to Jesus Christ must lack the ability, knowledge, mental capacity, and willpower to waive his constitutional rights to remain silent.

The motion was filed a few months after the incident and was to be heard on the first day of the trial. My client remained in jail without bail until the time of the trial. The police and prosecutors came to court confident that they couldn't lose. But all they really had were the statements.

Judge James McDermott started the trial. He said he would hear the motion to suppress later in the trial. A jury was picked and sworn in less than two hours. Halfway through the state's case, the DA tried to offer my client's statements into evidence. I objected. The jury was escorted out of the courtroom. The hearing on the motion would be held in their absence.

The homicide detective testified on direct examination to the facts surrounding the finding of the body. He went on to say that the defendant had waived all of his constitutional rights to remain silent and have counsel present. He then read the statement to the court. The DA said, "The Commonwealth rests on the motion."

Judge McDermott looked down at me and said, "Mr. Simone, you may cross-examine." I started, and it went something like this:

Q. Officer, do you believe the defendant's statement to be true?
A. Yes, but only the part about killing his wife.
Q. What does that mean?
A. I don't believe he is Bishop Neumann and I don't believe Jesus Christ spoke to him.
Q. Do you believe he believed he was Bishop Neumann and that he had a conversation with Jesus Christ?
A. I don't know.

Q. You can't tell the Court that he didn't believe those things, can you?
A. No.
Q. Did you or any other police officials take steps to have the defendant examined at about the time of his arrest to determine if he was of sound mind?
A. No.
Q. Has he been examined, from the time of the arrest until now, by any psychiatrist to determine his state of mind at the time his statements were made?
A. No.
Q. Do you believe he was mentally competent to understand the warnings you gave him?
A. I don't know.

At this point, the trial judge interrupted, "That's enough. Motion to suppress granted. Bring in the jury."

Once the jury was seated, Judge McDermott said to the prosecutor, "Bearing in mind my recent order, you may continue with your case." The DA, an older, white-haired man, asked for a sidebar conference. The judge nodded, "Yes, approach the bench." The following colloquy took place:

DA: Your Honor, we have no more evidence to present.
Judge: You have only proved that the woman died as a result of carbon monoxide poisoning. There is no evidence to implicate this man.
DA: We want to appeal your ruling on the motion to suppress.
Simone: I object.
Judge: This case is now on trial; the jury has been here for a couple of days. The trial will continue now without any postponements or continuances.
DA: Judge, we demand a continuance so we can appeal.
Simone: I object.
Judge: I demand you go back to your table and proceed at once.

The DA and I left sidebar and returned to our respective areas of the courtroom. Judge McDermott looked at the DA and said, "Please continue."

The prosecutor said with a hushed voice, "The Commonwealth has no other evidence," and then he said, "We rest."

I stood up, almost jumping out of my seat, and said, "The defense rests and moves for a directed verdict of not guilty."

The judge pounded his gavel and said, "Granted. The jury is excused."

As soon as the last juror disappeared out of the courtroom into the jury room, Judge McDermott said, "The defendant is released from confinement on these charges, and the no-bail order is lifted. However, he will be delivered to the proper authorities for a mental health evaluation for a period of 30 days. He is to be released only upon a finding of competency."

The defendant was released within two months. There was no longer any valid legal reason to hold him.

Over the next several months, I was constantly busy trying one murder case after another. A young male client of mine was acquitted of shooting and killing someone he said was prowling right outside his apartment door. The prosecutor alleged the victim was there to buy drugs. We claimed self-defense. The jury went our way.

Right before the verdict, the jury reported it was hopelessly deadlocked. I asked the judge to declare a mistrial. Fortunately, he refused, and in only five minutes the jury came back with their not guilty verdict.

A member of the Roofers Union Local 30 was alleged to have shot and killed a fellow roofer, who was sitting in the same automobile. My client testified that he had wrestled the gun from the hand of the deceased and that it went off accidentally.

An eyewitness sitting in the back seat of the car next to the victim testified that he saw my client with a gun in his hand immediately after he heard the shot fired.

I reenacted the scene in front of the jury, using a toy gun and my client and the witness as models. The defendant took the stand and told how he drove the shooting victim to the hospital. He dropped the motionless body in the parking lot and fled. He threw the gun in the river and then burned the car. After admitting his arson and destruction of evidence, he vehemently denied he intended to kill anyone. He, too, was acquitted but only after his first trial ended with a hung jury.

John McCullough, who was the rough and tough business manager and chief executive officer of the toughest labor union in the area, congratulated me. His union members were always in trouble with the law. He was glad that he and his union now had a lawyer they could trust and rely on when trouble arose. He promised me a lot of future work. He made good on his promise, and I never let him down. We became good friends and drinking buddies.

Aside from the general public, I now had the feared and respected Italians from downtown and the strongest union in the area looking to me for help and counsel when law enforcement people came knocking on their doors. The knocks came often, and I was there to answer.

"Skinny Razor" frequented the same golf course as I did—Iron Rock in Pennsauken, New Jersey—only a few miles east of Philly. One day we were playing in the same foursome with two friends, Paul King and Manny Oxman. Paul was the maitre d' at the Saxony Restaurant in Center City Philadelphia. Paul, a great host, was known for his remarkable sense of humor and quick wit.

Manny, one of the restaurant's owners, and Paul were using the same golf cart. I rode with Skinny. Both carts were stopped a few feet behind a large patch of hard, tan dirt that had absolutely no grass on top of it. Paul,

Manny, and I were sitting in our respective carts watching Skinny line up his second shot to the fifth green. Unfortunately, his ball sat right in the middle of the grassless plot. After a few easy practice swings, Skinny pulled his iron back and then swung it along with his arms and body. First came the loud grunt, and then the blade of his iron hit the dirt a few inches behind the ball. A mass of dirt flew forward 20 to 30 yards. The white golf ball moved only a few inches, leaving a six-inch-deep divot.

The three of us didn't dare laugh out loud. That is until Paul said with a straight face, "Yo, Skinny. If you swung any fuckin' harder, you might have dug up one of your victims."

Skinny turned his neck around, smiled, didn't say anything, and then addressed the ball again. He hit the shit out of it. Poor ball. But Paul was off the hook.

Later that day, Skinny asked me to represent him in connection with a subpoena he received to appear before a federal grand jury investigating organized crime. You know the bit, "round up the usual suspects." I convinced the U.S. attorney that DiTullio was suffering from serious heart problems and he therefore withdrew the subpoena. When I informed Skinny and also told him he didn't owe me any money for a fee, he promptly bought me the most expensive putter in the pro shop.

Unfortunately, Skinny was not feigning his illness. He passed away soon after, the victim of a heart attack.

CHAPTER SIX

▼

Justice Will Out

As the sixties were coming to a close, I lost my first murder trial. I had won seven or eight in a row. A jury found my client guilty of first-degree murder. Four others were convicted of the same murder in separate trials.

During the trial, however, the prosecutor made the same mistake that the DA in Pottsville made several years earlier. He introduced a tacit admission. He put a Royal Canadian Mountie on the stand to testify that when he arrested the defendant in Montreal, Canada, he read the charges to the fugitive. He went on to say, over my objection, that the defendant failed to make a statement denying the accusation. By this time I was somewhat of an expert in this area of criminal law. The trial judge reversed himself before sentencing and granted the defendant a new trial.

In the first trial, I had cross-examined the one eyewitness for over a day and a half. His prior criminal record, involvement with drugs, and inconsistent statements must have gotten lost in the lengthy cross. I changed my strategy the second time around. I spent less than an hour in the total cross-examination, zeroing in on only the important things. Again, I put the witness on trial.

The witness had given the police three previous statements. In effect, he said that he and the deceased were kidnapped, blindfolded, and bound at the feet and hands. They were taken to an abandoned house in North Philly and told to kneel down. Suddenly, the witness heard the loud reports of several guns. Four or five men surrounded the two men and opened fire. Unbelievably, they all aimed at the same guy. As the blood and flesh flew, covering the witness, he lay down and acted as if he, too, were dead.

Seeing all the blood on the two motionless bodies convinced the gunmen that they had killed both. Their mistake resurrected an eyewitness.

Fortunately for my client, in one statement, the witness had told the police that there were five gunmen. In another he said there were four, and in yet another he said there were only three shooters. If there were in fact three or four shooters, then it would necessarily follow that my client was not there. The jury was not convinced beyond a reasonable doubt, and my client was found not guilty. His mother cried when the verdict was announced. She kept hollering, "Thank you, Jesus. Thank you, Jesus." I finally turned around, looked at her, and said kiddingly, "You're welcome." Criminal lawyers, what egos.

One courtroom success after another brought favorable publicity, and thus more clients. My life in court became more important to me than my personal life. The more time I spent in court or interviewing new clients, the less time I spent at home with my first wife, Arlene, and my two children, Scott and Kim. My daughter was born on July 1, 1968, too young to really miss my presence at home.

I remember Scott saying he wanted to talk to me about something. He said it was important. "As soon as I am finished this case I am on," was my reply. After the same thing happened several times, Scott told me, "You are always going to be on a case."

He was right, and I knew it. Instead of going home at night after leaving my office, I found myself wandering from one mid-city bar to another. On off days I went either to a ball game to watch my huge bet go down the drain, or to the racetrack where the action was even faster. Drinking and gambling were my releases when I needed a break from the tensions of a constant heavy trial schedule. I was making thousands of dollars a week but spending and gambling twice as much. It was easy for me to borrow money at high rates of interest on the strength of future earnings. Too easy.

▼ ▼ ▼

Bill Malone stopped in my office one day. I thought he came to interview me about one of my up-and-coming trials. I was wrong. Bill was still a fine reporter with plenty of connections and sources in law enforcement circles. But above all he was a true friend. He came to tell me he had picked up reliable information that I was being investigated again by the Philadelphia DA's office and by the FBI as well.

He was worried and wanted to alert me. I immediately called Dick Sprague, the same DA who had represented the prosecution in the Brooks fiasco, and made an appointment to see him the next day.

I was told when I arrived that both the District Attorney's Office and the FBI had information that I was involved with an attempt to ransom some valuable stolen coins that belonged to the very wealthy Willis duPont. Without hesitation I told Sprague, the first assistant district attorney, and two county detectives of my involvement in the coin transaction. I explained that I was acting as an agent on behalf of duPont's investigator and that Joe Nardello was acting as my agent.

Several months before, a private detective from Miami, Florida, called me. Ed Stanton was both a private eye and a bail bondsman. "Bob, I am representing the duPont family in an effort to recover an extremely valuable coin collection that had been stolen in a robbery at their southern Florida mansion. I have information that these coins may be in Philadelphia." He added, "You know just about everybody up there who might have the coins or some information as to their whereabouts." Ed knew me as a result of my referring Lillian Reis to him to post bail in Miami when she was arrested for possession of one stick of marijuana. She would later serve two years for having just that one joint in her handbag. Unbelievable!

I didn't give his words much thought at the time. A couple of days later, Joe Nardello, a busy bail bondsman himself, came to see me. Joe, always well dressed, looked the part. He bore a strong resemblance to the ruggedly handsome forties actor George Raft. Joe came to the office to talk to me about the status of Paul Vargo's case. Paul was a client referred to me by Nardello only a week before.

Joe was a very proficient bondsman. If you had the money, you were out of jail immediately. Very few of his clients made it from the station house to the prison before their bail was posted. There were not too many thieves and burglars living and working in the Delaware Valley that he didn't know.

I mentioned the phone conversation I had with Ed Stanton. Joe said, "I'll keep my eyes open."

In less than a week, Joe came in again and said he heard about the robbery in Florida and that he might be able to get some of the coins back for the right price, but it would have to be paid to whomever it was who had the coins. Joe would settle for a piece of my commission.

In Joe's presence, I called Stanton in Miami and told him of this hot lead. After a few telephone calls back and forth to Miami, arrangements were made for Stanton to fly to Philadelphia to buy five of the stolen coins as a test run in the hope of having them all returned to Mr. duPont. They were part of the "Russian Collection," dating back to the days of the Czar, and they were valued at millions of dollars.

Stanton was going to give $50,000 for the five coins. It was supposed to be a good-will transaction. If everything worked out okay, arrangements would be made to recover the balance of the rare and expensive coins.

Stanton arrived on a late flight from Miami. I picked him up at the airport and drove him immediately to a designated secret hotel to protect the hoard of cash he carried with him. After he checked in, he and I had a drink in the bar. He then told me his wife was on the same plane and that she, not he, had actually carried the $50,000. *The son of a bitch didn't trust me,* I thought.

I showed him where my office was located in the Robinson Building at 15th and Chestnut Streets. He would come there the next morning to arrange for the swap.

Early that morning, after Stanton arrived at my office, I asked him if he had anything in writing to show that he was actually working for the duPont family. He quickly opened up his attaché case and pulled out a two-page typewritten document attached to a blue, legal-type backer.

I read it carefully and noted that Willis duPont had signed the bottom of the second page. It was an agreement between Stanton and the duPonts that provided that Stanton was working on their behalf to recover the stolen coins. He was to receive 10 percent of the value of any coins recovered. I thought to myself, *he doesn't trust me, so I better not trust him.* I said, "I need something in writing signed by you certifying that I am working for you in the pursuit of these coins."

He agreed. I promptly prepared a handwritten agreement stating that I was working on behalf of Stanton and the duPonts, and further, that Stanton and I would share any fee he received for any coins I helped get back.

We both signed the document. I made copies of the agreements and gave one to him and stapled the other to his agreement with duPont.

Later that day, Joe Nardello brought the five coins to my office. Stanton brought a numismatist with him. The coins were examined and orally certified. Stanton gave Nardello the $50,000 in cash. Nardello left my office first. Then Stanton and the coin expert departed ten minutes later.

I explained all of this to Dick Sprague and his associates. I gave them a copy of the written agreements. They took a couple of minutes examining the documents. Then Sprague looked at me and said, "Bobby, it seems to me you did nothing illegal, and I will not take any action against you. But how the hell could you get involved in this after being arrested in the Sidney Brooks matter?"

I answered, "You yourself just said I didn't do anything illegal. I have to earn a living, and I am a criminal lawyer."

Sprague went on to tell me how his office and the FBI were monitoring the entire transaction from start to finish. He further told me that Stanton was working both for the duPonts and with the FBI. He asked me about Nardello's involvement, and I told him that I showed Joe my written agreement and that as far as I was concerned, he was working as my agent—just as I was working as Stanton's agent. My agreement with Joe was that he and I would share any fee I was to receive from Stanton and the duPonts.

The very next day two FBI agents came to my office with a warrant of arrest charging me with receipt of stolen property in interstate commerce. I was taken to the federal courthouse, fingerprinted, and photographed.

I was brought before federal magistrate Tullio Leomporra for a bail arraignment. The mid-size courtroom was full. There weren't enough seats for all the media people from newspapers and television and radio stations.

The magistrate announced, "The United States versus Robert F. Simone."

I stood alone at the bar of the court. Leomporra said, "I am sorry to see you here as a defendant."

I replied, "Justice will out!" The headline for the evening news.

I was released on my own recognizance to appear at a hearing the following week. Again, my photograph and name were plastered all over the newspapers and TV newscasts.

Arlen Specter, who was still the District Attorney of Philadelphia, and Richard Sprague, his first assistant, told the reporters I should not have been arrested. The headlines read, "Specter Says Simone Gets Bum Rap." Sprague volunteered to testify as my witness at the coming hearing.

The federal law enforcement people were licking their chops. They were now in a position to nail that smart-ass lawyer, Bobby Simone.

I called Stanton in Miami to ask him if he was a witness against me. He said, "No, as a matter of fact the feds don't want me near Philadelphia when your hearing goes on."

Stanton showed me he wasn't all bad when he agreed to come to Philly and testify on my behalf at his own expense.

Both Ed Stanton and Dick Sprague appeared to testify on my behalf. An FBI agent testified to what he knew from wiretaps and surveillance of Stanton and me. There was no other evidence.

My old mentor, Max Klinger, who was representing me at the hearing, asked Stanton to explain my innocent involvement in the whole affair. He then asked Stanton to produce our written agreement proving that I was working with him on behalf of the duPonts.

Sprague then testified that his investigation revealed no criminality on my part. Fortunately, the Assistant United States Attorney wasn't sharp enough to object to Sprague's testimony. It was clearly inadmissible as it was nonfactual and amounted to being a conclusion. He was just too overcome by the carnival atmosphere that always seemed to surface whenever I appeared in court as a defendant or an advocate.

Magistrate Leomporra took no time in ordering the case dismissed. He released me in a most apologetic manner. It was certainly the correct legal thing to do.

Joe Nardello was later arrested by the DA's office. The prosecution did not want me as their witness, and why should they? However, I did testify as a defense witness. Nardello was convicted by a jury of receiving stolen goods, but the judge acknowledged the weakness of the case when he sentenced Joe to probation rather than prison.

The remaining coins were never found. No one would take the risk of helping the duPonts or Stanton retrieve the multimillion-dollar collection. The FBI and many career federal prosecutors would harbor a grudge against me forever.

CHAPTER SEVEN

Making Friends for Life

Frank Sindone, a friend of Angelo Bruno, was lending money to many people who needed it fast. The approval for a bank loan involved too much red tape and took too many days. Frank was tall—about six-three—slender and mean-looking despite his constant grin. He said few words, but often they were gems of dry humor. He had a sarcastic wit about him, but on occasion he could sound tough to the point of being frightening. John Berkery of Pottsville fame introduced me to him on one of those dark days when I needed instant cash to pay a few bookmakers. I was already at my limit with my three sharks. If I did not find a new source now I would be shut off from betting, a rough proposition for me during football season. Sindone obliged and from that day on I never lacked for cash in my pocket to spend or gamble.

One day, Frank Sindone called my office. It was not my day to pay on the loan, so I saw no need to duck the call. "Bobby, I am at the FBI office. I need you to get me the fuck out of here," Frank said very seriously.

"Let me talk to the agent who arrested you."

There were two seconds of silence and then I heard, "Special Agent Haggerty here. What do you want?"

I identified myself and was told Frank and a few others were arrested on a complaint and warrant charging extortionate extensions of credit transactions—loansharking. A preliminary hearing was scheduled for 1:00 p.m. the same day. Within minutes I hopped a cab to the federal courthouse, and I waited outside the magistrate's courtroom for Frank and the others to arrive.

The elevator door opened on the second floor of the courthouse and out stepped six men. Three of them had their hands cuffed behind their backs. The first off the elevator was Frank. A shorter, stockier, pock-faced man followed him. I recognized him immediately as Phil Testa, one of the men I had met a few years earlier at the Friendly Lounge. I did not know the third gentleman wearing cuffs. The three others were FBI agents. Once inside the small courtroom the agents removed the handcuffs.

I spoke to Frank and the other defendants for a few minutes before the hearing. Frank introduced me to Testa. He probably did not know that I had already met him. When Phil smiled as we shook hands, I was sure he remembered me from the Friendly Lounge. He was extremely cordial and calm. Frank introduced me to the third gentleman, who I will refer to as Al Smith. The man did not utter a word.

Sindone told me that Testa could not reach his lawyer on such short notice and that more than likely my services would not be needed beyond this hearing. I had no problem with that since I was busy with scores of other cases, and besides I felt a little funny about owing him twelve grand. *How would I be able to represent a guy that I owed that much money? If we lost the case he might think I dumped him. Then I would be in deep shit.*

Agent Haggerty testified to facts surrounding several loans made by Frank Sindone and to alleged threats that were made to enforce collections. I objected to a lot of hearsay and opinion evidence even though I knew it was admissible at pretrial hearings, only to be overruled by the magistrate. I argued with the prosecutor, the agent, and the magistrate. I did not give in on any point. Once I caught the agent in a gross inconsistency and I pounced on it and made him look like a liar. He gave me a threatening look but I did not back away.

The defendants were all held for action by the grand jury, but I was successful in getting them out on reasonable bail over protests from the Assistant United States Attorney. Sindone and Testa were grateful to me for putting up the good fight, but more so for getting them out on bail without even having to spend a single hour in a cell. The third defendant kept shaking his head as he murmured over and over again, "What the fuck am I doing here?"

The next day, Frank Sindone called me. "You were great in court yesterday. How much do you want to represent me at the trial?"

"How's 7500 sound?" Within 15 minutes of this conversation, a stranger came to my office and handed me a small, brown-paper parcel. In it was $7500, all in $100 bills.

A few days passed, and I drove down to Frank's Cabana, a small luncheonette specializing in Philadelphia steaks, hot coffee, and the quickest loan service on the East Coast, to deliver my weekly payment of $600 to Sindone. As I tried to hand him the money, I said, "I owe you 12,000. You didn't need to pay me the 7500. You could have just deducted it."

He totally shocked me by refusing the $600, stating, "One thing has nothing to do with the other. Plus, no more payments from you until after the case. I don't want you under any pressure while you're working on my case." I thought to myself, no matter what the feds accused him of doing, he was an all right guy in my book. This was to be the first of many important trials I would handle for an alleged member of La Cosa Nostra, the so-called Mafia.

In Philadelphia, as in most of the other large cities throughout the country, the United States Attorney's Office had a special section devoted to organized crime defendants and cases—the Strike Force. Frank Sindone and Phil Testa were prime targets. Only Angelo Bruno was considered to be a bigger fish. After all, according to them, he was the boss.

I received scores of tapes of telephone conversations between Sindone and several of his borrowing customers. In addition, typewritten transcripts of those conversations were provided to me in pretrial discovery. It appeared that Frank had threatened a few people who were late in their payments. On one such tape, Sindone is overheard saying, "If you don't bring me my fuckin' money, I am going to beat your fuckin' head in with a baseball bat." On another he says, "If you don't pay me, I'm gonna chop your fuckin' head off with an axe." *Is this the same guy that I owed twelve G's?*

Phil Testa was merely overheard speaking with Sindone on the telephone several times. The conversations were limited to their saying to each other, "I'll meet you in an hour for a cup of coffee."

The government's theory was that Frank was getting his loan money from Testa, the alleged underboss of the Philly mob, and putting it on the street at exorbitant interest rates—"juice loans." Interesting theory but where was the evidence, the proof?

The organized crime division of the local FBI and the Strike Force were confident that they finally had the goods on Frank Sindone and Phil Testa. They fully expected a conviction that would result in crippling Angelo Bruno's crime family. After all, loansharking was the family's biggest money-maker. It was its life's blood.

The trial started with banner headlines: "Mafia Underboss Testa and Chief Lieutenant Face Trial on Loansharking Charges." The third defendant was hardly mentioned.

Several witnesses took the stand and testified that they had, in fact, borrowed money from Frank Sindone. One gentleman, who owned a steel company, said he borrowed $10,000 from Sindone and paid $1,000 a week interest for over 20 weeks. He further testified on direct examination that he still owed the original $10,000.

On cross-examination I asked him, "Did the defendant, Mr. Sindone, ever threaten you in any manner?"

He answered, "No."

I continued, "Didn't you use the money for your business?"

"Yes, we were short of cash, and we needed it for payroll."

"I assume, then, that this was a business loan to the corporation. Am I correct?"

"Yes, it was."

"Did Mr. Sindone or anyone else ever threaten you in an effort to collect on the loan?"

"No."

I said, "No more questions." Then I sat down as my anxious client breathed a sigh of relief.

The specific crime charged in the indictment excluded any and all business or corporate loans. The excessive interest rates were of no consequence, absent a threat or use of physical violence.

The prosecution proceeded on other fronts. The damaging tapes were played to the jury, who seemed to be listening attentively.

An insurance broker who owed Sindone some money was the individual to whom Sindone was speaking on the phone when the remarks about the baseball bat and the axe were made. I cannot give a physical description of the man. He never appeared to testify for the government. So, I don't have the faintest idea of what he looks like and neither did the jury. I do know that he hired a lawyer who proved he was too ill to appear.

The prosecution naturally claimed he was too frightened to appear, and they implied he had been threatened. After a brief investigation and hearing, the judge quashed the subpoena, and the witness was ruled to be "legally unavailable."

Agent Haggerty testified that when he and fellow agents went to Sindone's apartment to arrest him, they saw a baseball bat and an axe in the back seat of his car. That testimony was naturally intended to corroborate the threatening telephone conversations and further convince the jury that Sindone intended to make good on his threats allegedly made to the absent insurance man.

The cross-examination went something like this:

Q. How many agents were present on the date and time of the defendant Sindone's arrest?

A. Approximately eight.

Q. Were you the case agent . . . meaning were you the agent in charge of this investigation resulting in the indictment?

A. Yes.

Q. Were any photographs taken of Sindone's residence?

A. Many. Maybe 75 to 100.

Q. Show the jury the bat and the axe that you seized from Sindone's vehicle.

A. I don't have it here.

Q. Did you seize it that day or any other day?

A. Well . . . not actually.

Q. What do you mean "not actually"? Did you take them [the bat and the axe] or not?

A. I didn't take them.

Q. Well, since you had at least seven other agents there, excuse me, special agents, how many of them took pictures with a camera?

A. One, maybe two.

Q. At whose direction were these pictures taken? I think you said between 75 and 100, right?

A. Yes. I believe I ordered the taking of the photos.

Q. Show the jury the pictures of the bat and the axe.

A. I don't have them. They were never taken.

Q. You heard the tapes in this case, didn't you?

A. Yes.

Q. Well, would you consider the bat and the axe, if they really did exist, to be important pieces of evidence in this case?

A. I don't know. I . . . I guess so.

Q. In spite of that, you didn't seize them when you allegedly saw them in plain view, correct?

A. Yes.

Q. And further, you didn't have photographs taken of them either, did you?

A. No, I didn't.

Loudly, I said, "I have nothing further to ask of this very special agent, Your Honor," as I glanced at the jurors. I thought I picked up a favorable reaction by observing certain jurors' body language. Some of them nodded at me. I only hoped they, too, did not suffer from any nervous affliction.

A rather attractive, voluptuous blonde also took the stand in the government's case. The expensive electronic surveillance equipment used by the FBI in their elaborate phone-tapping procedures had intercepted her, like the others. She smiled at Sindone and winked at me as she swore on the Bible to tell the whole truth. My mind traveled back in time to those nights at the Saxony, sitting at the bar inches away from the very sexy lady who was about to fuck the government better than she had done any of her long list of admirers, present company included.

Yes, she had borrowed $600 from Frank when her "public relations" position was unfruitful. "Interest?" she answered, "No way did he charge me even a penny. We were friends. He did me a favor, that's all." Her direct testimony ended when she answered the last question. "Threats? Are you kidding? Frank may yell but he's a real pussycat, he wouldn't harm a fly." A disgruntled prosecutor slid slowly in his seat. I thought she was going to ask him if he needed a towel. There was no cause for me to ask her a single question.

A few agents testified that they observed Sindone and Testa having coffee together at South Philly coffee shops on the same days as the intercepted telephone calls were made. In addition they offered a document that had been torn into many small pieces and then put back together at the FBI crime lab in Washington, D.C. The piece of paper was, according to an agent, found on the pavement in front of Testa's house. The government expert witness testified that the writing on the paper contained loansharking records.

The evidence against "Mr. Smith" was even weaker. One of the people who borrowed money from Sindone testified that Smith had introduced the two.

"The jury will have to decide Mr. Testa's guilt or innocence," the trial judge answered in denying Testa's lawyer's oral motion to grant an acquittal. Smith's lawyer's motion got the same response. I did not even bother to argue for Sindone's case to be dismissed. I was content to rely on the jury.

The FBI, the prosecutors, the press, and most of the general public believed that Sindone would be found guilty based on the very strong evidence against him. They also opined that Testa would meet the same fate, because everybody knew he was the second banana, right under the Don, Angelo Bruno. They also felt that the third defendant might be acquitted, but possibly might be found guilty by association.

When it came time for me to make my closing argument to the jury, I suppressed the butterflies in my stomach, took a deep breath, and went after the FBI and the prosecution with both barrels firing. I pointed out the convenient coincidence between the alleged intercepted threats by Sindone and the agent's testimony about seeing the bat and the axe in the car. "Why," I asked, "didn't they bring in the bat and the axe? Where are the photos? Why didn't they take any? The answer is obvious. They didn't exist. I do not relish calling anyone, let alone a Special Agent of the FBI, a liar, but there just isn't any other explanation."

Although I didn't represent Testa, I did allude to him and the lack of evidence against him. "Is it a crime for someone to have coffee with a friend," I asked the jurors, "or just if your name ends with a vowel?" I harped on how absurd the government prosecution team was in indicting Testa. I hoped that I would deflect the minds of the jurors off of the very damaging evidence against Sindone.

Just as I was about to complete my close, I looked into the eyes of several jurors, one at a time, and said in a hushed tone, "Recently, you have read about the FBI taping the phone calls of the Reverend Martin Luther King . . . eavesdropping on the Catholic Church and untold scores of other unpopular defendants and organizations. I tell you now, if you vote to convict my client, or for that matter any of these defendants, you would be granting the government carte blanche to listen in to the private conversations of your loved ones and yourselves."

The prosecutor rose to his feet and screamed, "I object . . . objection . . . objection."

The trial judge quickly responded, "Objection sustained. Counsel approach the bench."

Ordinarily, having my closing argument interrupted for even the shortest time would have peeved me. This time it didn't bother me. The judge looked at me coldly and said, "Mr. Simone, you know better. Your comment about wiretapping was way out of line. The electronic surveillance was ruled legal and proper in this case by another federal judge, and the propriety of it is not a question for this jury." He then glanced at the prosecutor and said, "If you wish, I will instruct the jury that the wiretapping in this case was authorized by the court, and therefore was proper and legal."

"I would like you to do that, sir, and right now," the prosecutor said as his eyes wandered over to the jury box where the jurors all seemed to be whispering to each other.

We resumed our seats at counsel table as the judge stated, "Ladies and gentlemen, our courts have ruled that wiretapping under certain circumstances is lawful, and another United States Court District Judge has already determined that wiretaps in this case were performed in a lawful manner. Therefore, I want you to remove Mr. Simone's last comments from your minds. It is irrelevant that the government on prior occasions has wiretapped the Catholic Church or Dr. Martin Luther King. You should not consider that your verdict would cause any of you to become the subject of a wiretap." Several of the jurors winced as the judge finished by saying, "I instruct you not to consider the remarks of counsel as evidence and especially his comments about Dr. Martin Luther King, the Catholic Church, and yourselves."

I rose and faced the jury box, continuing my close, "I apologize for making the statement of how I personally feel about wiretapping. Even if you feel the same way, you should erase from your minds Dr. King's and the Catholic Church's bad experiences." I smiled at the jurors. Some of them smiled back at me. They got the message. The judge, by repeating my words, ensured that they would not forget what I said. Hearing it a third time from me just about guaranteed they would remember.

I sat down next to my client, Frank Sindone. He whispered in my ear, "How the fuck can they erase that from their minds?"

I whispered back, "Let's hope they can't."

The not guilty verdicts were loudly announced, and again I enjoyed the scene as prosecutors and law enforcement officers (in this case FBI agents, special agents as they called themselves, as if there is a lower rank in the Bureau) left the courtroom with their heads down, and their tails between their legs.

That night, Frank called me at home to invite me to dinner. I met him at one of South Philly's best Italian restaurants, the Villa Di Roma on Ninth Street in the heart of "Little Italy." Phil Testa was there, and he and Frank each gave me a hug and a kiss on the cheek. Phil slid an envelope in my hand and said, "Here, kid, take this. It's a tip; you earned it." I later found 50 $100 bills in the envelope.

Frank also told me, "You're even on the 12,000. You don't owe me nuthin'."

The next day, a Saturday, the phone rang at my home in Cheltenham. "Bobby, do you know who this is?"

"Yes," I replied. I recognized the voice from television news clips of Angelo Bruno taking the Fifth Amendment on numerous occasions when he appeared before several witch-hunting investigating legislative bodies. I also recalled his voice from the short conversation in the Friendly Lounge when he congratulated me for winning Luther Fleck's case.

"I called to thank you for saving Frank's life in court. I told him not to use you, because you were known to be too reckless with your gambling and drinking. I was wrong. You must be a great lawyer. You have me as a friend for life. Take my advice. Stop gambling!" The phone went dead.

A couple of weeks later I walked into the Saxony, sat at the bar, and ordered Cutty on the rocks. I felt a warm hand on the back of my neck and then a kiss on the cheek. "Hello, Bobby, I've missed you, where you been?"

"Hello, Nina. I missed you too. Have you seen Frank since the trial?"

"No, but you'll never believe this story. A couple of days after I testified, I was sitting at a bar at the airport and that big, blond-haired prosecutor from Washington comes in with his suitcase for a quick drink. He sees me and comes over, buys me a drink, and before you know it we're in the sack. He canceled his flight. He gave me $100 and he told me he wanted to fuck me from the minute he first saw me in his office."

"I bet he liked you better in bed than in court." I could not stop myself from laughing. "Have a drink with me. No, have a dozen drinks with me." It was destined to be one of those nights.

CHAPTER EIGHT

▼

Just Us

Within a couple of weeks of the not guilty verdict in the Sindone-Testa case, I was summoned to the law office of Jacob "Jake" Kossman. Jake would become my second and last mentor. When I arrived, Phil Testa, Frank Sindone, and Angelo Bruno greeted me. They rose from the brown, leather-backed chairs that surrounded Jake's large, dusty, and paper-littered desk. He sat still, almost ignoring me. One of the others introduced me to Kossman. I raised my right arm, attempting to shake hands. He did not reciprocate. I learned later that Kossman shook hands with no man. He had this weird thing about the spreading of germs by skin contact. Another Howard Hughes?

I had heard that Bruno, who was called "Ange" by his friends and associates, spent many of his afternoons in Kossman's office. Those afternoons he missed were usually the result of a subpoena to testify before numerous state and federal grand juries and the Pennsylvania and New Jersey Crime Commissions.

I was told that a subpoena was recently served on Phil Testa to ensure his appearance before a federal grand jury investigating organized crime in the Philadelphia–South Jersey area. Bruno told me that Jake could not represent Testa, because he was then representing Bruno in connection with yet another organized crime investigation in New Jersey. These multitudinous witch hunts kept hundreds of people on the public payroll in our backyard alone and thousands all over the country.

It seemed that Bruno, Testa, Sindone, and Kossman had agreed among themselves that I should represent Phil Testa. Of course they knew that I would have to agree to take the case first—a no-brainer. My basic training was over, and I was now a major player in their war for justice. The constant battle cry was "just us."

Jake said, "I can't handle Phil because they will only say there is a conflict of interest. I can't do Phil much good anyway. They probably already have immunity for him and that means he will be held in contempt when he takes the Fifth and refuses to testify. It looks like he's going to jail next week."

I looked at Phil as Jake spoke and noticed he showed no emotion despite hearing that his incarceration was right around the corner. Ice water.

Ange said to me, "It's bad enough that I have to go back in because of this contempt thing, but in Phil's case he already did time for exercising his Fifth Amendment right. Enough is enough."

Jake interrupted, "Ange goes before the judge this Friday. He's been examined by the state's doctors and despite all his internal bleeding, they say he's faking."

Bruno had already pled the Fifth Amendment in New Jersey. He was in prison for a while when he suffered internal bleeding, resulting in his temporary medical release. He was about to return to his cellmates from New York and North Jersey—Anthony Ziccarelli, Jerry Catena, and several others whose last names I can't remember or spell, but you can bet they all ended with a vowel. They were all incarcerated for merely exercising their constitutional right to remain silent. They had committed no crime, but they lost their freedom anyway. It's called civil contempt.

In New Jersey there was no time limit on how long one can be incarcerated for refusing to testify. Bruno was to spend about four years in prison for contempt. One of his friends was locked up for over six years. That's a hell of a lot of time for someone who has not even been convicted of a crime.

Rather than discuss Phil's situation in the same room with the others, I made an appointment for him to come and see me the next day in my office. Testa seemed to appreciate the fact that I showed concern for his right to confidentiality, which he would have lost had we had our discussion in the presence of others.

As I left the office, Kossman and Bruno approached me at the door. Ange again expressed his gratitude to me for saving Sindone from prison.

Jake said, "This is a tough one for you, but after what I heard about you, maybe you can keep Phil out for a couple of weeks. If you need my help, call or come here any day. I am at your disposal."

I thanked both of them and left the office in the area of Broad and Spruce Streets. I walked back to my office. During the five-block walk, I tried to figure out a way to keep Phil, "The Chicken Man," out of prison for a while.

Phil Testa, at one time in his life, owned and operated a chicken store on the southwest corner of Ninth and Christian Streets, right in the heart of

South Philly's Italian Market. The local newspapers picked up on this, and it was some overzealous reporter who tagged Phil with the nickname "The Chicken Man." Fortunately for that reporter, his identity remains a mystery.

When Phil arrived the next day, I half expected him to come with Frank Sindone, but he walked in alone. We spoke about the loansharking trial victory, and we agreed that Frank got lucky and that Phil should not even have been indicted.

Phil then filled me in with some facts concerning a similar subpoena he received two years earlier. Back then the Strike Force had him brought before a grand jury. Phil took the Fifth, and he was held in contempt. The United States Marshals took him directly from the courthouse to the federal penitentiary in Lewisburg, Pennsylvania, where he was confined for 18 months.

Federal law provides that a person found in contempt for refusing to testify before a grand jury after having been granted immunity can be imprisoned until he agrees to testify. There is, however, an 18-month maximum period of incarceration. Small consolation for someone not proved guilty of any crime.

Testa was only two days away from his appointment with the grand jury. I did not need to ask him whether or not he would answer any questions for the prosecutor. As a matter of fact, from the time of his recent trial he carried my card in his pocket at all times. Written on the back was the following: "I refuse to answer any questions on the grounds of the Fifth Amendment, my right to remain silent, and to prevent you from using my answers to identify my voice on any tape recording."

I thought it was extremely unfair for the government to send Testa to jail for refusing to testify before a grand jury a couple of years ago. Then he had to defend himself in a criminal trial, and after being acquitted, was required to appear before yet another grand jury. The federal prosecutors knew he would never answer their questions, but they were about to extract their retribution from Testa for having embarrassed them in court.

"I refuse to answer the question on the grounds of the Fourth and Fifth Amendments of the United States Constitution." That is how Phil answered all questions except for his name and address.

I told him to use the Fourth Amendment since recently the government was forced to admit that they conducted illegal wiretaps on two Catholic priests, the Berrigan brothers, who were avid anti–Vietnam War protestors. In addition, an illegal electronic bug had picked up Angelo Bruno and others at some New Jersey garage several years before discussing "family" business. The Fourth Amendment to the United States Constitution protects citizens from unreasonable searches and seizures, and illegal wiretaps and bugs, usually without court authorization, come under this umbrella.

These instances were clear violations of the Fourth Amendment. We had a right to determine if any of the proposed questions which Testa was required to answer were the result of information obtained from illegal electronic surveillance procedures.

The day before the scheduled testimony I decided to phone the Strike Force attorney, Steve Stein, to find out whether or not he had already obtained an immunity request from Washington, D.C. He assured me in no uncertain terms that he had not yet obtained the necessary authorization from his superiors. He told me, "It will take me about ten more days. You can tell your client he's not going anywhere yet."

Early the next morning, Phil and I were dropped off by Sindone in front of the United States Courthouse, then located at Ninth and Chestnut Streets in Center City Philadelphia. As expected, we were greeted by about half a dozen reporters, some with cameras dangling around their necks and others holding and pointing video cameras.

The first stop was the grand jury room on the fourth floor. We were there together for only a matter of minutes. Phil and I separated when he actually entered the grand jury room. Lawyers are not permitted in the room when their clients are questioned. Another rule that should be abolished as far as I am concerned.

After Phil read from the three-by-five card I had prepared for him in response to several questions, we were ordered to appear before the United States District Court judge assigned to the grand jury. There he again pled the Fourth and Fifth Amendments of the United States Constitution as we planned.

Contempt hearings are usually over in less than an hour, just a matter of form. The witness is asked again if he will answer the questions before the grand jury. If the witness remains mute or states again that he will not answer the questions before the grand jury, the prosecutor will say, "I have an Order for Immunity and the authorization to ask Your Honor to sign it."

Steve Stein told the judge he had the authorization and the proposed order. "The bastard lied to me on the phone yesterday," I whispered to Phil.

I argued that we were not prepared to attack the immunity order and asked permission to call a witness. The judge asked me, "Who and where is your witness?"

I replied, "Steve Stein, the attorney for the government."

The judge permitted this highly unusual move. Stein admitted that he lied to me the night before. As you can see it is perfectly okay for their people to lie, but if it had been a defense lawyer, that would be obstruction of justice without a doubt. To my surprise and delight, the judge then continued the hearing for 30 days.

This not only delayed Phil's incarceration, but the clock was ticking on the grand jury's 18-month term. The effect was that we had just saved Testa from spending one month in prison. "Bobby, you have balls, calling that prosecutor to the stand. Great move."

By the time we returned to court, 30 days later, Angelo Bruno was in Yardville Prison in New Jersey for contempt. I was able to contest the legality of certain electronic surveillance information compiled by the federal agents who were investigating Testa prior to the grand jury proceedings. As a result, the judge held several hearings over a period of approximately four months. During this time, Testa was free to go about his business.

When the string ran out for Phil, he was able to enjoy about five months of unexpected freedom. He ended up doing 13 months in jail—better than 18. Two of those months were spent in a private room at Hahnemann University Hospital in Center City Philadelphia. Testa's high blood pressure necessitated the move. In the long run, we didn't fare too badly. Easy for me to say; Phil had to do the time. Back then I believed the courtroom door swung both ways for the lawyer.

Steve Stein resigned from the United States Attorney's Office several years later. He now actively practices criminal law in Las Vegas. I am sure he doesn't trust any U.S. Attorneys. Why should he? He knows how deceptive they can be.

When Phil was released, he, Sindone, and I shared many delicious dinners together at Dante and Luigi's Restaurant at Tenth and Catharine Streets in South Philly. Frank Sindone often bragged how he discovered me, and Phil would smile and wink at me on those occasions. If representing these guys and breaking bread with them made me a "mob lawyer," then I guess that's what I was.

The word seemed to spread like wildfire, "Bobby Simone represents the mob." Some people thought it was a put-down, while others concluded, "He must be a sharp lawyer if 'those guys' use him."

Personally, at the time, I was too busy going from one case to another to wonder about my reputation. I just continued to do what my oath as a lawyer required and that was to defend the accused to the fullest extent in an ethical and legal manner. Lest we forget, I do have cause to empathize with my clients.

▼ ▼ ▼

A few years before the dice ever rolled in the first legalized casino in Atlantic City, many of my friends and I spent the summer weekends there and in the adjacent communities of Ventnor, Margate, and Longport along the South Jersey shoreline. Our motel of choice was The Strand with its approximately 40 large, comfortable rooms surrounding an Olympic-sized pool. A cozy, cabana-style bar sat near the end of the pool close to the Boardwalk overlooking the wide, sandy beach and the Atlantic Ocean.

The Strand was home to one of the finest restaurants at that time in Atlantic City. The cocktail bar was always crowded as hungry, well-dressed diners drank martinis and champagne, waiting for their names to be called by the maitre d'. The vacation homeowners and renters joined The Strand's residents for the weekend ritual of dining and people watching. The diners all seemed to know each other. It was like going to a family reunion every weekend. Ninety percent of the clientele was from Philadelphia.

Lawyers, doctors, businessmen, thieves, burglars, bar owners, racetrack enthusiasts, and entertainers mingled, ate, drank, and spent hours talking every Friday and Saturday night. I reserved two rooms every weekend, one for my wife Arlene and me, and the other for Scott and Kimberly.

On one of those hot summer nights, I was on my first Bombay martini when a short, dark-haired, rather handsome and well-dressed man started a conversation with me. Arlene had gone to check on the kids. He acted like he knew me and indicated by his friendly manner that I knew him. I hadn't a clue as to his identity.

He wore a tan suit, a white shirt with noticeably long collars, and a black, tan, and white tie. He was dark-eyed, smooth-skinned, and tan, very tan. The sun had not harmed his complexion at all.

After only a few minutes of idle talk about The Strand, the beach, and the climate, he said in a low voice just above a whisper, "Do you mind if I ask you a legal question?" Rarely did a night pass without that same question being asked of me at least half a dozen times no matter where I was.

I looked at him and answered with a smile, "No problem."

The stranger then stated his situation. "I got a subpoena from the State of New Jersey to testify about so-called organized crime. I'm a friend of Ange's, so I thought I would ask you for some advice." Ange, of course, was Angelo Bruno, known throughout the East Coast as "The Docile Don." The press tagged him with that name some 20 years before. He allegedly became the new boss of the Philadelphia–South Jersey La Cosa Nostra family in the late 1950s.

For over 20 years, Angelo Bruno surrounded himself with only a limited number of friends and associates that he trusted. But just about the entire population of the Philadelphia area knew him and respected him, either through personal experience or what was continually written about the man.

Angelo Bruno once said to me at one of the many dinners we shared, "Bobby, please be careful. There are very few people you can trust. You are a devoted lawyer always looking out for your clients, but I want to tell you, you can't trust even your own clients. The only people I would swear for, the ones that wouldn't hurt you, are myself, Phil, and Frank."

He was dead serious when he said this to me. He also told me many times, "Don't do anything illegal." Angelo was a smart man. Odd as it might seem to many, he was a virtuous man.

As the story of how he acquired the nickname "The Docile Don" is told, someone else wanted his position and the power that went with it. That person wanted it so bad that he put out a contract on the life of Angelo Bruno. But before anyone had the opportunity to carry out the dastardly and dangerous deed, Bruno received a life-saving tip.

Supposedly, the big bosses in New York, who also got wind of the treacherous plot, gave Bruno the green light to have the ambitious mobster killed. Bruno declined and instead called the frightened man in for a sit-down. His life was spared, and he was relegated to some minor position as a bookmaker for the family.

Bruno's reputation for continuing to settle as many disputes as possible in the same kind of peaceful manner earned him the title of "The Docile Don."

The gentleman with whom I was engaged in conversation would much later acquire his own reputation as a boss. When I asked him his name, he replied, "Oh, Bob, I'm sorry. I thought you knew who I was. I've seen you with Ange, Phil, and Frank a couple of times. I'm Nicky Scarfo."

We shook hands, and he continued, "What I want to ask you is if I plead the Fifth, will I have to testify or go to jail?" He added, "You and I know Ange and Phil are already in jail, but is there a way I can stay out without testifying?"

I looked at him and responded, "You are going to jail—no ands, ifs, or buts—unless you answer the questions." I knew without having to ask that Scarfo would plead the Fifth.

He smiled and said, "I appreciate your telling me outright. I mean with no bullshit. Thanks for being honest." Years later he would remind me of that first short meeting and the way I answered his question immediately and honestly without pulling any punches. Down the line, Nicky Scarfo would become a major client, a good friend, and the source of tremendous animosity between the United States Department of Justice and myself.

▼ ▼ ▼

A couple of years later I found myself representing Frank Sindone, again charged with collecting money through extortionate means as well as extending credit for excessive interest rates, another loansharking case. And again a jury of his peers would acquit him. His co-defendant, Al Hartzell, was convicted. During the trial the jury heard several conversations on tape between the wired-up informant, Sindone, and Hartzell. Sindone said very little of an incriminating nature. His co-defendant hung himself when he spoke to the informant alone. Apparently, Frank had learned from his first case that "the walls had ears."

During the trial, the jury heard the co-defendant say to the informant, "This isn't my money. This belongs to Frank Sindone and the mob downtown. They lay out big money and never have trouble getting paid. Bobby Simone and Eddy Reif borrow 50,000 at a crack."

My buddy, Eddy Reif, by now no longer my partner but still a close friend, represented Al Hartzell, who was speaking on the tape. Eddy's face turned red, and he hardly spoke to Hartzell the rest of the trial. Sindone and I both looked at the jury when the gratuitous remarks were being played, and neither of us caught anything that would indicate he was in trouble.

The trial was winding down in late April, around Easter time. I ended my closing address to the jury with this: "Around 2,000 years ago there was another trial involving an innocent defendant. He was convicted and put to death. That defendant made one fatal mistake. He waived a jury trial." I stared into the eyes of the jurors, stepped back, said nothing else, and sat down.

When the verdict came in clearing Sindone, he went to the telephone and invited several of his friends and associates to the bar at the Benjamin Franklin Hotel where we all ate and drank to celebrate the big win.

Hartzell was released on bail pending appeal. He was eventually sentenced to five years in prison. Had Frank been convicted, he would have gotten no less than 20 years.

I had proved myself again to the powers that were supposed to rule the underworld in Philadelphia. I had also made some new enemies in the FBI and the United States Attorney's Office. Sore losers.

Angelo Bruno and Phil Testa again expressed their gratitude. I was often invited to join Ange, Phil, Frank, and Jake Kossman at dinner. More times than not, I accepted the invitations. The conversation was always stimulating and never about anything of an illegal nature. And of course we all laughed while watching Jake eat his spaghetti with his fingers. There was usually more gravy on his tie than on his plate.

These people, their associates, and their real families became more than clients. They were friends as well. And, of course, there was no end to the number of new clients that they sent me.

CHAPTER NINE

Roofers Local 30

The roofers, members of the powerful Roofers and Composition Workers, Local 30, continued to work and play hard. It was a rare weekend when one of their members wasn't arrested, usually after a couple hours of serious drinking. They were known as a tough group of guys and that reputation caused many bar owners in Northeast Philadelphia to close their doors when inclement weather forced the men off the roofs and into the saloons.

John McCullough was still the chief officer of the union with the title of "Business Manager." John was about six foot one, with an erect posture, and he carried his 200-plus pounds well. His crew cut and chiseled features were a dead giveaway; he was an ex-marine. McCullough's medals were won in the South Pacific during the Second World War.

The slightly over 1200 men who carried a Local 30 card were all extremely loyal to the union, but even more so to McCullough. John earned the loyalty and respect thrust upon him. He always went to bat for his rank and file. He didn't bother to make excuses for their errors in conduct; he merely defended them to the best of his ability. When they could not afford to pay me, he did so himself out of his own pocket. On some occasions he persuaded me to represent his men without a fee. Either way they got the best legal service I could supply. He also made sure that the optimum safety measures were in force at the job sites.

McCullough's support was much sought after by all those running for political office in Philadelphia and throughout the Commonwealth of

Pennsylvania. He donated his men to work the polls and canvass the neighborhoods to get out the vote. He was also responsible for large cash contributions to many campaign funds, mostly Democratic. He was able to deliver his friends who headed some of the other trade unions along with their pockets filled with PAC money, and he arranged numerous fund-raising events as well.

The word was on the street was, "If McCullough and the roofers were in your corner, you were a shoo-in." Many of the local judges owed their robes to "JJ," as he was affectionately called.

John asked me to represent one of his men in his upcoming murder trial in Philadelphia's City Hall. I met with the man, John S., over a few drinks at a local bar in the Northeast section of the city where most of the roofers resided and hung out. John had been released on bail, which is allowed in murder cases where the prosecutor does not seek the death penalty.

A decorated veteran of the Vietnam War, he joined the union and spent his time sweating on the rooftops of Philadelphia and picketing non-union construction jobs. He, too, was perfect for his position. He was tough, streetsmart, and loyal.

The Commonwealth's evidence consisted almost entirely of the testimony of a young man in his mid-twenties. He claimed that he and his friend, the deceased, were in a crowded bar when the roofer, upon entering, physically bumped into them. Words were exchanged and, according to the witness, "The next thing this guy does is pull a gun and he fires at my friend and then points it at me. He fired again, but he missed. I ran the hell out of the bar."

My client told a different story. "I walked into this bar alone, and these two guys were drunk and they started hassling me. They were cursing at me, and I told them to leave me alone. One of them pulled a gun. I grabbed it, and they both started to wrestle with me. They tried to take the gun, but it went off. I ran out. The gun fell to the floor."

The District Attorney had no gun to show to the jury; it had mysteriously disappeared.

I argued that the witness probably picked up either his or his friend's gun and got rid of it before the police arrived. The jury believed our version and rendered a not guilty verdict. McCullough and at least 20 of his entourage of roofers were in the courtroom for most of the trial. They loudly applauded the verdict, causing the judge to clear the courtroom. "Order in the court! Order in the court! Sheriff, get them out of here!"

A year or two later, John S. was arrested and charged with another murder that occurred in a shopping mall parking lot a few miles outside of Philadelphia. I represented him at a preliminary hearing before a district judge. The charges were dismissed after a lengthy cross-examination of the one eyewitness. He reluctantly agreed with me that he could not swear it was the defendant who actually fired the fatal shot. It was a classic case of mistaken identity.

Several months later a third murder charge was brought against John S. in Bucks County, Pennsylvania. The facts were similar to those in the bar shooting, only this time it was a house party. After a two-week trial he was convicted of third-degree murder and imprisoned for ten years. You can't win them all. Two out of three hits for a baseball player makes for a phenomenal batting average. A defendant must bat a thousand percent if he hopes to remain free. A heavy burden to say the least.

The stakes were so high in most of my trials—jail or freedom, life or death. The time spent waiting for a jury to decide the fate of any one of my clients was torturous. All I did was walk, pace back and forth, smoke, and worry. Very rarely if ever would I be able to leave my client's side while his or her fate was being decided by a jury behind those closed doors. I treated every client like a best friend, or a brother or sister. Some of them appreciated that, and some didn't. Not guilty verdicts came from heaven, and guilty verdicts from hell.

I firmly believed and fought for the presumption of innocence, innocent until proved guilty. I couldn't speak to a jury unless I really felt my client was in the right. Jurors can see through the acting and the lies, and they will react favorably to honesty and logic.

At around the same time there were two other roofers, both members of Local 30, who got into a fight. I had previously represented both of them in a burglary case that was dismissed before trial. They were good friends, working partners, and drinking buddies. Their fistfight erupted into a gunfight. Both of them had been drinking and both had been carrying. One of them died on the spot, a small bullet hole in the area of his heart.

The survivor came to me for representation. He was acquitted in a non-jury trial when the judge found the defendant to have acted in self-defense. The other guy fired first. When the DA asked the defendant on cross-examination, "Why did you fire your gun?" the answer came almost as fast as the fatal bullet traveled.

"Well, let me put it this way, if I didn't fire the gun, he [the deceased] would be sitting here answering that question."

I found myself drinking scotch and beer at night with McCullough and other Local 30 guys in the Northeast. The Branding Iron and the Princeton Bar were usual haunts. I did not realize it at the time, but now I am sure that these nighttime activities were taking a heavy toll on my home life and marriage. Arlene was very patient, but I know I did not appreciate her willingness to put up with all my bullshit. Looking back now, I can easily see that everything in my life took a back seat to my clients and their problems. Yes, "the law is a jealous mistress."

▼ ▼ ▼

In the suburbs of Philadelphia, near the site of Valley Forge National Park, a non-union builder by the name of Leon Altemose was making plans to build a Sheraton Hotel, a connecting movie theater, and a small shopping center.

The Philadelphia Area Building and Construction Trades Council was an organization consisting of officers of most of the building trade unions. The Council often negotiated union contracts with the area's builders. Carpenters, plumbers, sheet metal workers, concrete workers, iron workers, laborers, operating engineers, and, of course, roofers all belonged to the Council.

After several attempts to negotiate contracts with Altemose on behalf of the Council and some of its member unions failed, Altemose decided he would go non-union. After all, he had succeeded in completing several other non-union jobs in the past. This should not be a problem. Or so he thought.

Those tradesmen who belonged to a union earned anywhere from $18 to $25 an hour. Not bad for the early seventies. They also were paid time and a half for overtime and double pay on Saturdays, and some received triple time on Sundays. Their liberal fringe benefits helped them and their families live the American Dream. But now they felt threatened. Their jobs and their future were in serious jeopardy. If Altemose could get away with hiring men at the rate of $5 to $10 an hour, what would prevent the other contractors in the area from trying to go non-union?

On June 5, 1972, at dawn a dozen or so charter buses pulled up to the job site. The men hustled out of the buses where John McCullough met them with several of his burly business agents, Thomas McGrann, the president of the Building and Construction Trades Council, and other leaders of the individual trade unions. Picket signs were handed out to most of the anxious men.

The hotel had only been partially built. Work had not yet started that morning. Scores of pieces of heavy equipment were clustered inside the cyclone fence surrounding the job. Over 1,000 men began picketing around the perimeter of the building site. They walked slowly and peacefully for almost half an hour, carrying their signs protesting the low wages being paid to the non-union workmen.

Suddenly, without warning, as if a silent signal had been given, the men in packs of ten or more changed direction and went straight for the fence. In a matter of minutes the fence was completely flattened. What little had been completed of the hotel was ripped down, leaving only the foundation. Every piece of heavy equipment—forklifts, cranes, earthmovers, and trucks of all sizes—was engulfed in flames.

The few security guards hired by Altemose, along with township and state policemen on hand, were taken by surprise. No arrests were made at the scene, but they did manage to take hundreds of photographs. These would surface in future court proceedings.

Thick black columns of smoke rose from the burning equipment, filling the sky and covering the entire area. The smoke screen allowed the men to leave the scene, board the buses, and get the hell out of Valley Forge without incident. Was all this planned or spontaneous?

The newspapers covered the story on their front pages. "Union Vandals Destroy Building Site" was a typical headline. Altemose and Bill Nicholas, the District Attorney of Montgomery County, Pennsylvania, went on television condemning the Philadelphia Area Building and Construction Trades Council and its members' unions, especially Roofers Union Local 30. There were two separate points of view. The union people in the area, even those in non-construction employment, seemed to side with the building tradesmen. However, most other citizens thought their conduct outrageous. Emotions ran high on both sides.

The law and order people were out for blood. It would take Nicholas, his assistants, and the police a couple of weeks to review the photographs in an attempt to identify the perpetrators. Several informants were retained to point out faces and attach a name to the guilty individuals. These few turncoats refused to testify in court, but they did cause enough damage to help the District Attorney make a case sufficient to obtain arrest warrants.

Less than two weeks passed before the DA's office was able to obtain 23 warrants charging the photo-identified participants with crimes ranging from conspiracy, riot, and arson to malicious damage to fences and disorderly conduct. The police did not pick up the men. Instead the Building and Construction Trades Council's office was notified that the men were wanted and that they would be given a chance to surrender to the authorities in Upper Merion Township.

I received a telephone call from John McCullough and Tommy McGrann asking for a meeting to discuss legal representation for the accused men. I met them at the Building and Construction Trades Council's office in Northeast Philadelphia, a few blocks from the Delaware River. John and McGrann brought me into a room where several union bosses were seated around a large conference table. The painters, carpenters, plumbers, operating engineers, cement workers, laborers, roofers, and several of the other trades were there.

A discussion took place relating to how much it was going to cost to get the best representation possible for their 23 men. In about an hour it was agreed that I would bring in two other well-known criminal lawyers to work with me in defending the case. I chose Cecil B. Moore and Charles "Chuck" Peruto, Sr.

I encountered no resistance with regard to Peruto, because a few of the union guys had used Chuck in some personal criminal matters. He had performed well and had an excellent reputation. He was sharp, clever, fast on his feet, and a veteran in handling high-profile cases.

Getting the okay for Cecil Moore presented some unusual problems. Local Union 542, the Operating Engineers, were involved in a civil suit in federal court concerning violations of the civil rights of black workers who, it seemed, could not get a union card or were being denied work despite their union membership. The case had been pending from the early sixties.

Cecil Moore had been for many years the president of the Philadelphia branch of the NAACP. He was one of the black leaders who fought hard for the civil rights of his members and other African Americans. He had confronted the Operating Engineers and their leaders on many occasions.

I wanted Cecil on the defense team because I thought he was one of the best trial lawyers in the area. He was great at cross-examination, and colorful and persuasive in his closing arguments. We had worked smoothly together in the past. Cecil loved the good fight and more so when there was an underlying cause involved.

It did not take much convincing on my part to show how valuable Moore would be as co-counsel in this high-profile, emotional legal proceeding. The Laborers Union had mostly black members and leaders. Carlton "Browny" Brown, a smiling but tough black, was one of John McCullough's top business agents. With this kind of pressure, the Operating Engineers consented to Moore being retained.

When the newspapers reported who was going to represent the 23 defendants in the upcoming "Altemose" case, they referred to Moore's appearance as an indication that maybe the Operating Engineers had decided to open up their ranks to blacks. That would come later. But, at the time, the union's consenting to use Cecil as an attorney and his active, 100 percent commitment to the case, or should I say the cause, at least resulted in a truce between the union and the black community.

I had been told that the 20,000 members of the Building Trades Council would contribute $50 each to raise a million-dollar defense fund. If more were needed later, it would be raised in the same manner.

The three of us visited the Council's office the next morning and met with McCullough and McGrann. They had already received authorization from all of the union bosses to make the financial arrangements.

The agreement reached called for weekly payments of $35,000 once the actual court proceedings commenced. Chuck and Cecil were to be paid $10,000 a week. I, as lead counsel, would receive $12,500, and $2500 a week would be available for investigators and miscellaneous expenses. A lot of money in the early seventies, a lot of money today. But we had to consider that we were going to be absent from our Philadelphia offices and unavailable to most of our clients. We would also lose quite a bit of new business as this was going to be a long, long trial.

I hired Stanley Branche, a dear friend and drinking buddy, along with his partner, Gus Lacey. They would be the investigators we so sorely needed. I rented a suite at the Valley Forge Hilton for the duration of the trial.

After a lengthy preliminary hearing lasting a couple of weeks, including night sessions, the case was bound over for court. The evidence presented at the hearing consisted mostly of eyewitness testimony from security guards and policemen. They could not identify the actual perpetrators, but they were able to describe the general scene, the mass destruction, and the violent mood of the swarms of men infiltrating the building site. Then there were the hundreds of photographs showing some of the faces, the clothing, and what the men were doing at the instant the pictures were taken.

The thing I remember most about the preliminary hearing had little to do with the evidence. One night after a dinner break, Cecil Moore put a bottle of Old Grand Dad in his briefcase and brought it into the auditorium where the hearing was being conducted.

A small man dressed in work clothes walked up to the prosecutor's table and whispered something into the ear of Bill Nicholas, then he left the table and disappeared into the crowd of spectators who were seated quietly, listening to the proceedings.

Nicholas rose and interrupted my cross-examination of one of the security guards. "I must see Your Honor at sidebar."

Cecil and I joined Bill Nicholas at the bench. Peruto was not there that night. He did not start participating in the defense until we went to trial in Norristown, since he was busy with other pressing legal business. Nicholas said, "Your Honor, I have just learned that they are drinking at counsel table," as he pointed with his dark, piercing eyes first at Cecil and then at me.

There were white Styrofoam cups on both the prosecutor's and defense counsel's tables. Evidently, Cecil had poured some of his Old Grand Dad into his coffee cup. We vehemently denied the charge. Our words were spoken loud enough for some of the spectators to hear.

Then Cecil hollered, "What is he talking about? We are drinking coffee just like him. I wish there was some good bourbon around here, because I am getting bored with these lying witnesses repeating each other." The spectators cheered.

Nicholas retorted, "The janitor told me he saw them pouring something from a whiskey bottle into their cups."

The audience heard all that was being said. Then Cecil loudly replied, "I knew it was the janitor, because all janitors are informers! Goddamn!"

The spectators started laughing. Even the judge and Nicholas had trouble controlling themselves. The judge bellowed, "Court is in recess; Court reconvenes at 9:00 a.m. tomorrow."

On the way back to Philly, Cecil finished half the bottle. He could drink, but he sure could handle himself in court.

The case against the 23 men was severed into two separate trials. The first trial was to have nine defendants. Cecil, Chuck, and I would each represent three. Seven of them were roofers—naturally, all members of Local 30. One defendant was a small roofing union contractor. He had been paying union scale and lucrative benefits. He did not want someone cutting into his territory. The ninth defendant was an officer of the Roofers Union.

As lead counsel, I had to make some decisions on behalf of all the defendants and their counsel. I assigned the roofer Carlton "Browny" Brown to Chuck Peruto for two reasons. First of all, Browny knew Chuck and preferred him as his lawyer, and secondly, I thought it would be better if the only black defendant had a white lawyer. It also made more sense to me to have Cecil Moore represent three white defendants. We wanted to show that the issues involved in this case cut across racial lines. It was the workingman's struggle against union-busting big business. The Roofers Union did not have the same minority problem as the Engineers.

I filed a motion to suppress the identification evidence. We claimed that the identification evidence was tainted as a result of suggestive photographs and procedures, which in some instances only depicted one or two men at the scene. In addition, when the witnesses identified the defendants in the photographs, it was in the absence of counsel, in violation of the Sixth Amendment to the United States Constitution.

In my heart I knew we were not going to win the motion. But I knew it would be much better for the defense if we knew the identity and number of eyewitnesses and what they were likely to testify to at trial once the jury was in the box. Discovery rules were not as liberal at the time this case was pending, and the prosecutor would not have been required to give the defense this information. By having a hearing on the motion we were now getting what we would normally be denied.

We knew from the preliminary hearing that most of the evidence would consist of testimony from photographers, Altemose's security guards, local police, state police, and people who just happened on the scene. They were probably going to testify as to what they observed and point out the defendants both in the pictures and in the courtroom. Of course, there was to be other evidence including a history of Altemose's other non-union jobs, the constant bickering between him and the unions, the failed negotiations, and the deadly photographs themselves.

Filing the motion turned out to be a good strategic move. The trial judge, Robert Tredenick, listed the hearing on the motion "immediately before trial." Since the Commonwealth had only called about half a dozen witnesses at the preliminary hearing, we were all surprised to learn that there were approximately 100 witnesses for the prosecution.

Each eyewitness would have to testify as to what he saw, and then identify the culprits from their photographs and their appearances in court. All law enforcement officers present when the out-of-court identifications occurred would have to testify to the actions of each one.

The hearing took approximately a month and a half. The triple cross-examination—first by Peruto, then Cecil, and finally me—was grueling and exhaustive. The three of us showed no mercy to any witness. We could ask almost anything without fear of the answer. After all, the jury, not yet sworn, would not be there to hear any damaging answers.

After the lengthy informative hearing, the judge denied our motion. However, we now knew the strengths and weaknesses of the prosecution's case. We also learned that there were at least a couple of informants helping the prosecution. Try as we did to learn their identities, the prosecutor refused to divulge this information.

The nature of the case, a violent struggle between labor and management, attracted a tremendous amount of press coverage. This would prove to be harmful during the trial but potentially helpful in the event an appeal would be required later.

No witness was able to point the finger at John McCullough, Tom McGrann, or any other union boss. The FBI and the Department of Labor had investigators on hand to aid the prosecution and watch the proceedings for possible federal violations, with one eye always on McCullough.

The trial took an additional seven months, including jury selection which lasted about a month, owing to the pervasive publicity. At that time it was noted that this was the longest criminal trial in the history of Pennsylvania.

We all did our share of effective cross. Chuck played with the witnesses. Cecil argued with them. I pointed out inconsistencies on many major points. Many witnesses had given prior statements that were markedly different from their testimony on the stand before the jury. Others testified differently than previous witnesses on the same set of facts and circumstances. Some of the photographs were damaging, and naturally, you cannot cross-examine a photograph.

Judge Robert Tredenick did a reasonably good job of keeping control of the courtroom despite the antics of the three defenders. We did, however, try to make life tough for him on many occasions. Often, when there was a legal issue to be resolved on a question of evidence or procedure, Chuck, Cecil, and I agreed that we would all take a different position on the law. Then no matter how the judge ruled on the objection there would always be some defendants left with an issue for appeal to a higher court.

This happened time and time again. On one specific occasion the judge decided to hear evidence without the jury present. One of us said we wanted the press present in an open courtroom. One of us objected and asked for a closed hearing. The third lawyer took no position.

The jury in this case was not sequestered. They went home every day after court. The press, both television and newspapers, was anything but kind to the defendants.

Despite the fact that we were trying this case in Montgomery County, Pennsylvania, which was known to be a conservative Republican and anti-union area, the jury had difficulty reaching a verdict and deliberated for many days. When they were finally brought back into the courtroom to announce their verdict in front of a couple of hundred union sympathizers, the jury foreman announced that they found five defendants guilty and four not guilty of the charges.

There were mixed emotions as the separate verdicts were announced. The four who were acquitted did not even smile. They knew that five of their "brothers" were facing time in prison and separation from their families.

Shortly after the verdict and the hounding questions from the press corps, John McCullough, several of his business agents, Cecil Moore, Stanley Branche, and I drove to the Valley Forge Hilton Hotel bar, where we proceeded to get smashed.

Stanley Branche and I spent many nights drinking with John McCullough, but never did we drink as much as on that occasion. He and I had become the best of friends from the time I met him in City Hall while trying Lillian Reis' case in front of Judge Weinrott. Stanley, like Cecil, was a president of a local chapter of the NAACP. His territory was Chester, Pennsylvania.

We spent many evenings during the trial at the same hotel bar discussing strategy for the next day. It was close to the suite I maintained as an office and used as sleeping quarters several nights a week. This case and that suite spelled the beginning of the end of my marriage. It was too easy not to go home after a long day in court followed by dinner and drinks.

The five convicted defendants received sentences ranging from two to five years in prison. They were, however, granted bail while their appeals were pending. The case came to be known as the "Altemose I" trial.

Shortly thereafter the Building Trades Council and the member unions decided to hire me to represent the five convicted men in their appeals. After a lengthy, expensive, and drawn-out appellate court process, the Pennsylvania Superior Court reversed the convictions of all five. One of the defendants was completely exonerated as a result of lack of sufficient evidence. The remaining four were granted a new trial.

The District Attorney, Bill Nicholas, was upset, but no more than the county commissioners who knew they would be faced with a second trial of these four and the exorbitant costs and loss of law enforcement personnel hours that would accompany the retrial.

Before the opinion reversing the convictions of the Altemose I defendants was published, we were obliged to deal with the impending trial of the Altemose II defendants. Fourteen of them. I was summoned to McGrann's office where I met once more with him, McCullough, and the other union officials to discuss finances for the remaining defendants. After a couple of hours it was decided that I alone would represent the remaining 14 defendants in the upcoming Altemose II trial. The fee agreed upon was $17,500 a week, just half of what the first trial had cost for legal services. I agreed to pay the investigators out of my weekly check.

Bill Nicholas and I agreed to postpone the trial for those defendants who had just won their appeals. The appellate court, in reversing the convictions in Altemose I, stated that due to the immense amount of prejudicial publicity both before and during the trial, the trial court erred in not sequestering the jury. The court further stated that absent sequestration, the trial court should have questioned the jurors every time they entered the jury box to determine if any of them had heard or read about the case. The opinion also stated that the jurors should have been warned each time they left the courtroom not to read or view television, or anything relating to the trial.

During the period between the two Altemose trials, I was able to dig into my heavy backlog of cases created by the first nine-month trial.

Judge Louis Stefan of Montgomery County was assigned to try this second group of defendants. He was intelligent, rather smooth, and mild-mannered. The judge had read the opinion reversing the Altemose I verdict and adhered to the ruling by carefully instructing and questioning the jurors on every break. Instead of lasting nine months, the trial was concluded in four. The issues and the nature of the eyewitness testimony were pretty much the same as in the first trial. Nicholas again prosecuted the case.

At the conclusion of the case, the jurors who had been deliberating asked by written note if they could come back into the courtroom to compare the photographic exhibits with the actual faces of the defendants. The judge over-ruled my objection to this procedure and ordered the defendants to sit in the courtroom while the twelve men and women, who held scores of photos in their hands, began scrutinizing the defendants to try to match up the faces with the names and finally with the pictures. One of the defendants, a roofers union organizer, was on parole for a crime he committed many years ago. If convicted he would have to spend his remaining years in prison. When the jurors approached him, he lifted his right arm above his head and then dropped his jacket over his head, covering his face. Hard as they tried, the jurors could not see his face. My intuition told me that his actions would get him convicted, but I was wrong. He was one of the five defendants acquitted.

Again we had a split verdict. The defendants and the entire membership of the Philadelphia Area Building and Construction Trades Council were determined to continue the fight. Altemose II was appealed. I was retained to prosecute the appeal on behalf of the nine roofers who were convicted.

In the meantime no action was being taken against the four defendants who were awaiting their retrial in Altemose I. I had plenty of time to work on the appellate cases and take on some new clients.

The Pennsylvania Supreme Court affirmed the convictions in Altemose II. Judge Stefan had exercised extreme care in order to avoid error by constantly reminding the jurors of their oaths. The sentences of nine roofers in the second case also ranged from two to five years' imprisonment.

The nine convicted men finally surrendered to begin serving their sentences. They were incarcerated at Graterford State Prison, not too far from the site of Altemose's building project. While there, with the aid of John McCullough and Roofers Union Local 30, they put a new roof on the prison.

I am pleased to say that within a couple of months, I obtained their release because of a legal defect in their sentencing procedure. No presentence report was prepared for any of these convicted men. The sentences were vacated, and on resentencing they were given time served.

While these guys were in jail, John McCullough made sure their families received weekly paychecks just as though they were still out on the street working. All the defendants in both cases had also been paid their normal wages during the length of the trials, thanks to "JJ."

I now had to deal with those four defendants who were up for retrial in Altemose I. The county was almost broke as a result of the tremendous amount of money spent to prosecute the 23 men. They were open for a plea bargain that would get them off the hook financially and keep their relationship with the unions friendly.

Morris Gerber, a former Montgomery County judge who was now practicing law, approached the District Attorney's Office to plea-bargain on behalf of the four roofers. Without much difficulty the DA agreed to probation for these four men. There was no need to retry the case.

The members of the Building Trades Council, the union leaders, and most importantly, the 23 men were all more than satisfied with the final result of this case. The union workingmen in the area continued to earn their top wages and fringe benefits.

Shortly thereafter, Leon J. Altemose declared bankruptcy. He had built his hotel and shopping center but he was unable to survive financially in the area.

William Nicholas, a worthy adversary, was elevated to the bench in Montgomery County, where he now sits as a fair and impartial judge.

From the day of the incident at the Altemose job site, in June 1972, through several pretrial hearings, two lengthy trials, and several appeals, I spent a little more than ten years working on this case on behalf of the individual men, the Roofers Union, and all 20,000 members of the Philadelphia Area Building and Construction Trades Council.

CHAPTER TEN

You Can't Win Them All

In the early seventies I spent most of my days in a courtroom. At night I often cruised the bars, restaurants, and after-hours clubs in Center City with close friends Stanley Branche, Tony DiSalvo, Ed Reif, and a few others who could keep up with us. I also maintained my relationships with John McCullough and the roofers from Northeast Philly. I continued to see Sindone, Testa, Angelo Bruno, and of course, Jake Kossman, often dining with them, usually at Dante and Luigi's or the Villa Di Roma where the Italian food was the next best thing to home cooking.

One of Frank Sindone's many friends, Louis, was arrested for bank robbery. It seems he was playing a high-stakes poker game in one of the many social clubs in South Philadelphia. He had been losing badly when he was finally dealt a full house.

Someone bet right into him. He was about to call and raise when he noticed he had no more money either on the table or in his pockets. He got up from the table and said, "I need a five-minute break."

Lou walked hurriedly around the corner where the neighborhood branch of one of Philadelphia's largest banks stood. He walked in with no disguise, no mask, and no note.

A young female teller had no one in her line, and she motioned Louis over to her window. "What can I do for you, Louey?" she asked.

Without hesitation he said, "Just give me all them bills you got dare in the drawer."

"You're kidding," she said. "Aren't you kidding me?"

"No, I'm in a hurry," he said as he also told her he had a gun in his pocket that he never showed.

The teller had known Louis for many years. They had gone to school together. Rather than argue with him or risk serious harm, she handed him a pile of bills. He grabbed them up in his hands and shoved them into his jacket pockets. Then he turned around, ran back to the club, and raised the bet. Before the next hand, the police arrived at the scene to lock him up. He never got to spend the money.

This was a case that Perry Mason couldn't win. On my advice he pled guilty. With the benefit of a psychiatric examination and report, Lou received probation.

I lost a couple of important cases within months of each other. My clients were to suffer dearly. Two federal arson and mail fraud trials resulted in guilty verdicts. Ralph Natale, whom I had defended successfully a few years before, went down first. He was the chief executive of the Culinary Workers Union in South Jersey.

After the verdict, and again after the imposition of the stiff sentence of twelve years, the prosecutor failed to move to revoke Ralph's bail. I smelled a rat, and I warned my client to be careful while he was free on bail during the appeal. As it turned out, my sense of smell was working fine. The government didn't just forget to move for bail revocation; an informant had alerted the FBI that Ralph was involved in a drug transaction in Florida. The federal authorities wanted Natale free so that they would be able to catch him in the process of buying a large quantity of drugs for resale.

Months later, Natale was arrested on a small yacht docked in Fort Lauderdale, Florida, making a buy of a substantial number of Quaaludes. His bail in the arson case was immediately revoked, and in addition he was held without bail on the new drug charge. He pled guilty, and 20 years were added to his arson sentence. Ralph Natale was one of several clients I couldn't save from years in prison. He spent approximately 17 years in custody before being released in the early nineties.

A government informant, Charles Allen, managed to gain the confidence of Ralph Natale and many others involved in union causes. Allen had been at one time an associate of James R. Hoffa, the charismatic and tough boss of the Teamsters. Allen also knew and spoke to many different people in South Philadelphia. More often than not he wore a wire. Allen's cover was blown during the appeal in Natale's arson/mail fraud case in the late seventies.

Reports began to trickle into the offices of the local FBI and Strike Force Division of the United States Attorney's Office that certain alleged organized crime figures were looking to stockpile small-caliber guns for use in what looked like a fast-approaching mob war in Philadelphia.

In the other arson/mail fraud case I lost, the government's evidence was based mainly on the testimony of a turncoat informant and the informant's girlfriend. After the verdict the government informant/witness tried to recant his testimony by saying he lied about my client's involvement. I would not file the moving papers. I felt the informant would only flip back to the government and make matters worse for my client. The Sidney Brooks case was still burning inside me. My client got pissed at me and he fired me and hired a lawyer who would follow his instructions even if it meant certain harm. Again my gut feeling was on the money. When pressured by the federal agents and prosecutors, the man flip-flopped and testified that my client had induced him to change his testimony. The recantation was partially the cause of the 50—yes, 50—year sentence.

After I had built a reputation for winning many difficult trials, numerous clients began to think a not guilty verdict was automatic. "All you had to do was hire Bobby Simone and you would win," they believed. Some of these people were not only disappointed when we lost, they were shocked. They just didn't realize how tough it is to win.

On December 7, 1973, reporter L. Stuart Ditzen of the *Evening Bulletin* wrote a feature story titled "Bobby Simone? He's the Defender of the 'Bad Guys.'" In it he states, "Bobby Simone has never been able to figure it out— which guys wear the white hats." After writing about some of my headline cases and celebrated clients, Ditzen quotes me saying, "There are no bad boys." He mentions that these were originally the words of Boys Town's Father Flanagan. His full-page article ends by quoting me saying, "I believe that as much as I believe there are no totally good boys." I still feel the same way.

▼ ▼ ▼

On October 30, 1974, Stanley Branche, Gus Lacey, and a few other friends walked with me into the Spectrum in the southernmost part of the city. It was a big night in Philadelphia, and for that matter in just about every other metropolis in the country. But it loomed even larger in Kinshasa, Zaire, where Muhammad Ali and George Foreman were going to fight for the heavyweight championship of the world.

Approximately 15,000 fight fans paid $40 to watch the spectacle on large-screen television. Millions more crowded into sports arenas and theaters all over the world. It seemed like the whole city was there to watch and bet. I was an Ali rooter from the early days. I admired the man and the athlete. I had dinner with him, Stanley, John Berkery, and Ali's friend Major Coxen. I had been a guest at Ali's beautiful home in Cherry Hill a couple of times. Coxen had purchased the Celebrity Room from Lillian Reis and Junior Staino. The settlement took place in my office.

In 1964, I bet $800 on Ali, then Cassius Clay, when he was a ten-to-one underdog to Sonny Liston. Ali won by a knockout. I went to Madison Square Garden in 1971 to see the first Joe Frazier–Muhammad Ali fight. I also attended the second Frazier-Ali fight in early 1974. When I walked into the Spectrum, I wanted to bet $500 on Ali.

There was enough cigarette and cigar smoke inside the arena to fill the entire fleet of Goodyear blimps. Fight fans need their tobacco fix. Underneath a thick cloud of that smoke I recognized the unsmiling face of Antonio "Tony Bananas" Caponigro. He was standing next to John Berkery.

Tony had recently been released from Atlanta Federal Penitentiary where he did a bit for assaulting a federal officer who was trying to serve a subpoena on him. Angelo Bruno had asked me a few years ago whether I would represent Bananas before the parole board. I declined. I knew he would never make parole, so why take the guy's money and add insult to injury.

John Berkery walked over to say hello to Stanley, Gus, and me. We exchanged pleasantries and then John asked, "Does anyone want to bet on Ali? Tony is looking to bet on Foreman." By now there were about six or seven men in our circle.

I was the only one to respond. "I'll bet on Ali. See if your friend will lay three to one. If he agrees I'll take fifteen to five."

John left our group and after whispering into Tony's ear, he pointed to me with his finger. Tony looked at me and nodded. John then came back and said, "You're down. Tony is laying you 15,000 to your five." *Thousand?* I thought I was betting 500. I was now in heart attack territory. I took a deep breath and said, "I do not have $5,000 on me."

Before I could say anything more to get out of the bet, John said, "That's okay, he trusts you. The loser will give me the money within a week's time and I will deliver it to the winner."

When Ali came off the ropes in the seventh round to beat the living shit out of George Foreman and regain his title, I went berserk punching the air. "Bop-bop-bop." We were all screaming our lungs out.

Three weeks later I received my fifteen grand from the North Jersey wise guy.

▼ ▼ ▼

Included in the multitude of cases and somewhat interesting clients, I'll never forget being summoned while mingling and drinking with lawyers and judges at a Philadelphia Bar Association cocktail party. The message was, "Go to your office. Linda Lovelace is there waiting to see you."

I thought it might be a prank, but I did not have it in me to pass up an opportunity to meet the one and only Linda Lovelace. What a title, *Deep Throat*. When I returned to my office around 7:00 p.m., there she was, sitting at my desk with some short guy with a long gray beard, her producer. She was thin, but put together solidly. She had light brown hair, and she was rather attractive. Her lips were all they were advertised to be—large, well shaped, and sensual.

She was being sued by two promoters for failing to honor personal appearance contracts. She also had some minor problem with the police in Las Vegas. I went to both Miami and Vegas to help her in resolving her legal problems. They never did refer to me as a "porn queen lawyer." I guess once a mob lawyer, always a mob lawyer.

This incident reminded me of the time Sid Luft, who was Judy Garland's manager and husband, called me to get her out of jail. Some misunderstanding about a hotel bill. I thought it was a hoax. When the gentleman called me and identified himself, the voice on the other end added, "I have been told that if you have a problem in Philadelphia, you're the man to see."

I said, "Yes, I know and by the way Simone isn't here. You are talking to Frank Sinatra." They ended up getting another lawyer and I read about the incident in the newspaper the next day.

▼ ▼ ▼

In the middle of 1975, I received a call from Mel Kessler, a criminal lawyer who practiced in Miami. He told me that a client of his, Richard Cravera, was in trouble in Toms River, New Jersey, and also in Miami. Kessler asked if I would be interested in representing him in one or both cases.

The state case in New Jersey never developed; he was not charged with any crime. His problems in Miami took a different turn.

I flew to Miami and represented Cravera at a bail hearing where he was charged in a huge drug conspiracy and also named as a kingpin under the Federal Continuing Criminal Enterprise Act. To my surprise, the United States Magistrate sitting in Miami set bail for Cravera, and he posted $50,000 and was released.

He didn't get much time to enjoy his freedom. In a few months, Ricky and four of his associates were charged with first-degree murder in Miami. Cravera's luck ran out. He was held on that charge without bail.

. I spent many weeks commuting from Philadelphia to Miami where I stayed at the Jockey Club on Biscayne Boulevard near 110th Street. I was preparing for the murder trial and enjoying the mild winter and Gulfstream Race Track. Ricky hired another lawyer, Jay Hogan, to represent him in the federal drug case.

It was at the Jockey Club that I met Rita Carr. I saw her pass by me in the lounge and walk around the bar with another taller young lady. I couldn't take my eyes off her as she quickly circled the large and boisterous crowd. She was stunning. Long, dark hair swept from the back of her head, past her shoulders, and down her back. Her large, brown, Asian-looking eyes lit up the whole room. She walked with grace, and even though she wasn't smiling, I could imagine how beautiful that smile would be.

I reached out and grabbed her arm as she was heading back to the front door of the club, about to disappear into the crowd. I did not want her to walk in and out of my life so swiftly.

Richard Cravera's best friend and partner in crime, Billy, became the main witness for the State of Florida. I lost my first murder case. The jury voted for the death penalty, but the trial judge reversed the sentence and handed out life sentences to the three guilty defendants. Two of the defendants were found not guilty by the judge before the case was submitted to the jury. The informant was given immunity and freedom in exchange for his testimony.

The deceased had been shot no less than 17 times. The informant testified that he participated in the shooting with Cravera and two others. He also said that the two who were acquitted had obtained the four guns used to complete the job. No client of mine has ever received the death penalty. Ricky came close. He would also eventually be convicted of drug charges in federal court and sentenced to a consecutive 45-year sentence.

I found myself returning to Miami even after Ricky's case was over. I was determined to continue seeing Rita. By this time I was madly in love. I did the best I could to change some of my bad habits. My gambling and drinking decreased, but didn't stop altogether. After all, I was now handling more clients, and the stakes were getting higher. I still had the need to unwind, to blow off steam.

By now I had finally realized I had to put my clients' welfare to the side for just a short period of time and get my personal life straightened out. I needed a divorce; more urgently, I needed to marry Rita.

It was easier than I imagined once I devoted a little time and effort to the problems of working out a fair settlement with Arlene. I managed to obtain an agreement in only a couple of weeks, and then I was off to Santo Domingo, where I got a one-day, quickie divorce.

Soon afterwards, Rita and I were preparing our wedding, which was to take place in Miami. We selected the Cricket Club for both the ceremony and the reception. Now we had to work on the guest list.

We narrowed the list down to about 200 people. Most of those on my side of the aisle were from the Philadelphia area. Many of them failed to show even after we received their RSVP saying they would come.

CHAPTER ELEVEN

▼

Viva Las Vegas

The substantial money I was earning in the Altemose cases allowed me to pay off most of the balance I owed to various sharks. I tried hard to keep current with the IRS, but that was not so easy for me. I still had a serious gambling problem. Las Vegas was on the other side of the country, but only a five-hour flight away. The complimentary airfare and hotel room, along with the free food and beverages, made it very tempting.

One Labor Day weekend in the early seventies I was invited to the MGM Hotel and Casino with everything on the house. The bargain included first-class airfare for Arlene, the two kids, a baby sitter, and myself, plus two luxury suites, all meals, liquor, and wine. We could not say no when they added front-row seats to the hottest show around—the Jackson Five featuring the young and talented Michael.

I recall that "free" vacation costing me about $20,000.

▼ ▼ ▼

Ralph Staino, Jr. was indicted by the Feds and charged along with a friend of Stanley Branche's, Sonny Viner, with conspiracy to possess and distribute counterfeit money. Sonny, a thin, handsome, smiling African American, was a well-known man about town. He frequented the fine restaurants in Philadelphia and the Clubhouse at the Garden State Racetrack across the river in Haddonfield, New Jersey. I spent many afternoons there near the finish line with Junior, Sonny, and several other hardcore horse bettors. The touts had a field day with us. Oh, how I miss those days.

During the trial, several wiretapped conversations were played for the jury. In one such conversation, while Junior was discussing his gambling with Sonny Viner, he said, "Did you hear about Bobby Simone? Last week he won twelve out of thirteen football games and beat the bookie out of a shit pot full of money."

I gave Junior a dirty look, then smiled and said, "It was thirteen out of fourteen."

The trial was winding down, and I was about to argue a Rule 29 motion for Judgment of Acquittal before the trial judge who happened to be the Chief Judge of the United States District Court for the Eastern District of Pennsylvania, the Honorable Alfred Luongo. He changed his mind about staying late and told us to come back the next morning at 9:30 for oral arguments.

That night, Stanley Branche and I did the town up real big. We started about 6:00 in the evening and went to about 4:00 a.m. when we closed the 2-4 Club in Center City. Stanley prevented some woman weighing about 250 pounds from kidnapping me and taking me to her home.

He dropped me off at my small apartment at 17th and the Parkway, maintained for nights like this. I wandered into the building and miraculously found my way on and off the elevator, into my apartment, and into bed. Within minutes I was asleep.

The next time my eyes opened, I saw Stanley's full, pleasant face staring at me as he shook my shoulders. "Come on, Bobby, get up. You're supposed to be in court at 9:30. Get your ass out of bed."

"What time is it?"

"It's 10:30. They have been calling from the courthouse all morning," he told me as he helped me gather my clothes.

I found myself putting on the same dirty shirt, socks, tie, and rumpled suit. My body and the clothes smelled of Remy Martin. That figures since I drank enough of it the night before. I quickly washed my hands and face but didn't waste time brushing my teeth. There definitely was not enough time to shave either.

Stanley dropped me off at the courthouse about 11:10. "Good luck, partner. What time tonight?" He laughed and sped away. What a laugh he had. What a friend I had.

Judge Luongo was sitting behind the bench, and the prosecutor and Secret Service agent sat at counsel table near the empty jury box. My buddy, Eddy Reif, was whispering to his client Sonny Viner and Junior.

"Well, Mr. Simone, I hope you have a good excuse." I felt as bad as I looked and smelled.

"Your Honor, I have no valid excuse."

Judge Luongo looked at my client, then at me, and said, "I find you in contempt of court. You are ordered to pay a fine of $600."

Fortunately, Judge Luongo did not take my tardiness out on my client. He kept the jurors in the dark as to the reason for the delay. The jury was called into the courtroom and told that we had been going over some legal matters, and then they were dismissed until 1:30 when testimony was to resume.

Judge Luongo then ordered me to argue my Rule 29 motion. The basis for the argument was that there was insufficient evidence to prove beyond a reasonable doubt that Staino was involved in either the conspiracy or the act of possession of the counterfeit bills with intent to distribute them. His phone conversations were not really incriminating. He was never heard discussing phony money.

After listening intently to both arguments, Judge Luongo did not hesitate. "Motion granted as to the defendant Staino" were words as sweet as a jury saying, "Not guilty."

Ralph Staino smiled as we left the courtroom. "Bobby, you are fucking crazy." When I awoke the next day in Cheltenham, I picked up the *Philadelphia Inquirer*. The headline read, "Staino Acquitted, Simone Convicted."

A couple of weeks later, I received a call from Chief Judge Luongo. He wanted to see me in his chambers. I was concerned that he might want to give me a speech about holding up the trial and the jury that morning. I was wrong. He gave me his brother's phone number and asked me to call him about a personal family matter that he and his brother wanted me to handle. I must have done something right during the trial.

As it turned out, I was in more trouble with Arlene than with Judge Luongo. After she read about my being held in contempt of court and the reason for it, she was livid. Her patience was wearing thin.

▼ ▼ ▼

One Sunday afternoon, while I was at Liberty Bell Racetrack in the Northeast section of Philadelphia, the strangest thing happened. I can't remember if I was winning or losing at the time, but I am sure I was enjoying myself. Out of the clear blue came a loud announcement over the public address system. "Will Mr. Robert Simone please report to the business office immediately."

The message was repeated two more times. Now everybody at the track, thousands of people, had to know I frequented the racetrack. Whenever I went there alone, I told my wife and everyone else that I was going somewhere on business. This time I was caught dead. Trying to get these thoughts out of my mind, I switched gears and hurried down the back steps to the office area. It finally dawned on me that something major had occurred. They never page anyone at the racetrack.

A young secretary seated behind the desk in the lobby gave me a hand-written note. I hurriedly opened it and read, "Robert Simone, call Al Pagano at once. Emergency!" The young lady was kind enough to let me use her telephone, and I reached Al Pagano on the line.

By the way, he too had a nickname, just like most of my clients. His moniker was "Al Pajamas." Vincent, Albert, Al Pajamas; I called him by all three names on different occasions.

He sounded unusually excited as he tried to tell me, "Cookie's in jail. She was just arrested for murder. You gotta get her out. I need to see you right away."

It was serious, but I must admit I was somewhat relieved that no one in my family was involved in an accident or deathly ill. I promised myself I would never sneak to the racetrack alone on a Sunday again. Just like a New Year's resolution, it only took a couple of months before I was back at the windows betting with both hands, Sundays included.

Pajamas, who was over six feet tall, built like a lean linebacker, and had short-cropped dark hair, owned and operated a few restaurants and bars in Center City. He was distantly related to Angelo Bruno, but up to this time, law enforcement officials considered him to be semi-legitimate and not involved in organized crime activities.

Cookie, whose real name was Dolores, was blonde, pretty, extremely well built, and always tan. She and "Albert," as she called him, were an item for many years. However, during one of their separation periods, she met a young, successful businessman. They married and settled into a luxurious modern home in Huntingdon Valley, a yuppie neighborhood adjacent to Northeast Philadelphia.

When I met Pajamas over a cup of coffee that Sunday afternoon, he told me that Cookie had been physically abused by her husband for some time. He went on to tell me that earlier that morning, Cookie and her husband were arguing in their kitchen. A pot of hot water was being heated for tea at the time. He slapped her in the face, then punched her with his fist. She screamed. He told her to shut up. When she continued to holler, he reached for the pot of hot water. She ran from the kitchen, up the stairs, and into the master bedroom. She closed and locked the door behind her in one swift motion.

Within seconds she heard the pounding at the door. Frightened and crying, she yelled for him to leave her alone. He continued to bang on the door. She knew where he kept his .38-caliber revolver. Scared to death, she pulled it out of his drawer. Immediately after, she heard the sound of cracking wood as the door and its jambs gave way. At a glance she saw the fire in his eyes and the pot of boiling water in his hand.

She pointed the gun in his direction and when he was about three or four feet away, she fired. It was a lucky shot for her, unlucky for him. The bullet pierced the left side of his chest and continued through his upper body, exiting the rear of his trunk. It passed directly through his heart. He fell to the floor, and the pot of boiling water landed within inches of his body.

Cookie took a couple of real deep breaths as she dropped the gun where she stood. She called the police and then called Albert to tell him what happened. "Can we get her out on bail?" he asked. "What will it take?"

I told him I would do what I could and call him as soon as possible. Sunday is not a good day to get arrested, as if any day is. By the time I got to see her late Sunday afternoon, she had already given a statement, telling the police detectives basically the same story Al had related to me.

The first policeman on the scene made note of the broken door and the teapot and water-soaked rug. The detectives wrote in their report that the water in the pot was still warm when they arrived.

Early Monday morning I managed to get the DA's office to agree to a reasonable bail. After Cookie was released on bail, I advised her to make no more statements and stay home until the preliminary hearing. She said she couldn't sleep in that house and would feel better staying with relatives. I also told her and Pajamas to stay away from each other. No sense in giving the other side a potential motive.

At the preliminary hearing, I stipulated to the cause of death. I saw no need to have the coroner testify to prove something that we were not contesting. The assigned assistant district attorney put the policeman who first arrived at the scene on the stand. They introduced the gun and a report from a fingerprint expert that positively identified her prints as being on the gun handle. The prosecutor rested.

Normally, it is not to the advantage of the defendant to offer evidence at a preliminary hearing. I decided to disregard the norm, and I called the detective who interviewed and obtained the statement from Cookie. I made him read her entire statement on the record. I knew that the press would put it out there for everyone to see.

The district judge refused to dismiss all the charges but dismissed the first-degree murder charge and held her for trial on third-degree murder and voluntary and involuntary manslaughter. He permitted Cookie to remain free on bail.

Just before the case was listed for trial, the DA called me to offer a deal for a plea to voluntary manslaughter. I told him I couldn't plead her even to involuntary manslaughter. We stuck to our guns, and as I had hoped, the DA moved to dismiss the case rather than go to trial. He had tried to bluff us (as if I never played poker before).

Cookie and I appeared in Norristown and the judge dismissed the case. After court we enjoyed a nice lunch and a bottle of cold white wine—Cookie, Pajamas, and me.

▼ ▼ ▼

By now I was able to handle the pressure of my constant courtroom battles. Drinking and gambling were my "outs." There were periods of several days at a time that I did not go home. And yes, there were women. I am not proud of it, but there were always plenty of them around. Arlene wasn't buying it, though. Soon, I moved out of the house, and our marriage was dead. It would take a few more years before we gave it a decent burial.

I continued to stop at Jake Kossman's office at least a couple of times a week, usually late in the afternoon after court. Jake never ceased to amaze me with his knowledge and grasp of the law. I loved talking with him — mostly listening to him expounding on the law and some very interesting theories about strategy. He was a master. His list of past and present clients included Angelo Bruno, Frank Costello, James Hoffa, Sr., and Anthony Corrallo, also known as "Tony Ducks."

Jake had few, if any, inhibitions. He always spoke the truth and rarely held back his opinion on any topic of discussion. Angelo Bruno and Kossman were as close as brothers. There was a mutual respect between the two of them. I believe I learned a great deal each time I was in their company. Jake often advised and helped me with my difficult trials, and Angelo liked to lecture on life in general. He preached moderation.

One day, Kossman took the Metroliner into Manhattan. It seemed he had an appointment with Joseph Colombo, who was interested in retaining Jake to represent him in a grand jury investigation. Colombo was allegedly the boss of one of New York's five organized crime families.

Jake was picked up at Grand Central Station and driven by limousine to a restaurant on Mulberry Street in Little Italy. He was instructed to walk into the restaurant where he was told "someone" would be waiting for him.

A tall, well-dressed man wearing a dark suit approached Kossman and ushered him through the kitchen and out the back door. He got into a large sedan in which a driver sat with the motor running. Once seated in the rear of the car, Jake asked, "What the fuck is going on?"

The driver turned and smiled at both Kossman and the fellow in the dark suit. "We're taking you to see Mr. Colombo right now." He stepped on the accelerator, and the sedan sped off. After a drive of about 20 minutes, the car pulled into the driveway of a rather large garage.

The three men got out of the car, and Jake was ushered through the doorway into a huge, open, vacant area.

Off to the side there was another doorway, which led into a space about four feet wide and ten feet long. Standing by a white sink was the man Jake had come to see. Colombo put his index finger on his lips, motioning Jake not to speak. Then he turned on the faucet, and the water came pouring out. The sound of the running water made it difficult to hear a conversation, especially through a bugging device.

Before Jake left Philadelphia, he had been promised a fee from Colombo of $20,000. Jake walked over next to Colombo and the sink. The noise of the running water caused Jake to speak a little louder than normal. He said, "Did you bring the fucking money?"

Colombo whispered to Jake, "Speak softer, the walls have ears."

Jake repeated, "Did you bring the fucking money?" He was already aggravated for having been bounced around like a pinball.

Colombo opened a small briefcase and put his hand inside to remove some legal documents he wanted Jake to examine. "Look at these, will ya."

Kossman said, "Is the money in there? Do you have the fee?"

Colombo whispered with just enough volume to allow Jake to hear him over the sound of the running water, "I'll get it to you later."

Jake looked at Colombo and said in a clear, loud voice, "Turn the fucking water off," then he turned and left the room.

After all the mystery and trouble they put Jake through he wasn't about to say another word without first getting paid—in advance—as they had agreed. In five minutes he received his fee.

One afternoon Jake told us he would be a little late for dinner with the usual crew. He had an appointment with a wealthy businessman from New York. The man entered Jake's office, opened his briefcase on top of Jake's untidy desk, and pulled out numerous news clippings. "These will give you some idea of what my problems are," he said in a rather excited manner.

"You were supposed to bring me $50,000," Jake said as he put the newspaper articles back in the case and closed it. The businessman, embarrassed, grabbed his briefcase, turned around, and left the office in a hurry.

The very next day, the same man returned to Kossman's office, opened his briefcase, and plunked $50,000 in $100 bills on Jake's desk.

Jake looked at the man and smiled. "Am I glad to see you," he said. "When you ran out of here yesterday, I thought you went to call the cops to have me locked up for extortion."

Around the same time, Frank Sindone called me at my office and said, "Bobby, Ange would like to see you over at Jake's. He's got a new client for you."

I finished what I was working on and started the familiar walk over to Kossman's office a few blocks away. On the way over, as I passed a corner newsstand, I noticed a headline in one of those weekly tabloids that read, "U.S. Government Has New Mind-Reading Machine."

I purchased the newspaper and read this absurd story about an invention that enabled government law enforcement personnel to read a suspect's mind. This, of course, would create a tremendous headache for people like my friends and clients who already had their share of problems with the electronic surveillance equipment currently being used by the government.

When I walked into Jake's office, I dropped the tabloid on Bruno's lap and said, "I suggest you read this."

Kossman read the headline over Bruno's shoulder and quipped, "Well, Ange, some of your buddies won't have anything new to worry about since their minds are always blank anyway."

There was another gentleman seated next to Bruno facing Jake's desk. I could tell he was short and stocky, even though he was not standing. He had gray hair, a prominent nose, a thick moustache, and this strange habit of biting his lower lip and then sucking on it.

Bruno introduced me to the gray-haired man. "Bobby, this is 'Pappy.'

He's my cousin. His real name is Carl Ippolito. He just got a subpoena to testify in New Jersey. He was served in Philadelphia, not New Jersey." Angelo was free for the moment only because of his internal bleeding.

I shook hands with Pappy, who seemed nervous. He didn't say much at all. He just kept biting and sucking his lip. I read the papers he handed me, and I noticed that he was scheduled for a hearing in City Hall right here in Philly.

We agreed to meet in my office the next day to discuss his case privately. Before we met, I did some research on the Interstate Uniform Witness Act that provided for the appearance in court of witnesses who were located out of state. I found what I thought were a couple of good legal issues that I could present on Ippolito's behalf. Just maybe, I could get the subpoena quashed.

I was able to postpone a ruling to order Pappy over to New Jersey to answer questions. The Pennsylvania judge agreed that there was some merit to my argument questioning the validity of the New Jersey subpoena being served in Pennsylvania. After all, my client was not wanted as a witness in a criminal trial or hearing. He was wanted only as a witness before the State Commission of Investigations (SCI), an administrative body that had been investigating organized crime for several years in New Jersey.

The ruling against Pappy didn't come for over a year and a half and when it did I was able to appeal the order and obtain a stay which held up his appearance before the Commission while the appeal was pending. I knew that Ippolito would do the same as Bruno, Ziccarelli, Catena, and several others including Nicodemo Scarfo. Rather than answer questions, he would subject himself to prison for contempt of court. It was a matter of principle with these guys.

At least another year went by before the appellate courts in Pennsylvania ruled against us. Pappy now had to go to New Jersey and answer questions. He pled the Fifth Amendment on most of the questions. Many of them were of the "Do you know?" variety. Unlike a grand jury proceeding, I was permitted to remain with him during questioning.

Some of the questions asked of Ippolito went like this:

Q. Are you a member of La Cosa Nostra, or the Mafia?
Q. Do you know Angelo Bruno?
Q. Do you know Philip Testa?
Q. Do you know Frank Sindone?
Q. Do you know Frank Narducci?
Q. Do you know Nicodemo Scarfo?

To all of the above, Pappy followed my advice and answered, "I plead the Fifth Amendment of the United States Constitution on the grounds the answer might tend to incriminate me."

The Assistant Attorney General decided to move the proceedings before a judge for further action. He argued that the answers to the "Do you know?"

questions could not be incriminating. The state's attorney pushed the court to order the witness to answer the questions without being given immunity.

I had done my homework and was therefore able to cite a few cases holding that similar types of questions did call for a potential incriminating answer. To my surprise the judge agreed with my position. This was the same judge who ordered many of Pappy's friends and associates to jail.

The state appealed the judge's order. Six months later the Appellate Division of the Superior Court of New Jersey reversed him and ordered Ippolito to answer the questions without immunity.

I hit the law books again, and spent considerable time discussing the case with Jake Kossman. I appealed the decision to the New Jersey Supreme Court. Months later, Jake Kossman, Carl Ippolito, and I drove to Trenton, New Jersey, where I argued the appeal on Pappy's behalf.

Another year went by before the court decided that our position was correct. The New Jersey Supreme Court ruled in a case of first impression that Ippolito did not have to answer the "Do you know?" questions without first being granted immunity.

By the time the final decision was handed down, the SCI had lost most of its steam. The others had already been released from prison. Pappy did not have to testify. He was the only one of his friends and associates who did not answer questions. He was the only one who did not go to jail for not answering.

Pappy, my buddy Frank Sindone, and I celebrated by taking a long weekend in "Sin City"—Las Vegas, Nevada. It was not the first time Frank and I had gone to Las Vegas for the weekend, and there would be many more weekends to enjoy the night life and the casino gambling out there. None of us seemed to mind the fact that most of the time we lost thousands of dollars. Sick, compulsive gamblers usually don't give a damn.

There were times when we won at the tables, and on those occasions one win made up for five losing trips. On one of those winning weekends I won several thousand dollars shooting craps, my favorite game. A lovely, long-haired blonde, trim but built like a topless dancer, worked her way over to where I was standing at the craps table at Caesar's. I was in my glory, drinking and gambling with stacks of black chips in front of me. *Of all the joints in Vegas and all the tables in town she picks this one.*

I was too involved with the roll that was into the eighth pass to notice that she was not wearing a bra. I would get to that later. And "Chickie," Joseph Ciancaglini, would make sure. Sindone had earlier told Chickie, "Keep your eye on Bobby, don't let him get in trouble."

Chickie was always with Frank Sindone. Philadelphia, New Jersey, Vegas— it made no difference. They were together all the time, or so it seemed. Chickie was another guy with a magnificent body—muscle, nothing but muscle. Over six feet tall and powerfully built, always smiling or at least grinning. He was doing what Sindone asked, keeping an eye on me. His other eye was on the bombshell whose right arm was now snugly wrapped around my waist. The whole world loves a winner.

After three more line numbers, about eight more box numbers, $12,000 more in winnings, the dreaded seven arrived. By then it did not matter too much. I had just finished my fourth Bombay martini and taken my first good look at the 22-year-old beauty, Gale. I was almost hoping the seven would show.

Chickie looked at me and said, "Let's go. We gotta get changed for the Sinatra show tonight." He, Sindone, Phil Testa's son, Salvatore, a few others, and I were staying across the street at the Holiday Casino, owned by a friend of Angelo Bruno from back in the fifties, before Castro, when Havana was the preferred spot for gambling and sun worshippers.

Gale asked, "Are you guys going to the Frank Sinatra show tonight?"

Chickie picked her up and gently put her on his right shoulder, her fantastic ass facing the ceiling. He said, "Yes, and so are you."

I stuffed handfuls of chips into my pockets, all different colors, but mostly black 100s with about a dozen or so pink 500s. "Let's get some new clothes first," I said as we hustled out of the casino area and made for the clothing stores. Easy come, easy go.

Later that night, Chickie dressed in a new tux. Salvy Testa was wearing a dark blue suit and a beautiful redhead on his arm. Gale, in a shiny, tight, low-cut, silver sequin dress, smelled as great as she looked. I was all decked out in a tan silk cardigan suit, chocolate-colored sport shirt, and matching dark brown suede shoes. Another couple joined us as we walked into Caesar's show room where we were comped for the sellout show and drinks.

Sindone made the arrangements for the show and our ringside table, but he preferred to stay in the Holiday Casino and shoot craps until he went broke or he couldn't stand anymore. Our group drank several bottles of Dom Perignon and a score of snifters filled with Martel Cordon Bleu. Frank Sinatra sang at least as well as he had at any other time. I had seen him at least a dozen times at the Fountainbleu in Miami, at the Latin Casino in Cherry Hill, New Jersey, and elsewhere, but there was something about the electricity he created whenever he appeared in Vegas that made him sound and look so special.

A few minutes after the show ended, our waiter handed me a long check sitting on a white piece of china. I glanced at it expecting to see "Comp" or "No charge." To my total surprise it read "$850.00 due." Without thinking I hurled the dish straight up in the air. A crystal chandelier broke into several pieces upon contact. Chickie rushed to my side and said, "Bobby, calm down. I'll straighten this out." He did. The maitre d' apologized for the error as Salvy quickly secreted Gale and me out of the show room.

The next morning one of Caesar's casino hosts called Sindone and said, "I'm sorry, Frank, but your lawyer busted a $5,000 chandelier last night."

Quickly, Frank replied, "That's impossible. He was with me, here at the Holiday Casino, all night. It has to be a case of mistaken identity."

"Okay, Frank, if that's the way you want it to go." The host gave in rather easily. But he added, "It would help me square this beef if you and Simone came in and gave us a play before you head back to Philly."

"No problem," Frank answered.

When he told me about his talk with the host I said, "The tables are turned. It seems you are now representing me."

He answered, "I think it might be cheaper if you just pay them for the chandelier."

You know, he was right. We both dropped about ten grand in less than an hour. Justice.

CHAPTER TWELVE

▼

Marriage and Murders

In the late seventies, Philip Leonetti, Scarfo's nephew, was arrested for the gunshot murder of Pepe Leva, an Atlantic City wannabe wiseguy. The killing occurred in the early morning a few miles northwest of Atlantic City. After Uncle Nick was able to get his beloved nephew released on bail, he brought him to Philadelphia to meet with me. It was the first time I saw the dark-complected, handsome young man. Nick Scarfo did all the talking. Philip was eerily silent.

At the time, New Jersey courts were still not permitting out-of-state lawyers to represent defendants in criminal cases. Nevertheless, I managed to help in getting Philip off the hook by bringing him to a young attorney licensed to practice in Pennsylvania and New Jersey, Robert Sigal. With the help of Harold Garber, who by this time was a prominent lawyer in Atlantic City, the charges against Philip Leonetti were dismissed.

Harold managed to get the sole eyewitness to recant his original statement in which he identified Leonetti as the shooter. Sigal utilized the new statement of the witness at exactly the right time. Jeffrey Blitz, the First Assistant District Attorney of Atlantic County, New Jersey, had no choice but to drop the charges before trial. I merely advised Sigal, Garber, and Philip from the sidelines. Nick gave me more credit for the result than I deserved.

In this instance justice was served. Philip Leonetti was truly innocent. Years later the authorities learned the identity of the actual killer.

▼ ▼ ▼

George Botsaris, better known as "George the Greek," was alleged to be the top man in "The Greek Mob." Actually, I never saw any evidence that such an organization existed. A jury in City Hall found him not guilty of assault and attempted murder when I was able to show that the only damage the prosecution proved was to a telephone that somehow was shot in a scuffle between George and another Greek. The incident amounted to no more than a minor argument over a bill owed to George—no big deal.

In a more serious case, George was the only one of about twelve indicted defendants who refused to plead guilty to drug charges in U.S. District Court in Camden, New Jersey. The evidence was thin, and the Honorable Stanley Brotman granted my motion for Judgment of Acquittal after the government rested. There wasn't sufficient evidence to take to the jury. George did use drugs, but they were unable to prove he dealt them.

I had met George in his large convenience store located at 20th and Spruce Streets in Center City Philadelphia. He was always kind to Scott and me, often filling our kitchen with food he sold at his market. He never charged us for anything. He was constantly arrested, and I was always there for him and usually I didn't charge him. My daughter, Kim, moved to Florida with Arlene shortly after the divorce, but Scott chose to remain in Philadelphia with me.

A day after George was acquitted in federal court, he drove a new Toyota to the front of my Lombard Street address and gave me the keys. He also handed me a title for the car made out in the name of Rita Carr.

Rita and I were engaged at the time, and we spent a great deal of time together in Philly and Miami.

▼ ▼ ▼

Jake Kossman's office was still a hangout for Bruno and some of his friends and associates. When Sindone and Testa were busy, Ange was usually driven by Mario "Sonny" Riccobene or Raymond "Long John" Martorano. Sonny was half-brother to Harry Riccobene, reputed to be a card-carrying member for many years. His nickname was "Hunchback Harry." Need I say more? Long John was associated with Bruno in the extremely successful cigarette and vending machine business. Both Sonny and Raymond were at Jake's office with Ange and Jake when I stopped by one afternoon in mid-March 1980.

"Hi, Bobby, good to see you. You gonna have dinner with us tonight? We're going to Franky's," Ange said as I entered Jake's office. Sindone was now the owner of a fine Italian restaurant at 11th and Christian Streets in

South Philly. It was called Cous' Little Italy, named after the popular chef known by everybody as "Cous." Nicky Scarfo's uncles, the three Piccolo brothers, had owned it for years.

"No, thanks," I said. "I got to catch a plane for Miami in a couple of hours. I just stopped by to see how you guys were doing."

Bruno told me he was going to try to be in Miami for my wedding. I didn't really know if he meant it, but I said, "I am glad to hear that, and we really hope you and your wife can make it." Before leaving for the airport, I shook Angelo Bruno's hand and said goodbye to the other guys. Jake, of course, still did not shake hands.

Rita, as usual, was waiting for me at the Miami airport. After a big hug and an affectionate kiss, she drove us to a quiet restaurant in Coconut Grove where we shared a bottle of red wine and some delicious French cuisine.

We were home by about 10:00, 10:30, and no sooner had we walked into the house than the phone rang. I answered it, and the voice on the other end said, "Bob, did you hear about it? Angelo Bruno has been murdered."

I can't recall anything else about the conversation. I don't even remember who it was that first called me to give me the news. I do recall being on the phone for over an hour that night talking to several other people in Philly, getting many of the gory details.

Angelo Bruno, the man who once told me, and I am sure many others, "Always do the right thing, and you won't have to go through life looking over your shoulder," was struck down, ironically enough, by a blast from a shotgun fired from behind, over his shoulder, into the back of his head. Ange was seated in the right front passenger's seat of an old-model car, and John Stanfa, like Bruno, born in Sicily, was seated in the driver's seat. The right front window was open just enough. The car was parked directly in front of the Bruno home in the 900 block of Snyder Avenue in South Philadelphia.

That fatal night Jake Kossman was driven home from the restaurant by Sonny Riccobene, leaving at the same time Ange left with Stanfa. Long John begged off driving Jake or Angelo home that night.

I flew home to the City of Brotherly Love the day before the funeral and went immediately to the Bruno residence where I paid my respects to Angelo's widow and children as I sat at the dining room table with Jake Kossman, Salvatore Avena (a criminal lawyer from Camden, New Jersey), and several of Bruno's close relatives. I was reminded of a happier time on the past Easter when I stopped there for a hearty meal and some good conversation. My sadness could not compare with Kossman's despair. He was like a lost soul. Never again would he be able to sit down and exchange ideas with intelligent and understanding dear friend Angelo. Never again would Jake be able to zing his buddy and get zinged in return in such a friendly, noncombative manner. Never again would they sit together listening to the classical music they both loved so much. He had truly lost his best friend.

The crowds flocked to the evening wake. Thousands of people waited in a line a couple blocks long just to get inside the funeral parlor to be near the casket. To these people this was not a viewing of some mobster. It was a trib-ute to a fine gentleman who had earned the love and respect of many people in all walks of life. Several judges, throwing caution to the wind, came to show their respect and admiration. None of them was ever criticized for it.

Hundreds of beautiful and colorful wreaths were transported from the funeral parlor to the cemetery the next morning as part of the procession of more than 100 vehicles. Many of Bruno's close friends did not attend the wake or the funeral. They had paid their respects at the home in the few days before. There was no need to give the reporters, photographers, and television cameras more fuel for the sensational fire that was burning out of control. The police and the FBI, cameras in hand, were disappointed by the absence of the members of Bruno's other family.

Jerry Blavat, the "Geator with the Heator," was one of the pallbearers. Jerry loved Bruno, and he did not give a fuck who knew it. He often ate with us and usually paid the check. Jerry was a disc jockey, club owner, and friend of all the stars. His Margate, New Jersey, nightclub, Memories, was constantly under surveillance by law enforcement agencies merely because he was friendly with the "wrong people."

Already there was widespread speculation about who had ordered the murder and who would be the next "Don."

John Stanfa, the Sicilian who was seated next to Bruno when he was shot, was subpoenaed before a federal grand jury. He testified, after being granted immunity, about his whereabouts shortly after Bruno's death. Subsequently, he was indicted, tried, and convicted of perjury in connection with his grand jury testimony when he forgot to reveal that he was in New York City shortly after the assassination. He was sent to federal prison to do an eight-year sentence. A blessing in disguise for Stanfa. It beats the death penalty he was facing from some of Bruno's friends who believed Stanfa was involved in the assassination.

Within the next couple of months, Bruno's friends from Philadelphia and New York did what the police and the FBI couldn't, they solved the Bruno murder. Antonio Caponigro, "Tony Bananas," and his driver were found dead in two separate automobiles in the Bronx. They had both been shot. Caponigro's rectum was stuffed with $20 bills: a sign of greed. A clear indication that Tony Bananas planned the Bruno murder so that he could replace the dead Don.

I remembered how concerned Bruno was about his friend Caponigro making parole. Some friend. I felt even better now about winning that bet.

The Bruno era was over. Things remained the same but only for a short period of time before the shit would hit the fan.

▼ ▼ ▼

Philip Testa was anointed by law enforcement personnel and the power-ful press as the new boss of the Philadelphia La Cosa Nostra. He remained close to Frank "Chickie" Narducci and Nicky Scarfo. Somehow Frank Sindone did not fit into the picture they were drawing. Frank had been extremely tight with Angelo Bruno, but he also had been associated with Tony Bananas while Angelo was still alive. Sindone continued the close relationship with Caponigro after the murder. A no-no.

Phil Testa called me one morning and said, "Bobby, Chickie's locked up by the FBI. Will you see if you can get him out on bail?"

Within a couple of hours, I stood before a United States Magistrate and successfully argued for reasonable bail for Narducci. He was charged, along with an associate, with running an illegal card game in South Philadelphia. He and his co-defendant were also charged with paying bribes to two Philadelphia policemen in an effort to keep the game running without interference from the police.

After a two-week trial, both defendants were convicted. It was the first time I ever heard the sound of someone counting new, crisp $100 bills on tape. I lost another case. It was becoming more difficult to win in federal court, and I began to wonder whether I was burnt-out or not. Narducci was permitted to remain free on bail while he appealed the conviction. This would turn out to be a bad break for him.

▼ ▼ ▼

On May 25, 1980, Rita and I were married at the Cricket Club in North Miami Beach. I well recall my feelings, as Lou Gehrig said many years earlier, "Today I am the luckiest man on the face of the earth." I was surely the happiest.

Rita, holding on to her dad's arm, walked down the aisle as the words and music to "What I Did for Love" were being sung and played on the piano by the popular and talented Lenny Perna. Rita selected the song from the Broadway show *A Chorus Line* to substitute for the traditional wedding march. I still get goose bumps when I think of that moment.

Many of my clients couldn't or wouldn't come to the wedding. Some of them were not allowed because of bail restrictions forbidding them to travel to Florida. Others thought it best to "go to the mattresses" because of what they feared might happen if they were seen in public. Nicky Scarfo feared nothing. He came with a whole entourage including his nephew, Philip Leonetti, Chuckie and Larry "Yogi" Merlino, Nick "The Blade" Virgilio, Salvy Testa, Bobby Lumio, Saul Kane, and one or two others. They rented suites at the Cricket Club for the four-day Memorial Day weekend. They had a ball.

The day after the wedding, Rita and I flew to the French side of the island of St. Martin in the Caribbean. We spent a glorious two weeks at the laid-back resort known as La Sammana. It was just what the doctor ordered for both of us. Rita needed the R&R to recover from the hectic days before the wedding and all the details she handled so marvelously. As for me, I needed to unwind and recharge my batteries to face the battles waiting for me upon my return. There was another trial on my calendar, listed for September 1980 in Mays Landing, New Jersey.

PART TWO

"Every trial is a trial for life.
Every sentence is a
sentence of death."

Oscar Wilde

CHAPTER THIRTEEN

Witness for the Prosecution

On December 21, 1979, the police answered a call to investigate a strange odor coming from the trunk of a Mercury Cougar sedan parked on a residential street in Margate, a seaside suburb of Atlantic City. Inside was the frozen-stiff corpse of 30-year-old Vincent Falcone, a cement contractor and friend of Nicky Scarfo and his nephew, Philip Leonetti. Falcone had been shot twice with a .32-caliber gun, once in the back of the head, once in the chest. Hog-tied with rope and wrapped in a blood-soaked blanket, it was the portrait of a professional hit. The official focus would narrow in on rumored mobsters in the area before the tape around Falcone's Mercury was taken down.

If you're beginning to suspect that what we have here are all the ingredients of a mob murder trial, then we have to have a stool pigeon. Enter Joseph Salerno, a dead-broke plumber and self-described "gangster," picked up by Atlantic City Homicide for questioning shortly after the body was found. A friend and associate of both Scarfo and Leonetti, Salerno's ties to Falcone were also close. He gave several statements to the homicide detectives, admitting not only that he was involved in the murder, but also claiming that he'd actually witnessed the hit in a Margate beach house on December 16. With the threat of hard time and the promise of witness protection, Salerno not surprisingly flipped, ready to hand over anyone the state wanted on a silver platter.

The news of Salerno's deal and induction into the Federal Witness Protection Program came as swiftly as the arrests of Scarfo, Leonetti, and another alleged member of the Philadelphia family, Lawrence "Yogi" Merlino. The Atlantic City Police and the District Attorney were thrilled, news cameras and reporters crowding around as the men were hauled in for booking. And if this was a dragnet, Scarfo and Leonetti were flapping in the middle of it, two of what the authorities considered the biggest and most elusive fish in town.

While I was not a member of the New Jersey bar, Scarfo asked me to represent Merlino in the upcoming murder trial. Scarfo was often referred to by friends and associates as "Little Nicky" or "The Little Guy," a reference to his five-foot-five frame that he understandably took as an insult.

As the result of the March 21, 1980, unexpected execution-style slaying of Angelo Bruno (the reputed low-profile boss of the Philadelphia–South Jersey La Cosa Nostra), the upcoming trial would take on increasing significance. The media and law enforcement declared Scarfo a rising star in the family.

The prosecutor, Jeffrey Blitz, the DA of Atlantic County, New Jersey, was confident (perhaps overly so) that he would convict all three defendants of the murder, especially given the lurid account provided by Salerno, safely tucked away in witness protection and ready to sing. Scarfo and Leonetti would be represented by two prominent Atlantic City attorneys, Harold Garber and Eddie Jacobs, who had successfully gotten all three defendants out on bail pending trial. I was granted special permission to represent Lawrence Merlino by the New Jersey Superior Court judge sitting in Mays Landing, New Jersey. A small, rural community about 13 miles outside of Atlantic City, Mays Landing was the Atlantic County seat and was the site of all trials involving crimes committed in the Atlantic City area.

Scarfo made it clear from the start that he was expecting me to act as lead counsel. He told me he was depending on me to make most of the important decisions whenever Garber, Jacobs, and I couldn't agree. Thinking about it now, I can't recall even one instance when we had a major disagreement. Our preparation for trial was long and tedious, often requiring us to chase down the minutest detail. Key to our preparation was the eyewitness testimony of Salerno, star witness for the state, and we knew the defense would hinge on the extent to which his credibility would survive cross-examination. It went without saying that we were in for the fight of our lives and, not at all unlike the casinos I've admittedly spent too much time and money in, the odds were decidedly with the house.

After reading all the documents obtained through discovery, the first thing I did was hire two additional investigators to work with Stanley Branche, my longtime private eye, Ed Harrell, a recently retired captain from the Philadelphia police force, and the lawyers who'd try the case. It was decided early on that we needed a full background investigation performed on Salerno, who we anticipated would be painted as a choir boy by the state despite his wannabe wise-guy reputation. We needed to convince the jury that he was a paid-off informant trying to avoid hard time and a liar to boot.

Our investigators gathered a thick file confirming Salerno's involvement in several shady financial dealings. For instance, we had written proof that his bankruptcy petition included sworn affidavits containing numerous false statements. We also had documentation that his father, Joseph Salerno, Sr., took out a bank loan in order to give his son money to pay off a hefty debt to Falcone. There was no evidence that Joseph Salerno, Jr. ever used this money to repay Falcone, so a possible motive of his own for the murder began to emerge. In addition, our investigators obtained statements from several residents of Atlantic City who were willing to testify that during most of the time Salerno said he was with Scarfo, Leonetti, and Merlino on the day of the murder, they were actually with the witnesses at other places. Our alibi witnesses would not be able to cover the defendants for the full day, but what we had could possibly cast doubt on Salerno's story and credibility.

In pretrial proceedings, the trial judge from Cumberland County, New Jersey, William Miller, granted a media motion to televise the entire trial. I remember that Miller's face, in sharp contrast to his white hair, was always flushed, and to this day I do not know if it was from sun or booze or possibly both. I do recall that this was one of the earliest cases to be tried on live television in New Jersey, and it would prove to be one of the most publicized and sensational trials there in many years. Every television station in the area covered the three-week trial, and several newspapers had reporters there every day. The trial was front-page news, the lead story on every nightly newscast. When we arrived at the courthouse the first day, we were surrounded by reporters and cameramen, at least a dozen microphones in our faces. "No comment" was our standard response as we muscled our way past them.

Jury selection began as scheduled in early September 1980. Every day until the verdict was announced, Harrell drove the three defendants and myself up to the courthouse in the same big, black Cadillac sedan driven by both Scarfo and Leonetti at the time of the murder. While our daily arrival before the jurors in this conspicuous fashion was questioned at the time by many, especially given the stereotypical shades of mob bravado it conjured, this was a tactical move on my part from the start. Before I was admitted into the case, Garber had obtained a statement from a Margate police sergeant who stated that he was on duty on the day of the murder and was in the area for about 20 minutes at the time Salerno said the shooting occurred. He also said that while driving past the beach house he did not see the Cadillac. This statement was in direct contradiction to Salerno's claim that the Cadillac had been parked adjacent to the beach house the entire time of the murder. So while every cop in town recognized the car on sight and had tailed it numerous times, this one had not seen it parked outside the beach house around the time of the murder as the state would insist. The jurors would see the Cadillac every morning before court, and I figured they would realize that if the car were parked in their presence they would have seen it.

Another factor we had to consider was the jurors' reaction to these defendants, or rather the reputations the media would cause them to have, painted as we knew they would be by the state as ruthless and power-hungry gangsters, capable of mixing cocktails over the still-bleeding corpse of

Vincent Falcone, luring him there for the hit not ten days before Christmas. Then there was the matter of the sloppy gift-wrapping. I suggested that the defendants wear suits and ties every day. And I told Scarfo to tone down his ties a little, reasoning that the jurors would not respond well to his loud but sharp Leonardos, made of hand-painted silk and obviously expensive as hell. All three defendants were handsome, each in his own way, and they all looked even better dressed in business suits, or in the case of Leonetti and Merlino, an occasional blue or brown blazer.

Leonetti looked like Rudolph Valentino. He was about five foot ten with short, razor-cut black hair, combed back and always perfectly in place. His sharp features and dark eyes were complemented by a deep tan. Women jurors were sure to notice his handsome appearance, and more than likely, they would at least listen to his defense. I remember one of our alibi witnesses, a waitress at a nearby diner, testified at trial that while she did not know the defendants, she remembered they'd been in the diner on the day of the murder. When asked how she could remember, she said with a dreamy sigh, how could she forget a man as handsome as Mr. Leonetti?

My client, Lawrence "Yogi" Merlino, was a couple of inches shorter than Leonetti and several pounds heavier. With slicked-back hair and a straight Roman nose, his face was dark brown from the summer sun on the Atlantic City beach. I thought he was nicknamed Yogi because he was built a little like Yogi Berra, and every once in a while he'd come up with conversational gems that sounded like Berra being quoted by some baseball writer.

Scarfo was older than the other two, but his hair was still jet-black. He wore it back and short, eyes dark and piercing. I remember Scarfo's allergies were acting up throughout the trial, his eyes watering with an occasional sneeze into a handkerchief. He wore a pair of black-framed reading glasses whenever he had to read something in court.

"My name is Harold Garber," said Scarfo's lawyer to the jury after the prosecutor, Jeffrey Blitz, finished his opening statement. "And I represent Nicodemo Scarfo. I am telling you now the evidence will show that he is not guilty of these charges." To my utter surprise he said no more, and just sat back down. If I were Nicky, I remember thinking, I'd be petrified.

On the other hand, Leonetti's lawyer, Ed Jacobs, took his time telling the jurors what he expected the evidence to show. He responded to each of the points Blitz had raised in the state's opening, including the contention that Leonetti was the triggerman acting on Scarfo's orders. He reminded the jurors that the defendants were presumed innocent, that the state had the burden of proving their guilt beyond a reasonable doubt.

I introduced myself as Merlino's counsel, then said there was so little evidence against him I didn't know why we were even there. I went on the attack immediately, telling the jurors to beware of accepting the testimony of Salerno, who not only had a motive to lie, but also had a motive to kill Falcone. It was my usual strategy—put anyone but the defendant on trial.

I spoke of all the pretrial news stories, how these men were being tried and convicted in the press without the benefit of a trial, a lawyer, and, more importantly, an impartial jury. I often zinged the press for being unfair, and they seemed to take it as a compliment. I asked the jurors to listen to the evidence, to decide the case solely on what they heard and saw in court. "Please do not consider what you may have read or heard elsewhere about this case or any of these defendants," I said. "Should you accidentally hear or read something, you are bound and you promised you would disregard it." I sat down after thanking them for their undivided attention, hoping my sincere belief in the innocence of the defendants came across.

Blitz first called Salerno to the witness stand, which was not ten feet from our defense table in the mid-sized courtroom. While I had never seen Salerno before, I did know his father, Joseph Sr., a court officer in City Hall, Philadelphia. The son was about six foot two with wiry, dark hair and a thick beard. The little skin that showed on his face was covered with pockmarks. Not exactly what you'd call a good-looking guy. Casually dressed, a blue sweater and slacks softened the edges of the cocky and streetwise Salerno. Nice touch, I remember thinking. Blitz knew what he was doing.

I couldn't help but stare at him as he took the stand, watching the nervous way he avoided the eyes of our clients, and I wondered what was racing through his mind. I'd find out much later, in a book called *The Plumber*, about this case and Salerno's life on the run in the Federal Witness Protection Program. Surrounded by heavily armed police and marshals who had escorted him to the courthouse that morning in a bulletproof vest, Salerno was reportedly "nervous to the point of collapse" at the prospect of coming face to face with the "killers" of Falcone:

> I'd never been in a courtroom before and I was nervous, but when I saw them I was petrified. I hadn't seen them in over a year; and even though they were on my mind all the time, thinkin' about them and facin' them were two different things. It was a kind of fear I'd never felt before. It was like I was seein' them, but they weren't really there, like in a dream.

Blitz guided Salerno through a long but smooth direct examination. It was obvious to me that the prosecutor and the police had spent many hours preparing him. He answered questions slowly and deliberately, trying to impress the jury with his memory and honesty.

Salerno told of his relationship with Leonetti, whom he met while he was a plumber and Leonetti was a cement contractor. When Salerno was having tough times financially, Leonetti, with his Uncle Nick's approval, let him use the space and the telephone in the offices of Scarf, Inc. to conduct what little business he still had. While the authorities considered Scarf, Inc. nothing more than a front for shady Mafioso dealings, it was a successful cement contracting business during the construction boom of the seventies. Oddly enough, on the office walls of Scarf, Inc. hung poster-sized photos of three dubious figures—Alphonse Capone, Benito Mussolini, and Pancho Villa. Stranger still, next to these photos hung a shot of President Ronald Reagan shaking hands with Jake Kossman.

It was at Scarf, Inc. that Salerno said he met Merlino, who also shared the office facilities at the time. Soon after, Salerno was introduced to Falcone, a local cement contractor. He went on to explain that, in addition to doing construction work, he often socialized and drank with Scarfo, Leonetti, Merlino, and Falcone. He told the jurors he was impressed with all of them and initially enjoyed being in their company. This much was true, everyone knowing that Salerno was a wannabe prone to exaggeration, bragging about his supposed connections in the mob and borrowing money faster than he could lose it.

One day, while riding in a truck with Leonetti, Salerno testified, he was shown an article in *Philadelphia* magazine about Scarfo's alleged rise in the Philadelphia La Cosa Nostra. He recalled that Leonetti pointed to it, said something to the effect that the article was true, that Uncle Nick was a gangster, that they all were. After defining the term "gangster" in the most traditional and bloody sense, Leonetti allegedly boasted, "We control the gambling, numbers, the horses, and the loansharking. We loan a guy five Gs, he pays us back six. Everyone pays. If they don't, forget about it."

It sounded to me like some story a cop would make up just to nail Scarfo and his cronies. And there was no question that the state was hell-bent on making this a mob murder trial. But if this was the case, then where were the key elements? Instead of a hit on a major underworld figure, we had a two-bit cement contractor. Instead of a turncoat underboss or consigliere appearing in dark shadow, we had a deadbeat plumber with a motive all his own, someone even organized crime would not have.

Salerno went on to say that he drove Scarfo to Philadelphia one day, and while there they went to Virgilio's restaurant in Old City. There, he said, he met the owner, Philip Testa, who appeared to be a close friend of Scarfo. While in the restaurant, Salerno claimed that Scarfo asked him if he could get hold of some untraceable guns, which he took to mean guns with no serial numbers. He said he later gave Scarfo an old .32-caliber pistol belonging to his father, the gun that Salerno would testify at trial was the murder weapon. However, the murder weapon was never offered into evidence, and the jurors would therefore only have Salerno's word on this claim.

Before going into the facts about what occurred on the day of the murder, Salerno was allowed to testify to something I vehemently objected to as being irrelevant and highly prejudicial. The judge overruled my objection, and Salerno went on to tell the jury that Scarfo admitted killing a hulking Irishman named Billy Dugan several years before when he, Scarfo, stuck a long knife into Dugan's gut at a local diner. "Yeah," he recalled Scarfo saying dismissively of the crime, "I took out a knife and stuck it in the Irish son of a bitch." The stabbing was purportedly over the stool Dugan was sitting on at the time, the seat Scarfo demanded though there was plenty of room at the counter. According to Salerno, Scarfo said he wished the guy had come back to life so he could kill him again, fry his guts, and eat them.

The jurors sat there emotionless as Salerno continued. I remember the sinking feeling as the gory details came out. Devastating, I recall thinking. We're dead in the water.

Blitz finally moved on to Falcone. Salerno testified that Falcone was very friendly with Scarfo, Leonetti, and Merlino, but at some point he noticed, "the guys started to cool on him [Falcone]." At about the same time he claimed that Leonetti said to him, "If my uncle asked you to do something like help him get rid of somebody, would you do it?"

Salerno said he never gave Leonetti a direct answer, but it was then that he started to get scared and also started to sense that Falcone had a serious problem. He went on to say that he was asked soon after to take a ride with Leonetti and Merlino. He recalled sitting in the passenger seat of the black Cadillac, all the while wondering if he was going to get shot in the back of the head. He described how they drove south on Atlantic Avenue to the end of Atlantic City, continuing through Ventnor, finally making a left turn on Decatur Avenue in Margate where the famous elephant, Lucy, stands two stories high. They parked the car in the driveway of a new, unoccupied beach house owned by a friend of Scarfo's named Philip "Disney" McFillin. He was nicknamed Disney because Nicky and his buddy, Chuckie Merlino, joked that he spent more time at Disney World in Orlando, Florida, than Mickey Mouse. Phil loved to take his family and friends there to tour the resort for days.

Salerno said Scarfo let them into the beach house with a key, turned on the television set, and they left after having a few drinks. The next day, he went on to say, Leonetti and Merlino told him they were going to watch the Eagles football game at the same house they'd been to the day before. "Would you drive there with Falcone and us?" Merlino allegedly asked. Salerno testified that he was too frightened to say no. He added that he took a walk in the woods with his wife before leaving that day, and told her he thought someone would be killed.

It was a typical, cold afternoon just before Christmas when, according to Salerno, they picked up Falcone at his girlfriend's house, which was directly across the street from the Scarfo compound in Ducktown, Atlantic City. At the time, unknown to his wife, Falcone was seeing a 15-year-old girl, a fact we would later be sure to emphasize before the jury in the hopes of deflecting their sympathy from the deceased. Salerno said they followed the same route as the day before, and knocked on the door when they arrived.

Scarfo was waiting in the living room, Salerno recalled. After they all exchanged greetings, Scarfo rose and said, "How about a drink, everybody?"

There were new kitchen cabinets surrounding a window facing the desolate beach, the steel-gray Atlantic lapping at the shore. Salerno said that Scarfo next asked Falcone to get a few glasses from one of the cabinets over the sink. Blitz had Salerno go through the next few moments in excruciating detail.

Q. At this point I want you to relate to the jury what happened, what you saw.

A. I had a drink up to my mouth, and Philip Leonetti pulled a gun out of his jacket and shot Vincent Falcone, extending his arm, and shot him in the back of the head.

Q. What did Mr. Falcone then do?

A. He turned halfway around and slid down in the corner, and sort of sat with his hands on his stomach.

Q. Did you recognize the gun?

A. Yes.

Q. Whose was it?

A. Mine.

The courtroom was silent, I noticed, the jury hanging on his every word. Salerno looked at the jury box as he seemed to be getting increasingly comfortable with his role as the prosecutor's star performer. He went on to describe Scarfo, one ear pressed to Falcone's chest, listening for a heartbeat. "Give me the gun," Scarfo allegedly said to Leonetti. "I want to make sure the motherfucker is dead."

Leonetti was allegedly quick to reply, "Nah, let me do it." Salerno described how Leonetti took quick aim and fired the pistol at close range into Falcone's chest. He said that while he feared that he might be next, he complied with Scarfo's directions to tie up the body "cowboy style." While Salerno was wrapping the body in a blanket, Scarfo allegedly exclaimed, "I love this, I love this! The big shot is dead!" Salerno said that Scarfo added he wished he could bring Falcone back to life so he could kill him again. The story about the stabbing of the big Irishman came racing to mind just as the prosecution had no doubt intended, another murder victim Scarfo wanted to resurrect so he could kill him again. As for the motive for this murder, however, little was ever offered. Salerno said that as far as he could tell, Scarfo wanted Falcone dead because he made some belittling comments a couple months before about Scarfo and Leonetti, something to the effect that Scarfo was "crazy" and that "Leonetti shouldn't be in the concrete business." Hardly a plausible motive for such a heinous crime, we would be quick to point out when our turn came.

Salerno described how they cleaned the house, how Merlino and he carried the body out in a blanket, stuffing it in the trunk of Falcone's Mercury, and how Scarfo fished the keys out of Falcone's pocket. There was a gun to dispose of, as well as bullets and clothing in plastic bags. Throughout Salerno's testimony, Blitz produced some startling visual aids for the jury: the bloody blanket, color photographs of the corpse, Falcone's blood-splattered shirt and jacket, and some bullets retrieved from a sewer where Salerno said he was directed to dispose of them.

While he would say several times how fearful he was, he also said he was permitted to leave the house twice to call his wife from the pay phone down the block. He said he was supposed to go to see her and his kids, who lived in Brigantine, across the bay from the northern tip of Atlantic City. He admitted to returning both times before he and Merlino allegedly carried the body outside, a fact we would be sure to hammer on during cross-examination.

Salerno described how the Mercury was abandoned on a quiet corner a couple of miles away from the house, and how he had dinner that night at Scarfo's Georgia Avenue apartment. According to Salerno, Salvatore "Chuckie" Merlino joined them for dinner as he usually did on Sundays. He didn't implicate Chuckie, but Salerno claimed that Chuckie said something like "lights out" at dinner when Falcone's name was mentioned.

In an attempt to take the sting out of some of our upcoming cross-examination, Blitz asked Salerno about his present situation in the Witness Protection Program. Salerno readily admitted that he was not charged with any crime in connection with the murder. He also admitted to being transferred away from the area and being given a new identification, money, a job, and a new residence, all at the taxpayers' expense. By the time Blitz rested, Salerno had testified for six hours.

CHAPTER FOURTEEN

Thank God for the American Jury System and an Honest Jury

It was finally our turn to cross-examine Salerno. We knew this would be the most crucial part of the trial. Garber and Jacobs took him first; it had been decided beforehand that I would go last. Garber focused his questioning on whether or not the black Cadillac sedan was parked outside the house during the murder. When Salerno answered affirmatively, he seemed satisfied and asked only a few additional questions, leaving the rest of the cross to Jacobs and me. He was content to rely on the forthcoming testimony of the Margate police officer to prove Salerno a liar.

Jacobs was tall and husky, looking more like a defensive end than a criminal lawyer. I learned from working with him in this case that he spent hours in preparation, reading in meticulous detail every document and statement provided by the prosecutor's office and our own investigators. All these papers were underlined with thick colored markers to aid in his cross.

He pointed out dozens of discrepancies and statements that were inconsistent with Salerno's trial testimony. He brought out Salerno's bankruptcy petition and was able to show several lies which the witness tried to pass off as "mistakes." He asked several questions about how the initial shooting occurred. After all, he was Leonetti's lawyer, and the evidence was thus far more damaging to him than the others. Jacobs' cross-examination covered nearly the full day. It seemed to me that Salerno's credibility was severely weakened but not yet destroyed. I remember anxiously waiting my turn when Jacobs finally said, "I have no more questions."

The judge called a recess, and the defendants and defense counsel left the courtroom to meet in a small room the court personnel had provided for us. I couldn't help but notice two familiar-looking FBI agents and Joel Friedman huddling in the hallway. Friedman was the Chief of the Philadelphia branch of the Department of Justice's Strike Force, the section of the U.S. Attorney's Office that concentrates on the investigations and prosecutions of organized crime cases and defendants. They waved to me, smiling as though Salerno's testimony had sealed our clients' fates.

I do not recall feeling any differently knowing that my every move and word were being televised. I do recall feeling the eyes of all those spectators packing the courtroom, the weight of their collective silence at my back as I started my cross.

> Q. Mr. Salerno, isn't it a fact that you were just about broke when these defendants took you in and let you use their office for your business without charging you even one penny in rent?
> A. Yes.
> Q. When your wife threw you out of the house, didn't Nick Scarfo let you stay in his mother's apartment building without charging you rent?
> A. Yes.
> Q. Now you are testifying against these men, blaming them for a murder that would put them in prison for the rest of their lives. Is that the way you are returning their kindness to you?

I waited for an objection at this point, but it didn't come. Salerno answered that he was just trying to do the right thing. I rose from my chair, moving as close to him as I could. The judge didn't stop me. "You have not been charged with any crime in connection with anything you say occurred on the day in question, have you?"

He said he didn't commit any crime, but I reminded him of his testimony about disposing of the body after the shots were fired. Ultimately he relented, but added weakly that he still could be charged. I asked him if he believed that, and he responded that he didn't know. I would remind the jurors later that being an accessory after the fact to a murder is a gravely serious charge.

I switched gears and got him to tell the jury how many days and hours he spent with the prosecutor and the homicide detectives in preparation for his testimony, all the while moving about the courtroom as I spoke, between the tables and chairs, back and forth in front of the jury box. To my surprise, he admitted to numerous days and scores of hours going over his testimony with the police and the DA. I hoped that the jury would infer that he was coached and in some instances told what to say.

There is an art to effective cross-examination, not at all unlike boxing, complete with its own rhythm and footwork, and in this case the challenger was well coached. Beyond this there is the stamina required to wear your opponent down, sometimes questions and other times answers connecting squarely as an unexpected hook to the jaw. I jumped back to the subject of his poor financial condition just before he agreed to go into protective custody, modulating my voice, loud and soft, fast then slow.

Q. You already said you had no money when you began to cooperate, so I would like to know how are you now supporting yourself and your family?

A. The State of New Jersey and the United States Marshal give me money every month, but now I also have a job as a plumber.

Q. You didn't have to work for the money they give you other than cooperate and tell them all these things you told the jury, correct?

A. I cooperated and told the truth!

Q. In other words, you have been paid for your testimony?

A. You could say that.

Q. You owed a lot of people money when you went with them. (I pointed to the police as I asked the question.)

A. Yes.

Q. Did you ever pay any of your creditors who, by the way, included working men who were owed wages and suppliers who gave you material to use in your business?

A. I filed for bankruptcy.

Q. Isn't it a fact that after you filed for bankruptcy, you continued to conduct business and accumulated a lot of bills and debts that you still owe and which were not included in your bankruptcy?

I was holding a long list of Salerno's creditors that included the dates of several unpaid bills, proof positive that Salerno owed quite a few people a significant amount of money and that this indebtedness was neither satisfied nor discharged in bankruptcy. Our investigators had done their job well. I could see that Salerno didn't want to give in on this one, though by this time he was visibly rattled, looking increasingly perplexed by this line of questioning. The former polish of the prosecution's script was beginning to wear thin. He often glanced toward the prosecutor's table as though begging for an objection that never came.

He hesitated and said something to the effect he guessed he owed some people some money after his bankruptcy.

"Have you heard from any of these people who you owe this money?" I asked.

He answered, "I now have a new identity and for security reasons my creditors, just like everybody else, can't get in touch with me."

"Would you not then agree that by going into the Witness Protection Program you have been able to avoid the payment of thousands of dollars of personal and business bills?"

Salerno sat there silent for several seconds, trying to think of an answer. Then he stated, "I'm sorry, but I have to follow instructions and not contact anybody unless they [the cops] approve."

I finished this line of questioning with, "You made no effort to get these people approved for contact and really didn't care if you beat them out of this hard-earned money, did you?"

Still, to my surprise, no objection from Blitz.

Salerno, now in a much lower and less steady voice, said, "I can't help the way that turned out."

On the second day of my cross-examination of Salerno, I had him go over the minute details of the shooting. I pinned him down to having Leonetti pulling his right arm up straight, parallel to the floor, when the first and only shot to the head was fired. I was trying to predict how the medical examiner was going to testify about the bullet wound to the head.

"Are you sure that Leonetti's arm was pointed straight ahead when the gun was fired?" I asked.

"Well, his arm might have been pointing up a little at the time of the shot," he said as I thought he would, the relevance of this answer obviously a mystery to him. This is one of the secrets to effective cross-examination, masking a question so that the witness does not realize the significance of his answer. By getting him to say Leonetti fired straight, he was walking right into a trap I'd snap closed later—the fact that this testimony was inconsistent with the medical evidence and the ballistics, both of which confirmed a downward trajectory to the bullet as it traveled through Falcone's skull, a fact incriminating to Salerno since he was undeniably the tallest of the men allegedly in the beach house.

I moved to another area at this juncture, asking him if he knew when he brought Falcone to the beach house if he, Falcone, was going to be killed.

He swore he didn't know even though earlier he testified he'd told his wife he thought somebody might get killed. "I might have suspected something was wrong, but I didn't know."

"Then all you did was wrap the blanket around the body and help to put it in the trunk, isn't that so, Mr. Salerno?"

"That's correct."

"Well, wouldn't you agree that Lawrence Merlino did the same as you and no more, according to your testimony?"

He thought for a few seconds and then said, "That's right."

The two FBI agents and the Strike Force attorney winced when still there was no objection from Blitz. Merlino breathed a sigh of relief when he heard the answer. He even had to suppress a smile.

I then asked Salerno if it appeared that Falcone was dead after the first shot and before Leonetti fired the second bullet into his chest. Blitz did object to this one on the grounds that Salerno was not qualified to offer an opinion on this subject. The objection was sustained, so I moved to another subject.

"Mr. Salerno, you did not contact the police to report the murder you claimed you merely witnessed, did you?" I asked.

"I told the police what happened," he said.

I was ready for this response. "Mr. Salerno, please answer the question, did you contact the police or did they in fact contact you?"

He admitted he hadn't gone to or called the police, insisting that he was frightened to do so.

I reminded him that he testified on direct examination that he was "scared to death" after Falcone was shot while he was still in the house with the three defendants. I also reminded him that he'd admitted they had let him leave on two occasions to call his wife. "If you were afraid of being hurt or killed yourself," I asked, "why didn't you use the same phone to call the police?"

Salerno surprised me and I am sure the whole courtroom with his next statement to the effect that there was a police car parked near the corner where the phone booth was located.

This is precisely the type of surprise you learn to pounce on for effective cross-examination, how to fire the next question before the witness knows he's walked into a trap. "Why didn't you walk over to the police car and get the officers so that they could go and arrest the defendants?"

Again he said he was too frightened, and I recall he looked like hell by this point, forehead sweating, visibly angry, and increasingly argumentative.

"Wasn't it because Scarfo, Leonetti, and Merlino were not present when the murder was committed?"

He denied this as I'd expected, but I'd accomplished my goal. I planted the seed.

Salerno took the witness stand the following morning for what I hoped would be the last day of cross-examination. I got him to admit that he borrowed $10,000 from his father to pay Falcone the money he had taken on his "juice" loan. I pressed him on whether or not he actually used the money to repay Falcone.

At first the testimony was confusing on this point, but finally he admitted that he didn't use his father's money to pay Falcone. I was trying to establish that Salerno had a motive to kill Falcone, a more likely motive than the one the prosecutor presented against the defendants.

At dinner the night before, a friend of Scarfo, Nick "The Blade" Virgilio, casually remarked that Salerno was the arm-wrestling champion of Brigantine, New Jersey. With this in mind, I asked Salerno if this was true.

"Not Brigantine," he said to my surprise. "All of Atlantic County."

"Arm-wrestling takes a great deal of strength?" I asked.

"Yes," he said proudly, clearly romanced by the question, unaware he was being led to slaughter. "You can say that."

"Would you consider yourself a very physically strong person?"

I remember anticipating an objection, but none came.

"Yes, I would," he answered.

"You knew Falcone well and knew how he was built, didn't you?"

"Yes," he said, again before any objection could be made.

"Now, as a strong fellow, you would have no difficulty dragging that body and rolling it down the steps, wrapped as it was?"

"No."

"With your strength, if you really put yourself to it, you could have done that if you had to?"

"Possibly," he finally said.

"Couldn't you have?"

"Yes, yes."

"Mr. Salerno, you had the strength to pick up, carry, and dump Falcone's body into the trunk alone." I made sure to make him repeat his previous answer so the jury would know how important I considered it. "And further, you had a motive to kill Falcone since he was threatening you when you became delinquent on the loan you made from him, isn't that also correct?"

He replied, "I guess you can say that."

I concluded this line of questioning, knowing full well he'd deny the next logical question. Of course he'd never admit to killing Falcone, but my implication was clear enough. Keep in mind that it was not my burden or goal to prove my client's innocence, but rather to create reasonable doubt every bit as forcefully as the state was aiming to establish guilt beyond it. Many years later I would again face Salerno on the stand and, exasperated, he would refer back to this day in court, accusing me and Jacobs of "making a liar out of him" in front of the jury.

▼ ▼ ▼

Whenever we returned to Scarfo's Georgia Avenue compound late in the afternoon after court and on the weekends, I would notice a couple of unmarked vehicles circle the block and drive slowly past before moving on. Every time we entered or exited a restaurant after lunch or dinner, the same cars would be in the area. Sometimes the occupants even came into the restaurants and sat as close as they could to where we were eating. We were only free from the constant surveillance when we dined at a restaurant owned by a friend of Scarfo called Scannuccio's.

I was familiar with this type of action by law enforcement personnel from my many dinners in South Philadelphia with Angelo Bruno, Phil Testa, and Frank Sindone, but in the middle of a murder trial, I thought, enough already.

I filed a motion with the trial court to enjoin the homicide detectives and any other New Jersey officers from following us in this manner, arguing that this sort of harassment was interfering with the defendants' right to a fair trial. The judge granted the motion, and all the tailing came to an abrupt stop. The state, confident of a victory at trial, did not want to give the defense possible grounds for a reversal on appeal.

Blitz and the State of New Jersey were not finished by a longshot. We were encouraged by the cross-examination of Salerno and we felt the tide was changing, though the jury was tough to read. I do recall one juror in particular, an attractive African American woman whose body language seemed to be in our favor—an occasional nod of the head when we made a point and a shake of the head when we showed an inconsistency in the state's case. The press seemed to have had a sudden change of heart and started reporting the action in the courtroom in a much less prejudicial manner.

The state's objective was to rehabilitate Salerno by presenting evidence supportive of various facts testified to by him. For instance, the prosecution proved that the owner of the house where the murder was allegedly committed was in fact Scarfo's friend "Disney," and that Scarfo had a key as Salerno had stated. We didn't make an issue of these facts, since it was clear enough that Scarfo had access to the beach house. As another example, Blitz offered evidence supporting Salerno's claim that he went to a casino with the guys after the shooting, and to a dinner prepared by Scarfo's wife later that evening. Again, these relatively inconsequential facts were not questioned by the defense.

The Medical Examiner of Atlantic County next took the stand and testified that the cause of death could have been either gunshot wound. He couldn't say the death was the result of both wounds.

On cross-examination, the doctor agreed that if Falcone was shot in the head first, the second bullet may have been fired into a corpse and, if so, it couldn't have been the cause of death. This was a fact critical to Scarfo's defense, since there was no testimony from Salerno that Scarfo had ordered Leonetti to fire the first shot. In contrast, Salerno's testimony tied Scarfo to the second shot, Leonetti allegedly pumping the bullet into Falcone's chest as though to save his Uncle Nick the inconvenience. I recall that later that night Leonetti was morose, remarking that while it looked good for Scarfo and Merlino, he was still very much on the hook.

In my opinion, the most important and effective part of the doctor's cross dealt with the path or trajectory of the bullet. I demonstrated how Salerno said Leonetti stood, arm extended, using my glasses as a prop for the gun. He had to agree that the path of the bullet through Falcone's skull was markedly different than he'd expect if the gun was fired in the manner Salerno had described. He had said in his autopsy report and repeated in his direct testimony that the bullet, after entering the back of Falcone's head, took a downward rather than an upward path. Salerno was the tallest of all the individuals involved in the trial, including Falcone and the three defendants. Again, the inference I wanted the jurors to draw was that Salerno was the one to fire the gun, that his story was concocted to escape blame for a murder he committed alone. We'd shown motive and opportunity, and now the medical examiner himself had at least raised the prospect of scientific probability.

Blitz next offered into evidence the grotesque color photographs of the crime scene and the body. There was an abundance of blood and a pained expression on the face of Vincent Falcone. The bullet wounds were depicted at gory close range, and then there was the condition of the body itself to consider, looking like something out of a horror film. Beyond this there was the knotted rope tying Falcone from head to foot. The prosecutor might as well have screamed mob rodeo. I objected to these photos being admitted into evidence, arguing that they were too prejudicial and were offered solely to inflame the passions of the jury. Judge Miller denied the objection. So the eight-by-ten photos were passed among the jurors, and I couldn't help but feel we were losing ground as each juror's eyes widened upon viewing them.

As is customary in a murder trial, the state put Falcone's widow on the stand to testify as to the last time she saw him alive, describing through her tears her last conversation with her husband, their loving relationship, and the traumatic ordeal of identifying the body. Only a fool would cross-examine such a witness on these matters, though I was determined to convey how inac-curate her version of her relationship with Falcone was. There was the evidence of his 15-year-old girlfriend, for instance—how he'd spent his last day with her rather than his wife. I would remind the jurors to render a verdict based on the evidence rather than sympathy, which is a very real risk in criminal trials. A runaway jury may be swayed in one direction or another by any number of human emotions, from sympathy to anger or even revenge. I would do this later in my closing address rather than by cross.

When Mrs. Falcone's questioning was completed, Blitz rose and said, "The state rests, Your Honor."

Judge Miller then excused the jurors and announced a 20-minute recess after which he would entertain defense motions to dismiss the case or motions for Judgments of Acquittal.

Garber, Jacobs, and I went with our clients to our small room across the hall from the courtroom entrance. We needed to discuss the oral motions and arguments that were about to take place. We all agreed that Leonetti didn't have a prayer of taking the case out of the hands of the jury, and that Scarfo was a longshot to win a motion to dismiss. Garber, Jacobs, and I did, however, believe that Merlino might very well walk if I argued that the state failed to produce sufficient evidence against him.

We talked openly and frankly, as it was always our strategy that these three guys would sink or swim together, our defense united throughout. This notwithstanding, I had to tell Merlino that I believed that if he authorized me to make the motion and argue on his behalf, the chances were good that he would not have to sweat out the jury's deliberations and verdict. I also explained to Scarfo and Leonetti that if Merlino won his motion, I would be out of the case as well. That meant I would not be able to participate in questioning or in rehabilitating defense witnesses, and I would not be allowed to make a closing statement to the jury. This was a major consideration given my reputation as a "C&C," or "cross and close," man. I was known for effective closing arguments as well as cross-examination, and we were all keenly aware that a good closing could often win a losing case.

I will never forget the gesture Merlino made on behalf of his two buddies. "If you guys feel you need Bobby to speak to the jury at the end of the case, then fuck it, no motion for me." Scarfo, Leonetti, and Merlino spoke alone for a few minutes, and then Merlino said there would be no motion. He was determined to take a big gamble to help out his friends.

Outside the presence of the jury, Garber and Jacobs argued for a Judgment of Acquittal for their respective clients. I sat there and listened until they were finished. Judge Miller looked my way and said, "Mr. Simone, I'll entertain your motion now."

I stood and answered, "Mr. Merlino has no motion."

I didn't know who was more surprised, Blitz or the judge. Blitz then argued against the dismissal of the charges involving Scarfo and Leonetti. Judge Miller took no time in denying the motion. So the fate of all three defendants was now in the hands of the jury. The defense would start its case the next morning.

We began by calling several "clean" witnesses to the stand, meaning those without criminal records. While none of these witnesses could account for the whereabouts of any of the defendants during the hour the murder and disposal of the body allegedly occurred, they contradicted key portions of Salerno's testimony. While Garber and Jacobs felt we needed to call these witnesses, I felt that we should quit while we were ahead and not take any chances of losing the case should one witness or another slip up. Often even the most honest of witnesses will appear to be lying under the stress of cross-examination, and for this reason I am generally against putting them on the stand unless their testimony is absolutely necessary.

Garber then called the police officer from whom we'd obtained the earlier statement. He testified that he had been a police officer for several years and that he had an excellent record on the force. He further described his jurisdiction, Margate, New Jersey, the same community in which the beach house stood. He said he was familiar with Scarfo, Leonetti, and Merlino, having seen them many times in Margate, and that he was also familiar with the black Cadillac which he often saw them driving. At the time of the alleged murder, he said he was in the area of the beach house, just across the street from Lucy the Elephant. He was there for about 15 minutes, he said, sometime between 3:15 and 3:30 p.m. He observed the house and the parking lot, but did not see the Cadillac, adding that if it was there, he would have remembered it.

Blitz was enraged, tearing into the officer on cross-examination. He continued to bombard the witness with question after question, often not waiting for an answer to his previous question. There were times that I thought the officer was going to crumble and say, "I couldn't be sure if it was there." I had never spoken to the officer, but Garber had assured me he was telling the truth.

Blitz kept him on the stand for two days, suggesting he was lying or at least mistaken. Garber took the witness back on re-direct examination and undid the minimal damage inflicted by the cross. We were all relieved when the officer left the stand. Later he would be fired, reportedly for providing testimony helpful to the defense.

Next I called my photographer, Joseph Petrellis, to the stand. Joe had taken many pictures of the interior and exterior of the beach house. I had him identify them for the jurors. I was trying to show the spot where Salerno said the shooting took place, and also how short a distance a single person would have to walk to carry a body to a car outside.

I had earlier gotten Petrellis to recite all his experience and credentials. I wanted to show that he was more qualified as an expert in the field than the policeman, who didn't really specialize in photography. I then asked Petrellis if he had seen the photographs of the body of Vincent Falcone. Again, he said no, and again I handed him a stack of photos.

This time when he looked at the first picture, he turned his head in disgust and threw the stack of them on the small stand in front of him. He acted as if this was making him sick, like he might vomit in front of the jury, and for a moment I thought he might do so.

"Mr. Petrellis, have you in your experience ever acted as an expert witness for law enforcement and the prosecution?"

He answered calmly, "Several times."

"In your opinion, would black and white photographs depict the bullet wounds as to the spot and size of the wound as well as color photographs?" I asked.

"No question about it."

"Why, in your opinion, did the state choose to take and then offer into evidence the color photographs?" I asked, fully expecting a strenuous objection that never came.

"The only reason I could think of is that those color shots would inflame and prejudice the jury against the defendants." The flawlessly dressed and handsome Petrellis walked out of court, a serious expression on his face.

After Blitz finished his closing argument, it was the defense's turn. Garber went first. He stood up, walked over to the jury box, put his hand on the railing, and said, "I told you at the beginning that the evidence would show Nick Scarfo to be not guilty and now all I want to say is that the evidence shows Nick Scarfo to be not guilty." He sat down without uttering another word. Amazing, I remember thinking, Garber made the shortest opening and closing I'd ever witnessed.

Jacobs slowly walked before the jury box, scanning several large index cards. He was not going to rely on the jury remembering all the holes we'd driven through the state's case. One by one, he pointed out the inconsistencies between Salerno's testimony in court and his prior statements made to the police. He was truly an expert in this area; very few lawyers had his skill using prior inconsistent statements on cross-examination. He pointed to the testimony of the police officer who said he didn't see the Cadillac on the day and at the time of the murder. He showed the jury the pictures of the Cadillac, which they really didn't need to see since they all must have seen it at one time or another as we pulled up to the courthouse in it.

Jacobs also stressed that Salerno lied under oath several times in his bankruptcy proceedings. He asked the jury, "When does he tell the truth? Does an oath mean anything to Joseph Salerno?" He argued they shouldn't believe this man who was a proven liar. Jacobs concluded by covering reasonable doubt and the presumption of innocence, asking the jurors for a not guilty verdict for his client.

Before I began my closing address, I couldn't help but think of how Merlino had thrown away his chance to have his case dismissed, just so Scarfo and Leonetti would have the benefit of my closing argument. This better be good, I said to myself.

I started off by thanking the jury for the long hours and many days they served, as well as the attention and devotion they gave as jurors. Then I launched a full-scale attack on the character and credibility of Salerno. Jacobs had already pointed out most of his inconsistent statements, so I went straight for the jugular.

"No matter how much money the state gave him, no matter how much time they spent preparing him to take the witness stand, Salerno is still just a liar and a beat artist." I told the jury that it was no coincidence that he went into the Witness Protection Program at the same time he owed so many people so much money. In order to convict these three men, I argued, they would have to believe the testimony of Joseph Salerno beyond a reasonable doubt.

I rehashed the crucial testimony of the medical examiner, arguing that if the state's doctor was right, then Salerno must have been lying. The diagrams prepared by the medical examiner showing the path of the first bullet were documentary evidence supplied by the prosecution itself, and I argued that this alone was sufficient cause to reject Salerno's testimony. I returned to Salerno's answers on cross-examination, when he stated that he was strong enough to have carried and dumped the body alone, as well as his admission of a possible motive for the murder and the debt he owed Falcone.

"Yes," I told the jury, "I am putting Joseph Salerno on trial." I asked them, "Wasn't it more likely that he alone did the killing rather than he with the three defendants? Isn't there a reasonable doubt as to which theory is correct?"

I continued, "The judge will tell you in his instructions that reasonable doubt can be created by the evidence or the lack of it." I emphasized the lack of any evidence of a plausible motive on the part of any of the defendants.

Throughout the trial, Judge Miller was telling us stories about his boat docked in the rural waters of Cumberland County, New Jersey. Scarfo smiled from ear to ear when I told the jury that when Salerno falsely accused these men of this murder and then went into the Witness Protection Program, "He left a large wake behind him, almost drowning these three men, his own father, and all the people who trusted him enough to lend him money or extend him credit. If you look at the ocean, you can still see this wake on the horizon."

While discussing Salerno's testimony concerning the things that happened on the day of the shooting, I was sure to mention Falcone's 15-year-old girlfriend. Maybe just one or two jurors would have less sympathy for the deceased because of this fact.

"How frightened was Salerno?" I asked. "The police were there when he claims he went outside to call his wife. If he didn't do it alone, and if he really feared for his life, he would have walked right over to the patrol car."

I reminded the jury of the testimony of the Margate police officer who was just outside the beach house when the murder occurred, emphasizing the fact that he didn't see the big black Cadillac. "If it were there, he would have seen it." Then I asked the jurors, "Who are you going to believe, the police officer or Joseph Salerno? The medical examiner or Joseph Salerno?"

I blasted the prosecution team for trying to poison the minds of the jurors by bringing in evidence of an alleged killing of some Irishman by Nick Scarfo. In addition, I made reference to the alleged conversation between Leonetti and Salerno about "gangsters" as another ploy to prejudice the jury by bringing in the stigma of the mob. Finally, I reviewed Joe Petrellis' expert testimony about the color photographs of Falcone's body, "showing all that red blood as just another way of arousing the passions of the jurors. These things are only done in a courtroom when there isn't enough solid, credible evidence to convict."

After speaking for over an hour, I felt it was time to wind it down to a close. "It is obvious that these people," I said, pointing at the prosecution table where Blitz was surrounded by a few detectives, "want to get Nicky Scarfo, his nephew, and friend so bad they will do anything to get him convicted. This trial has proven that." As I spoke, I looked each juror squarely in the eye, one after the other, hoping to find a friendly face.

I repeated the law on reasonable doubt, adding, "In this case, not only do we have reasonable doubt, we have no doubt that these men are innocent." I thanked them again and sat down. I was exhausted.

Blitz then gave his rebuttal argument lasting over three hours. He went over every single fact and piece of evidence that he covered on direct examination. He neglected to cover almost any of the cross. He also seemed to be copying my style. The tone of his voice, for instance, and the footwork. While I remember being slightly annoyed at first, I decided to take it as a compliment.

Judge Miller gave one of the fairest, down-the-middle charges I ever heard in a murder trial. The jury went out in the afternoon and came back early the next morning.

A few minutes before the verdict was announced, all the lawyers, including Blitz, were sitting in the judge's chambers when the judge said to me, "Bob, there's a question I want to ask you after the verdict."

I looked at him and then at Blitz and said, "You want to ask me why I didn't move for a Judgment of Acquittal on behalf of Merlino, right?"

He smiled and nodded.

"Because you would have granted it."

As he was confirming my statement, a court officer knocked on the door and said, "The jury's got a verdict."

We watched the slow-motion way the jury filed in, the bailiff handing the verdict to Judge Miller, who handed it back, poker-faced, to the foreman to read. We rose with our clients, all of us tense—a lifetime in prison or free as a bird and nothing in between. Then we heard it. A not guilty verdict, for all three defendants, on murder, conspiracy, and weapons charges. A clean slate.

The television camera crews invaded the courthouse, breaking through the ranks of newspaper reporters and well-wishers to place their cameras and microphones in front of anyone with the defense. Jacobs, who had just tried and won his biggest case to date, was quoted as saying, "I was shocked that the jury found these guys not guilty, especially so fast." We still kid him about this statement now that he is one of the best and busiest criminal lawyers in the Northeast. I asked him that night if he wanted a new trial.

But the gem of the day occurred when a TV newsperson asked Scarfo, "How do you feel?"

It was the first and last media quote directly from Nicodemo Scarfo from that day to the present. "Thank God for the American jury system and an honest jury," he said with a wide grin and in his half New York, half Philadelphia accent.

Before we left the courthouse to join the victory party already in progress at the Scarfo compound on Georgia Avenue, I saw a few disgruntled FBI agents making their way to their cars. They glared at me and then abruptly turned away. I felt a slight chill, or maybe in retrospect it was more of a premonition of things to come.

CHAPTER FIFTEEN

▼

Sign of Respect

After his big win in the Mays Landing courthouse, Scarfo traveled from Atlantic City to Philadelphia on a much more frequent basis. I had dinner with him, Phil Testa, Testa's son, Salvatore, and Philip Leonetti. Chuckie and Lawrence "Yogi" Merlino were often with us when we broke bread in Old Original Bookbinder's restaurant at Second and Walnut Streets in Society Hill. On most of those occasions, Jake Kossman was there educating and entertaining us. John Taxin, the owner, would come over to our table and talk to Nicky, usually about the old days and the retired and deceased Jewish gangsters. Nig Rosen and Meyer Lansky were the names bandied about most of the time.

Scarfo was not given too much time to enjoy his big win, and neither was I. He was indicted by the United States Attorney's Office operating out of Camden, New Jersey. The charge—possession of a gun by a convicted felon. I was now officially Nicodemo Scarfo's lawyer.

When the Atlantic County detectives went to arrest Nicky for the Falcone murder, they found and seized a small derringer pistol in a bureau drawer in his bedroom. The gun was not introduced as evidence in the Falcone trial since it was a .22-caliber weapon, and Falcone was shot with a .32.

Scarfo remained free on bail until the trial. During this time, Philip Leonetti called me and asked if I would stop by "The Office" so they could show me something.

Ed Harrell drove me down the shore, and Leonetti, The Blade, Yogi, and Nicky greeted us. They couldn't wait to point out a video camera attached to a telephone pole just outside of the rear of the large yard that separated 26 and 28 North Georgia Avenue. The camera was aimed at the middle of the back yard that separated the office of Scarf, Inc. with several apartments above and the other building, owned by Nick's mom, that housed Nick's living quarters and several other apartments. The camera was mobile and able to maintain constant video surveillance over the entire exterior of the Scarfo compound. That meant that whoever installed that camera would be able to identify every person entering and exiting the premises. All visitors would have their names entered in a surveillance log.

Nicky put his index finger on his lips, motioning Ed and me not to speak while we were in the office. Once we were outside again, he told us, "The place is bugged." As we were talking, I noticed the same unmarked cars that followed us during the trial circling the block and slowing down as they passed us.

We all went to dinner at Scannuccio's where we retried the Falcone case and discussed the upcoming gun trial. Nicky had a great attitude. He knew he was only facing a maximum of two years should he be convicted, and he was grateful for beating a potential life sentence. He was also happy to be out on bail so he could, as he put it, "Enjoy some good friends and good food."

The United States Attorney assigned to the case sounded rather upset when he called me a few days later. He told me that federal property had been stolen from the area of Nicky Scarfo's residence in Atlantic City, adding that a government video camera was mysteriously missing from a telephone pole located near the residence. He mentioned a possible arrest on federal charges, indicating that the camera cost over $2,000.

I asked him to give me a couple of days to see if I could help locate the camera. He agreed to my request. Again, I had Ed Harrell drive me to Atlantic City where I told Nicky, Philip, and Lawrence about my conversation with the United States Attorney and the missing video camera. Ed was now my full-time investigator. He was mentally sharp, neat in appearance, but most of all, loyal.

Ed and I looked at the telephone pole, and sure enough, the camera was gone. Philip and Lawrence smiled as I explained to Nick that the Feds would surely prosecute anyone found in possession of this camera.

Nicky looked at Philip and Lawrence, and they promptly jumped into the familiar, big black Cadillac and left Georgia Avenue. An hour or so later, they brought a plastic bag into the office. In it was a slightly battered and water-soaked camera. One of them said to me, "We found this in the bay. We heard it fell off the pole and some kids threw it in the water." Then we all had dinner at Abe's Oyster House.

The next day, I went unannounced to the prosecutor's office in Camden and personally handed him the camera. I made sure I got a receipt, and the matter was never brought up again by the government or, for that matter, by any of my clients.

We went to trial in the early part of 1981 before Judge Stanley Brotman and a jury. Selecting that jury took longer than the trial. The newspaper and television stations continuously referred to the Falcone murder trial and Scarfo's alleged new high position in the mob. In addition, the United States Marshal's Office placed a security checkpoint at the courtroom entrance to screen for weapons and bombs. My objection to the device and the procedure of searching everyone who entered the courtroom was overruled.

As if that wasn't bad enough, we learned through the judge's clerk that among the reading material on hand in the jury room was a *Philadelphia* magazine with a picture of Nicodemo Scarfo on the cover. The related article mentioned his "penchant for violence."

In the middle of jury deliberations, the jurors were questioned about the magazine and what effect, if any, it might have upon them. The jurors all denied seeing or reading the magazine. Oh, really.

Of course, Nicky was found guilty, but Judge Brotman, a fair judge in my mind, denied the government's motion to revoke Scarfo's bail. In so doing, he agreed that we had a substantial Fourth Amendment issue on appeal. The search that led to the seizure of the tiny weapon may well have been illegal. Nicky walked out of the courtroom with me, and although injured, he was far from dead.

▼ ▼ ▼

John McCullough and I continued seeing each other at least once a week. Even when we did not have to discuss the legal problems of any of his men, we enjoyed each other's company, either at the bar or the restaurant table. On some occasions, I found myself at a political fund-raising affair at Palumbo's in South Philly or a banquet hall in the Northeast when I was obliged to purchase tickets to help pay off some deceased roofer's mortgage. John did an unbelievable job of raising money for the needy family members who were visited by tragedy.

As far as the United States Attorney and the FBI were concerned, John McCullough was a bad guy, violent in nature, who had too much power politically and otherwise. That made him a perfect target.

He and several other union officials, business agents, and organizers were indicted in a Hobbs Act extortion case. The government claimed that John and some of his associates roughed up a non-union New York contractor, and as a result, the contractor refused to complete his job, closed shop, and returned to safer territory in New York. In addition, the defendants were charged with forcing another contractor to keep a union employee on the clock 24 hours a day at an exorbitant wage.

After John McCullough told me he wanted me to represent him, I suggested that we retain Jake Kossman to represent one of his co-defendants. I wanted Jake's experience, knowledge, and good common sense as allies in the courtroom. It was finally agreed by everyone that Jake was to represent Steven Traitz, Jr. at trial.

The case was assigned to United States District Court Judge Clarence Newcomer, a former district attorney from Lancaster County, Pennsylvania.

The trial took almost three weeks. I remember often arguing with the judge, even after his rulings on the admissibility of evidence. The judge had no trouble putting me in my place when I went too far.

Kossman, in his close, referred to the testimony of the New York contractor who claimed that Traitz smacked him. The witness said, "I was afraid he would do worse to me, so I left Philadelphia and went back to New York."

Jake hesitated for a few seconds and then, looking at the jurors, said, "Big loss. Big loss for us Philadelphians. We have plenty of people who live here who can do the work and earn the wages."

The other lawyers for the defense then spoke for a few hours before it was my turn. I grabbed the photographs of this large piece of equipment that was used to burn tar and showed them to the jury. The crux of our defense on this point was that if these contraptions get too hot they will explode, and they are therefore a serious threat to human life and property.

Ron Kidd, the attorney for one of the other defendants, had accumulated several safety and injury reports showing that such accidents had occurred in the past. I argued that if someone weren't paid to keep his or her eye on the burner for 24 hours a day, the possibility of an explosion would be enhanced. The extra man would watch the temperature and control it even when the crew wasn't working. We had proved that the equipment had to remain "on" all the time.

Because of my personal relationship with John McCullough, I went the extra yard as I was making my closing argument. I pointed to the prosecutor and said, "Do you think this man would have brought these charges if this piece of equipment were working in his block or in his neighborhood? He would probably have required two men working around the clock."

I pointed to the defendants sitting next to their lawyers, and then said to the jury, "If you are going to convict these men and send them to jail for merely protecting our citizens, then convict me because I want to go with them."

The blond-haired, blue-eyed Judge Newcomer called all the lawyers to sidebar after he finished his charge to the jury. "Are there any objections or comments by counsel?" he asked.

Jake said, "No, Your Honor, and I want you to know that even Bob Simone says you were fair."

The judge grinned and looked at me as I said, "Yes, Your Honor. You're fair. You have the blond hair and blue eyes." Before he could react, I smiled and said, "Only kidding, Judge."

As a matter of fact, the charge was fair and down the middle, as much as any defense lawyer could hope for.

Jake and I went to the courtroom to hear the verdict after the clerk interrupted our lunch at a bar association function to call us. Scores of agents, marshals, and U.S. Attorneys rushed to be on time to hear the hoped-for news that one of their favorite targets and a client of Bobby Simone was going to the slammer for a long time. The jurors had been sequestered during deliberations, and after the second day they had reached a verdict. In my close I asked, "How do you like being locked up, separated from your families?"

McCullough was calmer than I was as we sat there waiting for the jury to walk into the box. I knew that John, in his mid-fifties, was looking at spending the rest of his life in jail if he lost.

The jurors walked slowly to their seats, but I saw one woman look at me and smile. I exhaled a deep breath and felt relieved. The foreman rose and said in a loud, clear voice, "Not guilty." He repeated the words for each defendant and for each count.

As usual, all the government people were stunned and pissed. McCullough supporters convened at John Berkery's Irish bar, Molly Maguire's, where we all drank, ate, and sang in honor of John McCullough, the other dedicated men, and the union. John was one of the good guys, no question about it. If he wore a hat, you could bet your ass it would have been a white one.

John hugged and kissed me. So did his wife. She repeated several times, "Thanks for saving my husband's life." Imagine how easy it was for the government, our government, to prosecute someone for merely looking out for his "brothers"—hard-working stiffs, protecting their safety and their jobs. *Give me a break! John McCullough was a saint compared to all the agents and prosecutors sitting on the other side of the aisle.*

▼ ▼ ▼

Two FBI agents walked into Frank's Cabana, Sindone's steak shop at Tenth Street and Moyamensing Avenue in South Philly, and handed him an official notice that the pay phone on the wall had been tapped for the past 18 months. Frank looked at the document and shook his head. Without saying a word, he walked over to the phone, grabbed it with both hands, and ripped it off the wall. The agents, seeing how angry Frank was, left without saying or doing anything more. For the next six months Sindone used the phone directly across the street at the gas station. The FBI would tap that phone also as they compiled evidence against Frank and his closest friends.

In February 1981, the United States Attorney for the Eastern District of Pennsylvania held a press conference and announced that the grand jury had indicted ten local members of the Bruno organized crime family, charging them with racketeering, gambling, and loansharking violations. The defendants in this indictment were Philip Testa, Frank Narducci, Carl Ippolito, Harry and Mario Riccobene, Joseph Ciancaglini, Charles Warrington, Pasquale Spirito, Joseph Bongiovanni, and another person that I never met. I purposely have not mentioned his name to protect his privacy.

Several of the defendants wanted me to represent them in this trial. I appeared for Carl "Pappy" Ippolito at the bail hearing when all of the defendants were released on bail. Judge James T. Giles, the assigned federal judge, put off the trial for several months due to the length of time counsel needed to review the hundreds of tape recordings the FBI had made during the five-year investigation. All of the defendants had no problem with the postponement.

This case was one of the first prosecutions of an alleged organized crime family under the Racketeer-Influenced and Corrupt Organizations act, better known as "RICO." Most criminal lawyers, including myself, were just getting familiar with the technicalities involved with the new anti-racketeering law.

▼ ▼ ▼

On the morning of October 30, 1980, John Berkery called me at home. "Bobby, Frank's dead." He didn't have to say any more. I knew he was talking about Frank Sindone.

I thought to myself, *Jesus Christ, I won his two cases, saving him from having to spend so many years in prison—only to have him gunned down in cold blood.* Frank's body was just found, wrapped in a large trash bag. He had been shot twice in the back of the head. His remains were left in a parking lot a couple of miles from his home. I was later told this was a sign of respect. Fuck all that respect, I wished it was a bad dream. No such luck.

A couple of days later, I went to Frank's wake on South Broad Street to say goodbye to an honest man and a friend. To my surprise it was relatively quiet, and the crowd was smaller than I thought it would be. I remembered all the good times we had—in Vegas and in a speedboat on the Delaware, how we both loved the feel of the wind and the splashing water in our faces. And no one I ever knew could stand at a craps table as long as Frank, sometimes for 16 hours at a stretch.

I knew I would miss sharing laughs and conversations with him over a warm dish of pasta at Cous' Little Italy. It did not seem so long ago when Frank, Phil, and I were horseback riding in New Jersey and Frank told me to bring Scott next time. He had bought my son, then twelve years old, a pony that was blind in one eye. We all broke up laughing when Scott named it "One Eyed Louie." The first time Scott sat on his sad-looking, black and white pony, Frank gave it a smack on its rear and away it went, Scott holding on for dear life until it returned on its own to the barn.

A few days after Sindone got "respectfully" whacked I received a phone call. Disguising his voice, the person said, "Bobby, you're next." Personally, it didn't bother me too much, but I didn't tell Rita or Scott about the call. Who am I kidding? Of course it bothered me.

▼ ▼ ▼

Less than two months later, in December 1980, while I was watching the six o'clock news, I was shocked again when I heard the TV anchor interrupt the news and tell the viewers, "Early this evening, the head of the roofers union, John McCullough, was gunned down while talking on the telephone in his kitchen. His wife, Audrey, who witnessed the vicious attack, had just let someone she thought to be a deliveryman into the house. The yet unidentified assassin was carrying two bouquets of Christmas flowers. He pulled a gun and shot McCullough twice in the head and calmly left the house." I learned later that John had just told his wife to give the deliveryman a bigger tip since it was Christmas.

I had a hard time accepting what I had just heard. John was just too good of a guy to deserve this. I couldn't help but think, *I did such a good job defending him—maybe if I fucked up his case he would still be alive.*

John, like Sindone, wasn't just a client. He was a good friend. Several thousand people waited in the cold to pay their respects. Congressmen, judges, mayors, lawyers, doctors, and union officials joined the rank and file of "John's men," the roofers, and all the other union construction workers in the tri-state area. They were all there to say goodbye to JJ, Philadelphia's most influential, accomplished, and loved labor leader. No one would ever be able to replace him in the labor movement. Not in a million years.

He was as kind as he was tough, and he was as loyal as he was stubborn. When they coined the phrase "man's man," they must have been talking about John McCullough.

The murders of Tony Caponigro, his brother-in-law and driver, and John Simone (no relation) had little or no effect upon me. But the violent deaths of three men who were clients, friends, and almost family were difficult to accept. Angelo Bruno, Frank Sindone, and dear John McCullough—all so close to me in so many ways, all gone now. Slain in 1980 in less than a year's time.

What a year! In the middle of all these assassinations I got married and tried and won the Falcone murder case. And people wonder why I drank and gambled so much.

CHAPTER SIXTEEN

Here Today, Gone Tomorrow

John Berkery and I had lunch in a popular restaurant in Palm Beach, Florida, over the Christmas holidays in 1980. We were both amused that the name of the restaurant was Testa's. John asked for a menu that he brought back to Philadelphia to give to Phil Testa.

Phil, still the alleged boss of the Philly mob, now owned a restaurant on Bank Street near Market in Old City, the artsy section of Philadelphia. The name of the place was Virgilio's. Berkery and I had dinner there when John gave Phil the menu. Testa quipped, "I heard a guy named Virgilio owns that place."

Phil's restaurant was a popular spot because of the fantastic Southern Italian food and the attendance every night of so many Damon Runyon–type characters. Believe it or not, the local office of the FBI had their annual Christmas party there in 1980. Testa smiled whenever he told anyone that tidbit.

Phil, like the late Frank Sindone, had a dry sense of humor that I guess came in handy in his rather serious line of work. Several years before, while I was trying a case in federal court, an informant admitted on cross-examination that the Secret Service case agent paid him $20,000 in exchange for his cooperation.

At the break in the proceedings, as I was walking in the hallway smoking a cigarette, the agent involved approached me and said, "Hey Bob, can I speak with you?"

"Sure," I said.

"You heard that testimony, and I wondered if you, too, would like to make 20,000. All you gotta do is take me downtown and introduce me to Phil Testa without telling him I'm an agent." He said this to me with a straight face.

I surprised him, I believe, by answering, "I'll let you know." That night, I happened to have dinner with Phil and a few others, and I told Phil about the proposition.

He said, without a smile, "Bring him down and we'll chop up the money."

It seemed that Phil wasn't as surprised as I that this agent would ask a criminal lawyer to sell out his client. I thought to myself, *those bastards talk about ethics and breaking the law.*

Nick Scarfo continued to enjoy his freedom while still on bail in the gun case appeal. On one of his trips to Philadelphia, he asked me to join him, Testa, Frank "Chickie" Narducci, Salvy Testa, and Frank Narducci, Jr. for dinner at Dante and Luigi's.

After we ordered our salads, veal picante, and perciatellis with brown gravy, Phil told me the purpose of the dinner meeting. "We got a problem, Bobby, and we need your advice." He went on to tell me that his son, Salvy, and Chickie's son, Frank Jr., had signed an agreement to buy an entertainment bar known as Le Bistro, at the corner of Missouri and Pacific Avenues in Atlantic City.

Chickie interjected that the Alcohol Beverage Commission, "The ABC," the state agency that had to approve liquor license transfers in New Jersey, was denying approval to Salvy and Frank Jr. This was being done on the basis that their fathers were "alleged to be members of an organized crime family." Neither Salvatore Testa nor Frank Narducci, Jr. had ever been arrested. They were being punished for the "sins of their fathers." Guilt by association.

Both Phil and Chickie wanted to know from me how we could fight the State of New Jersey and win. After hearing more details on the proposed sale, especially that the boys were paying $200,000 for the property and $50,000 for the license, I came up with a better idea.

Knowing that the corner they wanted to buy was right in the heart of the area where several new casinos were being built, one had to know that the property itself was a valuable asset. I said to all of them at the table, "Fuck the ABC and all the other law enforcement agencies in the State of New Jersey. Prejudiced bastards."

Boy, did they love that statement. Phil said, "Why don't you tell us how you really feel?"

I went on to tell them, "You have to buy the property even without the licenses. Trump Plaza Casino is right across the street. The corner is a gold mine. You don't need to sell whiskey there, and besides that's not a desirable way for your kids to earn a living. The law would be in the place every night harassing them." I grant you not too many people could have said that to them. "Go back to the sellers and ask them to just convey the real estate and make settlement." No ABC approval is required for a simple real estate transaction.

Someone asked, "What about the liquor license?"

"Tell the seller to sell it to someone else and deduct whatever they get off the sales price. It's worth 50,000, so you probably will only have to end up spending 200,000 for the property," I told them.

Phil and Chickie looked at their sons. "What do you guys think?" Phil asked.

Both Salvy and Frank Jr. nodded their approval; they now wanted to buy the property without trying to get approval on the license from the ABC and without all the aggravation and notoriety involved.

They took my advice, and within days they completed the deal and took title to the real estate. Less than a year later, Donald Trump bought the corner from Salvatore Testa and Frank Narducci, Jr. with a cashier's check for $1,100,000.

The advice I gave them was free of charge, but Sal and Franky asked me to go to the settlement with them. It took all of ten minutes, and at the end of the settlement, Salvy and Frank told the settlement clerk to cut a check in the amount of $50,000, payable to Robert Simone, as a fee.

▼ ▼ ▼

A short time before Nick Scarfo was to be sentenced for the federal gun violation, in the early hours of March 15, 1981, Philip Testa left his restaurant to stop at home and change his clothes. He intended to meet someone within the hour. He walked up the concrete steps onto his wooden porch, and he opened the screen door of his semi-detached home.

The explosion was heard for miles. I remember being awakened from a sound sleep by the loud, booming sound. I got out of bed and looked out my third-floor bedroom window expecting to see smoke, fire, and rubble. I could see nothing unusual. At that time, I lived at least four miles from Testa's home on Porter Street in South Philadelphia.

A couple of hours later, I was again awakened, this time by the ringing of the telephone. Rita picked her head up from the pillow and said, "What is going on, Bob?"

The caller, a friend of Sal Testa's, told me Phil was dead, "killed by a bomb." When I told Rita what I'd heard, she shook her head and went back to sleep.

It was difficult for me to believe that Angelo Bruno, Frank Sindone, John McCullough, and Phil Testa were all dead, victims of their way of life as much as their assassins. Naturally, I couldn't fall back to sleep. I tossed and turned and reminisced. *It was back in 1976 that my brothers and I had a surprise seventieth birthday party for Mom. Many of my clients were there. John McCullough, his wife, Audrey, and a few other bigwigs in the Building Trades Council had their own table. At another table sat Angelo Bruno, Frank Sindone, Sal Testa (who came on behalf of his dad, Phil), Carl Ippolito, and Johnny "Keys" Simone. And in the middle section was Lillian Reis, one of the only survivors, near many relatives.*

When Sindone and Testa first met Angelina and learned she was a Sicilian, they both said to me, "Now we know where you got your brains, your smarts, and your balls. Your mother, definitely." A few years later, Nick Scarfo, a Calabrian, learning that my dad was born in Calabria, said that those same attributes must have come from my father. Amazing!

Pennsylvania Burial Company, on South Broad Street, continued to do a booming business (no pun intended). I was ushered into the front entrance, past the large crowd of mourners, curiosity seekers, law enforcement officers, and the hungry press corps.

I walked through the crowd and down the aisle, then I knelt before the open casket. The undertaker had done an excellent job, considering the violent nature of the death.

Sal Testa stood near the casket and greeted me with a hug and a kiss on the cheek. He thanked me for coming, and I told him how really sorry I was. On the way out of the funeral parlor, Philip Leonetti and Lawrence Merlino stopped me.

"Nicky's sitting over there," one of them said. "He wants to see you."

He looked real serious as he shook his head in disgust. Everyone knew that Phil Testa and Nick Scarfo were close friends for many years. We chatted quietly for a couple of minutes, and I left.

On the way home that night, I thought about how so many of my clients were facing either a violent death or years in prison. There seemed to be a race between the law and the huge vacuum cleaner I equated with death to determine which would claim the body first.

It was only a matter of days before the news reports started trickling in announcing Nicodemo Scarfo to be the new boss of the Philadelphia La Cosa Nostra. Scores of press people and federal and state law enforcement officers appeared at Nicky's sentencing hearing, which was more like a side show than a court proceeding.

Judge Brotman permitted the government to offer a few witnesses who testified that they had reliable, unidentified informers who told them that Scarfo was now "The Boss." All this was just a show of power and a play to the press, because the judge could not sentence Nick to more than two years anyway—and that is what he did. The judge did, however, permit Scarfo to remain free on bail pending an appeal.

I rented a modern vacation apartment in Margate for the summer of 1981. I saw Nicky, Philip, Lawrence, and Chuckie several times a week. Philip Leonetti and I became close friends, and we spent many hours together—on the beach, riding in my small speedboat named *Next Case*, talking at the offices of Scarf, Inc., and drinking and eating at some of the better restaurants in Atlantic City.

Next Case was a 19-foot, fiberglass bowrider with a single, 175-horsepower engine. The boat was capable of doing 50 to 55 knots per hour. Philip Leonetti and Nicky Scarfo enjoyed taking rides on the open boat. Like Scott and me, they loved the feel of the splashing salt water on their faces and bodies. More effective than suntan lotion.

Nicky always insisted that we avoid the ocean's rougher waters and stay in the calmer bay area. He would often holler "no ocean" and "slow down."

I was impressed with Philip. He didn't talk too much, and he appeared to be a good listener. He went out of his way to thank me several times for my role in saving him from having to spend years in prison in both the Pepa Leva and the Vincent Falcone murder cases.

One day, while inside Scarf, Inc., Philip showed me the architectural plans for a new home facing the bay in Margate. "Look at these, Bobby," he said. "What do you think? Do you like it?"

I could only tell that these were the drawings for the construction of a new house, but I noted the prime location that was written at the bottom. I said, "It looks good to me."

Then he surprised me by saying, "My uncle wants us to build this house for you as a present." He went on to say that he, Lawrence, and Nicky would never forget the Falcone trial, and this was just a token of their appreciation.

Something inside of me told me to say "No thanks." I explained that I wasn't that crazy about the Atlantic City area, and that Rita and I were happier when we spent our leisure time in Florida or the Caribbean. I also knew that I couldn't accept this gift, worth hundreds of thousands of dollars, and then turn around and sell it later. Philip said he understood, and he agreed that Atlantic City couldn't compare to Florida and the Caribbean.

There was a certain undercurrent to the conversation which made me feel that Nicky felt the need to have me physically close to him. Close enough so he would have a lawyer he could trust available for him at all times. He might just have been right.

CHAPTER SEVENTEEN

The Court of No Appeals

Silvio Iannuccio, a handsome and charming builder of sorts, had done some work at my home several years before when I lived in suburban Cheltenham. He came to my office one day, minus his usual smiling face. As a matter of fact, he was extremely uptight, and his face was the saddest I'd seen in a long time.

Silvio, often called "The Count," told me he learned from the grapevine that he was about to be charged with conspiracy to murder a federal grand jury witness. He spoke with his slight Italian accent, which I always considered to be part of his act.

He explained to me that a friend of his, John Calabrese, had been a target of a federal grand jury several years before. The investigation concerned violations of the Internal Revenue laws. A witness who was supposed to testify for the government before the grand jury mysteriously vanished the night before his scheduled appearance. The body of that witness was found in a shallow grave in upstate Pennsylvania a number of years later. An informant told the authorities that Silvio had fingered the deceased to a drug dealer named William Knisley at the behest of Calabrese. Vincent Zabello, the informant, admitted that he participated in the "hit" with Knisley and that he shared some of the $20,000 payment. His story was given a great deal of credence when he directed the federal agents to the hidden grave.

John Calabrese, Silvio Iannuccio, and Bill Knisley were indicted and charged with conspiracy to violate the witness' civil rights and with actually violating his civil rights by killing him. They were all facing life in prison should they be convicted.

Calabrese and Iannuccio were granted bail, but Knisley, who was serving time on a prior drug case, remained in prison. Calabrese retained F. Emmett Fitzpatrick, a well-known and highly capable Philadelphia criminal lawyer. Knisley hired a lawyer from Washington, D.C., Roger Zuckerman, who came with an excellent reputation. We all figured that the case was going to be won or lost on the testimony of the informant, Vincent Zabello.

On October 6, 1981, a few weeks before the scheduled start of the trial in federal court, Calabrese was shot twice, once in the back of the head and once in the back. He died within minutes on a small street less than a block from Cous' Little Italy restaurant.

Several days later, I entered the elevator in the lobby of the United States Courthouse at Sixth and Market Streets and found Emmett Fitzpatrick standing there with his briefcase in hand.

"Well, Emmett, here is one you can't lose," I said to him.

He smiled and answered, "You never can tell about these things."

I couldn't believe my eyes when I saw him neatly place his file on the defense table as Judge Louis Bechtle walked in the courtroom to open the trial. Fitzpatrick said he was there to represent John Calabrese, who everybody knew was dead. The prosecutor didn't object, and the judge permitted Fitzpatrick to remain at counsel table for the duration of the trial. Very strange, but I guess it was better than having to return the fee.

The trial lasted about a week and a half, and every morning Silvio came to my townhouse residence about 7:00 to ring the doorbell and wake me up. While I showered, he drank about half a bottle of my Remy Martin each morning. Ed Harrell, who did most of the investigation on the case, would drive both of us to court.

The government had no trouble proving the identity of the deceased through dental records. The prosecutor put on a former IRS agent, Alan Hart, who testified about the investigation of John Calabrese and the subpoena served on the deceased a few days before he was reported missing. A few years later, Hart would become a very popular and able defense investigator.

Several other witnesses, including law enforcement personnel, testified to the facts surrounding the exhumation of the body. The medical examiner testified that the cause of death was "multiple bullet wounds to the head and body." Then the prosecution called their chief witness, Vincent Zabello.

He was able to tell his story without a problem on direct examination. According to Zabello, one morning they all met Silvio at his apartment, and he identified the target who lived in the same building. He testified that John Calabrese offered to pay him and Knisley $10,000 each to kill the witness and hide the body. He had very little else to say about Iannuccio.

Zabello told the jurors that a few days later they stopped the man in the parking lot outside of his apartment and pushed him into the car they were using. He and Knisley drove him to a remote location in upstate Pennsylvania in the Pocono Mountains. They had access to a mountain resort cabin where they drank and played cards with their captive.

Early the next morning they walked him outside to a wooded area where Knisley shot him. Then Zabello and the shooter returned to the cabin, cleaned it, and drove back to Philadelphia.

Compared to so many of the witnesses I had cross-examined in past trials, Zabello was a lightweight.

He contradicted himself at least a dozen times. His lengthy criminal record and his sweetheart deal with the government made it easy to impeach his credibility. After a three-week trial the not guilty verdicts came in only 90 minutes.

I had to stop in another federal judge's chambers, so Silvio left the courthouse with Ed Harrell. When I returned home an hour later, I found Silvio sitting at my kitchen table drinking from a bottle of Louis XIII cognac. He treated Ed and me to a fine meal and a couple of bottles of Dom Perignon. He loved to eat, drink, and sing, and for many months he sang my praises in scores of bars and restaurants throughout Philadelphia and South Jersey.

▼ ▼ ▼

Rita and I took our usual holiday vacation, spending Christmas in Miami and then taking off to the Caribbean. Miami was convenient since Scott could stay with his mom and sister who lived in North Miami Beach, while Rita was able to spend time with her folks who lived close to our townhouse in South Miami. And at the same time my mom, who lived in Hallandale, got a chance to see Scott, Rita, and me.

We found a new island in the French West Indies—St. Bartholemy. It was much different than St. Thomas, Puerto Rico, Martinique, St. Lucia, St. Martin, and the Dominican Republic, where we previously spent time relaxing and swimming both above and under the surface.

St. Barths, or St. Barts as it is usually called, is smaller and quieter with not much to do—no phones or TV. At least back then it was that way. It consists of only eight square miles, but the island is blessed with eight or nine beautiful white beaches. There were, and still are, no less than 70 places to eat the gourmet, mostly French, food with a bottle of white wine at lunch and a bottle of red wine at the dinner table.

It was here that I really learned how to relax. Every day Rita and I lay on one of the white, sandy beaches, reading a good book or a current magazine. Before the sun could bake us, we hit the calm, clear, blue ocean to cool off. I often think about lying on my inflated rubber raft, thinking about nothing except how stunning Rita looked in her bathing suit, and what and where we were going to eat that day.

▼ ▼ ▼

Back to reality.

The RICO trial was scheduled to start before Judge James T. Giles in early January, but without me, since my client, Carl "Pappy" Ippolito, had been excused from the trial. I was able to prove that he was too old, senile, and incompetent to stand trial. He was, in a manner of speaking, sent out to pasture, relatively safe from the wrath of the law and the violent group of gunmen who were changing South Philadelphia into a modern-day Dodge City.

Within hours of my arrival home, the doorbell rang and standing outside, blowing into his large, cold hands, was Joseph "Chickie" Ciancaglini. He looked huge at over six feet tall, with a very narrow waist below his very muscular upper body.

I ushered him upstairs to the kitchen where we drank some coffee and spoke about his trial that had just started. Chickie and I had been good friends for several years. He had been very close to Frank Sindone, and many times when he came to collect money I owed, he laughed when I sang, "I ain't got no money." He always let me slide, offering some good excuse for me.

Chickie asked me if I would work with his lawyer, Donny Marino. He explained that Donny was busy with his duties as either Chancellor or Vice Chancellor of the Philadelphia Bar Association at the time. He told me now that Frank and Phil were gone the government was concentrating more on him. I told him I would talk to Marino and get back to him later.

By the next day, Donny, who was and is an excellent criminal lawyer and a close friend of mine, told me that he would welcome my participation in Chickie's defense. Soon I was seated next to Ciancaglini and Marino as jury selection continued. Sitting to my right was Frank Narducci, Sr. I was sandwiched between the two Chickies. It was like being with the "Two Jakes," Jack Nicholson and Harvey Keitel.

I thanked Narducci for his most recent delivery of excellent Italian luncheon meat, cheese, round, hard-crusted Italian bread, and Dom Perignon champagne. Since his gambling and bribery trial, he had gotten into the habit of giving Ed Harrell two large baskets full of great food and drink, one for Ed and one for me.

I remember kidding with him, saying, "Hey, Chick, you missed us last week. What's the matter, you broke or something?"

He winked and said, "Tell Ed to come down tomorrow to pick 'em up."

That day he drove home from court himself and parked his Cadillac in the driveway behind his house, located not too far from Veterans Stadium in South Philadelphia. He had no sooner gotten out of the car than two young, hooded gunmen approached him and fired their revolvers into his body and head. They ran away, leaving him on the sidewalk, bleeding and mortally wounded. The Feds, the press, and several informants said that Narducci was killed in revenge for his alleged participation in the death of Philip Testa.

The next morning, the remaining defendants and their lawyers showed up in court at 9:00, wondering what was next. Several lawyers brought copies of the *Philadelphia Inquirer* and *Daily News* to show the judge in support of our motion to continue the case. Photographs of Narducci lying on the cement driveway bleeding, one depicting a priest administering the last rites of the Catholic Church, were plastered on the front pages.

Judge Giles reluctantly continued the case and rescheduled it to begin a couple of months down the road. Phil Testa and now Frank Narducci were killed before they had a chance to defend themselves. I doubt there was any lawyer that could have saved them from the death penalty they received in the "Court of No Appeals."

A couple of days later, Ed Harrell and I stopped at Narducci's wake, which was being held at the Pennsylvania Burial Company on South Broad Street. Before the week was over, we both stopped by the Narducci home, located further south on Broad Street near Veterans Stadium, to pay our respects to Mrs. Narducci and her three children.

We stayed for about an hour, and as we were leaving, Frank Jr. said, "Wait a minute. My dad had these here baskets for you guys." Sure enough, Chickie wasn't bullshitting when he told me that he wanted Ed to stop by and pick up the care packages.

I spent the next couple of months trying several cases and reading the transcripts of the intercepted conversations from the telephone calls and bugging devices that were going to be introduced in the RICO trial. *If the case did not start soon*, I thought, *would we have any defendants left?*

The media was having a field day with all kinds of stories about organized crime, violence, and Nick Scarfo. This came to a climax when both Nicky and Joseph Ciancaglini received subpoenas to testify in Washington, D.C., before the Senate Committee on Organized Crime and Labor Union Corruption.

The hearings were televised, and Nicky's fame and notoriety spread outside the Philadelphia–New Jersey area. I represented both men as they pled the Fifth Amendment to most of the questions. The trip was meaningless and wasteful as far as we were concerned, except for the great steak dinner we enjoyed at The Palm Restaurant.

Joseph Salerno, Jr. came out of his rat hole and repeated his testimony from behind a screen that hid his image from the spectators and the television cameras. This time there was no cross.

▼ ▼ ▼

Our second attempt at jury selection proceeded without incident, and the testimony started immediately after the opening statements of all attorneys in the RICO case.

Judge Giles permitted the prosecutors to play what is now called the "DeNittis Tape" for the jury. In early November 1977, two or three FBI agents broke into the offices of Tyrone DeNittis, a manager of musical groups who was associated with Harry Riccobene.

Harry, only about five feet tall, had a hunched back and you didn't have to be a genius to figure out why everybody referred to him as either "Hunchback Harry" or "Little Harry."

The agents wired the office for sound and placed a few pinpoint-sized cameras in the walls. Within a few days they hit pay dirt. The cameras and bugs picked up Phil Testa, Frank Narducci, Nicky Scarfo, and Harry Riccobene sitting around the office, involved in a conversation which was purported to be a discussion concerning an upcoming election of a new consigliere in the Angelo Bruno La Cosa Nostra family.

The government would later argue that the audio-video tape clearly established the existence of the enterprise they alleged in the indictment—the Bruno crime family. That argument was tough to overcome. The defense was more or less limited to attacking the government's evidence on whether or not any crimes were committed on behalf of the enterprise. We also argued whether or not the government could prove beyond a reasonable doubt that these defendants individually committed those crimes.

Now that Testa, Narducci, and Ippolito were not sitting in court as defendants, it would be permissible for counsel to point the finger at the empty chairs without fear of hurting someone at the expense of their own client.

Ciancaglini was charged with RICO and being involved in two gambling conspiracies on behalf of the enterprise. He was also charged with collecting unlawful debts—loans made at exorbitant interest rates.

The Strike Force prosecutors, who were originally aiming their guns at the deceased defendants, now changed direction and unloaded on Charles Warrington, Little Harry, Sonny Riccobene, Joseph Bongiovanni, Pat Spirito, and my client, Ciancaglini.

I remember hearing the voices of all the deceased defendants speaking, as it were, from the grave, as the tape reels rolled for the listening jurors. It was eerie to say the least. I also remember smiling as we were listening to a tape of a conversation that took place at Frank Sindone's steak shop—not his restaurant—where Pappy, Sindone, Testa, and Narducci were overheard talking about a crap game they were allegedly running just outside Philadelphia.

In the conversation, Phil Testa is overheard saying, "Maybe we should increase the limit from a hundred or two to five hundred."

Pappy says, "No, that's a bad idea. If a guy gets lucky, he could kill us . . . knock us out of the box in one night."

Chickie Narducci then says, obviously kidding, "So what? If they win we'll have someone follow them home and stick 'em up." Phil Testa and Sindone are overheard laughing, and one of them says, "You better be careful, the walls have ears." They all laugh. I held back my smile, remembering all the laughs I shared with those ghosts.

The prosecutor, in his close, jumped all over that conversation and argued to the jury, "These defendants couldn't lose. Even if a player won, it was their intention to rob them."

Give me a break, I thought. *How could any jury be so naive as to accept that argument?*

Another taped conversation played to the jury involved a conversation between "Chicken Noodle" Warrington and Pappy Ippolito. This conversation took place the day after the FBI raided one of the crap games.

Noodles is telling Pappy about the raid. "The fuckin' FBI nailed the game last night. They took all the dice, the money, and the table. I say we should open again tomorrow night. Why not? We got Bobby Simone who will get us out of anything."

I couldn't help but notice Judge Giles look up from his transcript book and stare first at Warrington and then at me. I could only imagine what was going through his mind.

The jury deliberated for a few days and sent a couple of notes to the judge. I especially recall an argument in court with regard to how the judge should answer one of the jury's questions. In the middle of the argument, I was watching the prosecutor, Joel Friedman. I saw him hand a piece of white paper to the judge's clerk, and I saw the clerk hand the note to the judge. He read it. I immediately stood up and said, "Your Honor, I object, and I request permission to see the note."

Judge Giles said nothing. He just stared at me without showing any emotion. I repeated my objection. "I saw him," I said, pointing at Joel Friedman, "pass you a note."

Judge Giles said, "So what?" He looked at me as coldly as anyone ever had—inside or outside a courtroom. I would match his stare against Sindone's. I have been accused of many things, but no one has ever suggested that I was blind. Ex parte communications are not supposed to be permissible in any legal proceeding.

Even though I might agree that the government had some evidence against the remaining defendants, I still feel that the publicity about the recent murders was what really convinced all the jurors that the defendants were guilty. There was only token satisfaction for Ciancaglini; he was the only one acquitted of one count. All the others went down on all counts.

So much for the token satisfaction—Chickie was sentenced to ten years in prison. Charles Warrington got the same sentence for being involved in illegal numbers and working at illegal crap games. Talk about an excessive sentence! Ten years for unlawful gambling does not equate with "let the punishment fit the crime." Harry Riccobene received nine years; his brother, Sonny, got four, and Pat Spirito and Joe Bongiovanni were each sentenced to three years in prison.

This time it was the FBI and the Strike Force lawyers who celebrated. They told the reporters, "This is for all intents and purposes the end of the Bruno crime family." They forgot to mention for how long.

The guilty verdicts and the sentences were appealed to the Third Circuit Court of Appeals while the defendants remained free on appeal bail. By the time the appellate court affirmed the guilty verdicts and the sentences, in June 1983, another one of the defendants, Pasquale Spirito, was shot and killed. I wondered why these defendants wanted to stay out on appeal bail anyway. The opinion in *United States v. Riccobene, et al.* states, "The Court does not have to decide the issues raised by the appellant Spirito since he was slain while this appeal was pending." The case ended in the same murderous manner in which it started. Several years later, Mario "Sonny" Riccobene was shot and killed and then stuffed into the trunk of his car, where his body was discovered in Camden County, New Jersey. He had earlier turned informant and testified against his brother, Harry, in a murder case.

As of this writing, the only defendants still alive out of the original group indicted are Charles "Chicken Noodle" Warrington, Joseph Bongiovanni, and Joseph "Chickie" Ciancaglini. Little Harry, close to 90 years of age, died in prison while doing a life sentence for the case in which his stool-pigeon brother testified against him.

CHAPTER EIGHTEEN

▼

La Tuna

One summer evening in 1982, the father of the chief witness in the Falcone murder trial, Joseph Salerno, Sr., answered a knock at the door to the motel he owned and operated in Wildwood, New Jersey. A short male, wearing a ski mask and a jogging suit, fired a couple of shots from point-blank range. Salerno was struck by a bullet in the neck, but he somehow managed to survive.

A day or two later, Nick Scarfo was arrested by FBI agents and brought before Judge Stanley Brotman, who revoked his bail. The gun case appeal was still pending, but the government prosecutor was able to prove that Scarfo had violated his bail conditions by associating with convicted felons. They couldn't prove that he was responsible for the shooting of Salerno, but they sure as hell tried.

Nicky was whisked away in handcuffs and chains. Under an assumed name, he was secretly flown to El Paso, Texas, where he was put in the La Tuna Federal Correctional Institution to begin serving his two-year sentence, approximately 4,000 miles away from his family and friends.

A few months later, the United States Court of Appeals, in a two-to-one split decision, affirmed his conviction and sentence. I learned from official sources in federal law enforcement that the government was able to convince Judge Brotman to send Nicky far away from the Philadelphia–Atlantic City area so he would not be able to exert any influence over any of his "criminal associates."

Nicky remained incarcerated for about 17 1/2 months. During this period, I went to visit him approximately eight times in the prison a few miles from El Paso.

I tried to get him transferred back to the Northeast to make it easier for him to receive visits from his family—his mother, wife, and children. As hard as I tried, the answer was always "No way!"

Nicky, who always suffered from a severe case of allergies, was put to work in the prison laundry. I had several medical reports mailed and even delivered to the prison officials in an attempt to get him a change of jobs. Again, I received a negative response despite a worsening of his medical condition.

I tried to have him transferred from the Federal Correctional Institution to the prison camp that sat right on the other side of the prison fence. Again, the answer, of course, was "no."

I discussed all of these things with him on my visits. We also needed to prepare the parole papers for submission to the parole board. In addition, I brought in a local attorney who would be physically closer, should he need one, without having to wait for me to make that long, tedious trip. In the end we were only successful in getting Scarfo out of the prison laundry.

Several times after visiting Nicky at La Tuna, I would head south to Mazatlan, Mexico, for a few days of R&R. Rita made the trip once or twice, and Scott went with me on another occasion.

The incident that stands out most in my mind about my jaunts to Texas to consult with Nicky was one of the times that Philip Leonetti accompanied me. I received a telephone call from Rita, who was now living and working full time in Philadelphia. Several months after we married, Rita left her job at Air Canada in Miami and now she worked at a travel agency in Center City Philadelphia where I purchased two plane tickets to El Paso. She told me on the phone that an FBI agent visited her office, and while there he was able to get the itinerary for my trip with Philip.

I telephoned the FBI agent from El Paso and told him I didn't like the idea of his intrusion into my attorney-client relationship with Nicodemo Scarfo. His explanation was that they were not keeping track of me and my visits to La Tuna, but that they had an absolute right to know where Philip was at all times. Philip was not allowed to visit his uncle, even though he did not have a criminal conviction up to that time. No legitimate reason was ever given for denying Nicky the right to see his nephew.

On one particular visit I represented Nicky at his parole hearing. After spending several hours at the prison, I returned to the new Marriott Hotel in El Paso, where Philip and I were staying in a large suite. I walked into the hotel lobby and then into the bar where Philip was having a drink.

"Hey, Bobby, how did it go for my uncle?" he asked.

"Parole denied," I answered, and then added, "What did you expect, something different?"

"Not really," he said as he asked me to join him for a drink.

I told him I wanted to drop my briefcase off at our suite on the sixth floor. "I'll be right back," I told him as I went to catch an elevator.

I walked to the door, put my key in the lock, and turned the knob. I had chosen the door that led into the large living room that sat between the two bedrooms. The door opened, and I started to walk into the room when I came face to face with two men wearing work clothes, each carrying a tool kit attached to his belt.

"What's going on, guys?" I said as I noticed they were moving to get past me out of the suite.

One of them said, "We just finished fixing the air conditioner," as they both jumped on the elevator.

I ran to the phone, paged Philip at the bar, and told him what just happened.

By the time I reached the lobby, the two men had vanished into thin air, but I saw Philip leaving the front desk. He told me he checked and was told that there was no work order for our rooms, and further that there were no maintenance men working in that area at the time.

I thought about how some FBI agents broke into the DeNittis office to bug it several years back, and I was convinced that the Feds were doing the same thing to Philip and me.

When I returned home, I filed a motion to release Scarfo from federal custody, alleging outrageous government conduct when the agents attempted to bug my conversations at the hotel. Judge Brotman denied my motion, but he seemed genuinely concerned about the incident. He ordered an investigation.

A few days later, two FBI agents came to my office to talk to me. I recognized them immediately as two of the many agents who also showed up whenever Nicky Scarfo had a court appearance.

"We're here to investigate your claim of a break-in while you were in Texas," one of the agents said.

The other asked, "Can you give us a description of the two men who you claim were in your room?" He smiled as he said this.

"You guys aren't trying to make a rat out of me, too, are you?" I asked. Then I said, "I can't identify the men who broke into my room."

"Well," one of them said, "I guess we are at a dead end." They both turned around and walked out of my office. The matter was officially closed.

▼ ▼ ▼

Two agents from the Internal Revenue Service stopped by my office unannounced to formally notify me that I was under investigation by the Criminal Division of the IRS. I had always filed my tax returns and fully reported all of my income from legal fees and any other sources, but there was a substantial amount of past due taxes in the approximate amount of $200,000. After the IRS tacked on interest, penalties, and costs, their figure came to about $900,000 due. A higher rate of interest than any of my clients ever charged. But the government had immunity.

Not particularly bothered by the IRS investigation, I felt certain I would be able to pay my back taxes in due time. Usually, whenever I finished a grueling trial, I would send the IRS a check and then fly to St. Barts, always with Rita. The sun, salt water, and rest were almost a necessity to me, breathing new life into my weary mind and body. St. Barts was an island paradise where I was able to put my clients and my personal problems on hold. Whenever I left there, I took a deep breath and thought, *Maybe I'll come back next month and stay longer.*

▼ ▼ ▼

The casinos in Atlantic City were all doing well. None of them did more business than the Golden Nugget, which stood on the same ground formerly occupied by The Strand Motel. I was there one Sunday night with George Botsaris and Stanley Branche. We were enjoying ourselves gambling at the blackjack and craps tables. When we finished, we went to the bar for a drink. While seated at a table, we heard and saw a disturbance of some kind on the casino floor.

Chuckie Merlino, Tommy DelGiorno, who then owned Cous' Little Italy, and Charles "Noodles" Warrington, who was still out on bail in his appeal in the RICO case, were being ushered out of the casino by a couple of security guards.

I left the bar and hurried over to ask what the problem was. When I told the guard I was an attorney and I represented these guys, he yelled to another guard, "Take him, too." I found myself being pushed into a room with the others. When I protested, I was picked up and thrown against the wall. It seems that my intervention only exacerbated the situation.

The four of us were arrested and charged with minor offenses. We were all found not guilty of the charges in the Atlantic County Municipal Court.

The Philadelphia and Atlantic City newspapers made a big "to-do" over the incident. Most of the headlines read, "Robert Simone, Scarfo's Lawyer, Arrested at A.C. Casino." I recall being embarrassed by the printed stories and also upset with myself for putting "heat" on Nicky Scarfo.

I suffered some rather severe injuries to my neck and back in this incident, so I retained James Beasley, the most talented personal injury lawyer in Philadelphia, and probably in the entire country, to file a lawsuit against the Golden Nugget.

The case was assigned to, of all people, United States District Court Judge James T. Giles, the same judge who had recently presided in Ciancaglini's RICO trial. Beasley and Giles had several confrontations during the trial. It seemed that Judge Giles didn't appreciate Jim Beasley telling him what the law was.

After several witnesses, including Stanley Branche, confirmed my version of the incident, I took the witness stand and told my story. An orthopedic specialist told the jurors that his examination, including x-rays, revealed that I had suffered permanent injuries to my neck and back.

Jim Beasley was able to prove that security guards and one of the main security officials of the Nugget used improper procedures when they evicted the four of us from the hotel-casino.

Judge Giles refused to give the jurors a legal instruction, submitted to him by Beasley, that dealt with loss of future earnings. It really made no difference. The jury found in my favor and awarded me $150,000 in compensatory damages and $1,000,000 in punitive damages.

As we walked back to Beasley's office, Jim said to me, "Bobby, when we get that check, I am going to give it all to you without taking any fee or costs. I want you to straighten out your debt with the Internal Revenue Service."

I was unable to respond, because I had a difficult time accepting such a magnificent gesture. I had known Jim Beasley for many years. He was one year ahead of me at Temple University Law School.

Several times during the trial, Jim remarked, "It seems like Judge Giles doesn't like you, Bobby." I recalled the incident in the RICO case when I brought the passing of the note to the judge's attention. However, at that time I personally thought that any animosity that Giles might have had was directed at Beasley, not me, because Jim, like me, did not take shit from any judge.

Lawyers for the Nugget appealed the verdict, asking for a new trial. Beasley said that he thought the trial was "clean" and that we should be able to keep the verdict. I was feeling real good. The jury had exonerated me of any wrongdoing that night at the Golden Nugget, and I would now be able to pay the Internal Revenue Service all my past-due taxes, including their shylock interest rates. It seemed too good to be true.

CHAPTER NINETEEN

Welcome Home, Boss

Raymond Martorano was the owner of a large, successful vending company and cigarette distributorship. Angelo Bruno had been for many years his leading salesman. The company operated under the name of John's Vending. All his friends, associates, and enemies called Martorano "Long John."

He was tall and thin with black hair and handsome features. He dressed rather well when not in the company of his employee, Bruno, who always tried to maintain a low-key image and expected the same from his associates.

Long John was picked up in taped conversations with a government informant, Ronald Raitton. The government was claiming that Raitton was the P2P king of the eastern coast of the United States. He snitched on at least 45 others in an attempt to avoid punishment for himself.

P2P was a liquid chemical that was hard to come by but necessary to manufacture methamphetamine, commonly referred to as "speed" or "crank."

Martorano was out of the country in St. Thomas in the U.S. Virgin Islands at the time his indictment was made public. A member of Long John's family contacted me about making arrangements to surrender him in the hope that we could get bail for him. Within a few days, a deeply tanned Martorano and I walked into the United States Courthouse at Sixth and Market Streets in Philadelphia and went straight to the U.S. Marshal's Office where Raymond surrendered. He was quickly processed, and after he was fingerprinted and photographed, he was taken before a U.S. Magistrate who granted bail pending trial. Long John's strong family ties and successful legitimate business were the basis for the magistrate to allow bail.

I spent many hours investigating the preparation of his case for trial. Raymond was agreeable to the hiring of no less than three investigators in addition to Ed Harrell. Between them, they were able to supply me with a great deal of information and documentation that I would be able to use to impeach Ronald Raitton, the clever informant.

Raitton had bribed police officers, sold furniture and a house at less than bargain prices to FBI agents, and even had made a loan of $50,000 to an Assistant United States Attorney who was involved in the government's investigation. If any defendant had done this, he or she would have been arrested and charged with obstructing justice at the very least. But government law enforcement agents, including prosecutors, engaged in such shenanigans are immune from prosecution and even reprimand.

If you don't believe me, then I suggest you read the book *Black Mass,* written by two reporters from Boston, Dick Lehr and Gerard O'Neil, who describe the outrageous conduct of the local FBI and U.S. Attorney's Office in detail. The misconduct of several federal agents, who permitted two mobsters to do pretty much as they pleased so long as they continued to supply questionable information, resulted in the murder of one person and hundreds of other crimes going unpunished.

Jake Kossman, who knew Raymond well from the many days that Angelo Bruno and Raymond sat in his office, was helpful to me in my trial preparation. We knew that I would be able to effectively diminish Raitton's credibility, but the question looming in our minds was whether or not I would be able to overcome the incriminating video and audio tapes.

Despite all of the impeachment material available, including the fact that Raitton had earned over $25,000,000 illegally, and the fact that he would be allowed to keep his ill-gotten gains when he was released shortly from prison, the jury convicted Long John of conspiracy and possession with intent to deliver a controlled substance. Raymond was sentenced to ten years in prison, had his bail revoked, and was whisked out of the courtroom within minutes.

▼ ▼ ▼

Subsequent to Long John's conviction and imprisonment, his rather good-looking son, George "Cowboy" Martorano, was arrested in Miami, Florida, by agents of the Drug Enforcement Agency. He called me in Philadelphia and asked if I would fly down to Miami for a bail hearing on his behalf.

When I arrived, I learned that George was indicted with about ten other males, all charged with being involved in a massive drug conspiracy. The young Martorano was also charged with violating the federal "Drug Kingpin" statute, which provides stiff sentences for those who manage at least five others in an enterprise involved in an illegal drug operation and who direct and/or control at least three transactions on behalf of the enterprise. There is no parole on any sentence received under this law.

The case was assigned to the United States District Court for the Eastern District of Pennsylvania in Philadelphia. We managed to get bail set, but at $2,000,000 it was not a feasible option for George Martorano.

His case was assigned to the Honorable John Hannum III, the wealthy blue blood from the Main Line. John Hannum had presided years ago at the trial of my old friend, Luther Fleck. I also tried several other cases before Judge Hannum, and up to that time, the result was always excellent—either an acquittal or a lenient sentence.

The judge had a reputation for being extremely harsh on lawyers and tough on sentencing. I considered myself lucky in that he always treated my clients and me fairly. He also was known for some strange conduct in court on rare occasions.

One morning, while I was seated in the courtroom, waiting for a status call on the Martorano case, a large group of Asian lawyers appeared before the judge in a civil matter having to do with several Japanese electrical companies that were being sued by an American firm.

The Japanese lawyers were asking Judge Hannum, an ex-marine who served with honor in the Second World War, to grant them a two-month continuance so that they could obtain local counsel to aid them in the defense of their case.

After listening to the arguments, Judge Hannum loudly announced, "You have ten days to get your local counsel. You've got to admit, that's more time than you gave us to prepare for Pearl Harbor." There were at least 25 other lawyers sitting in the court, waiting to appear before the judge. All of us were too stunned to laugh—until we finished our business and left the courtroom.

The prosecutors turned over copies of most, if not all, of the evidence they had to the defense. There were reams of documents, hours of tape recordings, and reels of videotape. In addition, several of the defendants flipped and chose to throw in their lot with the government. The case was postponed to give the defense lawyers enough time to review all the discovery material and otherwise prepare for trial.

▼ ▼ ▼

Over the previous couple of years, information had filtered back to me that often, when the FBI or DEA made an arrest or was in the process of interviewing a witness, the agent would ask, "What can you tell us about Robert Simone, the lawyer?" They would often add, "If you want to help yourself . . . save yourself time in prison, tell me what you know about Bobby Simone."

I also learned from some people who were being grilled by certain agents that they would be told, "What? You want to call your lawyer, Simone?

Forget about it. If you use him, you're gonna get 20 years in the slammer." It seemed that I had several enemies in federal law enforcement.

I recall that on at least two or three occasions individuals approached me in a bar or a restaurant with the comment, "Hey, Bobby, can you get any of your clients to get me some dope?"

Rather than start an argument, I'd answer, "No—definitely no, and please don't ask me again." I would love to know how many people were wearing a wire for the DEA or the FBI when they approached me in that manner.

Sometimes it was, "Hey, Bob, can you help me get rid of some bearer bonds?"

"Get the fuck outta here," I would answer, knowing they were either stolen or counterfeit. I would usually add, "And stay outta here, too."

A few years passed before I actually learned that the government was trying to set me up by sending wired-up informants into my office in an attempt to entrap me into committing crimes.

Despite the constant harassment, I was starting to feel pretty good about my future. I was happily married and still in love, I had just paid off a size-able portion of my debt to the Internal Revenue Service, and I was sitting on a $1,150,000 tax-free verdict. For the first time in many years, I could see myself totally out of debt and reasonably safe from federal authorities who continued to look at me through a microscope. My law practice and my reputation were flourishing.

It was at that period in my life that the sky seemed to fall on me. The United States Attorney's Office in Philadelphia held a press conference announcing that a criminal indictment had been handed down, charging me with four counts of willfully failing to pay income taxes.

Agents of the Internal Revenue Service and the United States Attorney's Office informed the media and the public that for the past few years they had been picking up and going through my trash and monitoring my mail. They claimed their investigation revealed that I had been concealing assets in an attempt to evade payment of my past-due taxes.

I read the indictment and knew at once that in order for me to defend myself against these serious charges, I would have to stop taking any new cases and concentrate on the open cases I had pending, and more urgently, on preparing my own case for trial.

In a matter of days, I received a collect call from Nicodemo Scarfo, who was still in the La Tuna Federal Correctional Institution. He screamed over the phone, "Those rotten motherfuckers indicted you just because you beat my murder case." As for the sign over the phone alerting the inmates that their conversations were being monitored, Nicky said, "Fuck them and their fucking signs along with 'em."

I didn't have much of a chance to speak; it seemed he was more pissed off than I was. Finally, I was able to say, "Don't worry about it, Nick. I didn't do anything wrong, and I know I will beat these bastards."

Before he hung up, he said, "I'll be out soon, so don't you worry . . . whatever you need, you'll be able to get it from me . . . if you need anything now, just see Philip."

I thanked him for his kind words, knowing they were said in earnest. There was no question in his mind that the real cause of my indictment was my attorney-client relationship with him.

The newspapers seemed to agree. Why else would their headlines read "Scarfo's Lawyer Indicted on Tax Rap" and "Mob Lawyer Faces Criminal Income Tax Charges."

During Nicodemo Scarfo's forced absence from the Philadelphia–Atlantic City area, there were several violent murders. Newspaper and television reports quoted "official sources" when these killings were referred to as "Mob Hits in the Ongoing Scarfo-Riccobene War." Word was out that Little Harry was making his bid to unseat Scarfo as boss. Good luck. Sal Testa was shot and seriously wounded by a shotgun blast fired by a Riccobene soldier. Frank Monte, a close friend of Scarfo, was shot and killed.

On the other hand, Bobby Riccobene, who was one of Little Harry's brothers, was shot and killed in front of his mother. Two other Riccobene associates were also shot; one survived, and the other died.

There were at least two attempts to kill Harry when anxious triggermen fired at the dwarf without success. Sir Winston Churchill was right when he said, "Nothing in life is so exhilarating as to be shot at without result." Soon thereafter a white flag was hoisted at the bar at Ninth and Morris Streets, the Riccobene base of operations.

One evening, while I was having dinner in Atlantic City with Lawrence Merlino and Philip Leonetti at Scannuccio's, Lawrence said to me, "Bob, I want you to know we're carrying." He then reached into his pants pocket and showed me the handle of a handgun.

Philip said he had a gun with him also, and then he apologized to me and said they were only carrying their guns for protection. His statement caused me to lose my appetite before the first dish of pasta hit the table. They obviously were expecting trouble.

I believe Nicky would have been upset by this incident. He never spoke to me about anything illegal, and usually Philip was of the same mindset. I never did tell Nicky anything about this. If anything was going on between these guys and the Riccobenes, I didn't know about it, and I didn't want to know about it.

▼ ▼ ▼

Late one Friday evening, a fight erupted at the bar in Sam "The Barber" La Russo's disco, Scruples. Some young friends of Riccobene started an argument with Joey Merlino and some of his friends. Joey, Chuckie's son, was a former jockey who won more than his share of races. He was one tough kid. Merlino was in his early twenties at the time. He was built thin and wiry, and did not take shit from anyone.

Salvatore "Torry" Scafidi was one friend of Joey Merlino who always denied he was present when that fight took place. Torry, also in his early twenties, was several inches taller, about six feet. He had dark, wavy hair, very similar to Joey's. The main difference in their appearance was that Torry was somewhat taller and huskier.

Hours later that night one of the young men who was in the fight at the disco rang his home doorbell at a corner house in South Philly. He did not have his door key, so it was necessary for him to awaken his mother so that she could let him in the house. He never made it past the front step.

His mom stuck her head out of the second-floor window and leaned over to see who was ringing her doorbell. She saw a single male at the corner, standing about 15 to 20 feet from her son. Her son turned to face the other young man, and a few words were exchanged, which she could not hear. Next, she said the stranger raised his arm, pointed a gun at her son, and fired it. She ran out her door and found her son lying on the sidewalk, still bleeding but no longer breathing. The cause of death was a single bullet wound to the aorta.

Although I was preoccupied with my own tax case, I just couldn't say no to young Scafidi, who I believed to be innocent. Several days after the shooting, Philadelphia homicide detectives secured an arrest warrant for Salvatore "Torry" Scafidi. The victim's mother identified Torry from some photographs, and the detectives obtained statements from several of the deceased's friends that put Torry right smack in the middle of the fight at the disco.

I made arrangements to surrender Torry to the homicide detective assigned to the case. At the arraignment, the prosecutor argued that this was to be a case of first-degree murder and that he was going to seek the death penalty. That meant there would be no bail.

At the preliminary hearing, the victim's mother testified, between tears, as she described what she claimed to have seen. She made a positive identification of Salvatore Scafidi and stated she would never be able to forget his face and the events that caused her son's death.

I only asked a few questions on cross-examination, but I got what I wanted from her for use at trial:

Q. Mrs. M., you testified that you observed this incident as you were looking out the window from the second floor which overlooked the entrance to your home. Did you actually see the gun in my client's hand?

A. Yes, I did.

Q. Did you observe the gun at the time it was fired?

A. Yes.

Q. Tell the court what, if anything, you saw at or near the gun when it was fired.

A. What do you mean?

Q. Well, I would like to know if you saw anything surrounding the gun when the shot was fired.

A. I saw the gun . . . I heard the noise. That's all I remember.

I then took a gamble and asked her, "Did you see any sign of fire or sparks coming from the gun when it was fired?"

Her answer, "I told you I saw the gun. I didn't see anything else. I was looking at the gun."

I asked her a few questions about her ability to identify my client's face, and she was adamant about Scafidi being the shooter.

I finished my cross by asking her if the doorbell awakened her, and she answered affirmatively.

"I see you are wearing eyeglasses now. You weren't sleeping with them on, were you?"

She said she wasn't, and then she even told me she didn't get them to put on when she went to the window. She swore, however, "I could see without my glasses." Surprise, surprise.

I asked no more questions. Scafidi was bound over for trial, and the real work in the case began for me.

My investigator, Ed Harrell, discovered the name of Mrs. M.'s optometrist. Then he took his statement: "Without her prescription glasses, Mrs. M. would not be able to sufficiently observe the face of a man from the distance between the window to where the perpetrator was standing."

I got a court order to enter the apartment and have my photographer take pictures from the window, aiming the camera at the sidewalk where the shooter and her son were standing. We also measured the distance from the window to where the head of the shooter would have been located at the time of the incident.

My photographer, Joe Petrellis, the same one who testified in the Falcone murder trial, blew the photographs up to life-size enlargements. I stood where Mrs. M. said my client, Scafidi, stood, and Ed Harrell stood where her son had been standing when he was shot.

The photographs were taken at night under lighting conditions similar to those existing at the time of the shooting. When we received the blowups, we were pleased to note that my features appeared rather fuzzy and unclear.

I then found a leading ballistics expert who conducted several tests firing a .32-caliber revolver at night with overhead artificial lighting, just as existed at the corner in South Philadelphia where the young man was slain. Petrellis photographed these firing tests.

As I expected, the photographs showed a great many red and white flashes, looking like lightning, coming from the spot where the gun was fired. We had these photographs blown up for use at trial.

We also learned, through discovery proceedings, that Mrs. M. was suffering from cataracts.

Torry's sister, brother, mom, and dad signed statements for Ed Harrell, swearing that he was at home with them at the time of the shooting; he had an alibi. Not an air-tight one, we knew, but with everything else we had, our chances of winning a tough eyewitness murder case were getting better.

When we were selecting the jurors who would decide this case, I asked each one individually if they could follow the court's instructions and not base their verdict on sympathy. I warned them that the mother of the deceased would take the stand and tearfully tell her story of how she witnessed her son being shot and killed.

In my short opening address, I asked the jurors to keep an open mind until they had heard "all of the evidence—the entire case," and I asked them not to decide to accept any witness' testimony until they heard the cross-examination as well as the direct.

Mrs. M. testified on direct as I thought she would. She described in detail what she saw, and her testimony had to be interrupted a few times when she lost control of her emotions and started to cry. I couldn't help but feel sorry for her myself, but I had a job to do and another life was on the line.

She admitted she wasn't wearing her glasses but protested she could see clearly enough to identify Torry as the shooter.

I questioned her about whether or not she saw anything resembling fire or sparks coming from the gun. Her answer again was "No." I didn't want to alienate the jury, so I tried to handle her with kid gloves—it wasn't easy since she was so emphatic about her positive identification.

The toxicology report attached to the typewritten autopsy noted that at the time of death the deceased had traces of marijuana and cocaine in his blood system. The medical examiner had not yet taken the stand, and I was reasonably sure that the DA did not inform Mrs. M. of the evidence of drug use by her son.

I asked her, "Did your son use drugs of any kind?"

"Absolutely not!" she exclaimed indignantly.

My last question to her was, "Are you as sure of your identification of my client as you are of the fact that your son didn't use drugs?" The objection I expected never came.

She confidently answered, "Yes, I am sure . . . My son was a good boy . . . He never used drugs."

I said to myself, "We will see." I felt a sigh of relief as Mrs. M. left the witness stand.

The medical examiner testified as to the cause of death on direct examination. I then asked him to read the toxicology report to the jurors. I saw no reaction and began to wonder if I overplayed my hand.

When it came time for the defense, I put on Mrs. M.'s eye doctor, who testified with his records in hand that in his opinion Mrs. M. could not have been able to identify the shooter.

My ballistics expert then testified that he performed firing tests with a .32-caliber revolver at night under the same lighting conditions. The enlarged photographs were shown to the jury. The fire and sparks were depicted very prominently. The jurors stretched their necks to get a good view of them before I had them passed around.

Joe Petrellis testified about taking the pictures of the gun being fired and the pictures he took from Mrs. M.'s window. He demonstrated how he measured the distance with his camera. My face, shown in the picture, was not discernible.

I followed up with the alibi witnesses, mainly to show the jurors that Torry came from a decent family. His father worked at the Navy Yard in South Philadelphia, and his mom was a slight but pretty woman who had raised several children without any problems with the law over the years, at least up to that time.

His parents insisted that Torry went to sleep early that evening and that they all had breakfast together as they did every weekend morning. According to them, their son could not possibly have been at the bar when the fight occurred, and he was sound asleep at the time of the shooting.

The DA called an ophthalmologist from one of the university hospitals as an expert witness on rebuttal to answer our expert medical testimony. He testified that he examined Mrs. M., looked at the enlarged photos of the scene of the crime and considering the distance involved, it was his opinion that Mrs. M. would be able to see well enough to identify the perpetrator. He said her cataract condition was not far enough advanced to cause serious vision problems.

After the prosecution rested again, I was allowed to call another expert witness — another ophthalmologist — an expert on cataracts. His credentials were far superior to those of the prosecution's expert. Naturally, he contradicted the view of that doctor.

This would not be the first time that twelve jurors with no experience or knowledge in a certain field decided a technical question when two so-called experts couldn't agree.

In my closing argument, I reminded the jurors of their pledge not to base their verdict on any sympathy that they might have for Mrs. M. The evidence, I said, clearly showed that she didn't see what she thought she saw. I was careful not to call her a liar.

The jury did not reach a verdict the first day. I spent that night with Joey Merlino, Torry's best friend. We were both worried.

The next morning, I noticed a large crowd of strangers in the hall outside the courtroom. This was quite unusual, because it was a Saturday, and there was no other activity in City Hall. Torry's brother, Tommy, told me that the crowd consisted mostly of friends of the deceased. He also said that most of these giant-sized guys were friends of the Riccobenes. They were there to taunt Torry if he lost or create serious trouble if he won.

The sheriff's deputies took notice of the whole scene that was unfolding. They called for backup men. They were probably needed. The jury came back early that morning with a not guilty verdict.

Torry was released after spending eight months in prison for a crime he was found not guilty of committing. He and his family were not as upset with that as I was. A couple of weeks later, I joined Torry and Joey for a drink, and they presented me with a gold medal showing two hands clasped together; on the back was inscribed, "Friends forever, thank you. Joey and Sal."

▼ ▼ ▼

Meanwhile, the more evidence I received and reviewed, the tougher the case against George Martorano appeared to be. Several of the co-defendants and their lawyers felt the same way about their own situations. People started to plead guilty, and some of them even agreed to testify for the government.

Judge Hannum called another status conference for the lawyers and their clients so that he could address scheduling problems. When he came out on the bench he said, "Mr. Simone, when we are finished with this meeting, please come to my chambers."

I walked into his chambers and was ushered by the law clerk to a comfortable leather chair across from the judge's desk. "Bobby, I am sorry to hear about your troubles with the IRS and your indictment."

"Thank you, Your Honor," I said quietly, not having the faintest idea of what was coming next.

"I called you in here to tell you I am going to testify on your behalf as a character witness," he stated, this without my asking him to do so.

I thanked him, and he told me to let him know when the trial was running so he would be available.

George Martorano's name or case was not mentioned in the entire conversation between the judge and me.

▼ ▼ ▼

Nicky Scarfo's release date, late in January 1984, was rapidly approaching, but three weeks before his scheduled release, he was put into solitary confinement for no apparent reason.

I flew down to El Paso with Scott and one of Nick's sons. Scott stayed at the hotel, while the younger Scarfo and I visited his dad. We were both relieved to see that Nick was physically okay. We didn't know if he was put in "the hole" because of a fight or for some other reason. They were probably just breaking his balls because of all the publicity he was getting.

His son stayed in El Paso for about three weeks until his dad was released. Scott and I went on to Mazatlan, Mexico, for a few days of sun and relaxation, and then back to Philadelphia.

The local newspapers and television news reports were mentioning Nicodemo Scarfo's imminent release and return to the Philadelphia–South Jersey area. Several days before the prison doors opened for Nicky, many of his friends and associates flew to El Paso to welcome him home.

Joey Merlino and Torry Scafidi flew down with Scott. From what I heard, they had a ball at all the steakhouses and discos.

Philip Leonetti, Lawrence Merlino, young Scarfo, and I pulled up to the entrance of the La Tuna Federal Correctional Institution in a large, black limousine. From the outside it looked like an old missionaries' home. That it was. We got out of the vehicle, and Nick's son, Philip, and I walked up the hill about 75 yards toward the front door.

There were approximately half a dozen television camera crews following us. Philip waited outside when I entered the prison. About half an hour later, after Nicky was finished being processed for release, we exited the prison and joined Philip.

As we walked back down the hill toward the limousine, the cameramen were following us from a short distance. No one stopped to answer any questions. When we reached the limo, Nicky gave his son and then his nephew a big hug and a kiss on the cheek. Lawrence was next as we entered the limo for the ride back to the hotel.

From the minute we left the prison grounds until we reached the hotel, we were followed by at least three unmarked cars. Nicky was to remain under constant surveillance for the next several years.

Unknown to me at the time was the fact that I was already being watched by law enforcement and that it was to continue for a longer period than my client had to endure.

There were about twelve friends, relatives, and associates of Nicodemo Scarfo waiting for him at the hotel. Harold Garber, his counsel in the Falcone case, Phil McFillin, Salvy Testa, Joey Merlino, Torry Scafidi, and several others were toasting with glasses of champagne—"Health and freedom." Philip and Lawrence also raised their glasses to join in the toast.

Nicky's main concern was my tax indictment. He expressed a great deal of worry about the outcome. It would be easy to say that he was worried for selfish reasons, but I know in my heart that his chief concern was my personal welfare. He repeated his offer of help, and made sure I didn't have to worry, particularly about money, when I went to trial.

That night, *ABC Nightly News* showed their video pictures of Nicky Scarfo leaving the prison, walking down the grassy hill, accompanied by his son, his nephew, and his lawyer, Robert F. Simone. The lead-in remarks to the one-minute story went something like this: "Nicky Scarfo, the reputed godfather of the Mafia's most violent crime family, is released from a federal prison in Texas."

The next day, the El Paso morning newspapers quoted a member of the Texas Rangers who was on guard outside the hotel: "Here we are, the local police, the Texas Rangers, and the FBI standing here doing nothing while there is a whole gang inside there partying."

Scarfo's mob myth was going through a process of rebirth. No matter what he did or didn't do from here on in, he would be front-page news. No matter whom I represented in court or whatever I might do, I would now be called "Nicky Scarfo's lawyer." It was easier and safer being Lillian Reis' lawyer.

Nicky needed to do about 20 days of parole before his sentence would be totally satisfied. I advised him not to associate with anyone who had been convicted of a crime, to avoid a violation and a short trip back to the slammer.

We decided that it would be best if he left the Philadelphia–South Jersey area until after he was finished with his parole. In a few days, Nicky took his son, his nephew Philip Leonetti, and several of his buddies, who had never been convicted of a crime, to the Sonesta Beach Hotel in Key Biscayne, Florida.

I went down to Miami and stayed at Rita's townhouse in South Miami, only 15 minutes from the Sonesta. Every day, I visited Nicky, Philip, Lawrence, Sal Testa, and several others at the hotel pool, and every day I saw the helicopters hovering just about a hundred yards above our heads. There was no question in our minds as to what they were doing there.

After two weeks of lying around in the hot sun and eating dinner with Nicky and his crew of friends, I knew it was time to go back to Philadelphia and the reality of defending myself against the Internal Revenue Service and the United States Attorney's Office. But first, I would have to deal with George Martorano's case.

▼ ▼ ▼

I read and reread every document the government gave me relating to George's case. There were mountains of incriminating evidence, but I wasn't ready to recommend that he plead guilty yet. I talked to both George and his dad about the case. Raymond suggested that another criminal lawyer should review the file with copies of all of the evidence, including tapes and transcripts, for the purpose of giving an independent opinion of whether or not George Martorano should plead guilty. After reviewing the entire file, criminal lawyer Dan Preminger recommended that young Martorano should plead guilty. He included his reasons that basically dealt with the overwhelming evidence of guilt.

George asked me what I thought about the potential sentence he would get. I told him I couldn't be sure, but that the prosecutor was only hoping for a 30-year sentence. That statement was made after I had talked to the Assistant United States Attorney.

After much soul-searching by both George and me, he decided to plead guilty. It was to be an open plea—meaning there would be no recommendation by the prosecutor, leaving the sentence entirely up to the judge's discretion. I told George about my past experiences with Judge Hannum and also his reputation for being tough on sentencing.

George Martorano pled guilty, and six weeks later Judge Hannum stunned him and everyone else in the courtroom when he announced a maximum sentence of life imprisonment with no parole. I will never forget that day as long as I live—I am sure that George won't either.

Judge John Hannum wore his black hat that day. He made up for all the fair sentences he ever pronounced.

Years later, George Martorano would get his sentence vacated only to have another judge re-sentence him to life in prison without parole.

To this day both Raymond and George claim I sold George down the river in exchange for Judge Hannum's character testimony in my tax trial. I am tired of denying this accusation and all the lies that go with it. It should be plain to see, after reading the next chapter, that I did not need the judge's help. As I stated earlier, I did not seek it.

I hope that George Martorano obtains his release from prison soon. I agree that his sentence amounts to cruel and unusual punishment. The sentence far outweighs the magnitude of the crime.

CHAPTER TWENTY

▼

Somebody's Watching Me

The indictment charged me with four separate counts of willfully failing to pay income taxes; each one carried a term of imprisonment of five years. This was no laughing matter; my ass was on the line. I was looking at 20 years in prison.

A young Assistant United States Attorney, Gary Glazer, was assigned to prosecute me. What better way to build a reputation? He gave me no less than nine cardboard file boxes full of discovery material, thousands and thousands of documents I knew I would have to read before trial.

Robert Madden, a former agent of the Internal Revenue Service and then a federal prosecutor, is now an excellent defense attorney. He was handsome and had a pleasant personality, but more important to me was the fact that he was extremely knowledgeable in the field of tax law. He volunteered his time, services, and expertise to assist me in the preparations for trial. His help was welcomed, needed, and accepted.

Jake Kossman called and asked to see me. I arranged to pick him up late in the day and take him and Rita to Bookbinder's for dinner. When we walked into the crowded restaurant, several customers, waiters, and the two bartenders, along with Anthony, the maitre d', and Albert Taxin, John's son, went out of their way to wish me well in the outcome of my case, which they had all read about in the newspapers.

We sat down in one of the large booths in the Presidents' Room where most of the locals ate. The intimate room was separated from the much larger dining area that was always full of out-of-towners, tourists, and business people loading up on their expense accounts. The paneled walls were covered with pictures of all the former Presidents of the United States and the Chairman of the Board, Frank Sinatra.

We ordered drinks and before the waiter returned with them, Jake started, "Well, Bob, how were you thinking of handling your defense, and who is going to represent you?"

I told him about Bob Madden's offer to get involved and then said, "I'm thinking of representing myself."

"Good idea. That way you will be able to speak to the jury and not have to testify and later be cross-examined."

I showed him the indictment, and he continued to read it as our drinks were placed in front of us on the table. I picked up my Bombay Sapphire martini and held the glass up to the tip of Rita's glass of Montrachet. Jake's eyes stayed focused on the indictment.

"Health and freedom," I toasted and then sipped. Rita smiled nervously as she glanced at Jake, who paid no attention to either of us.

"There's no fucking way . . . excuse me, Rita . . . that you should be convicted unless they have evidence that you have a stash of money laying in some safe deposit box or drawer. Knowing the way you have been living, I doubt you have any serious money laying around. I'm talking about fifty . . . a hundred thousand dollars."

"You're right, Jake. I either spent it all or gambled it away."

"Bobby, you got a pen? Write this down. I don't want you to forget what I'm telling you . . . in case I die or something." Jake wasn't kidding when he said this. He was covering all the bases. I took out a small notebook and a pen and wrote down what he told me. Then he grabbed his scotch and water and gulped it down. I swallowed what was left in my large, cold martini, and we ordered another one. Rita wasn't finished with her wine yet, but she didn't say no either.

Jake went on to tell me not to be embarrassed with the jury. "Let it all hang out. Tell them, show them where all the money went. You borrowed a lot of money from the loansharks, and you paid a helluva lot of interest. There's nothing wrong with saying you had to pay that money back. Look, Bobby, most of those guys are dead. You can't create any problems for them—and try to show all the money you lost gambling." Rita sat quietly, eating her seafood dinner, but she nodded as Jake was talking. Better than anyone, she knew that everything Jake said was true. Meanwhile I was taking notes as Jake suggested.

We finished our dinner, and Jake changed the subject while we drank our coffee. He spoke about opera, Broadway shows, art, and life in general. He was charming and delightful in his conversation and manner, but he couldn't conceal his deep concern for my serious legal problem.

I drove him home, and as he got out of the car, he said, "Everybody knows the only reason you got indicted is because of the way you keep beating 'them.' Don't worry, the jury will know, too." He ended by saying, "Come and see me anytime, before and during the trial. I'll help you as much as I can. If I wasn't so old, I would handle the case myself . . . but I still think it's better for you to represent yourself."

I kept the large cardboard boxes containing copies of most of the evidence the government planned to use against me at trial at my residence at 1709 Lombard Street. First I read each and every piece of paper, and then I numbered and re-filed all the papers so that I could retrieve any document I needed in a matter of seconds. Back then only a few lawyers utilized computers.

The voluminous material contained a fairly accurate history of just about every financial dealing I was involved in over the past 15 years. There were copies of all my tax returns and payments to the IRS and a schedule of what amounts were outstanding on any past-due tax bill.

There was a record of every bank account I had during the preceding 15 years with copies of every check and monthly statement. Another box contained all my credit card purchases and payments. There was a record of real estate purchases and sales in Philadelphia and Miami relating to Arlene and Rita as well as myself.

There was a separate box for stocks purchased and sold as well as other investments. There was even a record of my weekly living expenses, including cash spent for dining out and purchasing clothing. A small, elderly man, who runs a cleaning establishment, had told me that IRS agents interviewed him to determine how much I spent on weekly cleaning and laundry bills. I found his statement in one of the boxes.

I found one box that had material from airlines and travel agents, listing all my trips and vacations, including the frequent flights to Vegas, Miami, Acapulco, the Caribbean, and a few jaunts to Europe.

Another whole box of material listed all of Rita's bank accounts, checks, and expenditures.

There was one large file that contained only material relating to the purchase of 1709 Lombard Street and the bills and expenses for the improvements made on the house and the mortgage and utility payments.

The house actually belonged to my secretary of many years, Marianne Micoli. I paid the down payment and settlement costs. I intended the cost of its purchase to be a bonus and retirement fund for her. I agreed to pay all monthly mortgage payments, utilities, taxes, and insurance as monthly rental. The equity in the house would increase, and Marianne would have some security. It was the least I could do for her. She had been a hard-working, intelligent, and loyal secretary and a friend for over ten years. She never watched the clock, and my clients and I could always count on her when we needed her secretarial skills, evenings and weekends included.

The government's theory was that 1709 Lombard Street actually belonged to me and that I had put it in Marianne's name only to conceal my ownership to avoid IRS liens against me. Not quite a stash of cash as Jake had warned me about, but just as devastating if it could be proved.

The last box I examined contained copies of phone messages, notes, letters, and envelopes that I had discarded in my trash, believing it would be picked up and taken to the city dump. How wrong I was.

There was one box marked "Casinos," which had a record of many of my gambling episodes in Las Vegas, Puerto Rico, Atlantic City, and Monte Carlo. I was glad to see that the government agents did some of my legwork. I intended to use this material, and more, to prove that I didn't have any accumulation of money or assets.

Dr. Robert Blumberg, a psychiatrist and a friend, told me what I already knew—I was a compulsive gambler. He referred me to another psychiatrist by the name of Dr. Kenneth Kool, who was experienced both as a doctor and as an expert witness.

I was then referred to Dr. Stanley Levitt, a psychologist, for a battery of tests. In about 30 days, I received reports from Dr. Kool and Dr. Levitt, both of which stated that I suffered from being a compulsive gambler and that I had in the past sought, and was now actively seeking, professional help from Dr. Blumberg. All three would testify at my trial.

Ed Harrell pulled his black Oldsmobile Tornado up to the curb, directly in front of the entrance to the United States Courthouse in the 600 block of Market Street.

I jumped out of the front passenger's seat and then pushed the seat toward the windshield so Rita could move out of the back seat. Reporters and photographers immediately swarmed us. "Mr. Simone, do you think you were indicted because of who you represent rather than for doing something illegal?"

I thought for a second and then spoke into several microphones that were pushed into my face. "Let's put it this way . . . Nobody else has been prosecuted by the government in this area for owing the IRS money. You figure out why they are making a test case out of me." Jerry Lee Lewis was acquitted in a similar case somewhere in the South.

One TV reporter screamed over the voices of all the others, "We hear you are representing yourself. Is that true?"

"Yes, I am. Not only do I owe the IRS money, I can't afford to hire a lawyer."

As Rita and I finally reached the glass door leading to the courthouse lobby, another reporter asked, "Haven't you heard that a man who represents himself has a fool for a client?"

"I would rather have a fool for a client than a fool for a lawyer," were the last words I uttered as Rita and I walked into the building.

Judge Marvin Katz, recently appointed to the federal bench, was assigned to try the case. He moved through jury selection more quickly than I thought. The jurors all said they could be fair and decide the case strictly on the evidence, despite the fact that most of them had read or heard about the case or me before coming to court.

Gary Glazer, the Assistant United States Attorney, gave his opening address to the jury. He went over the charges as outlined in the indictment and told the jurors what he expected the evidence to prove. He claimed that I had earned a substantial amount of money and willfully evaded payment of taxes by concealing assets and ignoring my tax bills and attempts at collection by the IRS.

Some trial lawyers feel that opening addresses to the jury are not as important as the testimony and the closing argument. Personally, I have always believed the opposite to be true. A good opening address can jump-start a case and quickly put a defendant far out in front of the prosecution, making it very tough for them to catch up. It's like a racehorse with blinding early speed. In my opinion, no part of the trial is more crucial.

In the second week of July 1984, I stood for the first time to address a jury that was sworn to judge me, instead of one of my clients. I felt no differently than I had on the countless times before when I did the same on behalf of others, comfortable and confident. I believed in the innocence of my client.

I started off by introducing myself to the jurors, explaining that I would be wearing two hats, one as the defendant and the other as counsel. I asked the jurors to keep their minds open until they heard all the evidence.

I strolled back and forth in front of the jury box. "We all heard that the man who represents himself has a fool for a client. And let me say right from the beginning that you will see from the evidence that I was one of the biggest fools that you ever met in your life, but that doesn't mean I was a guilty fool as far as the law is concerned."

I told the jurors that they were going to hear from many experts in tax matters—Mr. Glazer, Mr. Mink, the agent in charge, my accountant, the government's accountant—and I added, "The only people who are not experts in tax matters in this case are you and me. We, in fact, are in the same boat." I was implying it was us against them, the IRS.

I repeated part of Glazer's opening where he told the jury that the government was having trouble collecting taxes from 1973 to 1984—twelve years. I pleaded that this case should be a civil case for collection of the money owed, not a criminal case. I asked the jurors to try to determine from the evidence why, after twelve years, they finally indicted me, only after I won a verdict in my favor in the amount of $1,150,000. I told them, "We will produce a letter sent to the IRS from Robert Madden and James Beasley authorizing payment out of my civil verdict of all money due the IRS. Two days after they received the letter, they convened a grand jury." Whenever I said "they," I pointed to the prosecution table where the IRS case agent and the Assistant United States Attorney sat.

I explained that I owed others and had to pay those bills as well as the IRS. I said that doctors would testify as experts and explain how I got myself "so screwed up financially." I advised the jurors that they would hear how I was a compulsive gambler, and told them they would be given the medical definition of the term "compulsive gambler" by experts.

The jurors listened attentively as I told them that once Dr. Blumberg convinced me that I was sick, a degenerate gambler, I started to change my lifestyle—a bit anyway. "The evidence would show that for the years 1981, '82, and '83, my taxes were paid in full." Those were the first three years of my marriage to Rita. I went on to say that I also started to pay my other bills on time—I was on my way to a normal financial life.

I argued that if they really wanted the money, they would not have indicted me. Now that I was close to having the ability to pay—with the funds from the Nugget case—they "thought they would lose their opportunity to stop me from practicing law, so here I am."

Ready to finish, I said that the evidence would prove that Marianne Micoli is the owner of 1709 Lombard Street, that I had not concealed any assets from the Internal Revenue Service. "Despite the fact that the government would like you to believe that a woman doesn't have the mental capacity or the ability to own a house, she can. And she does. And my rent is paid by me, paying her mortgage."

I didn't know it at the time, but I was now ten lengths in front in a five-furlong race.

The prosecutor presented evidence of my "lavish" lifestyle. The trips, the clothes, the cars, the boats, the restaurants, the casinos. They put a young lady on the witness stand to confirm that I had won $44,000 on a junket to Monte Carlo. They wanted the jury to infer that I did not use those winnings to pay the IRS, and therefore I must have concealed the money and had it stashed somewhere. I only wished.

In my mind, the highlight of the trial was when the IRS case agent took the witness stand and gave a summary of his investigation, including a list of all the documentary evidence he claimed to have uncovered. Part of the cross-examination went something like this:

Q. Agent Mink, in the course of your investigation, did you intercept and read my mail?
A. No. I did have a hold on your mail so we could make copies of the envelopes that you received.
Q. Did you have a court order to do that?
A. No.
Q. What gave you that right?
A. That's standard procedure in an Internal Revenue Service investigation.

I was hoping the jurors didn't like his answers. Maybe some of them started to worry about their own mail.

I continued.

Q. Did you pick up the trash from the front of my house?
A. Yes.

Q. For how long of a period of time did you pick up my trash?
A. For about two years.
Q. What gave you the right to go through and read my personal papers?
A. I didn't actually read those papers. I only spent about 15 minutes each occasion, just glancing at the material, not studying it.

Unknown to this mild-mannered agent, I had in my hand a copy of his chronology, a record of his time spent on the case and an allocation of his hours.

Q. Could you explain to the members of the jury what this document is?

I had the document marked as an exhibit. I handed it to Agent Mink and asked him to read it.

Q. Have you read the exhibit, and is it in your handwriting?
A. Yes. . . . Yes.
Q. Read this notation to the jury.
A. Spent five hours reading material from trash.
Q. Read this one.
A. Spent four and a half hours reading trash.

I continued to point out the various dates and hours in the chronology to show that Agent Mink had spent many more hours reading through my discarded documents than he had led the jurors to believe. His answers were now given in a lower voice and slower than before, with a lot less confidence. Now that I had him on the ropes, I moved in for the kill.

Q. Agent Mink, I am going to show you copies of some papers I received from Mr. Glazer that were included in the material you read from my trash, and I ask you now if, in fact, you seized this material from my trash?
A. [After examining material] Yes, these items were seized from your trash.
Q. I show you these three small pieces of paper and ask you if they are not copies of telephone messages from a federal judge who sits in this courthouse?
A. They appear to be.
Q. You read them, didn't you?
A. Probably.
Q. What, if anything, do these messages have to do with this case?
A. [No response]
Q. Well?
A. I don't know.

Q. [Handing him a slip of paper] Read this to the jury, Mr. Mink.
A. "Dear Rita: I have to work late tonight. I love you. I'll see you later. Love, Bob."
Q. Now read this one to the jurors.
A. "Dear Bob: I'm working tonight. I can't cook you dinner. I'm sorry. Look in the oven. There is something for you. Love, Rita."
Q. What right did you have to read personal correspondence between me and my wife?
A. You were under investigation.
Q. That gave you the right to invade my wife's and my privacy?
A. [No response]
Q. Is that standard operating procedure for the IRS?
Mr. Glazer: Objection.
Judge: Sustained.

At this point, the IRS and its agents were on trial. In my mind, every citizen and every juror could identify with having their mail examined and their trash gone through with a fine-tooth comb. It was offensive conduct, and I hoped that it would hit home with the jurors.

The prosecutor called Marianne Micoli as his witness. He hoped to prove that the house I lived in was really mine and that Marianne was merely acting as a straw party by having her name on the deed. The government was confident that this evidence would show that I concealed ownership in 1709 Lombard Street to evade the payment of my taxes.

Marianne Micoli stuck to her guns. She refused to bend to Glazer's grueling direct examination. She was declared a "hostile witness." Glazer was then permitted to cross-examine her, but that did not help him or his case.

On my regular cross, she testified about being my personal secretary for many years, and how I destroyed money by throwing it away gambling and being too easy with people who took advantage of me. She went on to say that when I started to straighten myself out by paying my taxes and other bills, I wanted to reward her for her loyalty and service through all the tough times.

The house was hers, she protested, and I paid the mortgage and the bills as a rental for living there. She went on to say that when I moved to an apartment a couple of years later, she sold the house and kept the proceeds of the sale, almost $100,000. Then she moved to Florida.

The government rested its case, and Bob Madden and I were ready to proceed with my witnesses. Dr. Blumberg testified that in the mid-seventies he saw me as a personal friend, rather than a patient, and he helped me see what I was doing to myself by constantly gambling my hard-earned money away.

He testified that in the last couple of years I had learned to control this sickness of being a compulsive gambler. Dr. Kenneth Kool and Dr. Stanley Levitt also testified as expert witnesses, a psychiatrist and a psychologist respectively.

Dr. Kool said I was still a compulsive gambler but that I had been learning how to control my habit. He said I had to take one day at a time. He further stated that when in the past I earned substantial sums of money and didn't pay my bills or taxes when due, it was because of the compulsion to gamble. He said that there was no intent to violate the law and that people who suffer as I did just could not control their actions.

Both he and Dr. Levitt testified that the prognosis was excellent for recovery if I would win this case, continue to earn money, and keep making payments on past-due bills and taxes. They said that by paying my bills and taxes in full from 1980 to 1983 I had shown that I was exercising control over my life and my affairs. They both credited Rita, my wife since 1980, with being a stabilizing force in my life.

A couple of friends of mine testified to my years of excessive gambling. One told the jurors I gambled "to lose." He added, "He is a demolition expert. He likes to blow money. He rarely wins."

One of my witnesses testified, "When Mr. Simone wanted to gamble, and he didn't have money available, he would borrow it from loansharks at the rate of three percent a week. If he borrowed $50,000, he would pay $1500 a week in interest alone."

We had to offset the evidence of the $44,000 win I made in Monte Carlo—explain what I did with this huge sum of cash. Larry Feinstein, who worked for me as a private investigator before Ed Harrell, testified that he picked up $44,000 from the office of the Monte Carlo casino in Manhattan. He delivered it to me in my office. He went on to say that I gave him another $6,000, and he then delivered $50,000 to the steak shop formerly owned by Frank Sindone. He wasn't sure if he gave the money to Sindone or Testa, both deceased at the time of the trial.

Gino Lazzaro took the stand, and when I asked him his occupation, he answered, "I am an investigator for the Pennsylvania Crime Commission."

I asked him what other law enforcement experience he had, and he stunned most of the jurors and spectators when he said, "I was a special agent for the Federal Bureau of Investigation, retired after 20 years of service."

He told a wide-eyed jury that in the course of his duties as an FBI agent he was assigned to monitor electronic bugging devices that had been placed in Frank's Cabana, the steak joint that Sindone used to own at Tenth Street and Moyamensing Avenue in South Philly.

He produced tapes and transcripts that I had given to him outside the courtroom. These were bona fide tapes and transcripts that were admitted into evidence at the RICO trial a few years earlier before Judge James T. Giles and a jury. He also had some tapes and transcripts of intercepted telephone conversations I had with Frank Sindone and Joseph Ciancaglini.

The tapes established that I had borrowed $50,000 from Sindone on a few occasions. Once the counting of bills could be heard on the tape. Lazzaro testified as my witness that he and the FBI could confirm that I had borrowed substantial sums of money in cash from Sindone. He further stated that I had made numerous payments of substantial sums of cash. Many jurors laughed out loud when the agent told them about my singing to Chickie, "I ain't got no money."

Approximately 20 witnesses testified to my "good character and reputation." Then Judge John Hannum III took the stand as a character witness, after Judge Katz overruled Glazer's objection. The courtroom became quiet as he was sworn in. He testified that he had spoken to many federal judges in the courthouse and that it was their opinion, as well as his own, that I had an excellent reputation for honesty and being a law-abiding citizen. Many lawyers had to scratch their heads when they heard about the "blueblood judge testifying for Bobby Simone, the mob's mouthpiece."

A day or two before the end of the trial, one of the many reporters who was covering it ran up to me in the hallway and said, "Did you hear the news about the Golden Nugget case?"

"No," I answered quizzically.

"Judge Giles reversed the jurors' verdict and gave the Nugget a new trial." It looked like my big lead in this trial was going to go right down the tubes just like my $1,150,000.

I was pissed, not so much by the reversal, but because the judge reversed the verdict during my criminal trial after I had been arguing for days that I now had access to the verdict and soon I would be able to pay my taxes in full. All of this was reported widely in the newspapers and on TV, and I had to assume the jurors read of the reversal of my verdict. And what about Judge Giles, had he not heard that I was on trial? The post-trial motions in the Nugget case were argued months ago and I thought it strange that Judge Giles reversed my jury verdict while I was defending myself in a major criminal trial.

Couldn't he wait to stick it to me? Timing is everything, they say, and at just the right time for the government, Judge Giles had dealt me a very severe blow—one that could cost me my freedom, my license to practice law, and my reputation.

My case was severely damaged but not as badly as the prosecution's after the motion to strike evidence relating to 1709 Lombard Street from the government's case was granted.

Before closing argument, Judge Marvin Katz ordered all of the evidence and argument that related to 1709 Lombard Street stricken from the record. He told the prosecutor and then the jury that the government did not prove by any standard of proof that the house was mine or that I concealed ownership from the IRS.

Gary Glazer felt this ruling destroyed his case, but he argued as well as he could. He implied that I was too smart to not know I was evading the payment of my taxes. He told the jurors that I had made a couple million dollars and was living off the fat of the land and the IRS. He asked the jurors to convict me of all four counts.

In my close I touched on just about all the evidence in the case, continuing to attack the IRS for their motives and their methods. I referred to them as "Big Brother." I added that they really didn't want me to pay what I now owed. They wanted me out of the courtroom and unable to defend others.

Near the end of my close, I held up the sheet music from a popular song and stated:

Some lawyers might quote poems, the Bible, from books, authors. Here I think a contemporary entertainer and songwriter, his name is Rockwell, might be more appropriate. Have you ever heard of him?

Well, Rockwell wrote a song, and he and Michael Jackson sang it, and the song is about . . . it's called "Somebody's Watching Me." Somebody Is Watching Me.

I then read from the sheet music:

"I'm just an average man with an average life. I work from nine to five. Hey, how I pay the price. All I want is to be left alone in my average home. But why do I always feel like I'm in the Twilight Zone? Just paranoid? I always feel like somebody is watching me. I have no privacy. Wow! I always feel like somebody is watching me.

"Tell me, is it just a dream, tricks on me? Just a dream? Who is playing tricks on me? Tell me who. Who can it be?

"Who is watching me, who is watching me? Well, is it mailmen watching me? Tell me who is watching me. I don't feel safe anymore. Oh, what a mess. I wonder who is watching me now: *The IRS.*"

I finished my closing argument with the following:

They have forgotten about common decency, they have forgotten about a lot of things. And that's what you are here for. You are here as a buffer between the IRS and every citizen that walks the streets. This is not a criminal case, this is not a case that requires invasion into privacy and an intrusion into the privacy and lives of citizens. It's a case where they are to do their job within reason.

There are two reasons why I am not going to comment anymore as to what Mr. Glazer said. Number one is that you have heard the evidence, and I have confidence in what your decision will be.

You have heard the evidence of the lack of willfulness and the lack of criminal intent. It's your interpretation, not Mr. Glazer's.

Despite the fact that they don't care if they destroy me, and maybe I don't care if they destroy me, I do care if they destroy my family and my relationships that I have had over the last several years.

In one way, I am a very happy person today, despite the fact of whatever you are about to do.

Who among us, who among all of us can say that they have the friends that I have and the wife that I have and the love that I have? I didn't need *them* to show it to me, but I feel very happy about that, and there is nothing they can do to take that away from me, as much as *he* would try.

They are willing again to suffer the loss of the money to destroy me, an attorney.

I'm not asking you for sympathy and I'm not asking you for pity. I'm asking you just for plain old ordinary American justice, and justice demands an acquittal of all charges.

Last but not least, they are talking about cunning and shrewdness. They have chosen in this case to charge me with four separate counts, hoping that maybe you would compromise this case and find me not guilty of three counts and guilty of one.

Well, I'm going to tell you, if I'm guilty of one count, it's the same thing: I'm a convicted felon, I'm disbarred, I'm destroyed.

So, I'm telling you, don't compromise this verdict. And when I say I'm telling you, it's not an order, but I mean don't feel that you are doing me a favor by finding me not guilty of three counts and guilty of one. If you feel that I am guilty, find me guilty of all. If you feel that I'm not guilty, find me not guilty of all. Because it will have the same effect on my life and the life of those that I hold dear.

My life is now in your hands.

I'm satisfied with the jury we picked.

Thank you very much.

Judge Katz charged the jury on the law, and after they went into the jury room to deliberate, he excused the lawyers for lunch saying, "Come back in an hour or so or be available by phone should the jurors have a question."

Bob Madden, Ed Harrell, Rita, Scott, and I went across the street for a sandwich, which I was unable to eat. My mind was on the jury. In about 20 minutes we walked back to the courtroom where I saw droves of FBI agents, U.S. Attorneys, IRS agents, and my two brothers, all waiting for the verdict.

The judge's clerk hurried over to Madden and me and said, "Come on. Get in the courtroom. There's a verdict." The foreman bellowed "Not guilty" four times. My friends and family cheered, and the government people shook their heads in disgust. Unbelievable, only 20 minutes to decide a three-week trial.

A woman juror came up to me in the hallway and hugged me. "Good luck to you and your wife. We knew you were going to be not guilty the first day."

I smiled and said, "Well, I sweated it for three weeks, but I thank you very much with all of my heart."

A group of friends, several members of my family, including my mom who just flew up from Hallandale, Florida, my office staff—Ed Harrell and Barbara "B.J." Futty—Scott, Rita, and I went to the Brasserie Bar at the Warwick Hotel to celebrate with champagne.

A few days later, Rita, Scott, Kim, and I were on a plane to Acapulco. There we celebrated for over a week, enjoying the beach, the Pacific Ocean, and most of all the margaritas in the lobby bar of the Princess Hotel.

CHAPTER TWENTY-ONE

Death Threats and Disqualification

Two gentlemen came to my office unannounced to see me within a week of my return from Mexico. I recognized them immediately as local policemen, one a detective with the New Jersey State Troopers and the other a Philadelphia cop. Both of them were assigned to the Federal Organized Crime Task Force, composed of FBI agents and members of local law enforcement agencies looking to put people with vowels on the end of their names in jail. Often they succeeded.

These two plainclothes men worked the Narducci gambling-bribery case a couple of years ago. They asked to see me privately, so I led them into my office and closed the door. I knew that they were not there to give me an invitation to the policeman's ball.

"Mr. Simone," they tried to be formal, "we have reliable information that your life is in danger."

This was no crank on the telephone talking. I didn't respond, I just sat there thinking.

One of them then said, "Our information is that the Martoranos are going to kill you."

"A pretty good trick," I said, "since they are both in jail."

"This is no joke. We think you should know this and be concerned," one of them answered. "We are here to take you into protective custody, with your permission, that is."

I told them to forget about my going with them or, for that matter, any law enforcement agent. I also told them I didn't believe what they were telling me.

Raymond "Long John" Martorano and his son, George, were not happy about the results of their cases, but they knew the score, and I figured if they were mad at anybody, it would be "the law." But to this day I continually receive warnings from law enforcement agents. Long John has since been released from prison, and I did hear that he told a civilian friend of mine, "If you see Bobby, tell him I didn't forget." George Martorano, still doing time, tells anyone who will listen that I was the one who put him there. Give me a break.

▼ ▼ ▼

Nicodemo Scarfo and his nephew, Philip Leonetti, continued to drive into Philadelphia from Atlantic City. On most of those occasions they stopped in my office and invited me to join them and their friends for dinner. I can't remember ever declining. Jake Kossman was often seated next to me at the table at Bookbinder's, Dante and Luigi's, The Saloon, or La Cucina, all great Philadelphia restaurants.

Nicky enjoyed good French wine, both red and white. He would usually order Montrachet—a smooth, dry, white burgundy—when at Bookbinder's, primarily a seafood restaurant. He also liked Ruffino Chianti Classico Reserva Ducale, Gold Label—a great Italian red. The expensive, red French wines were usually consumed when we ate at Nicky's apartment in Atlantic City. Every dinner cooked by his wife was an Italian feast.

Whenever we ate in a restaurant, Philip Leonetti would ask the maitre d' to turn off the air conditioning, so long as the other customers didn't complain too much. If the other diners complained, the air was turned down as low as possible. Nicky hated air conditioning and refused to subject his body to it, always complaining of his allergies.

It did not take me long to learn that wearing men's cologne was another no-no if you wanted to sit near Nicky. He always placed me in a chair next to him, so you could bet I wasn't wearing anything on my face or body that he could smell. I guess a few guys wore cologne so as not to sit too close.

Nicky usually ate with a large group. Chuckie Merlino, his brother Lawrence, Philip Leonetti, Sal Testa, Tommy DelGiorno, Frank "Faffy" Iannarella, Nick "The Blade" Virgilio, Phil McFillin, Tyrone DeNittis, Jerry Blavat, Jake Kossman, and I frequently dined with Nick. Sometimes all of us were present, but on rare occasions there would only be three or four of us.

Nicky liked his scotch and water, and so did Philip. Many times I noticed all of Nicky's friends ordered the same as he—Cutty and water.

One morning, Nicky called to alert me that he had just received another subpoena to appear in Washington, D.C. This was at a time before fax machines were popular, so I had to wait for him to bring the subpoena to me personally later that day.

He arrived at my office with Philip and Lawrence. The two of them sat in the comfortable, gray-leather chairs facing my desk. I read the formal-looking document, noticing a large seal on the bottom left-hand corner. It was from the President's Commission on Organized Crime. This executive body was formed at the direction of President Ronald Reagan, whose picture with Jake Kossman appeared on the wall of Scarf, Inc.

Nicky was given 30 days' notice of the date of his scheduled appearance in Washington, D.C. I called a good friend of mine, Harry Lore, a rather gifted and intellectual constitutional lawyer, and asked him to join me for dinner at La Cucina restaurant on South Street.

Harry, whose appetite for excellent Italian food, especially when free, was as great as his knowledge of constitutional law, needed no coaxing. I introduced him to Nicky at dinner, and we discussed strategy with regard to answering the subpoena.

Harry and I later joined forces and filed a motion to quash the subpoena in the United States District Court in Camden, New Jersey.

Judge John Geary ruled that the Presidential Executive Order allowing a division of the executive branch of our government to hold hearings for the purpose of studying for future legislation violated the Separation of Powers Clause of the United States Constitution. The subpoena was quashed. Harry wrote a convincing brief and argued the law brilliantly; I merely sat at his side. Several Assistant United States Attorneys and FBI agents left the courtroom rather unhappily when Judge Geary ruled in our favor.

The government appealed the decision to the United States Court of Appeals for the Third Circuit, and over a year later the appellate court reversed Judge Geary's decision, but by that time the President's Commission had finished its business, and no further hearings were held. Scarfo never had to testify in Washington, D.C., and he considered himself to have dodged the bullet, for which he was grateful. He just might have been held in contempt for not answering questions, and more than likely imprisoned. So much for the right to remain silent and the Fifth Amendment.

▼ ▼ ▼

Nicky and a few of his friends started making frequent trips to South Florida. He really loved the beach, the salt water, and the ocean breezes. Often he stayed at the Diplomat Hotel in Hallandale, and on one occasion he rented a suite at the Jockey Club in North Miami Beach. Another favorite spot was Turnberry Isle, a swanky resort along the inland waterway, just north of the Jockey Club.

On several occasions when Rita and I were at our townhouse in South Miami, we drove up to Christine Lee's Restaurant to join Nicky and Philip for dinner. Nicky loved Christine Lee's, a restaurant that served Chinese food along with the best New York sirloin steak available in Miami.

Nicky had told me that he would love to find a house in the area where he could spend more of the winter and visit frequently all year round. I knew of a place where a friend of mine lived that was available. Arrangements were made for me to drive Nicky up to Fort Lauderdale to examine the house, which I had never seen myself.

I pulled my four-door, gray Peugeot into the driveway of the Diplomat Hotel, looking for Nicky Scarfo to be waiting for me at the front landing to the main entrance. Sure enough he was there, talking to Salvatore "Chuckie" Merlino. I pulled over to the curb. Chuckie opened the front passenger's door, and Nicky slid into the seat. Chuckie then jumped into the back seat. The car was cool, as I had just made the half-hour trip from South Miami with the air conditioner going full blast.

I forgot to turn it off or even lower it, and as soon as we were all in the car, Nicky smiled and said, "We don't really need the air on, do we, Bob?"

I immediately turned it to the low position as I looked at Chuckie through the rear-view mirror. He was trying his hardest not to laugh. The temperature outside was about 95 degrees, and the air was filled with humidity. It was a hot fucking day.

After driving north on Interstate 95 for only about ten minutes, Nicky leaned over and said, "Do you mind if I turn this thing off?"

By that time it really didn't make any difference; both Chuckie and I were sweating bullets. I quickly turned off the air conditioner. With the windows still closed and the sun beating down on the metal car and through the windows, it felt like we were in a steam room.

I knew that Nicky didn't like the windows opened in a moving car either, so I didn't lower them. Chuckie was wiping the sweat off his forehead with his tee shirt, and I just let mine slide down my face.

Nicky looked at me and said, "It's okay to open the window a little, Bob, maybe half an inch or so." He wasn't kidding.

There was no relief, even with the window cracked open a little. I couldn't wait to get to the house in Fort Lauderdale. I drove faster than usual until Nicky told me to slow down.

Chuck said, "Yo, Bob, slow down," as he winked at me from the back seat.

When we arrived and entered the cool house, both Merlino and I were temporarily relieved until Nicky told my friend, "Would you please shut the air conditioner off."

Nicky examined the interior of the house, which was large, airy, and comfortable. The rear of the house led to a pool area and a dock right on the inland waterway connecting to Biscayne Bay and the Atlantic Ocean.

Nicky fell in love with the house, and he let the guy know it. "I want this house. You and Bobby negotiate and work it out."

We left after about 45 minutes, and Chuckie and I got ourselves ready for the hot, miserable ride back to the Diplomat. Nicky couldn't stop talking about the "dream house," while Chuckie and I did nothing but sweat.

When I pulled into the driveway at the Diplomat, both Chuckie and I jumped out of our seats into the comparatively cool air outside. The temperature was still about 95 degrees. The interior of the car was sizzling.

I looked at Merlino standing on the sidewalk, drenched in his own sweat. I told him he reminded me of the colonel played by Alec Guinness in *The Bridge on the River Kwai* after he was let out of the "hot house." Feeling pretty much the same at the time, I uttered my remarks loud enough so that Nicky, looking as fresh as a daisy in a refrigerator, could hear them.

The three of us laughed, but I couldn't wait around. I had to get back in the Peugeot and put the air conditioner on full blast. Driving south on Interstate 95, I relaxed in 70-degree comfort. What a relief!

Nicodemo Scarfo formed a corporation, Casablanca South, and the new company lease-purchased the property within a couple of weeks. Nicky had his dream house, which he renovated and refurbished inside and out. He called it, of course, "Casablanca South" and placed a large nameplate outside at the front entrance.

Shortly thereafter, a 40-foot yacht named *Casablanca* was docked behind the pool on the inland waterway. Underneath the name of the boat, the phrase "Usual Suspects" was written. Nothing could be closer to the truth.

Philip Leonetti was a natural behind the steering wheel of the *Casablanca*. He could maneuver the boat as if he were a seasoned captain. Nicky loved to entertain on the boat, but he never drove it, as far as I know.

At one point, as Nicky was enjoying his time in South Florida, he mentioned to me that there was another house for sale in the same block as his. He asked me if I would be interested in being his neighbor. "To tell you the truth, Nick, I need my space—away from everything—just to relax . . . me and Rita. You know what I mean."

Nicky, just a tad disappointed, said, "I understand, Bob."

There was a very good chance that if I'd said "yes," he'd have given me the house as a gift.

Before Nick was released from La Tuna, the United States Attorney's Office for the State of New Jersey called a press conference to announce an indictment charging Michael Matthews, the mayor of Atlantic City, Philip Leonetti, and a Teamsters Union official, Frank Lentino, with conspiracy to pay and accept bribes in connection with a land purchase scheme in which the mayor was to illegally profit.

An undercover FBI agent, posing as a land developer, caught Lentino and the mayor in tape-recorded conversations plotting to purchase city property for much less than market value. The plan was for them to first develop the land, then sell and split the profits among themselves.

Philip asked me to act as his lawyer. Nicky was worried about the case, not so much because he might himself be brought in later as a defendant, but mainly because he cared so much for his nephew, his sister Nancy's son.

It was apparent that Nicky loved Philip. He had practically raised him. I knew how important it was to Nicky for me to try to save Philip from a potentially long prison term. In addition, Nicky trusted Philip like no other. He needed him.

I appeared before the United States Magistrate in Camden, New Jersey, and had bail set for Philip. All three defendants were scheduled to appear for arraignment and plea before the Honorable Harold Ackerman, a U.S. District Court Judge who sat in Newark, New Jersey. Matthews, who was also released on bail, and Lentino, who was not, each had different dates to appear.

When I appeared in court with Philip, one of the prosecutors handed me a thick legal document just before the judge took the bench. I rifled through it and was able to determine that it was a motion to disqualify counsel for the defendant—in this case, Philip Leonetti.

This was a new device that federal prosecutors were using throughout the country to prevent certain defendants from using their competent lawyers of choice. The government never filed such a motion when they felt that the defense attorney might be a pushover. Damn the Constitution, the Bill of Rights, and especially the right to counsel.

The highly talented Oscar Goodman from Las Vegas, New York's Bruce Cutler, attorney for John Gotti, and I were constantly opposing motions to disqualify. The prosecutors wanted us out of their hair.

The judge took the bench and stated he had read the government's motion and brief. He postponed the arraignment for two weeks to give me an opportunity to review it and respond, or alternatively, have Philip Leonetti appear with new counsel. Did he really think I would give up without a fight?

I read the motion and brief very carefully as Philip and I sipped on our Cutty and waters as we rode back to Philadelphia in the club car of the Metroliner.

The prosecutors alleged that I was in fact "House Counsel" for the "Scarfo crime family." They went on to say there was a "conflict of interest" in that I had in the past represented Lawrence Merlino and Nicodemo Scarfo. They said that Philip Leonetti "deserved and was entitled to an independent lawyer—one who would only look out for his interest." As if they really cared about protecting his rights.

They went further. They accused me of being more than a lawyer for Scarfo. According to the moving papers, I was part of "The Family." The prosecutors accused me of conspiring with Scarfo and others, including Leonetti, to commit crimes. It would be difficult, if not impossible, to answer this allegation, since no specific crimes were described.

I was also "charged with" knowledge of the structure and workings of the "Bruno crime family," now headed by Nicodemo Scarfo, "The Boss of the Family." This despite the fact that every newspaper in the area contained articles on what was happening with the Scarfo family on a daily basis.

Philip was visibly upset by what we both read in the motion. He must have been thinking, *Where am I going to get a lawyer like Bobby, especially one that I can trust?*

Nicky hit the roof, screaming, hollering, and cursing the United States Attorneys and the FBI. Philip and I calmed him down as we explained that everything would turn out all right. I would file an answer and a brief, and more than likely we would win the argument, and I would be permitted to continue to act as counsel for Philip.

I retained Harry Lore again to aid me in this fight. Harry and I spent hours in the law library reading and briefing the law relating to a defendant's right to counsel of his choice under the Sixth Amendment of the United States Constitution.

Before Philip and I were scheduled to return to Newark, Harry and I completed our answer and brief and sent it off to the judge and the federal prosecutors.

Harry Lore, Philip, and I took the Metroliner to Newark on the afternoon of the hearing. Nicky Sr. stayed in Atlantic City, anxiously awaiting news of the hearing's outcome. There was enough media hype without his presence. The newspapers were having a field day writing about my alleged role in the "Scarfo crime family." The case against Philip seemed to be less newsworthy than my personal situation.

We walked into the courtroom. Harry sat on one of the wooden spectator benches in the rear. Philip and I sat at counsel table, separated by about five feet from prosecutor Peter Bennett, who sat at his table with another Assistant United States Attorney and an FBI agent.

After lengthy arguments from Peter Bennett and then me, it seemed that Judge Ackerman, who had a reputation for being tough on alleged mob defendants, was about to rule in the government's favor and disqualify me as Leonetti's attorney.

Suddenly, the mood changed. Judge Ackerman said, "Of course, Mr. Simone, if you testify that the government's allegations about you just aren't so, I might be persuaded to rule in your favor."

That was after Peter Bennett said that there was no denial of the government's claims on the record. "No way are these two guys trying to middle me," I said to myself. Stupid, stupid, stupid, stupid.

I took the witness stand, and Peter Bennett immediately started asking me questions about my relationship with Philip Leonetti, Nicodemo Scarfo, and Salvatore "Chuckie" Merlino.

"How many times did you visit Nicodemo Scarfo at La Tuna Federal Prison?" he asked.

"Many," I answered.

"Didn't you carry messages, to and from him, about his illegal crime family?"

"No, I didn't."

Then he asked me a series of questions about whether or not I made certain statements to "anybody" concerning Scarfo, Leonetti, and Merlino.

I started to think before I answered, and then I testified, "I don't recall making that statement, but if you have something to refresh my memory, maybe my answer would be different."

The same thing occurred about half a dozen times, but Bennett either ignored my request to look at whatever the government was relying on, or he asked the judge for help by making him order me to answer the questions.

Bennett asked if I was involved as a partner in any business with Nicodemo Scarfo. I said, "No."

He asked me if I ever told anyone Nicky Scarfo was the boss and Salvatore Merlino was the underboss of the Scarfo crime family. Again, I answered, "No."

Judge Ackerman then said he would review the testimony, study the briefs, and rule in a couple of weeks. During the train ride back to Philly, Philip, Harry Lore, and I discussed the procedure that had just taken place. We all wondered why certain questions were asked and just what might have provoked the asking. Philip Leonetti told me, "Bobby, I think somebody had you on a wire." I tended to agree with him.

I wasn't too concerned, because I knew I had done nothing wrong or illegal in all my dealings with Nicodemo Scarfo and his friends. I merely acted as his attorney, and I could not imagine how I was to be persecuted for doing my job too well.

Two weeks later we returned to Newark and Judge Ackerman's courtroom. He took only a few minutes to say, "I grant the government's motion and hereby disqualify Robert F. Simone as Philip Leonetti's lawyer. I find that a conflict of interest exists with the strong likelihood of Mr. Simone being called as a witness for either the defense or the government. And I must say that I find the conduct of Mr. Simone to be abominable, and in my opinion, criminal in nature ... Mr. Leonetti, I shall give you ten days to obtain other counsel, and if you don't comply, I will consider revoking your bail."

This time our side left the courtroom with our heads down. Our first concern was, "Who are we going to get to represent Philip?" and next, "What are these people going to do to Bobby?" In other words, "When is Bobby going to be indicted?"

Several years before, I represented a New York businessman in connection with a grand jury investigation involving both the Philadelphia area and New York City. My client was represented by an attorney from Manhattan named Gustave "Gus" Newman. I recalled that he was an excellent lawyer. I had a great deal of respect for his ability and his manner with people.

I mentioned his name to both Nicky and Philip, and a few days later we three went to New York to see Gus Newman. Philip and Nicky both liked him and arrangements were made for Newman to replace me as Philip's attorney to carry on with the defense.

It was an excellent choice. Through Gus Newman's efforts, an oral statement from Mayor Matthews implicating Philip was suppressed, and later the government was forced to dismiss the charges against Leonetti. Now there was not sufficient evidence to proceed against Philip. Interestingly enough, both Mayor Matthews and Frank Lentino pled guilty, and both were sentenced to long prison terms.

▼ ▼ ▼

It took a couple of months after my acquittal in the tax case for new clients to start coming back into my office. I'll never know how many potential clients and cases I didn't get because of the publicity and notoriety I received from the tax indictment and trial, as well as the verbal slap Judge Ackerman took at me at the conclusion of the disqualification hearing.

Another lawyer from "the Big Apple" referred me a case around this time. I received a call at home on a Friday night. "Mr. Simone, my brother is in jail at the lock-up in town. He will be having a bail hearing sometime tonight. Can you meet me there?"

Ordinarily, I would have said no since I did not often get into a case until after bail has been set. But in this instance the New York lawyer asked me to help his clients any way I could, so I agreed to meet the anxious man at the Roundhouse where the state case bail hearings were held.

The brothers were Russians who recently immigrated to New York. They both had very strong accents. It took me about seven hours to get bail set. It was high, $20,000 cash, because the defendant lived out of state, was not a citizen, and he was charged with robbery. Young, blond, and handsome, Rick and his brother were holding only $15,000 in their kick. Rick had been in lock-up for over twelve hours and in a lot of pain. Earlier that day he was shot in the stomach when he tried to pocket the money he had just won in a poker game. There was an argument over who was entitled to the pot. He was the type who preferred pain to talking to the police, so no thought of a hospital.

It was now about 4:00 a.m. I called my friend Tony DiSalvo. He brought the $5,000 to the Roundhouse and my client was released on bail. As we were helping Rick to walk to the car, I said apologetically, "I'm sorry it took so long to get you out on bail, with you being hurt and everything."

He looked at me, smiled, and said, "That's okay, Bobby. In Russia there's no bail."

On Monday, as the clock in City Hall struck 12:00, Rick and his brother walked into my office and handed me Tony's money along with a very substantial retainer fee. They had honored my trust—I just knew they would. Two months later, after three hearings, the case against Rick was dismissed.

▼ ▼ ▼

One of the new faces to enter my office around this time was Frank Gerace, the president of the Culinary Union in Atlantic City. Frank was about six feet two or three inches tall and carried around a lot of weight. He was at least 250 pounds. He had been indicted for embezzlement of union funds.

Frank sat across from my desk as he handed me a copy of the indictment. "Before you read this," he said, "I want to tell you that I already know I want you as my lawyer. But I have been warned by several of my associates in the union that you are Nicky Scarfo's lawyer and because of all the publicity you get and because of Scarfo, that I probably should use someone else."

"Frank, that is entirely up to you," I said.

"I told you I already made up my mind. But I wanted you to know that others think you bring too much baggage into the courtroom." He smiled, then added, "But if you're good enough for Nicky Scarfo, I want you next to me when my ass is on the line."

I read the indictment and then spent about half an hour discussing the facts with Gerace. The union had grown in size and power over the last several years. This was the result of the growth of gambling as an industry in Atlantic City. There were now approximately a dozen large hotel-casinos operating, each one employing hundreds of bartenders, waiters, waitresses, maitre d's, and kitchen workers. Just about all of them were members of the Culinary Union, Local 54.

Unfortunately for Frank Gerace, his mother happened to live at 26 North Georgia Avenue, the apartment building owned by Catherine Scarfo, Nicodemo Scarfo's mother and Philip Leonetti's grandmother. Frank was caught several times on video camera surveillance entering and leaving the building where his mother lived. Before now it was not a crime for someone to visit his mother.

What the hell, if they can pick on Nicky's lawyer, why not the president of a powerful union whose mother paid rent to Nicky's mother. That, as it turned out, was the only real evidence the United States Attorney's Office, the Department of Labor, and the FBI could garner against Frank Gerace.

The crux of the allegation against Gerace was that as the union grew, he was compelled to move the offices and hiring hall to much larger quarters. Acting on behalf of the entire union and authorized by the board of trustees, Frank acquired a large building, perfect in size for what the union had in mind.

Next, he retained a reliable general contractor to renovate the entire building to meet the busy union's needs. The building had to be gutted, new offices had to be built, and a complete mechanical contracting job had to be performed. Work on the exterior of the building was also required.

At about the same time, Gerace made some minor improvements to his home—rebuilding a den and putting in some new concrete. He used some of the same contractors as the union. He paid for his personal job by check, and he gave me copies of the canceled checks payable to the general contractor and some of the subcontractors.

That is really all there was to it. But his mom lived at 26 North Georgia Avenue and Scarf, Inc. did a small cement job at his house. Scarf, Inc., managed by Leonetti, had done a few jobs with the same general contractor that Frank had employed for the remodeling. It didn't seem like much, but

Gerace's union position and freedom were now in serious jeopardy. No one was more suited to empathize with his plight than I was.

The first time we went to trial, Frank insisted on testifying. I didn't want to put him on the stand, but when any defendant tells his lawyer he desires to take the stand, and after being shown the pitfalls, he continues to insist on doing so—well, that's it. The lawyer has to comply with the client's wishes.

The jury could not reach a verdict after two days of deliberations. Judge John Geary declared a mistrial, and the government, wounded by the hung jury, vowed to retry and convict Frank Gerace. I may have set the record for hung juries with this one.

The next time around, Gerace followed my advice and did not take the stand. He was acquitted. Frank thanked me. The union thanked me by paying a hefty fee that they would not have had to pay if Frank had been convicted. The truth of the matter was that Frank was a devoted, loyal, and hardworking union leader. The union grew to great heights under his direction and leadership.

Winning the Gerace case went a long way in re-establishing and enhancing my reputation as a trial lawyer, rather than as an alleged Scarfo associate as I was tagged by the Justice Department and Judge Ackerman.

◄ Private Joseph F. Simone in 1917.

▲ The Simone family in 1941. *Left to right:* Angelina, Ron, Joe Jr., Bobby, and Joseph.

Arlene and Bobby ▶
Simone soon after
their wedding.

Simone marries Rita ▶
Carr, May 25, 1980.

◄ Lillian Reis being arrested onstage for "lewd" dancing in an Atlantic City night-club, 1963.

◄ Lillian Reis and Captain Clarence J. Ferguson arrive at the Police Administration Building in November 1966. Police had found two pistols in Reis' South Philadelphia home. They were toy guns. *Courtesy of the* Philadelphia Daily News/*Lou Zacharias*

▲ Frank Rizzo *(second from right)* meets with fellow members of the Philadelphia Police Department in 1955. *Courtesy of the* Philadelphia Daily News/*Charles Myers*

▲ Ralph Staino, Jr. and Simone, circa 1975.

▲ Nicky Scarfo standing between Salvy and Philip Testa, 1978.

▲ *Left to right:* President Ronald Reagan, U.S. Senator John Heinz, and Jake Kossman.

Sam LaRosa *(left)* with ▶
newlyweds Dolores
"Cookie" and Al "Pajamas"
Pagano, 1988.

John McCullough and ▶
wife Audrey, 1978.

▲ Cecil B. Moore (with cigar) stands next to Dr. Martin Luther King, Jr. Ed Harrell is partially visible over Moore's shoulder.

◄ Frank Narducci in 1981. *Courtesy of the* Philadelphia Daily News/*Susan Winters*

▲ Angelo Bruno, "The Docile Don," around 1970. *Courtesy of the* Philadelphia Daily News/*Will Everly III*

▲ Joseph Ciancaglini in a wheelchair at Methodist Hospital in South Philadelphia, September 1967. *Courtesy of the* Philadelphia Daily News/*Charles Myers*

▲ Noah Robinson in the mid-1980s, when he owned several Wendy's restaurants.

▲ Frank Sindone.

CHAPTER TWENTY-TWO

Wired

The body of Salvatore Testa was found on the soft shoulder of a rural road in South Jersey on September 15, 1984. His hands and body were bound with a piece of rope, and he was found partially covered by a small, multi-colored blanket. He had been shot in the back of the head the day before.

I was requested to go to his Porter Street home in South Philadelphia's Girard Estate section to make arrangements to secure some of Salvy's personal property for his sister. I had been at the residence before, but mostly I remembered going there the morning the bomb blew the porch and Philip Testa away. I also remembered celebrating New Year's Eve there on two occasions with Rita, Frank Sindone and his girlfriend, Phil Testa and his wife, and many other good friends.

Several newspapers and magazines carried a picture of me sitting on one of the front steps of the house that Philip Testa once owned and in which Salvy was raised. There were also photographs of Rita, Scott, and me as we left the funeral home the night of the wake.

I recall that on that night a newscaster from Philadelphia's local NBC station asked me if I had any comment. I looked at him and he said to me in a rather civilized tone, "Bob, if you'd rather not comment, I'll understand and not bother you any further."

I answered, "Thank you." He left after he told the cameraman to shut the lights and camera off. The newscaster, Dick Sherran, was a complete gentleman while he tried to do his job. Many of his colleagues could learn a lesson from his ethical conduct. Little things mean a lot.

For the next year or so, I was busy with the retrial of the Gerace case and several other serious felony trials in both state and federal courts. I kept looking over my shoulder, wondering whether or not I was about to be indicted again according to all the indications I received in Newark some time before.

Nicky and Philip had no new problems with the law, except for constant surveillance. They always stopped in my office when they were in Philly. The fine dinners continued as before, only the topics of discussion were much lighter since we didn't have to worry about being in court the next day—that is, *they* didn't have to worry about being in court the next day. With rare exceptions, I always had to be there. Only now I had to worry about the Feds coming after me again.

▼ ▼ ▼

Late in July 1985, another well-known former associate of Angelo Bruno was shot and killed not far from his home. Frank D'Alfonso, who was known by everybody as "Franky Flowers," was the latest victim of violence on the streets of South Philadelphia.

I had known Frank for many years, and he was a complete gentleman as far as I was concerned. Back in the early 1960s, I traveled with Arlene, my first wife, and a planeload of Philadelphians to London, compliments of the Victoria Sporting Club, all arranged by Franky Flowers. He was on the same chartered flight. I also recalled being in San Juan, Puerto Rico, with him on another gambling junket several years later.

The murders of both Sal Testa and Frank D'Alfonso would be the subject of considerable hours in court for Nicky Scarfo and me, as his lawyer, three or four years in the future.

▼ ▼ ▼

Late in 1985, over 20 men and women were arrested by the Philadelphia Police Department and the District Attorney's Office, all charged with being involved in a large conspiracy to accept wagers in an illegal lottery and sports betting operation.

After being postponed many times, the preliminary hearing was listed before Philadelphia Municipal Court Judge John Scott. I represented one of the defendants, and many of my attorney friends represented others in the case.

There was a very large crowd in a very small courtroom when suddenly someone made a loud noise just outside the courtroom door. Judge Scott interrupted the proceedings and said with a straight face, "Oh my God, I thought the federal authorities were coming in here to arrest Bobby Simone and carry him out of the courtroom. We need to keep him here until this hearing is over."

Everybody, including me, laughed and then the judge said, "One of you court officers stand outside the courtroom and make sure these proceedings are not disturbed. You never know, maybe this isn't a joke." Judge Scott might have been a mind reader.

A few months after Judge Scott's joke, I was near the end of a lengthy murder trial when the judge broke for lunch. I rose from my seat and started to walk out of the courtroom when two gentlemen wearing suits and ties approached me. They showed me their FBI identification cards and asked to talk to me.

We had been in the hallway for a few minutes when the one who was doing the talking said, "Mr. Simone, we would like to show you something of importance to you, but isn't there someplace we can sit down and talk privately?"

I told them both, "Can't you see I am trying a murder case? Can't you see me at the end of the trial? It should be over in no longer than two or three days."

The agents both said that what they wanted to speak to me about was urgent, "It couldn't wait." We decided to go back into the courtroom that was now empty. We sat at the defense table as one of the agents opened his briefcase and retrieved a one-inch-thick stack of papers.

He handed me a copy to read. There it was, an indictment naming Robert F. Simone as the defendant. I read the document quickly but carefully. It alleged that I had committed perjury eight times when I testified before Judge Ackerman in the Leonetti disqualification hearing.

I noted with interest that no other crimes were charged, so I felt that whatever Peter Bennett, the Assistant United States Attorney, alluded to when I was on the witness stand was not altogether true and correct. He did indicate that I was criminally involved with Nicodemo Scarfo, and Judge Ackerman made a similar comment when he disqualified me from representing Philip Leonetti.

The agent then said, "We are here to tell you that you will be indicted by a grand jury tomorrow, and we thought after you saw these papers you might want to make a deal with us. We are prepared to take you into protective custody now."

"Are you fucking crazy? You don't have a case against me, and I am in the middle of a murder trial that has been in the papers every day. Besides, I would never go with you guys. Right now I'm concerned about my client on trial. I'll deal with my own problem later. Now, leave me the fuck alone."

They left after giving me the name of an Assistant United States Attorney from Newark. I couldn't believe this was happening in the middle of a murder trial. They had waited over a year, and now they couldn't wait another three or four days?

I hurried back to my office. I still had about an hour before court was to reconvene. First, I called Gus Newman in New York. He was genuinely concerned, but because he represented Philip Leonetti in the Atlantic City corruption case, he felt he would not be able to help me as an attorney. There was a conflict of interest.

Next, I called an old friend, Steve LaCheen, one of the best lawyers in Philadelphia and one who took a personal interest in everything he did for a client. I told him I needed to get the indictment held up or at least sealed so that my client and the other four defendants in the murder trial would not be prejudiced by the bad publicity that was bound to follow the arraignment on my indictment. Steve said he would do what he could, and I hurried back to the courtroom.

I asked to see the trial judge in chambers with the prosecutor and the other defense lawyers. I told them what was happening and of my efforts to hold everything up until our case was over.

A couple of hours later, I learned from LaCheen that the government was going to proceed as planned, and they didn't give a fuck about the rights of my client or any of the other defendants on trial.

Later that day, the judge called the federal prosecutor, and he was given the same answer. We had just reached the stage of closing arguments by counsel. What a headache for me, the other lawyers, the judge, but most of all, the five defendants who were involved in a life and death struggle.

Sure enough, an indictment was filed the next day, charging me with the eight counts of perjury. I was still presumed innocent of the charges, but you can imagine what a juror learning of these allegations would think. Especially so as I made my summation, attempting to persuade them that my client should be found innocent. Me, an indicted perjurer.

It took another full day before the newspapers and television stations blasted my name and photograph and the fact that I had been indicted for lying to a federal judge. The media could not resist adding, "The government further alleges that Simone is, in addition, criminally involved with Nicodemo Scarfo and his La Cosa Nostra family."

The state court judge was upset, but he refused to grant a mistrial. Instead, he chose to interview all of the jurors individually to ask them if they "heard or read anything about the case or any of the parties or attorneys involved." They all admitted reading about it, but when asked if they still thought they could judge the case fairly despite what they had heard about me, they all said, "Yes."

The case went to the jury, and after many days of deliberations, the jurors reported that they were "hopelessly deadlocked." The trial judge had no alternative; he granted a mistrial. I still wonder if any criminal lawyer has hung as many juries as I have. About a year later, without all of the negative publicity, the client was found not guilty of murder.

I was detoured away from my law practice once more, and my ability to earn a living was to suffer yet another blow. This time I was facing five years' imprisonment on each of the eight counts—a total of 40 years in prison. There wasn't much I would be able to do other than prepare my own case for trial.

Nicky Scarfo came to my rescue. He gave me a substantial sum of money, some of it chipped in by his friends and associates. This was to make sure I would have no problem paying my office expenses and taking care of personal and family needs as well. Nicky proved himself to be a loyal friend.

Steve LaCheen agreed to work with me as co-counsel. We both read the discovery material. It consisted mostly of a copy of the transcript of my testimony before Judge Ackerman in Newark and scores of cassettes of tape-recorded conversations and matching typewritten transcripts for most, but not all, of the tapes. The prosecution planned to present evidence that eight of my answers under oath were inconsistent with what I said in conversations with David Kurzband, who had been working as an undercover informant for the FBI for the past five years. Kurzband was secretly recording his conversations with me all that time, even when I was on trial in my tax case. Not very sporting behavior by the government agents.

I first met David Kurzband in 1980 at Resorts International Hotel and Casino in Atlantic City. Someone introduced me to him at one of the many lounges in Resorts. We had a drink and talked generally about gambling, junkets, and the great success casinos were enjoying on the East Coast.

Kurzband was—according to him—a "big man" at Resorts. He was running junkets for high-rolling gamblers from all over the world. He claimed to be earning big bucks from Resorts for bringing many rich customers into the casino and hotel.

He was a big man in another way, too. He must have weighed about 350 pounds, and he was only about five feet four or five inches tall. You can imagine what he looked like. However, he did seem to know an awful lot about casino gambling. And many, many times he would tell me, "Bobby, you should just come down here with your wife and have a nice dinner and see a show. Forget about the tables. If you need a comp, I'll get it for you." Considering my gambling habit at the time, it was like a fix to an addict. And he was certainly friendly enough. He fooled the hell out of me. Little did I know that he had a high-powered recording device in his briefcase.

LaCheen and I studied all the tapes and transcripts, and both of us concluded that I hadn't involved myself in any criminal conduct in my many conversations with Kurzband.

The gist of most of the conversations was that he was looking to get his wealthy gambling customers into other casinos. He wanted a "connection" with some hotel-casino executives so that he would be able to get his players comped: free rooms, meals, and booze. He also was looking for a substantial fee or commission by way of a certain amount of money for each player or some percentage of what they would lose.

He asked me if I could help, and he promised to pay me a fee. I consented at the beginning because I thought such an arrangement would keep me near the action in the casinos and at the same time stop me from blowing my own money gambling at the tables.

Dave acted like he was impressed with the people I knew and represented. He said he felt I could use my friends, clients, and connections to get him a meeting with top casino personnel to sell them his plan.

Kurzband often showed up at the Warwick Hotel where he knew I went for cocktails after court. The Brasserie was a popular spot for most of my friends as well. We met and drank there almost every day.

There were several occasions when I did make an appointment for him to come see me in my office where we discussed the progress of the venture. This went on for several years. It stopped abruptly when Dave suggested that he would be willing to pay bribes and kickbacks to the casino executives.

I read him the riot act! I made it clear that I would not become involved in anything illegal. I also clarified that all of my clients who had helped arrange introductions and appointments would also take a step back if there was any indication that something illegal would occur.

At one point, Kurzband introduced me to his associate, Ron Marino. He told me that Ron would be handling a good part of the business since he was familiar with many of the customers. Later, after the indictment was filed, I learned that Ron Marino was really Ronald Morretti, special agent of the Federal Bureau of Investigation.

Both Kurzband and "Marino" often suggested that they believed I was "fronting for the mob" and that any money I was to earn I would split with Nick Scarfo, Phil Leonetti, and Salvatore Merlino. When this topic came up, always initiated by them, I was quick to say, "Look, these guys are only doing me a favor. They are not looking for or expecting any money out of this." Coincidentally, I never was paid even one cent.

I had to utilize all my time and effort preparing this case for trial. My practice still was on the decline as a result of the IRS case, which had taken so much of my time only a year or so before. I felt that if I didn't concentrate all my efforts on this case, I would take the fall. Even before the outcome of the case, the government found itself in a no-lose situation. I was unable to take on any new cases. They were rid of me for the time being and they were busy preparing an all-out war against Nicodemo Scarfo—a war they felt they could win a hell of a lot more easily with me on the sidelines.

I thought to myself, *Philip Leonetti has got to appreciate the situation that I'm now in, because I tried so hard to win the motion to disqualify in his case.*

CHAPTER TWENTY-THREE

Hallelujah

United States District Court Judge Joseph Rodriguez, a recent appointee who sat in Camden, New Jersey, was assigned to try my perjury case. Camden is a small city known more for its Campbell Soup Company than as a place one should seek justice.

Steve LaCheen filed approximately 20 pretrial motions, and one by one they were denied by Judge Rodriguez, which led us to believe that we would be in for a tough time at trial.

On the eve of the trial, Stuart Peim, the assigned Assistant United States Attorney, filed a motion with the trial judge requesting a court order to limit me from having both Steve LaCheen and myself as counsel at trial. He alleged in his motion that when I went to trial in the income tax case, I had Bob Madden as co-counsel. Peim argued that the combination of another lawyer and myself created an unfair advantage for me. As if anyone could ever gain an unfair advantage on the government in a federal criminal trial.

Judge Rodriguez said he would reserve his decision on the government's motion concerning counsel for the defendant until after the jury was chosen and sworn.

Ed Harrell drove Rita, Scott, and me to the courthouse every day. Kimberly, my daughter, was still living in Miami with Arlene at the time, accounting for her absence. Scott wore a suit and tie every day, and I could tell he was nervous about the outcome of the case from day one.

Rita knew just how to dress—neat, low key, but in good taste. Actually, that was the way she ordinarily dressed. She seemed cool and confident, but I knew she was worried. She wouldn't let on, I am sure, for my benefit.

We would find out soon enough that Joseph Rodriguez was in fact a fair and impartial judge.

Ed Harrell, my trusted friend and investigator, had spent many hours both alone and with me studying the facts of the case and reviewing all of the tape-recorded conversations. He was ready to help in any way, even to the point of testifying—truthfully, of course. He would get a chance to do just that.

B.J., my loyal secretary, had done more than her share of pitching-in on this joint effort. We all knew that this was going to be a very rough case—one of the most difficult trials I had ever faced on behalf of a client or myself. I think it was Ed Harrell who said, "Let's face it . . . make no mistake about it. These people are out to ruin you professionally and personally."

We were greeted at the courthouse entrance by what seemed like the usual barrage of reporters and photographers. The headlines from the day before the start of the trial read "Mob Lawyer Starts Perjury Trial" and "Scarfo's Lawyer, Simone, on Trial Again."

Due to the mass media coverage, Judge Rodriguez agreed to have each prospective juror interviewed and questioned separately—one by one—in his chambers. The jury selection process took several days as most of the jurors had heard or read something about Nicodemo Scarfo, Robert Simone, or both. Individual questioning gave LaCheen and me the opportunity to weed out those jurors who we thought might be prejudicial. The truth of the matter is that you never know who the right jurors might be.

As soon as the final alternate juror was selected, Judge Rodriguez ruled that only one of us, Steve or myself, could act as counsel while the jury was in the box. I had thought about it before coming to court, should the decision be forced upon me. I told the judge that I would act as my own attorney. *If it ain't broke, don't fix it*, I thought to myself, remembering my last big win in the tax case.

The judge seemed surprised but said nothing except that Steve LaCheen would be permitted to assist me, and he would be allowed to sit at counsel table throughout the trial. The judge then stated that in the event of a side-bar conference, LaCheen would be permitted to participate and argue any points of law.

This minor concession was, in my mind, a big thing, because no one knew the law better than Steve. He had already established a good record for appeal, should I lose the case, by filing all the right pretrial motions. It was comforting for me to know he would be at my side throughout the trial.

It was time for Stuart Peim to make his opening statement. He stood before the jury for approximately two hours, letting them know how he felt about his case and me. He spent most of the time telling the jurors how the "Scarfo crime family" came to power and how it made a living through criminal and violent means. He was trying to poison the minds of the jurors against me by shifting attention to Nicodemo Scarfo and his undesirable reputation.

He told the jury he would prove that I was part and parcel of the organized crime scene in the area. He claimed he would prove that I was "more than just a lawyer for Nicky Scarfo." Near the end of his presentation, he said the evidence would prove that I lied under oath to Judge Harold Ackerman no less than eight times. It was obvious to me that Peim would do or say anything to convict me of these charges.

I sat there listening to his every word, thinking how I was going to overcome his strong, persuasive opening, bearing in mind my feeling on the importance of opening addresses. I rose from my chair, walked to the front of the jury box, and said to the jurors, "After hearing Mr. Peim's opening, I feel compelled to say to you that I am not now, nor have I ever been, a member of the Communist Party." I hesitated, then said, "Now, let's get to the evidence in this case."

I mentioned the many tape recordings the jurors would hear, and I apologized in advance for the many curse words uttered by the participants, including me. I told them the language used was the type you hear in a poolroom or a bar where usually only men were speaking. I added, "It was language that was not intended for you people." After all, I said, "I didn't know that I was on tape."

I tried to clarify for the jurors that I was not charged "with being a member of organized crime, or, if you will, La Cosa Nostra or the Mafia, as Mr. Peim would have you believe."

As I started to outline what I believed the evidence would show, Stuart Peim constantly and continuously stood and voiced loud objections and arguments in front of the jury. He was as tenacious as a bulldog. But I was not an easy prey for him. I answered him right back every time he objected. The judge voiced his concern early on about the "turbulence" that was evident between Peim and myself.

I told the jurors just how busy I was defending many people in court during the time I had my conversations with David Kurzband and the agent, Morretti. The inference was that I might have legitimately forgotten some of my earlier conversations when I was testifying before Judge Ackerman. This countered the allegations that I willfully lied on the witness stand.

I touched on the accusations that I acted as a messenger for the so-called mob by carrying information to and from Scarfo while he was in jail in Texas.

Peim continued to object, arguing that I was testifying before the jury. He said he was concerned about my self-representation. He saw the dangers to his case. But there really wasn't anything he could do about it except object. I could tell the jury was not happy with his constant loud interruptions. I would have to wait and see if I was right.

Near the end of my opening, I told the jury that the government's key witness, David Kurzband, testified under oath at the grand jury. I promised that I would prove that when he was on the witness stand, he was provided with written transcripts and other material so that he could refresh his memory before answering questions. I then said, "I was not treated the same when I testified before Judge Ackerman."

I completed my opening by saying, "You'll see from the evidence that David Kurzband can lie and lie and cooperate with the government and still lie and steal and cheat and walk out of the courtroom scot-free. Why should he be treated any differently than me?"

The battle lines were drawn. This time I was going to put both Kurzband and his protector, Peim, on trial.

Dave Kurzband testified for approximately five days on direct examination. In front of him were two loose-leaf books that contained transcripts of all the taped conversations that he had with me over a period in excess of four years. Actually, he did not have all of them—only the ones that the prosecutor would introduce into evidence.

Stuart Peim would play the tapes, and Kurzband and the jurors, who were also supplied with copies of the typewritten transcripts, would read them as the tapes were being played. But it didn't stop there. Peim would always ask Kurzband what he meant when he said certain things and then how he interpreted my answers and statements to him.

Between the two of them, they were doing a pretty good job of burying me. The tapes were painting a dark picture of me as Nicodemo Scarfo's confederate rather than his counsel. Steve LaCheen and I were not happy about the way things looked for me. Peim was obviously pleased during his direct examination of this oversized witness. Kurzband was getting more comfortable after each session on the witness stand. He was enjoying his role more and more.

I took Kurzband on cross-examination and immediately attacked his credibility. I was able to show that he was arrested in the Midwest and charged with serious crimes involving fraud and dishonesty. He admitted making a deal with the government to avoid prison. Coming to Philadelphia and Atlantic City was part of the deal. He also agreed to wear a wire so that he could record all his conversations while he acted as an informer.

I grilled him for two days. Sometimes I felt I was making headway and other times I felt like I was losing ground. Then I struck pay dirt.

Kurzband had testified on direct examination that he had a conversation in my office one day in which I made some very incriminating statements. He told the jurors that I bragged about my relationship with Nick Scarfo, Philip Leonetti, and Salvatore Merlino and that I also told him of their ranks in La Cosa Nostra.

No tape was introduced into evidence to corroborate Kurzband's testimony that the conversation occurred. Kurzband testified that he wasn't carrying the recording device on that particular day. His explanation for not wearing the wire this one day was that he did not have sufficient time to obtain the equipment from the FBI agent who was monitoring him. He stated that he received a call from me and that I asked him to come and see me about an urgent matter. He claimed that I said he had to be in my office "within two hours." He further testified that he attempted to reach his control agent but was unable to do so. He decided to visit me without the wire anyway rather than not come and create suspicion. Pure bullshit.

In an attempt to embellish his answer on this point, Kurzband said that for the first and only time, Ed Harrell searched him and his briefcase to make sure he wasn't wired on that particular day.

Lucky for me, I did my homework before the trial started. I located one of the tapes the government did not play for the jury. It was a short telephone call I had made to Kurzband, and the conversation went like this:

S. Hi, Dave. How are you?
K. Hello, Bob. How ya doin'?
S. I need to talk to you. Can you come to the office and see me?
K. How fast do you need me? Is it important?
S. No, not really. Why, are you busy?
K. Well, today right now I'm tied up. I can be there late this afternoon.
S. No, Dave. It will wait. How about tomorrow about 2:00 p.m. It's not that important.
K. Okay. You're on. I'll see you at 2:00 p.m. tomorrow. Goodbye.

I played the tape after giving Kurzband and the jurors copies of a written transcript I had prepared. Then I asked Kurzband if he remembered this conversation that was recorded on the day immediately preceding the day that he claimed to have been in my office—the one time he did not wear a wire.

He answered, "No." He did, however, admit that the voices on the tape were his and mine, and then he admitted that the conversation took place the day before he came to see me. He knew I received my copy of this tape along with all the others from his buddy, Peim, before the trial.

Kurzband was smart enough to know I had just caught him in a bald-faced lie. The jurors now knew that his excuse for not wearing the wire was false. Kurzband did not have only two hours to track the agent down, he had a whole day. The truth was that he always wore a wire when he spoke to me.

As this unfolded, I noticed Kurzband looking to the back of the courtroom where two of his friends were sitting, both FBI agents. I was standing as I questioned him, as I usually do on cross-examination. I moved my body between him and the agents to block his view.

He leaned to the left and then to the right, trying desperately to make eye contact with the agents. He was looking for help, a sign, anything. I asked, "Why are you looking at them?"

He answered, "What do you want me to do, look out the window?"

He was in over his head. I replied, "No, jump out the window."

Most of the jurors laughed. Dave squirmed. From that moment on he was my witness. I kept him on the stand for another day and a half and was able to get most of my defense into the record and before the jury through him.

When I asked him a question about what he said on a tape, Kurzband kept saying, "I can't remember—show me the transcript." I did just that. This happened over and over again. I would later argue to the jury that Kurzband was allowed to refresh his memory when he couldn't remember, but "they"— I pointed to the prosecutor's table—wouldn't let me see the tapes and the transcripts when I had to testify before Judge Ackerman.

I was able to show in no uncertain terms that David Kurzband was a con man, a thief, and a liar. I got him to admit he lied to the FBI even after he started to cooperate. During one of the breaks, I went to the men's room and saw one of the United States Marshals who was guarding the protected witness. He smiled at me and said, "How you doing?"

I answered, "I don't know."

He smiled again and said, "Don't worry, you are doing just fine."

Before I let Kurzband go, I pointed out those portions of the transcripts where he talked about paying bribes to the casino executives, getting hookers for the customers, and overcharging the casinos. In each instance, the tape revealed and the transcript read that I said, "No! No! No! There will be no wrongdoing here. Everything must be legal and legitimate."

The prosecutor put Ron Morretti, the undercover FBI agent, on the witness stand. In one taped conversation, another one not played by Peim on direct, I was able to show that Morretti offered to give me $50,000 for my role in helping him and Kurzband get their junkets into casinos. Since I had never succeeded in doing so, I refused the money. On tape, Morretti said to me, "Well, maybe you should take it and give it to your clients," meaning Scarfo, Merlino, and Leonetti.

I was firm in saying, "No, and besides, these guys weren't trying to help me for money, they were just doing me a favor. Once more, let me say, I didn't do anything to deserve this money."

Trying to soften the blow, Morretti looked at me and told the jurors, "Well, you knew you were being taped."

I replied instantly, "In other words, if I said something on the tape you thought you could use . . . I didn't know I was being taped. If I said something that would help me . . . then I knew I was on tape. I was damned if I did and damned if I didn't."

Morretti just shrugged his shoulders without answering. Peim asked him several questions on redirect, and soon after the government rested its case.

Steve LaCheen argued a motion for Judgment of Acquittal for over an hour. Peim responded, and the judge, without hesitation, denied our motion. Eight counts would go to the jury, but first we had our defense witnesses.

My old and dear friend, Stanley Branche, testified that I arranged a meeting for him with Mayor Matthews so he could get approval for a grand prix race in Atlantic City. He explained to the jurors that the meeting was arranged through an Atlantic City businessman, Kenny Shapiro, not Philip Leonetti as the government alleged. One of the perjury counts accused me of lying about Philip Leonetti being the one who arranged the meeting.

B.J., my secretary, took the witness stand and testified to the approximate number of cases I was handling. She had photographs showing stacks of files that were pending at the time. This was Steve LaCheen's idea. She went on to testify from the Nicky Scarfo/La Tuna file, which showed all the legal reasons I had to visit him in Texas. I was trying to prove that I was not his messenger boy.

I put on several character witnesses who, I thought, made a good impression with the jurors. Finally, I called Ed Harrell to the witness stand.

Ed had been with me since 1980, the year of the Falcone murder trial. From the time he started working with me to the very end, I was never again late for a court hearing. Aside from being loyal, trustworthy, and conscientious, he was extremely able and intelligent. Peim would underestimate his intelligence.

Ed, who is African American, looked at the two blacks on the jury as he sat in the witness box. I got right to the point and asked him if Kurzband was telling the truth when he testified that Ed searched him for bugging devices when the fat man came to my office.

"No, not on that day or any other day," Ed answered.

Peim stood up to cross-examine and tried to show the jury that Ed was biased and slanting his testimony in my favor. Ed insisted he was telling the truth, stating, "I was on the Philadelphia police force for 20 years, working my way up to captain before I resigned, and I know that you are supposed to tell the truth on the witness stand."

Peim countered, "Mr. Harrell, how long have you been working for Mr. Simone?"

Ed replied, "I work with Mr. Simone, not for him. And I work for other lawyers as well."

Peim, not believing Ed, then said sarcastically, "Are you trying to say that you were allowed to work for other lawyers while you are employed by Mr. Simone?"

Ed answered, "Mr. Peim, in case you haven't heard, Abraham Lincoln freed the slaves years ago."

The two black jurors beamed, and the rest of the jurors laughed out loud as Stuart Peim slid into his seat, embarrassed.

Every night after court I spoke to Philip Leonetti or Nicky Scarfo. They both voiced their concerns about the outcome. Nicky was relaxing at his Fort Lauderdale home, but he said he was having trouble sleeping, worrying about me. I let them both know that I wasn't sure about the outcome, but I had a chance of winning, depending on how the closing arguments were received by the jurors.

I knew in my heart and mind that Stuart Peim, who would speak to the jurors first, would attack Nicodemo Scarfo and then me in his closing argument. I also knew that he would spend more time trying to convince the jury that I had crossed the line as an attorney than he would in addressing the eight specific perjury counts. Before he started, I made a conscious decision to let him say what he wanted without objecting.

I knew from Peim's outrageous behavior when he continued to object to my opening address and by his conduct during the trial that he would interrupt me many times during my closing argument. Some lawyers would say that I should object when a prosecutor goes too far to protect the record. I say let him make an ass out of himself in front of the jury and then they may think, "Simone didn't object or interrupt him, why should he do this? It's not fair."

Peim did as I thought he would. It became clear to me, and I am sure to the jury, that Stuart Peim hated me. He ranted and raved for about two hours. He claimed that I not only represented my organized crime clients, "I was a part of the whole thing."

He mentioned Philip Leonetti and the mayor of Atlantic City, pointing out to the jurors that I too met with the mayor in an attempt to get my friend, Stanley Branche, the approval for his road race. A race which, by the way, never materialized.

Peim accused me of using the mob to get Kurzband and Marino-Morretti into the casinos. He said I was greedy. He forgot that I never took a penny from either of them. Peim insisted I was doing this for "Scarfo and his boys" as well as myself.

Stuart Peim, sweating profusely, touched his villainous-looking moustache and then asked the jurors to convict me of all eight counts in the indictment. Throughout his sometimes devastating closing address, I managed to control my emotions and myself. I did not object once.

Now for the second time in my career, I stood in front of a jury to argue for my own freedom. The first time it was comparatively easy. I had a lot more ground to cover this time.

The courtroom was packed with my family and many of my friends, at least a dozen defense lawyers included. All of them were worried about the dangerous precedent this case might set. On the other hand, there were also many FBI agents and Assistant United States Attorneys hanging in there, waiting for me to slip and fall. They all hoped that I would screw up the close and lose the case.

Early on, I reminded the jurors of the agent who testified that a tape recorder was used so there would be no question about what I had said. I followed with, "And then Mr. Peim said to you in his close, 'There is no dispute as to what Mr. Simone said on the tape.' Well, if Mr. Peim was being perfectly candid with you, why then did the words that I said have to be interpreted? Why did you have to hear the opinions of not only Mr. Peim in his questions, but Mr. Kurzband in his answers?"

Only a couple of minutes into my opening, I was interrupted by my aggressive adversary for the first time. He stood, objected, and then argued in front of the jury at least half a dozen times. That was within the first five minutes of my closing address.

After the fifth or sixth time, I turned around and walked over to the defense table, sat down, and looked at Peim, as he continued to rant and rave, and then I glanced at the jurors. When he finished giving a lecture on just what he thought a closing argument should be, I stood up and said, "I haven't had an opportunity to make one yet."

The judge then admonished Peim, "If you have an objection, just simply state you have an objection."

Peim didn't accept the judge's warning. He continued to object and argue in front of the jury. He accused me of testifying. He was probably right. To one of his objections, I answered, "Why is he doing this? I didn't interrupt him one time."

I covered a great deal of the evidence, keying on the cross-examination. In discussing David Kurzband, I suggested that "the government made a deal with the devil." Then I pointed out several lies he told the agents and the jury.

I was near the end of my argument when I dug down deep and said:

> I may not agree with what my clients say or do. And I'm not just talking about the clients you heard about in this courtroom; I have represented many more people. I don't necessarily agree with what they do or what they say or what they think. But I shall defend them and their rights to say and think it to my last breath. And that's terribly upsetting to the prosecutor. And that is why I've been picked on.
>
> In the United States during the '40s, the Japanese Americans were all taken off the street and put in concentration camps without regard to whether they were guilty or not guilty. In the '50s, the writers and movie directors were blacklisted, and the same thing happened in the '60s when civil rights advocates were put away. In the '70s, Vietnam protestors were also put away. Now in the '80s, the lawyers who represent unpopular clients have to worry. I'm not the first, nor am I the last that's going to be tried. If you permit the type of prosecution with this type of evidence, then in the '90s it may be you, your families. People you care about. It's got to stop. Only you can stop it. I can't stop it. I can fight every day in a courtroom, but I can't stop it. I'm just finishing now. Mr. Peim, he's going to have an opportunity to speak to you again, and I will not.
>
> Now let me say this. That I'm going to ask you to speak for me because I cannot speak any longer. After Mr. Peim, I can't answer. And in closing, let me just tell you something that some very wise person said, as I ask you to speak for me: "In Germany they came first for the communists and I didn't speak up because I wasn't a communist. Then they came for the Jews, and I didn't speak up because I wasn't a Jew. Then they came for the trade unionists, and I didn't speak up because I wasn't a trade unionist. Then they came for the Catholics, and I didn't speak up because I was a Protestant. Then they came for me, and there was nobody to speak for me."
>
> Ladies and gentlemen, you can speak up for me and you can stop it, what's going on that you don't like. Thank you very much.

The next morning, after the judge instructed the jury on the law, Rita and I walked the halls of the second floor of the United States Courthouse for what seemed like days. My two brothers, Ron and Joe, sat nearby, first inside and then outside the courtroom, talking to my son, Scott. We were all waiting for the verdict and were disappointed that it was taking so long.

Late in the day, the jurors asked for two exhibits. They were the two books containing the transcripts of the taped conversations I had with David Kurzband and Ron Morretti. Steve LaCheen and I both took it as a bad sign.

Shortly after the jurors received the transcripts, at about 6:00 p.m., Judge Rodriguez excused the jurors and all the participants until the next morning. Rita, Scott, and I left the courthouse, trying to avoid the raindrops as we rushed to Ed's car as it pulled up to the curb. There would be no celebrating this night.

Rita, Scott, and I went to dinner, but we were all so concerned and full of anxiety that I cannot remember where it was that we ate. There would also be no sleeping that night.

The first person I saw waiting at the courthouse the next morning was Steve LaCheen. He told me he saw Stuart Peim carrying some legal papers in his hand. Steve said, "Bob, I believe he has a motion to revoke bail." Yes, Peim was sure of himself, and he was going to object to my staying out on bail during an appeal.

For several more hours, I talked with Rita, and I had to tell her I thought I might be convicted. We discussed how we would both handle the loss and my going to jail. She was strong and supportive, telling me not to worry about her no matter what happened. Then she said, "Everything will work out for the best."

It was about then that everybody was summoned back into the courtroom. The crowd was larger than it was at any time during the trial. Relatives, friends, co-workers, lawyers, and I couldn't help but observe Judge John Geary slip into the courtroom. He sat only a couple of rows behind Rita, Scott, and my brothers, directly behind the defense table.

There were at least ten FBI agents and a dozen Assistant United States Attorneys sitting on the left-hand side of the courtroom behind the prosecutor. Every local television station was represented by a reporter, and at least seven or eight newspapers were covering the verdict.

In my opinion, a short deliberation period is usually better for the defendant, so I was not optimistic. The jurors had been out a rather long time — 16 hours.

The jury foreman rose and answered the court clerk's question. He looked at me and then toward the first row behind me where Rita, Scott, Joe, and Ron were sitting on the edge of their seats. I heard the first not guilty, but the other seven were drowned out by the loud and boisterous ovation coming from the spectators. I shall never forget the sound of the word "Hallelujah," repeated twice.

I turned my head and saw that it came from where Judge Geary sat just before he got up and left the courtroom by the middle door. Rita and I embraced and kissed, and Scott jumped in to give me a hug.

Stuart Peim and his entourage of FBI agents and United States Attorneys disappeared before the last of my supporters congratulated me. The media people gathered around me in the hallway, asking for a statement and a reaction to the verdict. It would be easier to speak to them all at one time, so I made a statement right there in the hallway outside the courtroom.

First I thanked the jurors for their verdict exonerating me. Then I said, "I feel I have been singled out not because of any wrongdoing, but because I continue to represent people who need lawyers perhaps more than anyone else. I will never stop fighting overzealous prosecutors, and I will continue to defend the constitutional rights of citizens. I also would like to voice my appreciation to all the members of the press who have reported this trial fairly and accurately throughout."

A question rang out from a young lady standing behind several other reporters. "Mr. Simone, do you think after winning two cases against the government . . . they will leave you alone?"

"Good question," I said. "I believe they [meaning the U.S. Attorney's Office and the FBI] are up there," I pointed to the floors above, "plotting and planning right now how they can indict me again, and soon."

A couple of television reporters gave me their cards and asked if they could interview me alone later. I consented, and Rita, Scott, and I left to join a smiling Ed Harrell, waiting in his car directly in front of the courthouse entrance.

That night, a relieved Rita and I made plans to jump on an airplane in a couple of days. We would stop in Miami to see her parents and my mom and Kim, and then off to St. Barts for ten days or so. We both needed to catch our breath.

The day after the verdict, before leaving for the Caribbean, I was in my office when the phone rang while B.J. was out to lunch. I answered it myself, and the voice on the other end said, "Simone, is that you, Simone?" No mister—no first name, just "Simone."

I answered, "Yes," and asked, "Who's calling?"

As soon as the person identified himself, I recognized him as one of the male jurors. He said in a loud voice, "Well, how are you doing today?"

"Perfect," I said, "thanks to you."

"I just wanted to call to say it was tough in that jury room. There were some people who wanted to hang you."

I thanked him again, but before he hung up, he said, "I told all the jurors they were never going to let you alone, and I'm telling you . . . so be careful and good luck."

Thank God for that one, I thought to myself.

The next day before Rita and I split for Miami, I received a note from another juror, a woman, which read:

April 25, 1986

Dear Mr. Simone:

I know perhaps this is not proper. However, I just feel the need to tell you that there is not a doubt in my heart or mind that we made the right decision.

These past six weeks have been an experience I shall never forget. I can only begin to imagine what you and your family have been through.

I know your future will not be an easy one, but I feel certain that you are a man of strong convictions.

Please know my thoughts and prayers are with you and your family in the days that lie ahead.

I have omitted the names of both jurors to protect their privacy and to prevent the rotten bastards from going after them.

Earlier on the night of the verdict, the phone at the apartment did not stop ringing until well past midnight. Nicky Scarfo called from Fort Lauderdale. I could hear the happiness in his voice as he cursed the Feds and praised me. "Please stop here before you go to St. Barts so I can take you and Rita out to dinner."

Anthony DeGregorio, who everybody called "Spike," got on the phone from Nicky's end. He said, "Yo, Bobby. Guess how we found out? Al Pajamas called and said, 'Bobby pitched a shut-out.'"

Spike was someone that Nicky trusted to look after the house in Florida and cook for him when he didn't want to go out for dinner. He was also sort of a court jester, always keeping Nicky and whoever else was around laughing.

Philip Leonetti drove in from Atlantic City the next day to make sure he congratulated me and to tell me how relieved he was. He knew I was being persecuted for defending him as well as his uncle.

The television reports on the evening of the verdict and the newspapers the next day seemed to agree with my statement about the reason I was prosecuted, and the *Philadelphia Daily News* ran a headline, covering the entire page, that read, "Jury Clears Simone: Innocent of All Eight Counts." When Rita and I arrived at Nicky's to meet him for dinner, we found a large cake on his kitchen table. The top of it, decorated like a birthday or wedding cake, had in pink, sugared letters, "Jury Clears Simone."

Before Spike drove us to Yesterdays, an excellent restaurant in Fort Lauderdale, he took several pictures of Nicky, Rita, the cake, and me. It was a happy occasion, and we made the most of it, champagne and all.

A day or two later, Rita and I were drinking a dry French white wine, eating fresh fish, suntanning, and swimming by ourselves in the Caribbean at our favorite spot in the world—St. Barts. The last thing I wanted to do was to return to Philadelphia and my office where I had hardly any clients, and those that I still had were sure to keep me bobbing and weaving.

CHAPTER TWENTY-FOUR

Tell Me, Are You Going to Kill Me?

I was back from St. Barts—tan, healthy, and broke. I sat in my office, waiting for the phone to ring or someone to walk in with an indictment in one hand and a check or cash in the other. No such luck. Instead, in walks James Maher, special agent of the Federal Bureau of Investigation. He was with one of the organized crime squads.

"Hello, Bob," he said as I offered him a chair near the corner of my desk. "I'm afraid I have some bad news for you."

"Don't tell me I am going to be indicted again. What am I supposed to have done this time?"

"Well, it's really more serious than that. We have reason to believe that you are going to be killed. There is a hit out on you."

"You're kidding." The last time it was supposed to be the Martoranos. I wondered who was going to kill me this time.

"No. Our information . . . from a reliable source . . . is that Nick Scarfo and some of his people feel that you know too much, that you can't be of any use to him now with all the publicity that came out in your last trial."

"Show me the tapes of the conversation where people are plotting to kill me," I requested.

"There are none," he responded. "But you must take this seriously. Our information is solid."

"Well, I'll just have to handle it, won't I? What do you expect me to do?"

"I didn't expect you to say you would go into the Witness Protection Program. But I gotta ask you to do that," he said with no smile on his face.

I just looked at him and shrugged my shoulders. He already knew what my answer would be. He lifted his tall body off the chair, wished me luck, and left.

I told myself, *This can't be. It's just another ploy by the Feds to get someone to switch sides. To become an informer!* I didn't have any more time to think about it. That same day a new client came breezing into my office with a serious state case involving drugs. I would eventually win his case in Media, Delaware County. Soon after my office was deluged with new clients, all with cash in hand and all expecting to win in court.

A week later Nicodemo Scarfo and Philip Leonetti arrived at my new office at 1919 Walnut Street in Center City Philadelphia. I heard their voices as they walked up the circular stairway leading to the second floor. No, I did not think they were here to do me in. But I wasn't sure if I was going to tell them about Agent Maher's visit and warning.

Nicky and Philip were in an unusually good mood. Both of them looked tan and rested. Nicky had recently returned from a three-week stay at Casablanca South in Fort Lauderdale. Philip was tan and trim all year from vacations in either Atlantic City or Florida.

Nicky brought in a bag of Philly's famous and tasty soft pretzels. He sat at my desk picking the insides out with his fingers, eating only the crust. After the usual greeting, a hug and a kiss on the cheek, I started the conversation. "Nicky, last week our FBI 'friend' Maher came here to see me. He told me you guys were going to kill me." I forced myself to look at their faces as I spoke those words.

"Jesus, Bobby, they don't know how much we love you, them mother-fuckers." Philip sat there appearing embarrassed about Maher's accusation. He managed a smile.

"I told him to give me the tapes of the conversation so I could hear with my own ears. But all he would say was 'we have information from a reliable source.' I chased him out, but I thought you should know what he said to me." This was probably the most awkward conversation I ever had in my life. Here I was having a little chit-chat with two guys that were supposedly going to kill me.

Although I felt that nothing could be further from the truth, I still had to tell them—to get it off my chest and out of my head. Not an easy task. I also wondered if by some chance it was true, in which case, how were Nicky and Philip to act? Were they going to admit it? No way!

The three of us sat there talking for a few minutes, all agreeing that this was a plan by the Feds to get people to "flip." We felt the plan went something like this: "Come in and cooperate, tell us what you know and worse, make up some lies to bring Nicky Scarfo down and Philip Leonetti along with him." The future would prove us right as several turncoats would use this type of warning as an excuse for becoming informants.

The distasteful subject was dropped. As it was late in the day, the three of us went to Bookbinder's. We stopped and picked up Jake Kossman, who joined us for a few drinks, some fresh fish, and a cold bottle of Meursault. I couldn't help but order and drink two of the largest, coldest, driest martinis I'd had in a long time.

A month or so later, I received a telephone call from Philip. He asked me to meet him a few blocks from my apartment at the busy corner of Fifth and South Streets. I couldn't imagine the purpose of the meeting. When I reached South Street, I saw Philip standing on the corner on Fifth Street, talking to Joe Grande. Joe was a younger man in his late twenties. He lived in South Philadelphia and was often seen in the company of Philip, Nicky, and Joe's brother, Salvatore "Wayne" Grande.

Philip greeted me with a smile, and I shook hands with him and Joe. "Let's take a walk. We need to talk to you," Phil said as he steered us east on South Street.

We crossed Fourth Street, filled with cars and pedestrians. The pizza shop on the northeast corner was full, and customers were lined up on the sidewalk waiting to order the brick-oven pizzas. "Joe has a problem," Phil said just before pointing to a narrow, deserted alleyway between Third and Fourth Streets. "Let's go up here," he continued, "where we can have some privacy."

Without thinking, I walked slowly between Philip and the husky, soft-spoken Joe Grande. In a few seconds, my thoughts went back to my conversation with Agent Maher. Suddenly, a cold chill filled my body and ran down both my legs. I slowed down, but I couldn't stop. *Was this it?* I thought to myself. *Should I try to run away? Were these guys going to kill me? Would they shoot me in this deserted alley? No way. Philip would never let anything happen to me.* Besides, it was too late. I could not get away, and if my fears were unwarranted, I would make a total ass of myself.

Then I thought, *If I run and these guys weren't looking to hurt me, I would make them think I was worried about them and that I didn't trust them. Then I would be ripe for killing later.*

We reached the end of the alley, and Philip said, "Tell him your problem, Joe."

"Well, you see, Bobby, me and my wife were in a car accident. She got hurt and the car is wrecked."

I couldn't follow his conversation. I was so relieved that he wanted to talk to me about a legal problem that whatever he said was music to my ears.

The FBI had planted a suspicious seed in my mind. Fortunately, I went with my gut reaction, which was right. Thinking about it now, I must say that no matter what their motives are, these law enforcement people can sometimes cause more harm than good. Can you imagine how many people may have been whacked because of fear caused by a warning based on a "reliable informant"?

Slowly but surely my practice started to grow again. I was getting some new federal cases as well as state cases in Philly and Delaware County courts. I also tried a couple of cases in Orlando and, of course, I went to Disney World.

A few months after Agent Maher warned me with his "reliable information" about my impending assassination, I walked up the steps leading to the U.S. Courthouse in Camden, the site of my recent big win. When I reached the landing, I saw James Maher standing there, waiting for me.

I said to myself, "Oh shit, not again."

"Can I speak with you for a minute, Bob?"

"Who is going to kill me this time?" I said.

"Nobody. I see you're still alive, though," he replied. At least he wasn't a hypocrite, telling me how pleased he was by that fact.

"I need you to do something for me," he said.

I could hardly believe my ears. *I have been battling with the FBI for over 20 years, and they have been trying to bury me as well as my clients. This guy, this special agent, is asking me to do him a favor.*

"We have information from a 'reliable' informant [here we go again] that someone in New York has ordered a hit on your client, Nicky Scarfo." He was dead serious when he told me this.

At least it's not me this time.

"I know that Nicky won't talk to me, so I need you to warn him. We have an obligation to pass on this information to him. You'll be seeing him soon, so will you give him this message for me?"

How about this guy, I thought. *He knows when I'm to see Nicky when I'm not sure myself.*

"Didn't you tell me a few months ago Nicky was going to kill me?" I asked. "Why should I warn him that he's going to be knocked off? If your information is as reliable and truthful as you say, why should I warn someone who is supposed to kill me that he is going to be killed?"

Agent Maher just looked at me. He had no answer. If he weren't an FBI agent, I would say he was embarrassed.

"I'm only kidding," I said. "I'll tell him."

Maher left without smiling and without thanking me. The next time I saw Nicky, I gave him the message.

"Those fucking people are crazy!" is all Nicky said. I couldn't agree with him more.

▼ ▼ ▼

I walked into the same courtroom in Camden where a jury had given me a new lease on life, but this time the defendant was someone other than me.

My client and I sat at the defense table, waiting for Judge Stanley Brotman to open court.

Judge Brotman was the trial judge in Nicky's gun case a few years back. He also presided when George "The Greek" Botsaris was acquitted. I had tried several other matters before him, and he always seemed to be a fair and deliberate man.

He opened the court session and within seconds, the young federal prosecutor from North Jersey handed up some papers to the judge. I read my copy and learned they were filing another motion to disqualify counsel for the defendant. The United States Attorney's Office was alleging that I was still a target of investigation, and as such there was a potential conflict of interest.

Judge Brotman asked the prosecutor, "What is the basis of this motion?" He wanted to know if it dealt with the facts that recently surfaced in my trial before Judge Rodriguez.

The young United States Attorney, whom I had never met before, told the judge that certain "facts" were uncovered as a result of my being captured on tape by Kurzband during the past four or five years. These "facts" were still being investigated, despite the not guilty verdict of less than a month ago.

Judge Brotman stated in no uncertain terms, "Motion to disqualify Mr. Simone is denied. Let me say this to you and your superiors in the United States Attorney's Office. Mr. Simone has appeared before this court many times, and he has always conducted himself in a lawful and ethical manner. I hold him in high esteem. Lastly, I personally spoke to Judge Rodriguez, who presided at Mr. Simone's trial. He told me there was no evidence of any wrongdoing on the part of Mr. Simone. So why doesn't your office stop persecuting him? Now, let's get on with this case." I could not have defended myself any better.

The Assistant United States Attorney came up to me after court and apologized to me. "I'm really sorry for having filed that motion, but please understand it was not personal. My boss insisted. I wish you luck and success in the future." I believed him. He said it like he meant it.

I am sorry to say that the jury convicted my client and I suffered one of my few losses in the Camden-based federal court. It did, however, seem to me that my career was back on track.

CHAPTER TWENTY-FIVE

The Beginning of the End

The retrial of the Golden Nugget case started before a new jury with Judge James Giles presiding again. The publicity and notoriety from the recent perjury trial in Camden surely didn't help my chances of winning another large verdict.

I recall Jim Beasley telling me after he made his closing argument on my behalf, "Bobby, I didn't like the way the jurors looked or reacted when I spoke to them." He was right on target. The verdict was for the defendant. We decided not to appeal and the IRS would have to wait for its money.

I tried to keep current with my taxes, but I found myself spending a great deal of the money I was earning. I started to drink a little more. Many of those drinks were consumed at whichever racetrack was open at the time. I needed a release. I couldn't just pick up and leave whenever I felt the need. So it was, have a drink and make a bet. It got to be that the only times I did not need these vices were when Rita and I escaped to St. Barts.

The surveillance increased. The Organized Crime Division of the Philadelphia Police Department maintained what appeared to be an around-the-clock watch on Nick Scarfo and his many associates. Those numbers seemed to escalate with all of the killings over the previous half-dozen years or so.

Frank Narducci, Jr. was stopped and arrested by police twice within a period of a couple of weeks. His car was pulled over by a uniformed police officer accompanied by an O.C.D. cop. The first time they claimed to have found a revolver under the driver's seat. The second time they said they found a blackjack.

Around the same time, the same squad stopped Lawrence Merlino. He also had a gun in his car. I represented Frank Jr. and Lawrence in separate trials. Frank Jr. was found not guilty both times. Lawrence also walked out of the courtroom a free man.

In one of these trials I asked the arresting officers if all they had to do was stop cars being driven by Italians in South Philadelphia. Believe it or not, one of the cops answered, "Yes." Strong evidence of "selective prosecution," I'd say. The judges agreed and acquitted. The harassment by the police stopped, but the taking of hundreds of photographs by the police and the FBI continued.

Often, when I walked into a restaurant or bar, I saw the flash of a camera from a parked van. It got so frequent that I used to wave hello to the O.C.D. cops. They often waved back. It all seemed like a game at the time.

I couldn't help noticing that when Nicky came into Philadelphia, he often saw Nicholas "The Crow" Caramandi and Tommy DelGiorno. They never discussed anything of substance in my presence. There was a lot about The Crow I didn't like, but I said nothing.

Many years ago, after he was released from prison, I discovered that he was making long-distance telephone calls and charging them to my office number. I hollered at him and had Ralph Staino talk to him about it. The practice stopped.

When Caramandi saw me having dinner with Nicky, he tried to make amends by talking to me in a friendly manner. I preferred it when I didn't see him at all. Many times we simply ignored each other.

It seemed as though all of a sudden Caramandi started asking me to do things for him. "Bobby, can you talk to this judge? My friend's got a case in front of him." Or, "Bobby, can you help me get this state legislator to do something for me?"

I always brushed him off. When he continued to bug me, I complained to Nicky. "Nick," I said, "The Crow keeps asking me to do things for him . . . which I refuse to do even though sometimes he says you okayed them. This guy and his requests could create problems with the law for the both of us."

"Don't do anything for him. Christ, I wouldn't ask you to do anything that would be illegal. I'll talk to him and stop it," he answered.

Within a few days, The Crow stopped bugging me. He always came off as a tough guy, but I knew him as a con man and a pathological liar. I never trusted the guy.

In June 1986, I bumped into The Crow at a Center City bar. He made his way over to where I was sitting alone and whispered into my ear, "Yo, Bob, how are ya?"

"Fine, Nick, fine."

"I got some news. I'm on to a good deal, could be a big score," he said as he ordered drinks for both of us.

"You're friendly with Beloff—Lee Beloff, the city councilman—and his flunky, Bobby Rego, aren't ya?" he asked.

"Yeah, so what?" I answered, feeling more uncomfortable with each second.

"Well, this multimillionaire Rouse is planning to do a big number down on Delaware Avenue. He wants to build shopping centers, hotels, office buildings, restaurants, and everything. It's gonna be a $100 million job. But guess what? He can't get the okay unless Lee puts the zoning bill in, because it's in his district."

I could hardly hear what he was saying because of his whispering. He wasn't the best public speaker I ever met. I said nothing but thought to myself, *what a fucking idiot!*

"I'm gonna work something out with the 'Little Guy' where I shake Rouse down for a million," he said in a bragging manner. "What do you think, Bobby?"

"I think you're fucking crazy! And if you try to do this, you're gonna go to jail."

"I already set it up. I've got Rego scared to death of me to make sure Beloff don't introduce the bill until I get the bread from Rouse's man, who I already talked to."

"Why are you telling me this?" I asked. "I don't want anything to do with it. And I'm convinced if you don't forget about it, you'll all go to prison."

I finished my drink and scooted out of the bar. That was the first time I heard about what was later to be called the "Rouse extortion."

Within days of my conversation with The Crow, I saw Bobby Rego in City Hall where I was trying a case. He approached me in the hallway outside the courtroom. Rego had survived up until now mainly because he was a lifelong friend of Lee Beloff. He was the councilman's legislative assistant, and nothing happened in Lee's office that Rego didn't know about. He was, as a witness would later describe him, "a sleazeball."

Rego knew that I was friendly with Lee, and was certainly aware that Lee had hired my son Scott as a legislative aide. He couldn't wait to tell me about his scheme to extort a million dollars from Willard Rouse, the city's top developer at the time.

"Rouse's people were talked to by Nicky Crow, but they won't pay unless they know Lee is involved and will be doing it for the money. They want a sign from Lee. What do you think, Bobby?" It was easy to see that Rego and The Crow, with their two great minds, thought alike.

"Look, Bobby," I said to him, "you are looking for big troubles. I told Crow to forget about it, and I'm telling you the same thing."

"Crow told me you thought it was a good move and also that Little Nicky approved it."

Now I was pissed. "The fucking Crow is a liar and an idiot. I don't want to hear any more about this lame-brained plan of yours. If you don't stop with this thing, you and The Crow are going to go away and you're probably going to take Lee with you. You're probably dealing with an agent and a sting operation."

About a week later, The Crow tried to talk to me again about Rouse and the plot to extort him. Before I could get away from him, he said, "Nicky's happy, because Scarf, Inc. is going to get all the concrete work on the job. It will be at least a couple of million."

That is when I decided to drive to Atlantic City and talk to Scarfo. I drove alone to Georgia Avenue, but Nick and Philip were out of the office. Nancy, Philip's mom and Nicky's sister, told me they went to the eye doctor in Ventnor, a couple of miles away. She gave me the address, and I left immediately to find them.

Nicky and Philip seemed pleasantly surprised to see me, until Nicky's mind registered. "What's wrong, Bob?"

"Nick, I got to talk to you. There's something bothering me."

He was trying on a new pair of eyeglasses when he said, "We'll go outside in a couple of minutes. Let me just get finished here." He put the glasses to his head and looked into the mirror to see how he looked.

"I'll take these, too," he told the optician. "Put them with the other pairs I like."

Philip, Nicky, and I went out the door, and we walked only a few steps away from the storefront window. I told Nicky about what The Crow was doing with Rego, Beloff, and Rouse and the potential problems. Nick said, "I'll talk to The Crow again, and I am sure he won't bother you anymore." Then Nicky asked, "Do you need any glasses? Come on, let me get you a couple of pairs."

"Wait a minute, Nick. I'm not through," I said. "It gets worse. Did you know that The Crow is trying to shake down this big builder by using Lee Beloff's office, and he's using your name?"

Nicky and Philip looked at me, then at each other, and then Nick exclaimed, "What?"

"I am warning you that if Caramandi continues with this, he is going to get Lee Beloff, Rego, and himself thrown in jail. And by using your name, you're gonna be in a shit pot full of trouble, too! I told them to stop—but they won't listen to me."

Nick then said, "If you see any of them, tell them it's probably a set up, and I told them to stop. When I get to Philly, I'll tell them myself."

Nicky changed the subject and said, "Come on, Bob, let's get you some glasses that look better than what you're wearing."

I stayed for dinner with Nick and Philip and returned to Philadelphia with three new pairs of eyeglasses on order, a full stomach, and a slight feeling of relief about The Crow.

In less than three weeks, FBI agents arrested Nick Caramandi, Leland Beloff, and Robert Rego. The complaint and warrant charged them with extortion under the Hobbs Act and conspiracy to commit extortion.

I represented Lee Beloff at his bail hearing. Bail was set for all of them, and they were all released from custody the same day.

Under the law there is a requirement for the government to bring an indictment within 30 days of the issuance of the original complaint, otherwise the complaint will be dismissed. That's exactly what happened in this case. The charges against Lee Beloff, Nick Caramandi, and Bobby Rego were all dismissed in one month's time.

The Rouse employee turned out to be an undercover FBI agent. He offered easy money, trying to ensnare Rego, Caramandi, and Beloff, and hoping for Scarfo and yours truly to enter the trap.

I have examined my own conduct with reference to the Rouse extortion many times. I am satisfied that I personally did nothing illegal. Yes, I knew what Caramandi and Rego were plotting, but I was never aware of Beloff's or Scarfo's actual involvement in the scheme. All I did was try to stop a crime by telling people they were crazy and warning them that they were being set up.

Nicky "The Crow" Caramandi had been trying for almost two years to get involved in the construction business with his new friend and associate, John Pastorella, who had recently moved from Baltimore.

Unknown to Caramandi, Pastorella had been arrested and charged with the distribution of heroin prior to moving to Philadelphia. Facing a long prison term, he agreed to cooperate with federal authorities and thus was recording his conversations with Caramandi and anyone else who happened along.

Caramandi, true to his nickname, did a lot of "crowing" in Pastorella's presence. He bragged about his criminal conduct which included extortion, drug dealing, swindling, and conning anyone who came in contact with him. He even mentioned a few assaults and murders.

When the time came for the FBI to pull the plug on Caramandi, he ran to me for advice. I didn't totally turn my back on him, but I made it clear that I couldn't represent him should he be indicted. I had already entered my appearance for Lee Beloff in the Rouse case that had been dismissed. It now became apparent that a new indictment would be forthcoming and would include the Rouse affair. After all, The Crow was overheard, on tape, bragging about his part in the extortion of Rouse. It was no surprise when FBI agents again arrested Caramandi, Beloff, and Rego. They were charged with several extortions, including the one involving Rouse's redevelopment of Philadelphia's waterfront.

Lee Beloff and Bobby Rego were released on bail. Caramandi was detained without bail because he had admitted so many violent crimes on tape to his partner, John Pastorella. The magistrate had no problem in finding The Crow a danger to the community and therefore ineligible for bail.

On the other hand, because fellow inmate Raymond Martorano had told Caramandi that Nicky and I had decided to "dump him and go with Beloff and Rego," he took this to mean that he was going to be killed. If Long John wasn't going to kill me, he would do what he could to see that I wasn't able to practice law again. Within days, The Crow told his FBI inquisitors that he, Rego, and Beloff were trying to shake down the Rouse people and that Nicky Scarfo authorized them to do it. He couldn't wait to tell the Feds that

"Bobby Simone was involved in the plan, and he was going to get ten percent of the score." And now as a result of Caramandi's lies I was forced to withdraw as Beloff's lawyer in the Rouse case.

▼ ▼ ▼

The other constant new face on the scene was Thomas "Tommy Del" DelGiorno. I met Tommy seven or eight years before when he spent a lot of time with Frank Sindone. He and Frank were partners in Cous' Little Italy, at Eleventh and Christian Streets, where Angelo Bruno had his last meal. Tommy also had a rather large sports book that was his main source of income.

Tommy was as short as Nicky Scarfo, and he loved to tell people how much he knew. Sports, politics, women, and everything else—just ask Tommy, he was an expert.

Tommy and The Crow would join Philip, Lawrence, Chuckie, and at least a dozen other guys for parties hosted by Nicky at his home in Fort Lauderdale. I never attended any, but I have seen hundreds of photographs of "the guys" at Nicky's pool, on the boat, and on the beach. I went to the house when Nicky, Philip, and Spike were there.

But it was sometimes tough for me to decline an invitation to go out to dinner at a restaurant with all of them. On these occasions Nicky would lead me to the chair next to him and say, "Sit here, Bob." I can't remember having a bad meal—or a dull one for that matter. Spike always kept everybody in a good mood, telling funny stories and jokes.

During the summer of 1985, Tommy DelGiorno rented an apartment in Ocean City, New Jersey. The apartment overlooked the bay and causeway that connected Ocean City to Somers Point, Longport, Margate, Ventnor, and eventually Atlantic City. His family stayed at the apartment for the entire summer while Tommy commuted by car every weekend from Philly. The Georgia Avenue home and office of Nicodemo Scarfo was convenient to Ocean City. Tommy stopped by Georgia Avenue frequently.

In 1986, Tommy rented the same apartment. Both years he got something extra that he had not bargained for in the lease. The apartment was wired for sound by the New Jersey State Police. Virtually every conversation that took place in Tommy's apartment was recorded. Aside from all the bickering and screaming of Tommy, his wife, and the kids, there were many interesting conversations.

Tommy and his friends—Frank "Faffy" Iannarella, Wayne and Joe Grande, and several others from the heart of South Philly—were overheard on numerous occasions talking about bets on sporting events. It was a toss-up as to whether Tommy bet or booked more action. In addition to all of the bookmaking, many of the conversations revealed "juice loans" made and collected by either Tommy or a member of his crew.

All this evidence acquired through electronic surveillance resulted in an indictment. It charged Tommy, Faffy, Nicky Scarfo, Philip Leonetti, Frank and

Philip (the Narducci brothers), Wayne and Joe (the Grande brothers), Yogi and Chuckie (the Merlino brothers), and several others with violation of the New Jersey State RICO Act, specifically racketeering based on illegal gambling and loansharking. Ed Jacobs, now more experienced, went to work in Atlantic County, New Jersey, and arranged for bail for Nicky Scarfo, Philip Leonetti, and all the other defendants. They were all released within a 24-hour period. In the next couple of weeks, all hell would break loose. The New Jersey State Police convinced Tommy DelGiorno that he was on Nicodemo Scarfo's hit list. Just the excuse he needed to become a turncoat and informant. DelGiorno also agreed to cooperate with the authorities and accept an invitation to be inducted into the Federal Witness Protection Program with his buddy, The Crow.

Scarfo sought refuge in Fort Lauderdale where he updated his tan and planned for the court battles he knew he would have to fight in the near future. The New Jersey RICO case seemed inconsequential now with the knowledge that Tommy Del and Nicky Crow might say anything to avoid long prison sentences.

▼ ▼ ▼

At this time in 1986, I received a call from someone that I had known since high school when we played against each other on opposing football teams. Saul Kane had been a bail bondsman for several years, springing people in Miami, Philadelphia, and Atlantic City.

At one time he was the co-owner of a small but popular bar on Pacific Avenue, not too far from Georgia Avenue. The My Way Lounge was an occasional hangout for the likes of Nicky Scarfo, Nick the Blade, and Philip Leonetti.

Saul, a rather personable guy, was always happy, always smiling, and always laughing. He drank moderately, dressed well, loved to play blackjack, and lived in a tastefully decorated, modern apartment. When he wasn't working or playing blackjack at Caesar's Palace, he spent a great deal of his time socializing with Nicky, Philip, and The Blade.

The phone call from Saul was from the United States Marshals' lockup room in Camden. I rushed over to see how I could help. Shortly after I arrived, Saul and I appeared before the United States Magistrate where an indictment was returned charging Kane and a few others with a massive conspiracy to import and distribute the precursor substance known as P2P, which was used to make methamphetamine.

Saul was in serious trouble due to the fact that he was named as a "drug kingpin." He was, therefore, facing a minimum of ten years to life in prison without parole. The indictment alleged that he managed a group of people in this illegal business on behalf of Nicky Scarfo. This made the case much more difficult, even though there was no evidence of Scarfo's involvement in the scheme.

The prosecutor was successful in getting the magistrate to deny bail. Weeks later Saul was released to help prepare his case for trial but without me as his lawyer. Immediately after the first bail hearing, Stuart Peim, the losing prosecutor in my perjury trial, now assigned to Saul's case, approached me in the hallway and said, "Mr. Simone, you will not be able to represent Saul Kane in this case." Before I had a chance to speak, Peim continued, "You are going to be indicted in the next couple of weeks yourself."

Saul was pissed. I was angry but not surprised. "These guys play for keeps, and they are sore losers," I said as we discussed what our next move would be.

We decided to bring in another lawyer to represent Saul without going through a formal hearing and a long-drawn-out fight on disqualification. We chose Miles Feinstein, an excellent criminal lawyer who practiced out of an office in North Jersey.

Peim did not make good on his threat to indict me, but Saul did not get his lawyer of choice—that is, his first choice. Saul's trial ended with a guilty verdict and a 95-year sentence. Yes, 95 years, and without parole.

Saul continued to fight his conviction and sentence. He had the sentence reduced first to 50 years and then again to 25 years. Scheduled to be released on August 1, 2001, Saul never got to taste freedom again. He died of heart problems early in 2000. Saul could have obtained his release merely by agreeing to testify against Nicodemo Scarfo and/or me. People like Nick Caramandi and Tommy DelGiorno, who were always quick to put Saul Kane down, proved themselves to be much lesser men and friends than Saul. Let me make myself clear on this. Nick Caramandi and Tommy DelGiorno were never friends of mine, but they had always sworn friendship and loyalty to Scarfo.

Saul Kane, who we all called "Meyer" (because of his Jewish faith, his knowledge of the street, and the fact that he so admired Meyer Lansky), surprised a lot of people by his "stand-up" ways. He did not lie or inform on anyone. That didn't surprise me one bit.

For the next six months, the FBI, the New Jersey State Police, and the local and federal prosecutors questioned DelGiorno and Caramandi on endless occasions. The grave was being dug to make room for the bones of Nicky Scarfo. During this period I was busy trying one case after another. Good practice for the many battles soon to come.

PART THREE

"In the halls of justice,
the only justice is in the halls."

Lenny Bruce

CHAPTER TWENTY-SIX

▼

Lawyer
of Choice

In January 1987, Nicky Scarfo flew from Fort Lauderdale to Atlantic City, arriving at the Pomona Airport, just 15 miles away from Georgia Avenue. When he and a few friends stepped off the plane late that night, they had to use their hands to shield their eyes from the glaring lights of the television cameras.

There were approximately 20 law enforcement officers, mostly FBI agents, waiting in the crowd to arrest Scarfo. A superseding indictment added him and Charles Iannece as co-defendants along with Beloff, Rego, and Caramandi. Of course, The Crow didn't have to worry since he had a deal with the Feds guaranteeing him leniency.

Iannece was nowhere to be found. Supposedly, he was in South America where he could not speak the language and just did not feel comfortable. He voluntarily returned and was arrested a short time later. For him prison was a better option. At least he'd be with his buddies and be able to see his family on visiting day.

I represented Nicky at his bail hearing the next day, but to no one's surprise, he was denied bail. He was held in custody pending the trial, a flight risk and a danger to the community.

Several months earlier, when I withdrew as Lee Beloff's counsel, Lee asked me if I knew Oscar Goodman, who originally lived and practiced in Philadelphia, but who was now residing and working in Las Vegas. I told him that I had several telephone conversations with the Vegas lawyer and that I might be able to get him to fly in to discuss the case with a view toward retaining him.

Lee Beloff, his wife, Diane, and I arrived at Bookbinder's restaurant about 6:00 p.m. Waiting for us at the bar was the tall, medium-built Oscar Goodman, wearing his Texas-made, Tony Lama cowboy boots.

We introduced ourselves and had a drink at the bar in the President's Room before we sat down to eat dinner. Oscar and I hit it off immediately, and Lee and Diane liked him very much. After a brief discussion of what we believed the evidence would be and some conversation about fee and costs, Lee gave me the green light to tell Oscar he was retained.

The meal, as always, was excellent, but Lee might have had one too many scotches. Near the end of our dinner, Lee pointed to three well-dressed men, all wearing dark suits, white shirts, and ties. He said, "Look, the FBI is even following us and taking notes while we have our attorney-client meeting."

He quickly rose from his chair. Before I could stop him, he started a shouting match with the three strangers sitting in the last booth. Oscar and I ran over and grabbed Lee about the same time that Anthony, the maitre d', arrived.

Anthony told Lee, "These guys are good customers from out of town. They are executives who work for IBM."

An honest mistake, more likely to occur after a few drinks. Everybody shook hands, we returned to our table, ordered another drink, and we all laughed except Diane, who seemed to be the only one of us to appreciate the seriousness of the problem at hand.

I entered my initial appearance on behalf of Scarfo. In a matter of days the prosecutor filed a motion to disqualify counsel. Nicky would never agree that I should withdraw voluntarily. It was the same old story. The government alleged that there was a conflict of interest, because I previously represented Lee Beloff. Again, they stated that I was a co-conspirator along with the defendants.

Nicky was well aware that the government was alleging that I was personally involved in the Rouse extortion, but he wanted me to fight like hell to stay in the case as his lawyer. He knew better than anyone that Caramandi was lying about my involvement.

I had several long talks with Nicky at the Philadelphia Detention Center where he was being held without bail pending trial. I convinced him, I thought, to use another lawyer, one who was not tainted by an informant's accusations. In the interest of giving him the best opportunity to win what we both knew would be a very tough case, it was the reasonable thing to do.

I brought the lawyer to see Nick and the three of us discussed the case and the bail hearing. Chief Judge John Fullam scheduled a new bail hearing shortly after I filed an appeal from the magistrate's order denying bail.

Oscar Gaskins, an excellent criminal lawyer who was formerly an associate of Cecil Moore, entered his appearance on Nicky's behalf and appeared in court for the full-blown hearing. Judge Fullam ordered the government to bring live witnesses to court to testify against Scarfo. He would not accept hearsay testimony from any federal agents who might tell the court what the informants told them about Nicky Scarfo.

The law had recently changed and federal defendants had the difficult burden of proving they were not a danger to the community or a risk to flee the jurisdiction in order to get bail.

Chief Judge John P. Fullam was perhaps the brightest judge sitting in the United States District Court for the Eastern District of Pennsylvania. He was also one of the fairest. The presumption of innocence meant something to him. He was not going to permit the government to keep a defendant in jail before that defendant was convicted unless the prosecutor could prove by legally admissible evidence that the defendant was a potential danger to the public.

The government brought one of their new star witnesses to court on the day of the hearing—Thomas DelGiorno. Ed Harrell and I provided Oscar Gaskins with a substantial amount of material to use on cross-examination. When the evidentiary hearing concluded, Judge Fullam denied the motion for bail. I must say that it was through no fault of Oscar Gaskins, who did a commendable job.

Nicky, however, would never be satisfied unless he had Robert F. Simone sitting next to him in court. I was the only one he truly trusted. If Clarence Darrow had still been around, Nicky would have preferred me to the great one.

After the hearing, I entered my appearance on Scarfo's behalf, along with an answer to the government's motion to disqualify counsel. Before the issue was decided, Nicky did something very unusual and without asking me. He wrote a letter in his own hand to Chief Judge Fullam. In the letter, Scarfo told the judge that he did not want any other lawyer but me to represent him at trial.

He wrote, "I think it's unfair for me not to have the lawyer of my choice. The government is very unfair. They keep trying to involve Mr. Simone in wrongdoing in this case and in the past. He has been admitted in my RICO case in New Jersey."

Nick continued, "He represented me before. I have all the confidence in him. I know he will be fully prepared on my behalf. If Mr. Simone was a surgeon, and I needed a life or death operation, I would make Mr. Simone operate on me."

I think now, just as I did when I first read Nicky's letter, how much better off I would have been if I had gone to medical school instead of law school. Oh, well!

Near the end of his letter, Nick stated, "It is not fair for me to be deprived of the lawyer of my choice just because the informants lie about him, as well as me. I am willing to waive my right to have a lawyer other than Mr. Simone, and I waive my right to have him as my witness. I believe he will be more important in my case as my lawyer."

Nick ended the letter with, "Respectfully yours, Nicodemo Scarfo."

If I were not personally involved, I would have believed that I wrote the letter for him. I did not, but I couldn't have said it any better.

Judge Fullam's decision surprised the prosecutors and me, as well. He signed an order stating, "The government's motion to disqualify Robert Simone is denied. However, Mr. Simone is ordered to retain co-counsel for the sole purpose of cross-examining the witnesses Caramandi and DelGiorno and arguing their credibility before the jury."

The effect of the motion was that I could continue as lead counsel and handle the entire trial except for the limitations that the court set. We would have to see how this would work for Scarfo as the trial unfolded.

With Nick's approval, I retained as co-counsel Miles Feinstein, the New Jersey lawyer who represented Saul Kane. The trial was put off for several months, and I had sufficient time to represent some other defendants while preparing the Rouse case for trial.

When I entered a courtroom to represent a client, I was always able to leave my personal problems outside. It was the client of the moment that mattered. It was a form of therapy for me. I loved it — the challenge, the action, and the high stakes.

In between trials and often at night, I drove to the Philadelphia Detention Center to see Nick Scarfo. Once in a while, since I was there already, I visited with one of my many other clients who were awaiting trial. More and more defendants were incarcerated without bail due to the new Bail Reform Act. Getting bail for a client was almost as big as winning a case.

Philip Leonetti and I spent more time than usual together now that his uncle was in jail. Philip loved the Saloon restaurant. He called me often and asked if I was free for lunch or dinner. He would pick me up at the office in either a Mercedes or an Audi four-door sedan. We never talked in the cars. We knew they had to be bugged.

After a drink or two we talked about the upcoming trial, and then we would settle in for a remarkable meal including a radicchio salad, fried calamari and shrimp, the best veal in town, and usually a bottle of Robert Mondavi Cabernet Sauvignon. After dinner or lunch, Philip would say to me, "Bob, I wish you were allowed to cross-examine The Crow and Tommy. Nobody knows them the way you do. I'm a little worried about my uncle." He had good cause to be.

Oscar Goodman filed a motion for a separate trial. He recognized the inherent dangers of going to trial before the same jury with Scarfo as a co-defendant. Judge Fullam granted the motion, and Beloff and Rego were scheduled to proceed to trial before Nicodemo Scarfo. Iannece was still tanning alongside all those topless South American beauties.

Oscar tried a great case on Beloff's behalf, and Rego's lawyer, Josh Briskin, also did a commendable job. The jury found both defendants not guilty of a few of the extortion charges, but they were unable to reach a verdict on the Rouse matter. Upset by the outcome, Edward S. G. Dennis, who was then the United States Attorney for the Eastern District of Pennsylvania, removed the assistant who tried the case. He announced that he would personally try the next one. He also let the world know that he would personally try Scarfo's case as well.

Judge Fullam decided to go with the Scarfo trial before retrying Beloff and Rego. I knew that Rego and Caramandi were overheard on several taped conversations asking the FBI agent, who posed as a Rouse employee, for money in exchange for City Council's approval to go ahead with the multimillion-dollar waterfront development. There was no conversation on tape that the prosecution could use to tie Scarfo to the conspiracy. The key evidence against Nick would be the testimony of Nick Caramandi and Thomas DelGiorno, the two that I was not permitted to cross.

We did supply Miles Feinstein with enough ammunition to use on cross. I hoped that he would be able to convince the jury that these two thugs should not be believed. Miles did as well as he could, but he just wasn't familiar enough with the two informants to handle them on the witness stand. The Crow and Tommy Del were a little too sharp and street-smart for Miles. I am not saying we would have won the case if my hands weren't tied. But I know we would have had a better shot at winning the marbles if I could have battled with The Crow and Tommy. I did know how to vex them to the point of unmasking the innocent facade they portrayed.

The party line was, "Yes, I committed all these crimes, but I learned my lesson and now I am a law-abiding citizen." They also testified that their reason for cooperating was that they were convinced that Scarfo was about to have them killed.

Be that as it may, Nicky was convicted. A couple of months later, Lee Beloff and Bobby Rego were also convicted of extorting money from the Rouse Company and several other local builders as well.

Lee hired Alan Dershowitz to represent him in his appeal. I was permitted to represent Scarfo in his appeal while Nicky remained in jail, unlike Beloff and Rego who remained free on bail during their appeals.

Judge Fullam had sentenced them all to lengthy prison sentences: Scarfo, fourteen years; Beloff, ten years; Rego, eight years. Meanwhile Caramandi and DelGiorno, who were enjoying their new roles as credible witnesses, continued to feed information to federal and local law enforcement. It was just a matter of time before additional charges were to be brought against Nicodemo Scarfo and most of his associates.

Several reporters asked Ed Dennis whether or not he intended to indict me for complicity in the Rouse extortion. It appeared that two juries had accepted the testimony of Caramandi and DelGiorno as truthful, so an indictment against me was logical. Without directly answering the questions, Dennis made it clear that since I had already beaten the government in court twice, they didn't feel they had a strong enough case to indict and win at trial against me.

Naturally, I was relieved. So were Nicky and Philip. They now felt that since no charges were forthcoming against me, I would be able to carry the banner on their behalf in the future battles.

The United States Court of Appeals affirmed Nick's conviction and sentence. Beloff and Rego also lost their appeals, and shortly thereafter, they too went to prison.

Philip Leonetti continued to enjoy his freedom for only a few more months. He traveled from Atlantic City to Philadelphia and Fort Lauderdale. One day, while Spike and I were sitting by the pool at Nicky's Florida home, we watched Philip walk and pace continuously around the pool. Spike said, "The man can't sit still. He prances like a tiger."

I thought to myself, *I wonder what's going on in his mind.*

▼ ▼ ▼

Before the year 1987 ended, the Organized Crime Division of the Philadelphia Police Department and dozens of FBI agents arrested Philip Leonetti, Salvatore and Lawrence Merlino, Joseph and Anthony Pungitore, Wayne and Joseph Grande, Frank Iannarella, Salvatore Scafidi and Joseph Ligambi, Frank and Philip Narducci, Nicholas Virgilio, Joseph Ciancaglini, Eugene and Nicky Milano, and Charles Iannece. All except for Anthony Pungitore were held without bail. Scarfo was served with warrants and indictments in his cell at the Philadelphia Detention Center. Ralph Staino, a fugitive somewhere "east of the sun and west of the moon," was not apprehended.

The arrests related to more than one case. The murders of Salvatore Testa and Frank D'Alfonso were treated as two separate matters, each requiring its own trial in state court. Both were death penalty cases. There were also two separate federal indictments. One charged Scarfo and four others with several drug violations, including continuing criminal enterprise, commonly referred to as the "Drug Kingpin Statute." A conviction in this case would more than likely bring a life sentence without parole.

Then there was the RICO killer indictment naming the Philadelphia branch of La Cosa Nostra as the illegal enterprise. Nicodemo Scarfo was named "the boss" and lead defendant. All of those named above were listed as defendants and members of the enterprise.

Nicky, already a sentenced federal prisoner, was now facing a New Jersey state RICO case, a federal charge of being a drug kingpin, two separate murder charges in the state court in Philadelphia, and a federal RICO indictment. I have never heard of any one defendant or group of defendants having to face so many separate trials in such a short period of time.

Scarfo's main complaint was that he believed it was totally unfair to subject him and his friends to so many separate trials, which would naturally cause them to deplete their resources, spend outrageous sums of money to defend themselves, and work their lawyers to death. Considering the availability of government funds and manpower together with the fact that in each of these separate trials the state and federal prosecutors used a different team of lawyers, Nicky may have had a legitimate beef.

Most of the evidence on all these charges came from the lips of Nicky Caramandi and Thomas DelGiorno.

Surprisingly, there were no moves by any of the prosecutors to disqualify me as Scarfo's attorney. That was probably because they were so sure of winning these cases. The battle lines were drawn and lawyers were chosen for every defendant in each case. The first thing to be done was not to "kill all the lawyers," but rather to determine which of these monster trials should start first.

CHAPTER TWENTY-SEVEN

Next Case

Judge Thomas N. O'Neill—short and dapper with white hair and a pleasant, red face—was to be the trial judge in the drug-related case. The most serious count in the indictment alleged that Scarfo, Leonetti, and Salvatore Merlino were involved in a "continuing criminal enterprise." It was alleged that they each organized, supervised, and/or managed at least five individuals in three separate drug transactions. There was no question in anyone's mind that if they were convicted they would never see the light of day again.

I convinced Oscar Goodman to represent Philip Leonetti. Ed Jacobs would handle Salvatore Merlino, and Bob Madden entered his appearance for Frank "Faffy" Iannarella. Joe Santaguida would take on Charles "Charlie White" Iannece, who was no longer a fugitive, only missing the Rouse trial. The other named defendant, Ralph Staino, Jr., was still at large.

This was the case the other defense lawyers and I chose to be first. It goes without saying that drug-related trials are perhaps the most difficult for a defense lawyer to win. Add the fact that this was also what is commonly called a "mob trial" and you have a case nearly impossible to win. A mob-drug case was just what the prosecution wanted.

The United States Attorney's Office thought that my colleagues and I were crazy to select this one as the first to be tried. They agreed to go forward in expectation of an easy win, thereby possibly forcing guilty pleas in the remaining cases.

Judge O'Neill saw no problem with my representing Scarfo and imposed no restrictions on my right to cross-examine The Crow and Tommy Del. The overconfident prosecutors thought better of objecting to having me represent Scarfo. They did not wish Nicky to have a strong appeal issue by being deprived of his lawyer of choice once he lost the trial. Since the Rouse conviction, Ed Harrell and Alan Hart, who was added to the investigation team, had compiled more impeachment material for use against The Crow and Tommy Del.

All the defendants in this case were charged with importation and delivery of drugs, but the evidence failed to show that they were involved in such conduct. Caramandi and DelGiorno would testify that they—on behalf of Scarfo, Merlino, and Leonetti, and aided and abetted by Faffy, Charlie White, and Staino—extorted from two major drug importers a "street tax" on all the drugs they imported and distributed. For some unknown reason the prosecutors failed to charge the defendants with extorting money from the dealers.

Jury selection took longer than usual. Fresh on the minds of most of the jury panel members were all the recent newspaper and television reports of the arrests and charges relating to Nicodemo Scarfo and his "Mafia family." After the arrests, the media disseminated Scarfo's picture and a summary of each pending criminal case along with the history of all the murders committed in South Philadelphia over the past decade. He was already convicted as far as the press and the majority of the public were concerned.

There were only a few jurors out of the first panel of 150 who claimed they had never heard or read about Nicodemo Scarfo. Those who swore that they could still be fair in deciding the case were considered as possible jurors. Another panel was called before we were able to select a jury.

During the jury selection process, a potential woman juror was questioned by the judge as to whether or not she, or to her knowledge any of the other potential jurors, had made a statement complaining about news leaks to the press.

The questioning by the judge went something like this:

Q. Did you hear any conversation among the jury panel relating to juror information that might have been leaked to the media?
A. Yes, I did.
Q. What did you hear?
A. I heard one of the jurors tell another juror [she went on to relate what she heard].
Q. Who was that juror? Please give me either the seat number or juror number if you know it.
A. I can't do that, Your Honor. I was taught by my family not to squeal on anybody.

All the defendants and their lawyers laughed, some out loud. Even the two prosecutors smiled at the remark.

To my total surprise the woman was selected as a juror. The prosecutors chose not to use one of their peremptory challenges to strike her. In all criminal cases both sides are permitted to strike a certain number of jurors without having to show prejudice or any other legal reason.

I thought to myself, *How lucky can we get? The government's whole case is based on informants, and we have a woman on the jury who obviously hates snitches.*

The prosecution presented evidence that a group of men from South Philadelphia and elsewhere were importing P2P from Germany for many months, and then reselling it at a huge profit. The purchasers, also in South Philly, used the P2P to manufacture hundreds of pounds of methamphetamine that brought $10,000 a pound. Both the importers and the manufacturers earned millions of dollars in profits.

Caramandi testified on direct examination that he was a "soldier" in the Philadelphia La Cosa Nostra. He claimed that his captain was Tommy DelGiorno and that Nicodemo Scarfo was "the boss." His testimony was similar to what he had said in the Rouse trials. He also identified the other defendants and testified what their ranks were in La Cosa Nostra.

Caramandi described how he learned of the business of each of the two groups that were making all this money from the P2P and speed. He claimed that he received the order and approval directly from Scarfo to demand money from both groups. He also told the jurors that he reported all his dealings to his captain, DelGiorno.

Caramandi testified that he was able to "shake down" or extort almost a million dollars from the drug dealers and that he turned the money over to DelGiorno. According to The Crow, the dealers were threatened with death or serious injury if they did not pay.

Scarfo, Leonetti, Merlino, and Iannece were not on any of the tapes played to the jury in which there were discussions about either this drug business or any plan to extort money from such a business. There was, however, one only slightly audible tape that was played to the jury on which The Crow tried to identify Faffy Iannarella as one of the speakers. Bob Madden, who represented Faffy, objected to the tape being admitted into evidence while the jurors were still seated in the courtroom.

Judge O'Neill said he wanted to hear the tape again. He asked the prosecutor to play the tape so the jury and he could listen to it. First, however, he had his clerk take all the typewritten transcripts away from the jurors.

The tape lasted only about one minute. It was nearly impossible to make out what was said or who the speaker was. As soon as the taped conversation ended, I walked over to where Faffy was sitting. I took special notice that the jury was following me with their eyes. I leaned over and whispered to Faffy, "Shake your head as if you are saying 'no.'"

He followed my instructions as I asked him in a low voice, "Was that your voice?"

At least a couple of jurors whispered to each other. I can't be entirely positive, but I would bet a good piece of change that they were saying and thinking, "Iannarella says that's not him on the tape."

Judge O'Neill ruled that the jurors could not use the transcripts as an aid in determining who was speaking or what was said. Then he announced, "I find the tape to be inaudible, and it is stricken as evidence." Judges often change their minds and opinions, but rarely in favor of a defendant.

This was a big plus for Faffy and all his co-defendants. There was now no solid evidence against any of them except for the testimony of Caramandi and DelGiorno, which was, to say the least, suspect.

I decided that I would cross-examine Caramandi first and the other lawyers would follow my lead and go after anything that I had either overlooked or not sufficiently covered. We brought an easel to the front of the courtroom, right next to the witness stand, and placed it in a manner that would allow the jurors to view it. Oscar Goodman, black marker in hand, stood next to the easel, ready to record Caramandi's life of crime. I then started my cross of The Crow. I had been looking forward to this task for a long time.

He was asked dozens of questions about his wicked past. First about all the crimes of which he had been convicted, including those to which he pled guilty. Then he was asked to tell the jurors how many crimes he had committed in instances where he was not arrested. In a matter of 15 minutes, the three-by-five-foot chart was filled from top to bottom with a career criminal's lifetime achievements. On the left-hand side of the chart we listed the crimes, including murders, conspiracy to commit murders, larceny, flimflam, extortion, counterfeiting, drug dealing, and bribery.

In the next column, Oscar wrote down the approximate number of times Caramandi committed each crime. As an example, "Murder and Conspiracy to Commit Murder—10 times; Extortion—200 times; Larceny—100 times." In the third column we listed the sentences he could receive for each crime: "Murder—life in prison or death; Extortion—20 years; Larceny—10 years."

In the last column we multiplied the crimes by the number of offenses and listed the total number of years his sentence would be if he hadn't made his deal. The examples read: "Murder—10 life sentences or executions; Extortion—400 years," and so on.

Caramandi had to admit that by testifying against Scarfo and the others he was actually saving his own life or at least avoiding spending the rest of it in prison.

Not only did I get him to admit to committing hundreds of serious crimes, he also was forced to confess to committing perjury in the past. I had documentation of that fact in my hand while I was cross-examining him.

He tried to deflect each question and answer by blaming Nicodemo Scarfo for his crimes. But as a matter of fact, most of his criminal conduct occurred before he ever met Scarfo. By trying to avoid and evade answers, he made himself look even worse in the eyes of the jury.

Ed Jacobs took The Crow through most of his interviews with the FBI agents, and he was able to show scores of inconsistent statements. His testimony and his interviews did not correspond. By the time cross-examination was finished, he wasn't a very believable witness.

Tommy DelGiorno then took the stand and pointed the finger at his "best friend," Faffy, and also at Nicky, Philip, Chuckie, and Charlie White. His testimony was marked by a huge difference in the amount of money he claimed they all earned from the shakedowns. This contradicted what The Crow had told the jury. One of them testified that the total amount collected from the drug dealers was over $900,000, while the other put the figure at around $500,000.

Tommy DelGiorno's record of criminal conduct was not nearly as extensive as Caramandi's. But he did admit to participating in approximately eleven—yes, eleven—murders and numerous extortions. Oscar Goodman repeated his performance at the easel as DelGiorno admitted he committed larceny a few times and also recounted a history of being an illegal sports bookmaker for many years. By the time this area of cross was completed, DelGiorno, like Caramandi, was the proud owner of a record of criminal conduct that filled the entire chart.

Our investigation also revealed that several years earlier, when Tommy was drafted to serve in the United States Army, he was rejected at the last minute. He failed his physical and mental exams by faking that he was mentally unbalanced. He admitted this fact on cross-examination mainly because he had no choice. If he testified that he did not lie to the Army psychiatrist, then the jurors would think he was nuts. If he admitted that he conned the psychiatrist, then they would know he was a liar. Tommy's ego made him admit to being a liar rather than a mental case. It worked for us either way.

When it came time for closing arguments, I chose to be the last defense attorney to speak. All of my colleagues gave superb and convincing arguments. They did a fine job of summation. That made my job that much easier.

I took my usual position up close to the jurors. I started, "My client, Nicodemo Scarfo, is happy and relieved to know that his guilt or innocence is finally going to be adjudicated by a jury of his peers. A group of impartial citizens like you. For the past several years, every newspaper and television station in the area has tried and convicted him without the benefit of evidence, rules of law, and most importantly, without the decision of a fair-minded jury.

"You have heard from my colleagues who have pointed out to you that the government is relying on the word of the likes of Caramandi and DelGiorno . . . who have, as Mr. Goodman said, 'violated every law and broken every commandment known to God.'" I did not want to put the jury to sleep by repeating what my very competent counsel already said. But I knew from my experience that it was possible for this jury, or any jury for that matter, to acquit co-defendants and still convict Nicodemo Scarfo. He was the primary victim of the massive onslaught of prejudicial news articles.

The prosecutor had already given his first closing argument. He had torn into Scarfo, calling him "a money-hungry killer who would stoop to the lowest levels of conduct for personal financial gain."

I countered with, "Let's talk about Caramandi and DelGiorno. Caramandi, as you can see," I pointed to the easel, "has been a professional criminal his entire life. He lies to everybody. You recall how many people he conned and flimflammed. He would promise them one thing and deliver something else. He committed perjury in at least one other case when it was for his benefit, and he is doing it here, again for his own benefit."

I hesitated and walked to his chart, marked "Defense Exhibit 1." I pointed to the crimes and years Caramandi should have been required to serve in prison. I then stated, "He told you he expects to be released from prison shortly. You know that would not happen unless he came in here to say all these things about my client and the others. The prosecutors have given him an invitation to lie. He is slick enough to know what he had to say to cut him loose from prison. He conned the FBI and the prosecutors just like he conned his victims. The question today is whether or not he is going to be able to con you people."

Next, I moved to DelGiorno. "Tommy fancies himself to have been a big man around town. Once he knew his number was up, he was smart enough to blame others, particularly Nicodemo Scarfo, for his crimes. He avoids responsibility, and, at the same time, he avoids spending more time in prison."

I argued that "He was clever enough to get away with lying to an educated psychiatrist to avoid serving time in the Army." I asked the jurors if they were going to let him get away with lying again.

Ed Jacobs had already pointed out the many inconsistencies between the testimony of DelGiorno and Caramandi, so there was no need to repeat that argument. Just about every other defense lawyer directed the jury's attention to the discrepancy between Caramandi and DelGiorno with regard to the total amount of money the "Scarfo organization" was supposed to have earned.

I did not tell the jurors that I felt the evidence might have proved extortion. But I did say, "If you find from the evidence that these defendants, or any one of them, committed a crime not charged in the indictment, and you find that they didn't commit any crime in the indictment, then you must find them not guilty." I added, "The judge will tell you this in his charge."

I pointed to the easel once more and said, "When prosecutors use witnesses like these to build cases and then pay them large amounts of money and reduce their sentences no matter how many crimes they have committed, then we have a situation where criminals are not being punished—they are in fact being rewarded. The use of people like Caramandi and DelGiorno as witnesses then does not deter crime . . . it encourages it."

I finished with, "You can see that people like Caramandi and DelGiorno know they can go out on the street and rob, steal, and yes, kill without fear of the law. All they have to do is deliver testimony against Nicodemo Scarfo and they are forgiven."

The jury was sequestered for their deliberations. They filed into the jury room to begin those deliberations late on a Friday afternoon in December 1987. They did not reach a verdict that afternoon, and they were sent to a hotel for the evening.

However, before they left, they sent a note to the judge requesting that Defense Exhibits 1 and 2 be brought to the jury room. They wanted to see the charts with all the crimes of Caramandi and DelGiorno. Over the objections of the two prosecutors, Judge O'Neill let the jury have them.

I spoke to Nicky and Philip in the U.S. Marshals' lockup before they were sent, along with their co-defendants, back to the Philadelphia Detention Center. It seemed to me that the defense lawyers were more pessimistic about the outcome than the defendants.

We were definite underdogs. As a matter of fact, in all federal criminal trials, the defendant's chances for an acquittal are less than 10 percent, and with so-called mob defendants, the odds on winning are even less.

Nick Scarfo knew that if he lost this case he would be sentenced to life in prison where he would probably die. Philip Leonetti acted like he would accept a guilty verdict and its ramifications, but he was also optimistic about the result. Both of them thanked me for the effort as they were removed from the lockup for transportation back to jail.

Even though Nicky had already been sentenced to 14 years, he and I knew that if we were able to win the remaining cases — including this one — he would be out of prison in five or six years.

Judge O'Neill told us to be on call for Saturday morning in the event of a question from the jurors or a verdict. The next morning I met Ed Jacobs, Bob Madden, Joe Santaguida, Oscar Goodman, and Milton Grusmark, a lawyer from Miami I had brought in to help us with the law during the trial, for breakfast at the Four Seasons Hotel on the Parkway in Center City Philadelphia.

Oscar and Milton were registered there for the duration of the trial. Before we had an opportunity to finish our eggs Benedict, we were interrupted by the waiter and told there was a phone call for either Milton or Oscar.

Within minutes we were all out the door and in taxicabs on our way to Sixth and Market Streets, the site of the U.S. Courthouse. Once in chambers, Judge O'Neill read a note in which the jurors asked for a copy of the notes of testimony of the witness DelGiorno.

I took that as a bad sign for the defense. I expressed that feeling to my associates and to the judge. Judge O'Neill, a true gentleman, said to me, "Bob, I think you are overreacting and worrying for no good reason," and then he said to me something I will never forget: "That was the best closing argument I ever heard . . . I mean it." Quite a compliment, I thought — but I was still worried about losing the case.

Around noon, after some eight hours of deliberations, the jury walked into the courtroom and said the magic words, "not guilty." All the defendants were acquitted of all the charges.

Nicky was so happy he screamed, "We beat you," as he looked at the two Strike Force lawyers and the FBI agents. One of the prosecutors screamed back, "Shut the fuck up," as if we were on the streets and not in "The Halls of Justice."

Nicky got the last couple of words in as he and the other defendants were ushered out of the courtroom by the U.S. Marshals. The spectators, many of whom were friends and family of the defendants, loudly applauded the verdict. Of course, the prosecutors and agents in the room left quickly and quietly without further comment.

After visiting with our jubilant clients for a few minutes, the other lawyers and I went back to the Four Seasons Hotel for a victory drink and a needed lunch. As we all sipped Louis XIII cognac from large snifters, many newspaper and television reporters requested interviews. They had been caught by surprise and most of them were not present in the courtroom to catch the verdict. One reporter asked us if we would come outside with our snifters to be videotaped and interviewed.

When we were all assembled in front of the Four Seasons on camera, the reporter asked us to give our names and the name of our individual winning client. Each lawyer stepped forward, raised his glass, and identified himself and his client.

When it was my turn, I said, "My name is Bob Simone, and I represent 'The Boss.'" The gentlemen in the United States Attorney's Office and their comrades in the FBI did not enjoy this scene. It was played over and over again on local news stations.

Nicky and his friends had won a big battle, but they knew that the war was far from over. Getting a jury to reject the testimony of Caramandi and DelGiorno certainly didn't do me any harm personally. If twelve people could determine that the likes of Scarfo and his associates should be acquitted, the thought of another jury of twelve people convicting me on the same type of evidence seemed far-fetched.

All we could think about now was the next case. Coincidentally, that was the name of the boat in which Nick, Philip, and I used to take our pleasure rides off Atlantic City. Maybe it wasn't a coincidence after all.

CHAPTER TWENTY-EIGHT

Almost Made

The Philadelphia District Attorney's Office got the next shot at Nicodemo Scarfo and eight of his associates under the terms of an agreement between state and federal law enforcement authorities. The Feds, having blown their opportunity to put Scarfo and "company" in prison for life, would now have to pass the ball to the local authorities. They were standing by, waiting with what amounted to a sort of ghoulish glee, to put Nicky and eight of his friends into the electric chair.

The Salvatore Testa murder trial was listed before Judge Albert Sabo only two months after the acquittals of Scarfo, Leonetti, Merlino, Iannarella, and Iannece. Judge Sabo enjoyed the dubious distinction of having presided over more murder trials that resulted in the death penalty than any other judge in the country.

One of the city's leading prosecutors at the time was a lady named Barbara Christie. Her trial record for winning was better than excellent. She had a reputation for being a tough, no-nonsense prosecutor who would do or say almost anything in a courtroom to win. Rumor had it that she never lost—except, that is, on appeal. Several of her guilty verdicts were reversed for "prosecutorial misconduct."

There was never any question about Nicky's right to have me as his attorney in this trial. The other defendants and their lawyers—Oscar Goodman for Philip Leonetti, Ed Jacobs representing Salvatore Merlino, Joe Santaguida defending Wayne Grande, Ed Reif for Joe Grande, Bob Madden for Frank Iannarella, Steve LaCheen representing Joseph Pungitore, Bob Mozenter for Charles Iannece, and David Chesnoff defending Salvatore Scafidi—all agreed that I should again act as lead counsel.

In the previous trial, I retained a sociologist who specialized in helping select juries. Jim Burgund, a short, bearded, handsome man, had done an excellent job in the case before Judge O'Neill. He would now be tested in the state court in a case that had received even more damaging publicity than the drug case.

As I wrote earlier, Salvatore Testa, who was only in his mid-twenties, was not just another victim of murder as far as I was concerned. I knew and admired his father for many years before his violent death. And I had spent considerable time with Sal as well. He was over six feet tall, muscular, and quite a good-looking young man.

A little over a year before he was shot and killed, Sal was one of many guests that Rita had invited to a surprise fiftieth birthday party she threw for me. It was held at the Elan Club in the Warwick Hotel in Philadelphia. Sal gave me an Ebel wristwatch engraved with the date and his and his fiancée's names on the back. I still have and treasure his beautiful and thoughtful gift.

I never considered saying to Nicky and Philip or any of the other defendants, "Look, Sal was a friend of mine. I just can't be involved in a case where his accused murderers are on trial." Not out of fear, but because I felt that Nicky and the others were presumed innocent. Just because Caramandi and DelGiorno said they were guilty didn't make it so. Besides, defense lawyers are not supposed to judge their own clients.

The two informants had told the police and the FBI that Nicky had ordered the hit on Sal Testa because he thought "Sal was getting too big for his britches." They said that Chuckie Merlino told them, "Nicky wants this done."

They also stated that Joseph Pungitore, Sal's best friend, lured Testa to a meeting in a candy store on Passyunk Avenue in South Philadelphia where Wayne Grande, another good friend of Sal's, fired the fatal shot to the back of his head. They claimed the other defendants tried to kill young Testa several times before he was fatally shot. They also stated that certain of the defendants moved the body from the store to a van. Others were alleged to have driven the van to the spot in South Jersey where the body was dumped. And two more men supposedly washed and cleaned the van.

The motive, if one existed at all, was thin. The fact that it took eleven men to pull off a single murder, and stranger yet, that it took several months to do the job, made one think, *Was this really a mob hit?*

It took the better part of a month to question and select jurors. Extensive questionnaires were prepared by our jury expert, Jim Burgund, and passed out to the panel members. The completed forms were returned to the attorneys on both sides. Burgund marked our copies with a number from one to four—the higher the number, the more favorable to the defense.

We had used the same forms and rating system in the drug case, and they seemed to work like a charm. One of the questions required the jurors to note whether they had an opinion of any defendant, and if so, what that opinion was.

More than half of all the prospective jurors wrote statements such as, "I have read about Nick Scarfo, and I believe he is a vicious murderer." Some wrote, "As far as I am concerned, Scarfo is guilty and so are the others." One comment read, "Scarfo is a gangster and a murderer . . . I would give him the electric chair." Another said, "Scarfo is a blood-thirsty killer, and he should never be let out of prison." One would-be juror answered, "The death penalty is too easy for Scarfo and his mob."

As a result of reading so many of these answers, I believed that we were not going to be able to obtain jurors with an open mind. The process became so tedious that I showed Nicky what we were up against. I let him read the answers on the questionnaires. He grimaced and then said in a low voice, "Let's get rid of that one," or "Where did these people come from?"

At one point Joe Santaguida, sitting next to me, started to smile. Before we knew it, we were both laughing. Joe seemed to get a big kick out of my passing the questionnaires to Nicky. We thought it funny. Nicky didn't. He sometimes cursed under his breath and whispered, "How the fuck are we going to get a fair jury . . . damn newspapers!"

I couldn't help but agree. But after a month we finally did have a jury of twelve and six alternates in the box. Several of the lawyers representing the co-defendants didn't appear in court every day during the jury selection. They more or less left it up to Jim Burgund and me.

Barbara Christie made her opening address to the jury, outlining what she expected to prove. She said that this was a mob murder, that some of the defendants who participated did so to earn membership in La Cosa Nostra. She claimed that a prerequisite to becoming a member was to participate in a murder. She portrayed her two key witnesses, Caramandi and DelGiorno, as former members of La Cosa Nostra. She further claimed that they were testifying mainly because they believed Scarfo had marked them for death. She laid out the plan and execution of the murder. She had received the information from her two turncoat informers. Christie promised that she would prove all the defendants guilty beyond a reasonable doubt.

All of the defense lawyers, including myself, chose to make opening addresses. The crux of our openings was the lack of credibility of the state's witnesses. I recall saying to the jurors, "Please keep your minds open until you have heard both the direct and the cross-examination of the witnesses."

All of the attorneys for the defense explained that their clients were presumed innocent and that the prosecutor had the burden of proving their guilt beyond a reasonable doubt. I begged the jurors to decide the case on the evidence or the lack of it and not on any news story they had read or heard, as they had promised while they were going through the jury selection process.

The large courtroom in City Hall was packed solid with family and friends of the accused, federal and state law enforcement personnel, and many representatives of the news media. Artists kept busy drawing pictures of the defendants, their lawyers, the prosecutor, and the judge. Pictures of the jurors were forbidden, as were the presence and use of cameras in the courtroom.

Aside from those people who had some direct interest in the case, there was always the usual crew of retirees who would come every day and share their views, opinions, and thoughts with the spectators. Even the lawyers frequently sought them out for advice. Some of these people spent more time in court than any lawyer. They were sometimes called "the roving jurors." They usually visited many trials in different courtrooms, but they stayed with this trial to catch every word.

▼ ▼ ▼

One day, while smoking a cigarette on a short break, I noticed two unfamiliar figures in the crowd. Both were African American. One was dressed in a sharp silk suit, white shirt, and color-coordinated tie. The other was dressed more casually, wearing a "Members Only" black jacket. They both looked at me and smiled, but neither approached, obviously respecting my need to be alone at such a crucial time.

I couldn't help but see these two men sitting in the courtroom, observing some of the heated exchanges I had with both Caramandi and DelGiorno. One day, after court recessed, the men approached me and introduced themselves.

The gentleman who was wearing the suit said, "Hi, Bob, my name's Noah Robinson, and this is my brother, Brooks Gray. I'd like to speak with you when you have time about representing me in a murder trial. I haven't yet been charged, but I expect it to happen real soon. I know you're extremely busy, so just let me know if you are interested, and if so, when we might speak."

We made an appointment for the next night after court. We planned to meet at a hotel in West Philadelphia. Ed Harrell told me, "That guy is Jesse Jackson's brother—the well-dressed guy. I don't know the other one."

After court the next day, Ed drove me to the hotel and walked into the bar with me. I introduced Ed as my investigator, and they were more than willing to talk in his presence.

We learned that Noah Robinson was expecting an arrest warrant to be issued against him. It would charge him with murder in connection with a shooting death that occurred many months before in Greenville, South Carolina.

Noah said, "This being an election year and seeing that my half-brother, Jesse . . . Jesse Jackson, is creating a lot of waves by declaring himself a candidate for president. Well, they're going to arrest me while the campaign is still hot." He added, "Did you hear anything about my problem? It was reported on national television within the last couple of days."

I told him, "No, I have been too busy with the trial I'm working on to pay attention to much else."

"I can understand that. I respect that. I heard what you did to Caramandi and DelGiorno in that last case in federal court and yesterday. You are just what I need."

As a result of our conversation, I called the authorities that night in Greenville and learned that charges were still being investigated, and it was safe to assume that nothing would happen until I was finished with the Testa murder trial.

Noah was relieved, and we agreed to meet again once the Testa trial was over. That, however, didn't stop him from coming to court to watch his new lawyer perform.

Later I learned that there were five witnesses, all of whom turned state's evidence against Noah. I would deal with that in the future. I got right back on track to handle the immediate problem—whether or not I would lose my first client to the state executioner.

▼ ▼ ▼

Caramandi took the stand, and he was as cocky as ever. He and Barbara Christie made a good team as she led him through his narrative description of the plot and his version of the actual murder. He told the jurors he purchased the rope that was used to bind Sal Testa at a hardware store in South Philadelphia. He also testified that at one point during the conspiracy he used an outdoor phone booth to call either Faffy Iannarella or Tommy DelGiorno to report the movements of Salvy, whom he was stalking.

On cross-examination, I got him to name the owner of the store where he claimed to have purchased the rope. Our investigator already had a statement from the owner, along with the records to prove that the type of rope used by the killer was never sold at his place of business.

The Crow squirmed as I asked him the exact location of the phone booth he used to report in to his alleged superiors. He answered the question, but he didn't know that we also had a statement from the owner of the cigar store where the phone booth was supposed to have been located. The owner said the public phone had been removed at least five years before the date mentioned by Caramandi. To be sure, Alan Hart obtained the records from the telephone company, which confirmed our evidence.

The Crow told the jurors that he received his direct orders from Tommy DelGiorno and Chuckie Merlino. Ed Jacobs would later show an inconsistency in DelGiorno's testimony on this point.

While I was questioning Caramandi, he often attacked me personally. I asked him, "Do made guys carry identification cards?" I was referring to his earlier testimony that an inducted member of La Cosa Nostra is referred to as a "made guy."

He answered, "You know how it's done. You've been around these guys so long. They wanted to make you."

I fired back, "I am not a member, am I?"

He said, "Pretty close . . . you're almost made."

There was now a new mob term—"almost made." There would be several more before I finished with Caramandi in this and future trials.

On further cross-examination by my co-counsel, we were able to recreate the chart of The Crow's life of crime. He admitted, "I hope to be released from prison soon." Free to walk the streets despite the fact that he had swindled, extorted, killed, and dealt drugs most of his adult life.

Next, DelGiorno went after Scarfo and Merlino. He kept saying that they both pressed him about why it was taking so long to kill Testa. He told the jury, as did Caramandi, of several foiled attempts before the job was completed. His testimony on the whole sounded incredible. When we were done posting his criminal record before the jury and letting them know how he lied to dodge his military service, I doubt that anyone in the courtroom believed him.

The DA had The Crow and DelGiorno identify hundreds of photographs of the defendants, who were often depicted in groups of three, four, five, and sometimes more. There were pictures of some of the guys on the beach at Atlantic City and Fort Lauderdale, partying on Nicky's boat, or standing outside the office on North Georgia Avenue.

When I examined the stack of photographs, I couldn't help but notice that several of them were taken in El Paso, Texas, just before Nicky Scarfo's release from La Tuna. I saw the faces of my son, Nicky's son, and Chuckie's son, Joey, as well as my own. I purposely didn't object—more ammunition for my closing argument.

Sal Testa's sister testified for the prosecution, but all she really had to say was that the defendants treated her brother's death much differently than her father's. "They did not pay their respects. None of them went to the funeral." I let that alone and asked no questions on cross.

An agent who worked out of the FBI laboratory in Washington, D.C., testified that the tire tracks found at the scene where the body was dumped matched the tires of a van driven by one of the defendants.

On cross-examination, I asked, "Agent, you can't tell this jury that the tire marks you examined were made by any of the tires that were connected to the van that is in evidence in this case, isn't that correct?"

"Yes, that's correct."

"Would you agree that there are literally thousands of vehicles in the Philadelphia–South Jersey area that have tires that would leave the same marks that you examined?"

"Yes, that's right." With that answer I asked no more questions. It was almost like it was done in *My Cousin Vinny*.

Both DelGiorno and Caramandi testified that the time of the shooting, and therefore the death, was somewhere between 12:00 p.m. and 2:00 p.m. The medical examiner testified that his findings were consistent with that testimony and time frame.

Before the trial, the DA's office examined the candy store where the shooting allegedly took place. The entire floor was ripped up to no avail. There was no evidence of blood anywhere. In addition, the van that the detectives seized, searched, and submitted to the crime lab failed to turn up any evidence of blood, fibers from the rope, or the blanket in which Sal Testa's body was wrapped and tied.

The trial, including jury selection, was going into its third month when Barbara Christie announced, "The Commonwealth rests."

On prior occasions when I represented Nicky or his nephew, Philip, there were always the happy hour cocktails and dinners. With this case, it was a crowd of defense lawyers meeting every night either at the Warwick or the Four Seasons. A few drinks and we were off to The Saloon, Bookbinder's, or La Cucina for a meal and some heavy strategy talk for the next day.

The lawyers, including myself, could only talk to our clients on weekends or early in the morning before court. Most, if not all, of the defendants were perfectly willing to rely on their attorneys despite the knowledge that if we lost, they would more than likely get the death penalty.

Several of the lawyers and all of the defendants were surprised that Judge Sabo, with his tough reputation, wasn't really treating the defense that badly.

He prevented the prosecutors from going too far with evidence of other crimes committed by the defendants on trial. He chose to follow the law as Judge O'Neill had done. He refused the admission into evidence of any other murders allegedly ordered by Scarfo and committed by the co-defendants. He also ruled Nicky's Rouse conviction inadmissible.

I had made a decision to keep our objections to a minimum so that when Christie objected, she was likely to look bad in front of the jury. Some of my colleagues fought me on this one, but their clients finally told them to abide by my decision. Their argument was sound though, because if we lost this case with a jury, the likelihood of a successful appeal was diminished. But my gambling instincts and past experience convinced me that I was right in my view as to how to try this case.

Christie moaned and groaned in front of the jury. She seemingly did not care about the impression she was making on those who would ultimately decide the issue of guilt or innocence. Barbara Christie tried this case not unlike the way Marcia Clark tried the O.J. Simpson case.

When the time came for us to put on the defense witnesses, I took a back seat to the other lawyers. The storeowner who knew that there was no telephone booth located just outside his front window so testified. The telephone company records were introduced as an exhibit to confirm that he was correct. The owner of the hardware store where Caramandi said he purchased the rope testified, with records and receipts in hand, that no such purchase occurred or could have occurred.

Then an elderly gentleman, who worked as a caretaker in the small city park directly across the street from the Testa residence, testified that on the day of the murder he not only saw Sal Testa leaving his home, he had a conversation with him. The caretaker said that the chance meeting took place about 5:15 p.m. That was at least two or three hours after both Caramandi and DelGiorno said that Testa was shot and killed.

Before the defense rested, I called Captain Frank Friel, who supervised organized crime investigations for the Philadelphia Police Department, to testify as a witness for the defense.

I started off by asking him if he was involved with the surveillance that took place at Sal Testa's funeral. "Yes, I was there," he answered.

The next few questions went like this:

Q. Did you observe any of the defendants at either the wake or the funeral . . . paying their respects?

A. No, they weren't there. None of them.

Q. Was I there?

A. Yes, you were observed entering and leaving the funeral parlor the night of the wake.

Q. A couple of years before Sal Testa's death, a man by the name of Frank Monte was shot and killed in Philadelphia, wasn't he?

A. Yes.

Q. Isn't it a fact that Frank Monte was a close associate and friend of Nicodemo Scarfo and some of the other defendants on trial?

A. Yes, that is true.

Q. Isn't it a fact that people other than these defendants were arrested and charged with the death of Frank Monte?

A. Yes. Some of the Riccobenes.

Q. You were involved in the investigation of Frank Monte's murder which resulted in that arrest, weren't you?

A. Yes.

Q. Nicky Scarfo and these other men were not present at Mr. Monte's wake or funeral, were they?

A. No, they were not.

Q. None of them are responsible for Monte's murder?

A. That's right.

Q. Would you agree that just because Mr. Scarfo and the other defendants did not attend Sal Testa's wake and funeral does not mean that they either killed him or conspired to do so?

A. I would have to say you are right.

Frank Friel was known to be an honest cop. That reputation was enhanced when he spent many, many hours over several months to prove the innocence of another murder defendant. One who had previously been wrongly convicted of another "mob-related" shooting.

Another reason I put Friel on the stand was to ask him if, during the course of his investigation, he uncovered evidence that Sal Testa was alive and well several hours after the time Caramandi and DelGiorno said the murder took place. He said that he did have such information from the park custodian and also from another police officer.

Next, I switched to the day of another murder and I asked, "Did you obtain a search and seizure warrant for the Testa residence after the murder of Philip Testa back in 1981?"

"Yes."

"Isn't it a fact that when you searched the residence, a few years before this homicide, you observed a blanket similar in color and size to the one found wrapped around the body of Salvatore Testa?"

He knew where I was headed, but he had to answer affirmatively. We had been given a copy of his report of that search in federal discovery documents. Then I asked, "During that earlier search, didn't you also observe a rope similar to the one used to tie Sal Testa's body?" I showed him the exhibits as I was asking these questions.

"Yes, that's true," he answered. At that point, I stopped and Friel was excused as a witness.

I was trying to show that Testa might very well have been shot, killed, wrapped, and then moved from his own house, not the candy store.

The prosecution couldn't very well argue that lying career criminals like Caramandi and DelGiorno should be believed while Captain Friel, an honest police officer with an outstanding record, should not be believed. Barbara Christie was in a bind, but there was nothing she could do about it.

The time for closing arguments arrived. As lead counsel, I determined the order of speeches for the defense. Oscar Goodman was to be first, and I would be last. Between our two closing arguments Joe Santaguida, Eddy Reif, Ed Jacobs, Bob Madden, Steve LaCheen, David Chesnoff, an associate of Oscar Goodman, and Bob Mozenter would argue on behalf of their clients.

The first closing address by Oscar started on Monday morning. His argument on behalf of Leonetti was much shorter than anticipated. Goodman chose to stay away from the facts. He attacked the credibility of the prosecution witnesses. All of the other lawyers reviewed the facts as they applied to their individual clients. I kept crossing out the subjects I had outlined in my notes as each lawyer dealt with that portion of the case.

Near the end of the summations, I asked to see Judge Sabo at sidebar with Barbara Christie. I told the judge that because Ms. Christie had the last argument, the defense wanted to have at least one summation on the same day. It looked like all my colleagues would be finished early on Friday morning. I wanted to avoid a situation where I would speak to the jurors on Friday afternoon, and then Christie could wait through the weekend and start fresh on Monday morning.

I was fearful that over the weekend the jurors would forget many of the things we had to say to them. A huge advantage for the prosecutor. I also did not want Christie to have too much time to review the transcript of my summation.

Judge Sabo ruled that even if the other defense lawyers were finished early, I did not have to speak until Monday morning. He allowed me an hour and a half for my summation, more than enough time. He gave Christie the rest of the day if she needed it. The important thing was that we both had to finish the same day.

Monday morning came, and Barbara Christie didn't show. I believed she was home, busy reading the transcripts of the other defense closings. Fortunately, she did not have mine. An associate from the DA's Office advised the judge that Christie was ill. The jury was returned to the hotel in which they had been sequestered.

We were now in the fourth month of trial, and the jurors had been sequestered, separated from their homes, families, friends, and jobs during all that time. They had to be getting restless. On Tuesday morning there was still no Barbara Christie. The message was, "She is still sick." The jury again was sent back to the hotel.

Wednesday morning arrived and so did Ms. Christie. I had been on hold since the previous Thursday and was anxious to get on with my summation. I planned to speak for about an hour—no more than an hour and a half, just as Judge Sabo had instructed.

The courtroom was so packed that the spectators with an interest in the case had to stand against and around both sides of the walls. The jurors filed into the box, took their seats, and listened to the judge say, "I am sorry for the delay, but believe me it was unavoidable. You will now hear from counsel for Mr. Scarfo and then Miss Christie will give her closing address. Tomorrow I will charge you on the law you must follow when you deliberate."

Judge Sabo glanced at me and said, "Mr. Simone." I rose from my seat and thought, *This jury has to be pissed. They've been locked up for four days doing nothing but waiting. All they want to do at this point is decide it and go home.*

"Ladies and gentlemen of the jury, I have been waiting, like you, for four days to speak with you, but the delay was unavoidable as Judge Sabo told you. Ms. Christie was ill and unable to be in court. But please don't hold that against her or the Commonwealth of Pennsylvania. If my case was as weak as hers, I might not have shown up at all."

Christie did not object. I think my opening remarks took her by surprise. But the jurors now knew that the delay was not caused by the defense.

I told the jury that according to Caramandi and DelGiorno, Nicodemo Scarfo was supposed to be a boss of some giant, sinister, criminal organization. I asked, "Does it make any sense—is it logical—that such an organization would need eleven men to kill one person? Would it take eleven men several months to succeed?"

I pointed out that both Caramandi and DelGiorno had a motive to kill Testa. "According to their own testimony, DelGiorno ended up taking over as 'captain' of Testa's crew in the family, and Caramandi was also promoted to a position where he could report directly to Scarfo."

I said that this case stood or fell on the credibility of DelGiorno and Caramandi. "One rat is here corroborating another. Two times zero equals zero. And that's what their testimony is worth, zero."

I repeated part of the argument I made in the federal drug trial. "These guys are testifying and lying to save their own skin." I reminded the jury that The Crow had committed perjury before and that Tommy Del lied his way out of the Army.

"Who would you believe . . . these lowlifes or Captain Friel and the fine gentleman caretaker? The two criminals say that Testa was killed early in the afternoon at the candy store on Passyunk Avenue. Friel says that because the same rope and blanket were at Testa's house for some time, he believed Testa was either killed in his house or taken from there with the rope and blanket and killed later. Both Friel and the caretaker say that Testa was alive late that afternoon or early evening."

I took the photographs in my hand and showed them to the jurors one by one. "Look at these when you go back to deliberate. Pictures of my son, Nicky's son, Chuckie Merlino's son, and me. Why do we have to be tainted by the prosecutors? All this surveillance, all these photographs! They don't care whose life they ruin. Enough is enough! You can stop this now with a not guilty verdict."

I then tried something different. "Let's take the so-called case against Philip Leonetti, Nicky Scarfo's nephew. I don't represent him, but I have to tell you . . . You saw and heard for yourselves . . . There was absolutely no evidence against him. Except that he happened to be the son of Nicky's sister. He was charged in this case only because he was related to my client.

"These photographs of men standing and talking, sunbathing, sitting on a boat, they prove nothing. These people," I pointed to the prosecution table, "don't care who they louse up or whose reputation they might destroy. Well, I am proud to say that I am a friend of Nick Scarfo. I might add that I am also proud to say that Philip Leonetti," I walked over and touched his shoulder, "is perhaps my best friend.

"The DA wants you to believe if you are Nick Scarfo, or Italian and a friend of his, or worse yet a relative, you must be guilty of something. Well, that's not how it works in this country."

I advised the jurors that if they wanted to keep killers off the streets, they should reject the testimony of Caramandi and DelGiorno so that others won't get the wrong message. That message is that they can kill, then testify against another person, and escape punishment. All these informants need to do to gain their freedom is blame others for their own crimes.

I reminded the jurors of their promise to vote "not guilty" if they had a reasonable doubt. I sat down to listen to Barbara Christie. She spoke for several hours, but I couldn't tell one way or the other if the jurors were listening to her. Most of them sat there with blank expressions. I know I listened. And I squirmed in my seat several times when I felt she was scoring points.

We broke for the day when she finally finished. I spoke to Nicky, Philip, and several of the other defendants in the cell room afterward. I couldn't believe how upbeat they all were. They knew that they were looking at the death penalty if we lost.

Judge Sabo instructed the jury the following day on the law. The jurors wanted the testimony of the FBI tire expert read to them. We were all worried by the request. After listening to a repeat of the direct examination, we asked each other, "Are they going to convict on the basis of that evidence?" We felt better when we heard the cross-examination, much better.

They returned to deliberate. Ten minutes later, they came back to their seats in the courtroom.

The verdict of "not guilty" was loudly announced by the jury foreperson. It was repeated eight more times. The huge throng of spectators cheered and waved to their victorious friends and relatives, all of whom were busy hugging and kissing their lawyers.

The defendants were guided out of the courtroom by several sheriffs. All of them smiling and laughing, they were overheard saying, "Nobody will believe DelGiorno and Caramandi."

A couple of our lawyers from out of town were again staying at the Four Seasons Hotel. They had said before the verdict, "If we win, we're gonna have a big bash." Somehow the word got out. An hour later, after I visited with the jubilant defendants, I drove to the hotel. Scores of people connected with the case—lawyers, relatives of the defendants, reporters, and cameramen—surrounded the bar near the lobby. Soon the crowd grew to over a hundred people. I stayed for only a few minutes and then left quietly.

I knew we had just won a huge victory. But I also knew there were several other cases yet to be fought. The defendants were still in jail, and I thought to myself, *It is too early to celebrate.*

CHAPTER TWENTY-NINE

What Ever Happened to Double Jeopardy?

A week or so after the stunning victory in the Testa murder trial, Rita and I took off to St. Barts for another glorious week of doing nothing but lying on the beach, swimming, reading, and dining in a different restaurant each night.

Our trip was delayed a few days only because I accepted a few interviews on radio and television shows in the Philadelphia area. Several people called while I was on the air, expressing their opinions about the multiple prosecutions of Nicodemo Scarfo and the use of murderers as witnesses by the prosecutors. I was surprised to hear people say, "Enough is enough" and "How can the government let people out of prison who have committed murders in exchange for their testimony?" My sentiments, exactly.

I started to believe that public opinion was beginning to sway in favor of the defendants. Could it be that we were going to win all these cases? What a dreamer I was.

Several new clients came to me for representation in criminal matters, including a South American drug dealer who had a federal case in Miami, two police officers charged with accepting bribes, and a couple of defendants charged with white-collar crimes. Most of my work and income were unrelated to Scarfo and the so-called mob, unlike most of the publicity. The tag "mob lawyer" followed me like a lost dog.

My good friends Diane and Lee Beloff came to me for representation; they were charged with vote fraud in a federal indictment. The government alleged that the wealthy and good-looking couple submitted scores of forged absentee ballots in the 1985 state and local election. Lee was the leader of the thirty-ninth ward and Diane was a committeewoman in their home district in South Philly. The amount of pretrial publicity caused Judge Thomas O'Neill to postpone the trial for a few months after we started jury selection. Just before the next trial date, Lee pled guilty and received time running concurrently with his Rouse case sentence. Diane pled to a lesser misdemeanor charge and was placed on non-reporting probation. Soon Lee lost his Rouse appeal and surrendered to do his sentence.

In between trials I started to prepare the upcoming federal RICO case for trial, scheduled to start in the fall of 1988. Nicky and 19 of his friends and associates remained in prison without bail despite the fact that they had already been found not guilty in the first two trials.

▼ ▼ ▼

The presidential election was heating up, and Jesse Jackson was becoming more viable as a candidate with each day. It was then that his half-brother, Noah Robinson, learned for certain that he was going to be arrested and charged with murder in Greenville, South Carolina.

Besides the many golfing retirees from the Northeast, thousands of employees in the textile, electronics, computer components, pharmaceutical, rubber, and tire industries resided in Greenville. Furman University and Bob Jones University were its best-known scholastic institutions. Ed Harrell and I flew to the small, quaint city with its population of less than 60,000.

We made arrangements to surrender Noah to the local authorities. They had charged Robinson with first-degree murder. The warrant and accompanying affidavit stated that he hired several members of a black street gang from Chicago to kill Leroy "Hambone" Barber because he allegedly started a fight with Noah several weeks before he was shot to death outside a Greenville poolroom.

It was a capital case, but despite that fact, Noah Robinson was granted bail. Many of his supporters from Greenville gladly pledged their real estate as collateral, and Noah was released from jail in a matter of a few days. The trial was put off until after the first of the year to give both sides ample opportunity to prepare. Before Ed and I left, I got my first taste of real down-home cooking and honest-to-goodness southern hospitality.

Noah returned to his home in Chicago where he owned and operated eight Wendy's restaurants and a successful construction company. Once back in Chicago, Robinson learned that two federal grand juries were looking into his business affairs and personal life. There were the usual news leaks mentioning Noah's problems with the law in some of the stories relating to Jesse Jackson's run for the presidency.

Meanwhile the federal RICO indictment charged Nicodemo Scarfo with ordering the murders of Judge Edward Helfant in 1978, and Vincent Falcone in 1979, both in Atlantic City. Other murders used as predicate crimes, committed in Philadelphia, were of Pat Spirito, John Calabrese, Frank Narducci, Salvatore Testa, Robert Riccobene, and Sammy Tamburrino (one a brother and the other an ally of Little Harry). Strange as it may seem, the prosecution was allowed to retry Scarfo and others on two murders for which they had already been acquitted. So much for the right to claim double jeopardy. Sorry, Nick, we cannot allow you to make use of too many constitutional guarantees.

In addition, Scarfo was charged with ordering the failed hits on Frank Martines, Harry Riccobene, Joseph Salerno, Sr., and Steven Vento, Jr. All were listed as attempted murders in the indictment.

Winning a single murder trial was certainly difficult enough, but now I dreaded the situation where one jury would hear all the gruesome facts surrounding multiple murders and attempted murders. I knew that a jury would have to be prejudiced by the constant flow of all these accusations of violent behavior. It made sense that they would think, "He's got to be guilty," or "He must be a violent person. After all, he knew all these victims." There were hundreds of photographs to prove association. This was not supposed to be sufficient, but in this instance I am not so sure.

The prosecutors also included counts of shakedowns, extortion, drug dealing, gambling, and loansharking. One defendant, Joe Ligambi, pled guilty to gambling charges, and the other more serious counts against him were dropped. He remained a defendant in the D'Alfonso murder that would be tried later in state court.

The illegal enterprise was identified as "the Bruno crime family," succeeded by "the Testa crime family," and finally called "the Scarfo crime family." Under the RICO statute, to convict the government needed to prove (1) the existence of the enterprise; (2) that a defendant was a member; and (3) that a defendant committed at least two of the predicate crimes on behalf of the enterprise.

The federal prosecutors had learned many things from following the trials in the Falcone and Testa murders and the conspiracy to commit extortion drug case. They did not rely solely on the testimony of Caramandi and DelGiorno, their two trained seals.

Lou Pichini and Arnold Gordon led the prosecution, and when they questioned The Crow and Tommy Del, they made sure that the many tape recordings were played for the jury as the witnesses sat in their chairs, facing the jurors. There were many incriminating tapes that originated from Tommy's summer residence and the two clubhouses where these defendants spent a great deal of their time.

Finally, the government was able to call witnesses to corroborate the testimony of Caramandi and DelGiorno. Some were victims of shakedowns and extortion, and others were co-conspirators in other illegal activities. Ralph Staino, arrested in the Dominican Republic and now on trial, was on

▲ *Left to right:* Dr. Martin Luther King, Jr., Detective Ted Jordan, and Ed Harrell in the mid-1960s, before Harrell began working as Simone's investigator.

▲ Simone and Tony DiSalvo toast in Miami, circa 1985.

Stanley Branche. ▶

Simone and Rita leave ▶
the viewing for Sal Testa
on September 19, 1984.
Behind them are
Gus Lacey and Stanley
Branche. *Courtesy of the*
Philadelphia Daily
News/*George Reynolds*

◄ Nicky Scarfo in Simone's office, 1986.

◄ Best friends Simone and Philip Leonetti on the beach in St. Barts, 1985.

▲ *Left to right:* Attorneys Ed Jacobs, Oscar Goodman, Milton Grusmark, Simone, Joseph Santaguida, and Robert Madden drink a toast to the "not guilty" verdict in the Scarfo drug trial, December 1987.
Courtesy of the Philadelphia Inquirer

▲ Leland and Diane Beloff with attorney Oscar Goodman, 1987.

◄ The defendants in the Falcone murder trial relax in the sun in Key Biscayne, Florida, in 1984. *Left to right:* Lawrence Merlino, Philip Leonetti, Nicky Scarfo, and Sal Testa.

◄ *Left to right:* Sam "The Barber" LaRosa, Simone, Spike DeGregorio, and Nicky Scarfo show off the cake inscribed "Jury Clears Simone," 1986.

◄ Salvatore "Chuckie" Merlino in Simone's office, 1984.

▲ *Left to right:* Simone, Bobby Rego, and Lee Beloff, circa 1985.

▲ *Left to right:* Philip Leonetti, Nick Scarfo, Nicky "The Crow" Caramandi, and Joseph Grande in Fort Lauderdale, 1986.

▲ This law enforcement surveillance photo shows Simone in discussion with Philip Leonetti, Nick Virgilio, and others on the sidewalk outside Nicky Scarfo's Atlantic City office.

▲ Simone's son, Scott, visiting him at Nellis Federal Prison Camp.

▲ Simone's daughter, Kim, often visited him at Nellis.

◄ Simone today.
*Photograph by
Bob Jones*

several tapes allegedly shaking down a few bookmakers along with the late Pat Spirito.

Pichini and Gordon were clever in the manner in which they presented the evidence in the murder counts. They chose not to include all of the facts in their direct examinations. This made it difficult for my colleagues and me to impeach the witnesses on cross, as we had done in the previous trials.

Here there was no mention of a phone booth, no store where the rope was purchased, and the witnesses were trained not to volunteer facts when answering the questions on direct. In addition, Joseph Salerno's testimony was tailored to limit the cross.

The cross-examination of the government witnesses, while as relentless as in the past, was not nearly as effective. You can't cross-examine a tape player or videotape, and some of the evidence on these devices was devastating.

An example of what the defense was up against can perhaps best be told by recounting the testimony in the murder portion of the trial. One cold, snowy, winter night in December 1978, Judge Helfant and his wife were seated in a booth in the restaurant of the motel they owned on Pacific Avenue in Atlantic City. A tall, thin male wearing a ski mask and carrying a snow removal shovel walked into the restaurant. He went directly to the booth where the Helfants were sitting, pulled a small pistol out of his pocket, and fired it into the back of Judge Helfant's head. The assassin left and disappeared into the snowstorm.

At the trial one person, who claimed he saw a male leaving the area, identified someone in the courtroom other than Nick "The Blade" Virgilio, the person that the prosecution claimed to be the hitman. Mrs. Helfant testified as a defense witness, swearing that The Blade was not and could not have been the shooter. "His eyes were a different color," she said.

The jury, which began their deliberations on Thursday, November 17, 1988, returned with their guilty verdicts on Saturday, November 19. All the defendants were convicted of all the counts despite the general unreliability of the government's witnesses. Virgilio was convicted of the Helfant killing despite the testimony that seemed to clear him.

The verdict was a devastating blow for Scarfo and most of his friends and a major victory for the patient prosecution team. The government had used every weapon at their disposal to win this conviction. They had granted immunity to many witnesses and promised freedom to a few cold-blooded killers. A handful of informants who testified were rewarded with large cash gifts. A substantial amount of evidence was derived from court-authorized electronic surveillance devices and procedures. The government asked for and got an anonymous and sequestered jury that couldn't help but think that their identities were being concealed to protect them from the "violent" defendants.

Immediately after the verdict, I went to the U.S. Marshals' lockup on the second floor of the courthouse. Nicky Scarfo had already been shipped back to the Philadelphia Detention Center, but I did manage to see Philip Leonetti for a couple of minutes.

"Bob, I never thought they would get me," he said. "What kind of sentence will I get . . . the max I guess, 40 years. Do we have a shot on appeal?"

"We'll have to talk later," I said. I was still unraveled from the verdict, even though I knew it was a tough case. It seems, however, that in every case I ever tried, I believed I had a good shot to win.

"Where's Oscar?" Philip asked. Oscar Goodman was his lawyer, and Philip was peeved that he didn't stop to see him. Philip added, "Tell him to come to the Detention Center so I can discuss the situation with him." Then Philip surprised me. "Agent Maher and another FBI guy just gave me a cup of coffee and a couple of donuts. I was starving, so I took them." He smiled as a United States Deputy Marshal led him away from me. *First a donut and coffee, then a steak and eggs. Before you know it, freedom on the table.*

I tried to reach Oscar Goodman by phone, but I learned he had already checked out of the Warwick Hotel. I went to the hotel lobby where I saw Philip's mother, Nancy. She asked me several questions about what might now happen to her son, and she, too, was peeved that Oscar was already in the air on his way back home to Las Vegas, while she and her son were frantically hoping to talk to him.

After the post-trial motions were denied, sentencing was scheduled for all the defendants in May 1989.

I still had to think about the appeal, the D'Alfonso murder trial was on the horizon, and the Noah Robinson case was listed for January 1989. I had little or no time to feel sorry for my clients or myself.

A month later I flew to Miami to spend Christmas with Rita. We would go to St. Barts for New Year's, where I would unwind and get myself physically and mentally ready for what seemed like a never-ending battle against the powers that be and the system that continued to stalk my clients and me.

▼ ▼ ▼

Ed Harrell and I arrived in Greenville, South Carolina, several days before the start of the trial. It was January 1989, but the weather was mild compared with Philadelphia. Actually it seemed like spring. Noah, still out on bail, greeted us at the airport and drove us to the Hyatt Hotel, only a couple of blocks from the small, brick building that housed the criminal courtrooms.

Members of the press from Chicago, Atlanta, and other major cities were already in Greenville, waiting for the all-important jury selection process to begin. The day after our arrival, the reporters wrote about the upcoming trial, prominently mentioning the fact that Noah Robinson was being represented by a "Philadelphia lawyer" who had represented "many mobsters including La Cosa Nostra boss Nicodemo Scarfo." The articles also made reference to my two indictments and acquittals. That was the baggage I brought with me.

Noah was not upset about the nature of the news stories, but I was wondering if they would adversely affect his chances of winning. This was not a bullshit case. We lose, and Noah was going to get the death penalty. I did not want Noah to be my first client lost to the executioner. As a matter of fact, I did not want anyone to be first.

That first morning in court I was taken by surprise by the local custom or rule of court which provided for the revocation of defendant's bail at the start of the trial. All further conferences with Noah would now be held either in the courthouse cellroom or the Greenville County Jail.

Jim Burgund, my jury expert, flew in to assist me in the jury selection process. Noah had also retained no less than three local lawyers to aid in his defense. He made it clear to them that I would be the lead counsel and have final say in the event we disagreed on how to proceed.

The courtroom was jammed with relatives and friends of Noah Robinson. Several of his brothers were always present, but Jesse Jackson never appeared. Noah and Jesse were born and raised in Greenville, and both later moved to Chicago.

When the first jury panel was brought in, I noticed that there were only about ten African Americans and maybe 90 whites. I knew race was going to be a factor in the jury selection. This trial was in the heart of Senator Strom Thurmond's conservative South Carolina, the Bible Belt, and of course, Bob Jones University.

The trial judge, Harry Moore, allowed quite a bit of leeway to the lawyers on both sides in the questioning of prospective jurors. Burgund gave me several questions to ask the prospective jurors about their personal lives and their likes and dislikes. I often relied on his ability to interpret and use the answers and information to determine a candidate's independence of the authorities' view of the evidence.

I recall one of the earliest prospective jurors testifying that she graduated from Bob Jones U. She went on to say that she went to Bob Jones High School before she entered college. To make matters worse, her two children were already matriculating at Bob Jones Elementary School, and she was planning for them to follow completely in her footsteps.

I was able to strike her for cause when she stated that she knew the wife of one of the local lawyers working with us. My colleague cautioned me that in his opinion she was probably too conservative and would be unsympathetic to the defense. Hello!

We only had seven peremptory challenges compared to 20 in a Pennsylvania first-degree murder case. In order for jurors to be qualified to sit, they must say that even if personally opposed to the death penalty, they would vote for it in an appropriate case. We lost several liberal-minded jurors who said they couldn't vote for the death penalty no matter what the evidence showed.

Because of the small number of challenges, I was forced to cross-examine jurors who I didn't want to sit in an effort to prove they were either prejudiced or held some bias against the defendant or in favor of the law enforcement authorities.

The prosecutor, Joe Watson, was a young, clean-cut man in his mid-thirties. He spoke with what I considered to be a southern accent. Of course, the jury would think it was I who had the accent. He was friendly to me and Ed, and he always seemed to have a smile on his face. He was an easy guy to like, and I knew that the jurors would consider him to be one of them.

The prosecutor, as expected, kept striking the black jurors, and we had ten white jurors already in the box with the hope of getting some African Americans fading fast. We were already through three panels, and Noah and I were both worried.

I knew from my notes that there were a couple of blacks on the tail end of the list who had not yet been called. This meant that I had to get the next couple of white jurors stricken for cause. Both the prosecution and the defense were almost out of peremptory challenges by this time.

The clerk called the next number, and a well-dressed white man, wearing a light blue seersucker suit, walked into the courtroom and took his seat in the witness box. The gentleman had gray hair combed neatly to the side with a part on the left. He was tan from playing a lot of golf.

Burgund and I read his questionnaire, and we saw that he recently sponsored a speaking engagement for Oliver North in Greenville. This guy had to go.

I started my interrogation:

Q. Were you one of the people who brought Oliver North to Greenville, South Carolina, to give a speech?
A. Yes.
Q. Do you adhere to most of his conservative philosophy?
A. Well, I agree with most of his ideas and what he had to say.
Q. Have you heard or read anything about the Reverend Jesse Jackson?
A. Of course I have.
Q. Would you agree that the Reverend Jesse Jackson's political philosophy is about 180 degrees from Oliver North's?
A. [He smiled] I would have to agree with that.
Q. You do know that the defendant Noah Robinson is the half-brother to Jesse Jackson?
A. Yes, I read that somewhere.
Q. Would that fact cause you to be unfair in deciding this case solely on the evidence?
A. Of course not.

Burgund and I huddled after the prospective juror answered all of the other questions in a manner that would make it impossible for us to strike him for cause. I whispered an idea I had into Jim's ear, and he nodded and whispered back, "Go ahead, try it. We have nothing to lose."

Q. You know that this is a death penalty case, don't you?

A. Yes, I do.

Q. Let me ask you, sir, if South Carolina passed a law abolishing the death penalty, would you approve of that?

A. I would move out of the state.

I couldn't help but smile when I heard this reply and heard the laughter from the spectator section of the courtroom. I heard Robinson whisper, "Thank God." I rose and addressed the judge. "Your Honor, I challenge this juror for cause. It seems this juror would vote for the death penalty no matter what the facts are."

"Granted," the judge said with no hesitation before the prosecutor could argue.

In the fourth day of jury selection, we finally landed a young African American woman as our eleventh juror. The prosecutor did not challenge her. He was well aware of the recent "Batson" decision in which the United States Supreme Court held that a prosecutor could not arbitrarily strike a black juror just because of race. To do so would result in a successful appeal and a new trial. By the next day, we had our twelfth juror and four alternates. The testimony would begin on the following Monday.

Downtown Greenville was very quiet at night. Jim Burgund, Ed Harrell, and I only ventured out of the hotel a few times. Most of the time we took our meals in the hotel restaurant. The food was excellent, and the people who worked in the hotel were extremely friendly. They offered us encouragement and always wished us luck with the case. For the most part these people were white. Not what I expected.

Over the weekend, I visited Noah a few times at the county jail. His spirits were high, and he was optimistic. The fact that he was a well-known black man about to be tried for murder in a southern city by a jury consisting of eleven white folks didn't seem to bother him. He kept telling me, "Bobby, this is your kind of case. You will destroy these witnesses on the stand."

Hambone Barber was shot and killed outside a poolroom-bar in downtown Greenville. Four black men from Chicago's South Side were supposed to have done him. All were members of the infamous gang called the "El Rukns." Three of the killers were going to testify that my client, Noah Robinson, paid them $10,000 to do the job. Two other members of the gang were also going to testify that they heard conversations between Noah and the four men in which the hit was discussed.

The leader of the gang was Jeff Forte. He was already serving a life sentence in Marion Federal Penitentiary for dealing drugs, weapons offenses, and several murders. Noah had hired many members of the El Rukns to work in his Wendy's restaurants as they were released on parole over the years. He claimed that he was trying to save these people from a life of crime by providing legitimate jobs for them.

A young black woman was a witness to the killing. Shortly after the shooting, she was stabbed by an individual named Freddy Sweeney. He would testify that Noah also paid him to kill the young lady. That testimony was his ticket to freedom.

Noah was also charged with that attempted murder and obstruction of justice. The state had evidence that Noah sent Sweeney a few money orders when he was running from the police that resulted in charges of being an accessory after the fact. I made the decision to try these cases together, at the same time. I knew we would be taking a gamble, but I thought this was the best way to save Robinson's life. I was really hoping that I could convince one jury that there was reasonable doubt on the murder count. I feared that a second trial and another jury of mostly whites might convict Noah of murder.

I was willing to concede that Noah sent the money orders to Sweeney, and therefore that he might be guilty of being an accessory after the fact. But we would strongly contest that he had anything to do with paying Sweeney to kill the young lady. Of course, Noah was denying any involvement in the Barber slaying whatsoever.

After Watson made his opening address outlining the charges and evidence, I strolled to the front of the jury box to speak. That, to me, is the most comfortable spot in the world.

I told them that Noah Robinson was a law-abiding citizen, a successful black entrepreneur who just happened to be the half-brother of Jesse Jackson. "And that is why he is here today . . . for no other reason." At that time "black" was politically correct. This jury would have thought Noah and I were from outer space if I said "African American." "You will hear, from the scum of the earth, nothing but lies about my client. Several men will testify that my client caused the death of Leroy 'Hambone' Barber when in fact these witnesses are only blaming my client to save their own lives." I spoke loudly and with emotion, a far cry from the manner they had just observed from the prosecutor. I definitely had their attention.

"Please wait until you have heard the cross-examination of these witnesses before you decide whether or not they are telling the truth." I held back some of what I expected to prove during the trial so as not to alert the opposition. This case was not unlike many others I had tried over the years, especially those in which Caramandi and DelGiorno had testified. I told the jurors that if they listened to the evidence they would have at least a reasonable doubt at the conclusion of the trial.

Noah was pleased with the opening address, but I was more concerned about the jury's reaction. I would have to wait and see.

The five El Rukns testified smoothly and effectively on direct examination. The cross-examination was easier than shooting ducks in a pond. They all had extensive criminal records including other murders, drug dealing, and extortion. All had been granted immunity as part of their deal. They knew that there would be no electric chair and a release from prison in the near future in exchange for their testimony.

Their stories were inconsistent on many points. Some of the jurors nodded when I pointed out the difference in the testimony of one as opposed to another. It seemed to me, although I couldn't prove it, that some of these informants were high from drugs while they were testifying. They, of course, denied this when asked.

At one point during the cross-examination, I was able to prove that on several occasions the five witnesses were in the same room at the same time while they were being prepared to testify. That would partially explain why their testimony was similar on some of the important facts.

Freddy Sweeney, a marijuana dealer from Greenville, testified that he tried to kill the young lady in her bedroom and that Noah put him up to it. He, too, was granted immunity from prosecution for the stabbing and several drug deals, just for saying that Noah asked him to do it.

On cross, I was able to trace him back to Chicago where he did some drug deals with the El Rukns. I tried to show that more than likely they, rather than Noah, hired him to kill the young lady.

Sweeney also admitted that Noah had helped a lot of black men by giving them financial aid in times of need. The inference was that Noah sent him money when he was on the run, but that by doing so, Noah wasn't automatically guilty of the attempted murder of either the witness or Barber.

Two police officers from Chicago testified that they were investigating the El Rukns for years and that Noah was deeply involved with the criminal organization. They played some tapes of conversations between Noah and Jeff Forte, trying to prove that Noah got the okay from the leader of the gang to hire these thugs to kill Barber. They failed.

Many character witnesses from Greenville testified on Noah's behalf. They said he was an honest man, a law-abiding citizen, and that he was born and raised in Greenville. Several of his friends and associates from Chicago also testified to his reputation and charitable work on behalf of the less fortunate.

The trial was close to the end. I walked into the courtroom after a lunch break. There were only a few people sitting there in the spectator section. There was no prosecutor or police official in sight. I looked for a court clerk or bailiff to find out if we had changed courtrooms. None was to be found.

Noah was not yet in the courtroom, and no one from the sheriff's office was around. It seemed mighty strange to me. Ed was out gathering some records for me, so I just sat there alone for about ten minutes.

One of the judge's secretaries stuck her head in the courtroom and then entered. "Oh, there you are, Mr. Simone. The judge would like to see you in his chambers." She left before I could ask her where everybody was.

I walked through the open space in the wooden railing, past the front of the bar, and opened the door leading to the judge's chambers. There was a crowd of about 20 people, some sitting in chairs and on the sofa and others standing. They were all leaning forward facing a small radio, listening attentively. The judge hardly acknowledged my presence. Joe Watson smiled and beckoned me to come over.

In a few seconds, I was able to discern that they were all listening to a basketball game. I heard the announcer say, "Time out." The judge looked up and said, "Welcome, Mr. Simone. Everything stops down here when Duke plays North Carolina. Come on in and listen to the game. We won't be starting until it's over."

This was a key game in the Atlantic Coast Conference. Noah Robinson's fight for his life had to take a back seat to a basketball game.

When the time arrived for the lawyers to make their summations, I knew that this was going to be just as important as the cross-examination of the state's main witnesses. I was more than ready. I had done this many times before, and even though the state was seeking the death penalty, there was nothing new here as far as I was concerned.

I tore right into the state's witnesses, calling them liars, rats, and lowlifes. "They informed to save their own lives. They should be on trial here, not Noah Robinson." I went over their crimes, including several murders, and asked, "How can you believe these people? How can he," I pointed to the prosecutor, "call them as witnesses, and deal with them . . . offer them freedom?"

I mentioned the amount of dope these witnesses admitted to putting out on the streets of Greenville and Chicago. How they were trying to ruin the lives of everyone with whom they came into contact. "This was a joke," I said.

"If my client wasn't Jesse's kin, he wouldn't be here. This is a political trial, and these people want to make him a political prisoner." The courtroom was quiet except for my words. The jurors were stone-faced, but they listened to every word.

The jurors had been sequestered for almost two weeks. I asked them, "How did you like being locked up in a hotel away from your loved ones, your families, and friends? Well, just imagine what they want to do to my client on the word of witnesses like these people." This was one of my familiar cries whenever I could get away with it.

Noah had not taken the stand in his own defense, so I told the jurors that it was my decision. I also reminded them that when they were being questioned, they promised they would follow the judge's instructions on the law, including not to draw any unfavorable inference from Noah's exercise of his constitutional right not to testify. I knew this was a tough sell, but it is one of those things a lawyer has to cover in his summation. Otherwise there would be a danger and invitation for jurors to allow themselves to think, "He didn't take the stand. He must be guilty."

I finished with, "Send Noah Robinson home to his family and community. Let the state know that you do not like the idea of freeing criminals . . . murderers . . . dope dealers who might just lie to get out of prison." Totally exhausted, I thanked the jury for their attention and took my seat.

Joe Watson would have the last summation—a tremendous advantage for the prosecutor in any trial. He spoke slowly and softly, and he covered every piece of evidence. "Thank God," I said to Noah, "that we have a couple of jurors who recently moved from the northeastern part of the country."

Watson's southern drawl wouldn't play well in a Philadelphia courtroom, but it seemed to be working here in Greenville. By the time he finished, I felt that our only hope was the one black woman juror. Would she be strong enough to hold out and cause a hung jury?

The judge charged the jury early Friday morning, and they were sent out to deliberate immediately. They stayed all day Friday into the early evening. Still no verdict. Judge Moore sent them back to the hotel and recessed court until Saturday morning at 9:00.

I saw Noah at the jail on Friday night, and I must say he was holding up better than I was. He was only a few steps away from the electric chair and yet his handsome face, with a strong resemblance to his famous brother's, managed to smile.

"What do you think, partner?" He sounded very much like my buddy Stanley Branche, who knew Noah and Jesse from the civil rights days of the sixties. Noah was extremely intelligent, and he had graduated with honors from the prestigious Wharton School of Business at the University of Pennsylvania.

"I don't know, Noah. Do you think our lady on the jury will crumble?"

"No way, partner. You did one helluva job."

If anything it seemed like he was trying to bolster my morale. He acted as if he was more concerned about me than he was about his own life. We talked for a while, hugged each other, and I left for the hotel. I knew I wouldn't be able to sleep.

I can't remember how many sleepless nights I had while waiting for juries to decide the fate of a client. The feeling never changes. My life would go into limbo. I couldn't do anything constructive or think about anything else. One would have to live through a similar experience to know the feeling.

On Saturday morning I made sure I was at the courthouse by 9:00. Ed and I walked the few blocks, and we speculated what the outcome would be.

The jury continued to deliberate for several more hours before the knock came on the door. That knock started a tremendous buzz that reverberated throughout the whole courtroom. I noticed several out-of-town TV crews were camped outside the courthouse next to the locals. Two cable networks, CNN and WGN, were there as well as a crew from CBS. Whatever the verdict, this was to be a big story.

Russell Ghent, one of my local co-counsels, heard that one of the jurors had a relative who personally knew Joseph Watson, the prosecutor. How he learned this and what it might mean, I didn't know.

The jurors walked in slowly, took their seats, and the foreman rose to answer the judge's question. "Your Honor, we have a partial verdict, but we are hopelessly deadlocked on most of the charges."

The judge asked the jurors, "Do you believe that further deliberations will result in reaching a verdict on the charges you have not agreed upon?"

The foreman said, "No, Your Honor."

The judge sent the jury back to the deliberation room and called the lawyers to the bench. Everything seemed to be happening very fast—too fast. In a matter of only a couple of minutes, the jury was back in the court-room.

The foreman rose again and answered the questions put to him by the judge's clerk:

> Q. Have you reached a verdict on the count charging Noah Robinson with first-degree murder?
> A. No, Your Honor, we are deadlocked.
> Q. With regard to conspiracy to commit murder, do you have a verdict?
> A. No, Your Honor, we are deadlocked.

Both Noah and I breathed a sigh of relief. The spectators, most of whom were friends and family of Robinson, cheered. I guess they were satisfied. I wasn't sure myself. Noah shook my hand under the table, concealing his gesture from the jurors. It was not over yet.

> Q. Have you reached a verdict on the count charging Noah Robinson with attempted murder of Janice Rosemund [The young lady who was stabbed]?
> A. No, Your Honor.
> Q. Have you reached a verdict on the charge of being an accessory after the fact in the attempted murder of Janice Rosemund?
> A. Yes, Your Honor, we find the defendant guilty.

Noah looked at me, and he shrugged his shoulders as if to say, "Now what?" or "So what?" I am not sure which.

Before I had a chance to respond, Judge Moore ordered Noah to stand up.

"I sentence you, Noah Robinson, to ten years in the state prison." Things were not just happening fast—now they were flying.

I asked the local lawyers, "What the fuck is going on here? We haven't had a chance to appeal to the trial court. There is no pre-sentence investigation, and I didn't have an opportunity to argue in mitigation of a sentence."

"That's the way we do things here, Bob," one of them said. "But don't worry about it, ten years means two years have to be served, and we can still appeal and get bail set."

I stood up and asked the judge to set bail for the appeal and the charges remaining open because of the hung jury.

He answered, "Bail is set in the amount of $500,000."

Noah whispered to me, "Ask if we can put up real estate."

I did so, and Judge Moore stated on the record that the defendant could post unencumbered real estate in lieu of cash for bail. I knew it would take at least a few days to arrange for the posting of bail, but at least Noah would be out while his appeal was pending.

That afternoon and evening, I ate and drank with Ed Harrell and Jim Burgund, who returned to hear the verdict. This was a big case for him and his résumé. I wasn't sure if I was celebrating or not. At that time all I knew was that Noah was not convicted of murder. His life was spared, at least for the time being. I have heard several lawyers say that "A hung jury is like kissing your sister." Ed Harrell, Jim Burgund, and I felt that the black woman on the jury saved Noah from taking the fall. I went to sleep early that night. I felt the need to stay at least until I was sure that my client would make bail. I was also there in the event that I was needed to review any of the complicated paperwork in posting real estate for bail.

Early the next morning the phone rang. "Congratulations, Bob. Great job. I told you, you buried those guys." It was Noah.

"What are you talking about?" I said. "What's the big deal in getting one juror to go our way?"

"You didn't see the paper yet, did you? The vote was ten to two for not guilty, and the prosecutor said he wasn't sure if he would try me again." The result was looking better now.

I jumped out of bed with the phone still in my hand. "I'll be over to see you in an hour."

The news articles quoted several jurors saying, "We just couldn't accept the word of all the state's witnesses. If we thought that the judge was going to give Mr. Robinson more than 30 days in jail, we never would have convicted him of that one charge."

I visited with Noah for a few hours, made sure he was getting out on bail, and then Ed and I left for the airport. We arrived in Philadelphia on Sunday night. You got it—in a couple of days, Rita and I were back in St. Barts, where I wish I were now.

Noah Robinson returned to Chicago. Within a matter of a few months he called me for representation again. The federal government did to him what they did to Nicky Scarfo. They charged Noah in a RICO case and included the Hambone Barber murder and the Janice Rosemund stabbing as predicate acts. Double jeopardy be damned! I shall never understand the legality of charging citizens with crimes for which they have already been tried.

There was still plenty of work for me to do in Philadelphia, not the least of which had to do with defending Nicodemo Scarfo in the Frank D'Alfonso murder trial and preparing appeal papers and legal arguments for the RICO case. I also had approximately 20 non-jury state trials on my calendar, but I knew that I'd be going to Chicago for Noah in the near future.

CHAPTER THIRTY

▼

Best of Friends

The D'Alfonso murder trial was assigned to Judge Herbert Clark, a short, thin, light-skinned African American jurist who had a reputation for being fair and mild-mannered. It was only four months since the guilty verdicts were returned in the RICO case when we started to pick a jury, which again took almost a month. It was a tough thing to do after all the recent prejudicial publicity.

Charles "Joey" Grant, a handsome, well-dressed, smiling prosecutor, was assigned to try the case. I knew he was going to be a worthy and dangerous opponent as soon as I met him. That was at the first status call before the trial started.

At first there were nine defendants: Nicodemo Scarfo, Joseph Ligambi, Frank Iannarella, and three sets of brothers—Salvatore and Lawrence Merlino, Frank Jr. and Philip Narducci, and Nicholas and Eugene Milano. Joseph Ligambi, one of the alleged shooters, was the only defendant who was not convicted of serious RICO charges in federal court. He made a wise decision to plead guilty to gambling charges before the trial started in exchange for a three-year sentence.

Just before the testimony was to commence, the prosecutor notified the defense lawyers that Eugene Milano had jumped ship and was going to testify as a Commonwealth witness. Yes, that meant he would testify against his own brother as well as the other defendants.

Up to this point, all the defendants, except Eugene Milano, and their lawyers felt the chances for an acquittal were good. As in the Testa trial, the jury would hear evidence of only one murder. But now we were faced with a new, likeable prosecutor with plenty of jury appeal and a new witness, Eugene Milano. Milano had been a good friend to Sal Testa and he was saddened by his murder. He was privy to most of the defense's trial strategy, having been locked up with all of his co-defendants for the past year.

I recall retreating with the other defense attorneys to Bob Madden's office directly across the street from City Hall where we discussed what action, if any, to take. We read several recent cases dealing with factual circumstances similar to what we now confronted. The decisions indicated that there was a strong possibility of "an invasion into the defense camp and an unfair look at its strategy."

Some of my colleagues wanted to request a hearing to determine what, if anything, Eugene Milano had told the prosecutors about how the defense intended to try the case. Besides his daily conversations with eight co-defendants he had sat with all the accused and their lawyers while jury selection proceeded.

I argued with some of my friends on the defense team about what we should do. I was in favor of doing nothing, because I firmly believed that if we were granted a hearing, Milano would testify that he did not divulge anything about defense strategy to the prosecutors. I also knew in my heart that Grant and those assisting him would swear that they purposely refrained from asking Milano anything that would compromise the defense strategy.

Most of the other lawyers and all of the defendants accepted the decision to go forward with the trial without such a hearing. Maybe the judge would continue with the trial without giving us the required hearing. If so, we had an excellent chance of winning an appeal should we lose. That is exactly what happened.

Caramandi and DelGiorno were their usual selves. They pointed the finger at each defendant and told the jurors what each had said and done in the plot to kill "Flowers."

The cross-examination by all the lawyers went well, or so we thought. By now we had more material and hundreds of pages of testimony from the other trials to use in attacking their credibility. The extensive criminal records and other crimes for which they weren't charged again were presented to the jury. The favorable treatment they received from state and federal agents was also explored.

Both Caramandi and DelGiorno were housed in expensive resorts where they ate and drank as guests of the government. They were each given large sums of money to pay for all their bills and to live the lavish lifestyle to which they were accustomed. At one point Tommy Del was even allowed the services of a hooker.

When Milano took the stand, the courtroom was as quiet as a church. The jurors listened to every word as he told how he and his brother stalked

D'Alfonso before he was shot and killed. He testified that the order came from my client, Nick Scarfo, and that the shooters were Philip Narducci and Joe Ligambi. He was deliberate and soft-spoken with every answer.

When asked, "How can you testify against your own kid brother?" Eugene Milano said, "I tried to convince him to come with me . . . go with the law into protective custody. But he wouldn't budge." Milano was a convincing and believable witness. He had no criminal record to speak of, and impeaching him was no easy task.

Joey Grant put on two eyewitnesses who testified that they saw Frank D'Alfonso shot by two men. The shooters then jumped into a getaway car that sped from the scene. Neither witness could identify the shooters, but this testimony corroborated the words of DelGiorno, Caramandi, and Milano.

Joey Grant stood before the jury in his dark blue suit, pale blue shirt, and red and blue tie, and argued that he had proved the guilt of each and every defendant. He said, "Mr. Simone tells you that these defendants are being treated like the union leaders in the '30s, the Japanese Americans in the '40s, the liberals in the '50s, the civil rights advocates of the '60s, and the anti-war demonstrators of the '70s. Well, these defendants acted like a bunch of wild criminal animals in the street . . . worse than the wolf packs who roam the streets of Philadelphia committing vicious crimes."

"Objection! Objection!" shouted a few of the defense attorneys.

"Overruled," answered Judge Clark.

By the time Joey Grant completed his final argument there was no question in my mind that the jury was going to convict all the defendants. The jury loudly announced that they found each one guilty of first-degree murder and conspiracy. Some of the spectators jeered and others merely moaned.

The judge excused us for the rest of the day but told us to return in the morning to address and argue the penalty phase of the case. Eight lives were on the line. All the lawyers went back to Bob Madden's office across the street so that we could discuss how we were going to handle the issue of life or death. I hadn't had a cigarette for over nine months, but as soon as I walked into the conference room, I said, "Somebody give me a fucking cigarette!"

The prosecutor had notified us before the trial that he intended to seek the death penalty in the event of a conviction. At that time he claimed there was an "aggravating circumstance," in that one or two bullets ricocheted at the time of the shooting, causing a danger to the witnesses in the area.

When court was reconvened the next morning, Grant added another aggravating circumstance in his bid to win a death penalty verdict. He said that since the defendants (except for Ligambi) were recently convicted of multiple murders in the federal RICO trial, they were candidates for the death penalty.

Joey Grant did not recall the eyewitnesses to the stand, but he did call a homicide detective to testify where he found bullet holes and markings in the vicinity of the shooting. My colleagues and I cross-examined the detective, and he had to answer that he couldn't be sure when the other holes or markings first appeared at the scene. They could have been there prior to the time that Flowers was shot. It also seemed to me that Joey Grant was not pressing as hard as he could have while he was questioning the detective.

Next, we went to sidebar to argue the admissibility of the RICO conviction. The jury sat stone-faced in their seats all the while. I argued that the conviction wasn't final under the law since the defendants still had motions for a new trial pending, and that they had not been sentenced.

One of my colleagues argued that the defendants had not even been arrested or charged with any of the other murders at the time D'Alfonso was shot. Grant remained silent, and the judge said, "I am inclined to agree with the defense and not submit the other evidence of the convictions on the RICO case."

Grant did not argue the point. Then several of the defense attorneys asked the judge to dismiss the death penalty from the case. They argued that the Commonwealth had not proved the first aggravating circumstance—danger to others. Grant again said nothing.

Judge Clark stated, "I am not sending the death penalty decision to the jury. There is insufficient evidence of any aggravating circumstances." He repeated his remarks to the jurors—for the record and for all the spectators to hear.

Nicky and the others smiled. They knew that their lives had been spared. I honestly felt that if the issue had gone to the jury there would have been a death penalty sentence. I was quoted in the newspapers saying, "I felt like we just came out of the grave."

Two years later the Superior Court of Pennsylvania reversed the conviction and granted a new trial on two major grounds. First, the trial judge erred when he did not hold a hearing to determine whether or not Eugene Milano disclosed inside defense strategies to the prosecutors. The second basis for a new trial was that Grant, the prosecutor, had gone too far in his summation when he referred to the defendants as "a group of wild criminal animals . . . worse than a wolf pack."

The defendants were retried in 1997 and all were found not guilty. I was not in the courtroom during any part of the second trial.

Shortly after the guilty verdict in the Flowers case and only days before the sentencing in the federal RICO case, Lawrence "Yogi" Merlino joined the list of defectors. He started to cooperate with local and federal law enforcement agencies. He supplied them with information relating to some of the yet-unsolved murders of the past decade.

In May 1989, the defendants in the RICO case were sentenced at separate hearings. Nicky Scarfo was last. Before the judge pronounced sentence, I told the court, paraphrasing Oscar Wilde, "Sometimes the people in the business of punishing criminals do more damage to society than the criminals themselves." I also said, "Mr. Scarfo does not need a speech at this time in his life."

Judge Franklin Van Antwerpen abided by my request and refrained from making any profound statements about Nicodemo Scarfo's "now proven" life of crime. He merely sentenced Nicky to the maximum sentence of 55 years.

It was to run consecutively with the 14 years Nicky was now serving as a result of the Rouse extortion conviction. The judge also stated that the 55-year sentence was to run consecutively with the life sentence recently imposed by Judge Clark in the Flowers case.

Strange as it might seem, Judge Clark had also ordered his life sentence to run consecutively with any sentence imposed in the RICO case. This confusion was to be unraveled in the future when the Flowers conviction was reversed on appeal.

Philip Leonetti was sentenced to 45 years in prison a few hours earlier than his Uncle Nick. The other 15 defendants received sentences ranging from 30 to 45 years.

I returned to my office to learn that Philip was on the line. I picked up the phone and he said, "The same FBI agents talked to me again. The ones that gave me the coffee and donuts. They want me to cooperate. They're asking me about 'The Apple.'"

Philip's comments took me by surprise. When I weighed his words, I came to the conclusion that Philip was telling me that the Feds were thinking about offering him a deal for early release in exchange for his testimony. "The Apple" meant New York. I also thought Philip was trying to tell me that he was going to give them information about John Gotti, then awaiting trial in a murder-RICO case in Manhattan. I deluded myself into thinking he was trying to tell me, "Don't worry, they are not asking about you. I wouldn't hurt you if they were."

I managed to see Philip and Nicky a few more times at the local jail before Nicky was shipped to Marion, Illinois. There Nick was locked in a small cell where he ate, slept, and watched television for $22^1/_2$ hours a day, seven days a week.

A month or so after Nicky's transfer, Philip Leonetti made his deal with the government. He went into the Witness Protection Program. I learned much later that his mom, Nancy, with the knowledge and approval of the FBI, went to Nicky's apartment on Georgia Avenue in Atlantic City where she had a section of drywall torn out. A safe was hidden behind the wall. The estimate of how much cash was in the safe ranges from $1 million to $3 million.

Nancy Leonetti, the only sister of Nicodemo Scarfo, joined her son, grandson, and Philip's girlfriend in the Witness Protection Program. With at least a million tax-free dollars at their disposal, they didn't have very much to worry about financially.

When these facts were confirmed, I made my first call to Marion Federal Penitentiary to talk to my client. It was not easy telling Nicky that his beloved nephew and his only sister had betrayed him. To this day, Nicky has not gotten over the shock. In his mind he has disowned them both. Whenever Nicky refers to Philip, he calls him "my lying ex-nephew."

A couple of months later, early in 1990, I received a telephone call from FBI agent Mike Leyden, asking to meet me in Rittenhouse Square, a park within a block of my office. The park is slightly larger than two square city blocks. Adjacent to it sit two hotels. The Barclay is located at 18th and Locust Streets, and The Rittenhouse stands at 19th and Walnut Streets. Surrounding Rittenhouse Square are numerous high-rise apartment houses, most of them exclusive. The neighborhood also consists of several fashionable townhouses and numerous trendy shops. From that time to today the neighborhood has changed with the addition of new sidewalk cafés, restaurants, and hotels.

The park itself is always crowded when the weather is decent. The grass is usually trimmed and watered to maintain its rich, green look. Colorful flowerbeds and benches sit on the sides of the winding concrete sidewalks. In addition there are numerous statues of animals spread throughout the park. Rittenhouse Square is a popular place for lovers.

Leyden and I agreed to meet at the statue of a ram. I walked to the park and there he was, standing by the horned statue with Klaus Rorer, the agent-in-charge of organized crime investigations in Philadelphia. We walked through the park for only a few minutes. Leyden said, "I want you to know that your buddy, Philip Leonetti, is saying things about you. He told us that you were criminally involved with him and his uncle."

"I can't imagine Philip saying I did anything illegal. He, better than anyone, knows that I just acted as his uncle's lawyer."

Rorer answered by saying, "You know when someone goes into 'the program,' they have to tell all."

I then said, "Well, I gotta tell you. I am disappointed in Philip. I always cared for him, and I thought he was my friend. I can't believe he is going to lie about me."

Leyden added, "We are here to offer you the Witness Protection Program. It might be the best thing for you."

I looked at both of them. I could tell they were just going through the motions. They did not believe for a minute that I would fold and embrace what they were suggesting.

"Well, thanks for telling . . . warning me. I guess I'll be seeing you guys around." We shook hands, and I turned and left the park. As I walked to my office, I said to myself, "Poor Philip. He must be desperate to turn on me like this. Angelo Bruno was right, 'you can't trust anybody.'" Yes, I was talking to myself.

As soon as I got back to the office, I rifled through several files containing letters I had received from Nicky and Philip during their incarceration. I remembered receiving letters from Philip thanking me for all I had done for him. He also wrote words to the effect, "It's a shame the Feds are always bothering you just because you're a good lawyer. Everybody knows you never did anything wrong."

I searched for over an hour, but I just couldn't find the letter I was looking for. I lit a cigarette, leaned back in my chair, and thought about my relationship with Philip Leonetti.

I was instrumental in saving him from life in prison and the death penalty so many times. But it was more than that. When his uncle went to jail back in the early eighties, Philip and I traveled to El Paso several times. We spent many hours sipping scotches and talking on those long flights.

We dined and drank in just about every fine restaurant in Philadelphia, Atlantic City, and Fort Lauderdale. Often it was just the two of us. Many times when he offered to compensate me for legal work, I declined to accept. I never took advantage of him.

I told the jury and announced to the world, in open court during the Testa trial, that "He was my best friend." I remember all the times that he smiled at me when his uncle said something that he thought surprised me. On rare occasions, when Nicky would seem angry or disappointed with Philip, I would intervene and straighten out the problem.

Then there was the case in Newark. I testified at the disqualification hearing so that I might continue to represent him as he so dearly wished. That gesture nearly cost me my license and my freedom.

My thoughts drifted to St. Barts a few years before. *I had left the beach and walked to the miniature airport terminal some small distance from the Filao Hotel. I decided to purchase a small, yellow jeep, called a mini-moke, for getting around on the island. After all, Rita and I were visiting St. Barts every couple of months. With the frequency of our visits, it was more economical to buy this vehicle than to rent one.*

I had just shaken the hand of the French salesman, Henri, after completing the deal on the car when I turned, in a hurry to get back to the beach, and literally bumped into Philip. He had been standing there with his girlfriend, watching me all the while. I couldn't believe it. He had never been to the island before. I wasn't expecting him.

"Bobby, look at you . . . no shoes, no shirt, in a bathing suit, driving a jeep," he said, smiling broadly. We hugged and patted each other on the back.

"Phil, it's great to see you," I said. "How long are you staying? When did you get here?"

Then it all registered. He was free on rather strict bail conditions set by Judge Ackerman in Newark. He was not allowed to leave New Jersey.

"Did you get permission to come here?" I asked.

"Well, Bob, it's like this. Right after you left I was arrested by the state for signing a false affidavit. It had something to do with a construction job. My uncle got really pissed because I didn't show you the document before I signed it. He hollered at me and called me stupid and other names. I couldn't take it anymore, so I left."

"Who knows you're here? Did you call Gus Newman, the court, anybody, to get permission?" I asked.

We walked over to the small, square-shaped bar in the terminal and ordered a beer. Philip and his lady looked out the large, open window to the twin-peaked mountain and the single-engine airplane that had just flown them into St. Barts. The view extended down the black-topped runway, ending at the beach and the smooth, clear-blue water of the Bay of St. Jean.

"This is even more beautiful than you said it was," Philip mused as he sipped his cold glass of American beer.

He went on to tell me that he left Atlantic City without telling anyone. He was in violation of his bail conditions. He was in the doghouse with his uncle, who by now was probably even more pissed because he disappeared. He didn't seem to care.

It took me the better part of two hours on the telephone, making international calls to Newman in New York and Nicky in Atlantic City, before I was able to salvage Philip's bail and square things for him with his uncle.

Philip couldn't get a flight back to Atlantic City for about 36 hours, so he was "forced" to stay in St. Barts. He came to see me because there was really no one else he trusted and in whom he could confide. He loved the white, sandy beach and the warm, clear-blue sea.

"Now I know why you come here so often," he said.

Little did he know that my main reason for coming to St. Barts was to get away from the everyday stress that came with representing him and his uncle, and the personal legal problems that went with the job—all of which I could put out of my mind while on this quiet, beautiful island.

Before Philip left the island, we took some pictures at the bar adjacent to the beach at the Filao Hotel. I gave him an enlarged copy of a couple of them. Months later, I saw one displayed prominently in his apartment in Longport. Anyone looking at the picture could tell we were the best of friends.

When I looked at the ashtray in front of me on my desk, I saw that I had actually smoked about ten cigarettes during the time I sat there thinking about Philip Leonetti, my friend.

I lit yet another cigarette. I just couldn't get my mind to focus on anyone or anything else. *I remembered the frequent rides he and I took on my small speedboats,* Next Case, No Problem, *and* Just Us. *Then I drifted to the many times we sat high up on the bridge of his uncle's 40-foot cruiser. He was in another world when he piloted that boat. He loved the water. I knew how much he missed the sea while he was in prison. Well, maybe not.*

I thought he was probably sitting in a boat right now because he did what "they" wanted him to do—deliver Bobby Simone on a silver platter. The Feds knew that they wouldn't be able to convict me on the testimony of Caramandi and DelGiorno or even some others that they had standing in the wings. All of them were lined up waiting to make a deal for freedom in exchange for testimony against the troublesome "mob lawyer."

There was no guarantee that I was going to be indicted again. But I also knew that if Philip lied about the Rouse case, I would be in a world of trouble. At this time I had no idea as to what Philip was saying. For some reason I still felt confident that he wouldn't lie. If that was the case, I really didn't have a problem.

The phone rang, and I picked up the receiver. It was Noah Robinson. "How ya doin', partner?"

I recognized the voice immediately. "Hi, Noah."

"Well, it happened. I've been indicted twice here in Chicago. I need you to come and talk to me about representation. There's an arraignment next week." He repeated, "I need you."

In seconds Philip Leonetti was out of my thoughts. "Sure, Noah. I'll see you in a couple of days."

Just what I needed, a cause other than my own.

CHAPTER THIRTY-ONE

▼

Is This the End of Rico?

I flew into the Windy City and took a cab directly to the Metropolitan Correctional Center in the heart of the Loop. Noah had copies of the indictments against him. I read them as he watched me and tried to supply additional facts relating to the charges and the cases in general.

Noah, two of his brothers, and his wife were charged with a RICO conspiracy. The gist of the allegations was that Noah ordered the cash registers turned off from 12:00 midnight to 6:00 a.m. every business day to avoid an accurate and full recording of the receipts in several of his Wendy's restaurants.

The government claimed that by doing so Robinson did not have to pay full state and federal taxes on the income and also was able to fraudulently lower the amount of royalties he was obligated to pay to Wendy's parent company. Noah's corporation had filed a Chapter 11 bankruptcy petition that caused an added charge of bankruptcy fraud. Noah's wife and brothers were charged with aiding and abetting Noah in the scheme.

The other indictment charged Noah and approximately 65 members of the El Rukns with racketeering. The predicate offenses were drug dealing, extortion, and multiple murders, including the murder of Leroy "Hambone" Barber and the attempted murder of Janice Rosemund, the same crimes charged in Greenville. Noah was the first and only client I ever had who was charged in two RICO indictments at the same time. It was the answer to

Edward G. Robinson's dying question as "Little Caesar": No, this is not the end of Rico.

The RICO-fraud trial lasted about a month. Rita came to spend about a week with me during the trial, just as she had earlier flown to Greenville for a long weekend. There was plenty for us to do in Chicago in the limited spare time I had. We visited the famous Chicago Art Institute and took in a breathtaking Monet exhibit, saw the *Phantom of the Opera,* went to Wrigley Field to see the L.A. Dodgers trounce the Cubs, and dined at Morton's, The Pump Room, and Rosebuds.

That was the good news. The bad news was that Noah, who remained in jail without bail, was convicted mainly on the testimony of his accountant and several employees. They testified that the cash registers were turned off in the mornings, and the sales were added up on hand calculators, but not added to the day's receipts.

The jury hung on Noah's wife, and she was granted a mistrial. She later pled guilty to avoid a prison sentence. His brothers were convicted and later sent to prison for a couple of years.

The judge in Chicago listed Noah's sentencing in the RICO-fraud case. The United States Attorney was looking to obtain a 12-to-13-year sentence under the harsh, new federal sentencing guidelines. Instead the judge gave Noah five and a half years. Noah also received credit for a few years he had already served, so the result was not that bad. I know, easy for me to say.

Later that day, Noah called me just as I was about to leave my hotel room for the airport. "Bobby, you won't believe this. No sooner did I get back to jail than the IRS agent on the case comes to see me."

"You're kidding."

"No, I am not," he answered. "And do you know what he wanted? You! He said if I tell him everything that I know about you of a criminal nature, I can get the sentence cut. Man, they really want your ass."

The government wanted me so bad it seemed that they were willing to let any of my clients who lost their cases out of prison just for information on me.

Noah continued, "I chased that motherfucker out of here. Man, you saved my life in South Carolina. I'm never gonna forget that. And besides, I ain't no rat." A better man than Philip Leonetti, that's for sure.

I returned to Philadelphia a few days after sentencing in early 1990. At about this same time, Philip Leonetti testified against John Gotti before the grand jury in New York City. He also appeared as a witness against several of his father's friends and associates in Philadelphia, Boston, and New Jersey. The government won convictions in all the trials in which Philip testified.

While in Philadelphia, I learned that the U.S. Attorney's Office had two separate grand juries investigating me as if I was Charles Manson. Leonetti was the main witness, and there were others against me who would also say anything to get out of jail.

Then it happened. Rita was served with a subpoena to testify before one of the grand juries. In addition the subpoena called for her to pose for photographs, give handwriting samples, and be fingerprinted. This was not some unusual ploy by unscrupulous prosecutors and agents. They do it all the time. "Hassle the family if we can't shake the target."

It wasn't long after that she flew to Florida to get away from it all. I couldn't fault her. She had stood by me for years. But it was now obvious that the situation was never going to change. Not until I was either shot or put in jail. I do not believe she wanted to be there to witness such an event.

Rita came back to Philadelphia a couple of weeks later, but it wasn't the same. We didn't make the final split until after the Christmas holidays of 1990, and our last visit to St. Barts. We spent a rather quiet New Year's, then parted company in San Juan. She flew to Miami, and I returned to Philadelphia to fight what had become "the never-ending battle."

A month or two later she returned to Philadelphia, but only to pack her clothing and personal belongings. I air-freighted them on to Miami after she left. I was devastated and in no mood to think about what I still had to confront. It definitely wouldn't be the same without Rita at my side.

▼ ▼ ▼

Marvin Aspen was a bright, experienced, and no-nonsense United States District Court Judge. He issued an opinion severing the El Rukns case into five separate trials. If all those indicted were to go to trial at the same time before the same judge and jury, the prospects of a fair trial would have been very dim indeed. A single trial also may very well have taken more than a year to complete.

Even with the severance, Noah went to trial with six others, all of whom were alleged to be high-ranking members of the El Rukns. The trial lasted approximately four months. The government's case depended heavily on the testimony of six former gang leaders, three of whom had already testified in the murder trial in Greenville. Between them they had killed over 50 human beings. "So what?" as Judge Giles would say.

The Ritz-Carlton, one of the finest hotels in Chicago, was home to me for the duration of the trial. When I was in Chicago for Noah's first trial, I stayed at the Ambassador East, also a great spot.

Noah agreed that I should fly back to Philadelphia every third weekend or so in order to make sure my office was in order. He also retained Anita Rivkin-Carouthers, a local criminal lawyer, to assist me in his defense. I found Anita to be pleasant and personable, and one of the best-dressed women I ever met. More importantly, she was a talented, devoted, and experienced lawyer. We got along beautifully from the very beginning.

I made the opening address on behalf of Noah and cross-examined most of the government's witnesses, particularly the six El Rukns. Anita handled several other witnesses on cross, but was primarily responsible for preparing and questioning the defense witnesses on direct examination.

I specifically recall that Ronald J. Clark proved himself to be an excellent lawyer in a very tough case. I spent many nights having cocktails and dinner with Ron and Anita. Chicago has more than its fair share of great restaurants, and I felt very much at home with Anita, Ron, and Adam Bourgois, Noah's civil lawyer, showing me their city. Adam also represented Dick Gregory, the comedian and former civil rights activist. Once I stood in for Adam at a hearing in federal court in Philadelphia. Mr. Gregory was very gracious in thanking me. The hearing involved a civil matter in which Adam's client was very much in the right.

At Noah's trial all of the prosecution witnesses testified, as these types usually do, that they had now "seen the light and were turning over a new leaf." The jury seemed to disregard all the answers we elicited on cross as it convicted all seven defendants. Judge Aspen sentenced Noah and four others to life in prison without parole. Two were sentenced to very long terms, long enough to guarantee they would not be able to get a driver's license due to age or infirmity. They'd never even get a traffic ticket again.

A few years later, all these convictions and most of the convictions in the other trials were reversed. The grounds of reversal were that several of the witnesses were doing drugs, selling drugs, having sex with furnished prostitutes, and receiving other special favors while they were cooperating with the prosecution. To make matters worse, the witnesses denied these facts in testimony at trial. Worse still, the lead prosecutor and some of his aides knew what was going on and failed to disclose this strong impeachment material to the defense. The prosecution willfully suborned perjury and obstructed justice.

Can you imagine what the government would have done to me if I had been caught treating my witnesses in the manner that this prosecutor treated his? They would have thrown away the key and piped sunlight down to me. But for the government this is business as usual, ultimately coupled with freedom for the witnesses to boot. The prosecutor in this case was merely transferred to another district after being censured. A slap on the wrist. And they call this justice and themselves the Department of Justice.

So what happens next? The prosecution buys some other criminals to act as their witnesses. They gain another conviction against Noah and his co-defendants. Appeals are now pending. And the beat goes on.

I recently learned that Noah, still fighting for his freedom and vindication, met Nick Scarfo in prison. There he told Nick, "Bobby saved my life and I shall never forget that. I'll never be able to thank him enough." *Do you get that, Philip?*

During the El Rukns trial in 1991 there were several three- or four-day weekends which afforded me the opportunity to fly back to Philadelphia, though now there wasn't much of a reason to do so. Rita was living and working in Miami.

On one such long weekend, while I was in Philadelphia, I received a call from someone in the U.S. Attorney's Office, asking me to meet him outside the chambers of one of the local federal judges. I was told that the meeting related to my own legal situation. I called my friend, Bob Madden, and he agreed to join me.

When we met in the judge's chambers and I observed a stenographer present, I knew this was serious business. The government was close to obtaining two separate criminal indictments against me — one for alleged non-payment of taxes, similar to the case I had won in 1984, and the other having something to do with my relationship with Nicodemo Scarfo and his nephew, Philip Leonetti. They refused to divulge any more information about the second indictment.

The prosecutors knew that I was presently representing Noah Robinson in Chicago, a case that was getting quite a bit of media coverage. Any publicity bound to come as soon as I was indicted could cause a mistrial. The prosecution was more concerned about the statute of limitations running out. Whatever it was they were going to charge me with occurred almost five years before. They did not want to lose another opportunity to take me from the courthouse to the jailhouse.

After talking it over with Madden, I agreed on the record to waive the statute of limitations. I further agreed not to object to the sealing and impounding of the indictments. That would prevent the newspapers and television stations from obtaining and disseminating the information and more importantly, protect my clients' right to a fair trial.

I also informed the judge and the prosecutors that while I was in Chicago I had been retained by another individual who was to proceed to trial shortly after the El Rukns case. The prosecutors agreed to wait until after the verdict in the second trial in Chicago before holding their usual press conference. Of course, this would be done before my trial in a blatantly obvious ploy to prejudice potential jurors.

My daughter, Kim, was living with me in my three-bedroom apartment in Independence Place. She had moved from Miami and was attending the Art Institute of Philadelphia. Whenever I returned from Chicago for a short stay, Kim would always ask, "How are you, Dad?" She was concerned about the recent separation from Rita and how I was handling it, although she never said so. I had not yet told her about my new legal problems.

One day I walked into the apartment, all smiles. Kim looked at me and asked, "Why are you so happy?"

I told her I had just met an American beauty on the elevator. "Gorgeous blonde" is how I described her.

Kim asked if I spoke to her. I said, "No." She shook her head and said, "Big deal. It looks like you are going to continue to mope around here forever."

Within days I saw the young lady again. This time I took advantage of the situation and introduced myself. The following weekend I flew back from

Chicago to take her out to dinner. Jennifer was not only beautiful, she was intelligent and pleasant as well. On our first date we drank champagne, ate strawberries, and even danced.

In a matter of a couple of weeks, she flew with me to Chicago. We wined and dined between court appearances. Unfortunately, she had to go back to work. I found myself very saddened by her departure. However, I now had a reason to come home on weekends. My black mood began to change. I felt rejuvenated. I stopped worrying about the problems looming in the future and started to enjoy life again.

Right after the verdict in the El Rukns trial, Jennifer and I flew to Naples, Florida, to spend a week relaxing in the sun. It wasn't St. Barts, but being with Jennifer more than made up for that. If only she didn't beat me in golf.

After stopping in Philadelphia for a few days, it was back to Chicago. I was representing my new client, Bobby Bellavia, in yet another RICO trial.

▼ ▼ ▼

Approximately 20 men were indicted in this massive RICO case. They were charged with multiple illegal gambling violations, a series of extortions, and two murders, added to give the case a touch of violence. Murder, whether real or even pertinent to the case, always helped the prosecutors in their claims of working to stamp out "organized crime."

The government was alleging that the defendants were part of "The Outfit," a name used in Chicago for the mob. The "crew" that was to go on trial consisted of Rocco "Rocky" Infelice (the alleged leader), Salvatore "Solly" DeLaurentis, Louis Marino, Robert "Bobby" Salerno, and my client, Robert "Bobby" Bellavia. The other 15 indicted defendants pled guilty to RICO and conspiracy before the trial. They admitted to participating in a giant bookmaking operation on behalf of "The Outfit."

My buddy from New York, Bruce Cutler, represented Solly DeLaurentis. Pat Tuite, a well-known and very capable Chicago defense lawyer, represented Rocky. Terry Gillespie was counsel for Bobby Salerno, and former U.S. District Court Judge George Layton and Joanne Wolfson represented Louis Marino. All the lawyers were experienced and highly qualified.

The key witness for the prosecution was William "B.J." Jahoda. A Chicago bookmaker and expert on illegal gambling, he would identify each defendant and try to explain his role in the operation. He would also testify that all the defendants on trial, except for DeLaurentis, participated in the murder of a competitive bookmaker, Hal Smith. Jahoda became a government informant after he found himself in trouble with the law for other illegal conduct. He agreed to wear a wire and managed to trap all the defendants on tape.

Jahoda claimed that some of the cryptic conversations were about the murder of Hal Smith. The prosecutors contended that one of the conversations he had with Bellavia "contained an admission by Bellavia that he participated in the murder." A second murder was charged but very little evidence was presented.

I again stayed at the Ritz-Carlton Hotel where Bruce Cutler also took up residence. Every night after court we would meet in the gym, work out, then meet again at the lobby bar for a few drinks before dinner.

Bruce and I had much in common, especially the nature of our clients. He represented John Gotti, a man even more infamous than Nick Scarfo. Unfortunately for Mr. Gotti, Cutler was disqualified from acting as counsel in his last battle against the government in New York. The government used their same bullshit reasons to get rid of the defendant's lawyer of choice.

Most of the evidence in our trial pertained to Rocky Infelice and Solly DeLaurentis. During the four-month trial, I doubt that more than one week's time was devoted to evidence against Bellavia. I tried to help Bruce as much as possible by writing questions on three-by-five cards and handing them to him as he cross-examined the witnesses. He welcomed the help. Whenever I became lax with the cards, he'd ask, "What's wrong?" There would be an ever-so-slight tone of disapproval in the question. But it was only when his client, Solly, gave me the "evil eye" that I reacted immediately.

Bruce was like a bull in a china closet, walking all over the courtroom, shouting the questions in rapid, machine-gun style. At one point he was held in contempt of court by the trial judge. He asked for my help again. I represented him in a contempt proceeding. Judge Ann Williams vacated the contempt order and fine after the hearing.

On several weekends while the trial was in progress, Jennifer flew to Chicago, as did Bruce's significant other at the time. The four of us would have dinner at one of the many great restaurants in town.

I remember Bruce telling me one night while just the two of us were having a drink, "Could you believe what they're doing to me? Holding me in contempt after I said some good and truthful things about John [Gotti] just after he was indicted. And that only happened after the prosecutor's press conference of the indictment, telling the world how guilty John was."

"Bruce, I know. Perhaps no one knows as well as I."

"Bobby, the wind-up is, 'they' are going to put both of us in jail. There aren't too many guys like us around, willing to give their all. We fight like hell for our clients and refuse to lay down or sell out."

"The last of a breed, like dinosaurs," Gus Newman told me once while we discussed the hazards of our profession.

John Gotti, the high-profile alleged boss of the Gambino family, went on trial without Cutler defending him. Gotti's friend and associate, Sammy "The Bull" Gravano, did what Nicky Scarfo's close associates had done—he flipped and made a deal for early release. Sammy's testimony, of course, was welcomed by the government and accepted by the jury. The fact that he had killed no less than 19 people made no difference. John Gotti was sentenced to life in prison without parole. Gravano, on the other hand, was released from prison and allowed to make millions more by selling drugs in some unsuspecting community.

The Infelice jury didn't buy Jahoda's testimony that he witnessed the defendants kill Hal Smith. Actually, the jury failed to reach a verdict on that murder count. The defendants were acquitted of the other murder in the indictment. Bobby Salerno was the only defendant to walk out of court with his victorious lawyer, Terry Gillespie. The jury found Infelice, DeLaurentis, Bellavia, and Marino guilty of RICO violations, basing their verdicts on the gambling and extortion.

This trial got its share of media coverage. When we got off the elevator in the courthouse lobby, the newspaper and television reporters swarmed Bruce Cutler (he was not disqualified in this case) and the other lawyers, asking the usual questions about the verdict.

I was the last to exit. I stood a few feet away as the grilling took place. Suddenly, one of the TV reporters recognized me. He ran over with his cameraman. "Mr. Simone, do you have any comment on the indictments?" He said indictments, not verdict.

The rest of the press reporters saw him interviewing me and promptly abandoned the other lawyers. In seconds I was mobbed. No pun intended. They threw questions at me right and left.

"Did you know you were indicted months ago and the indictments were unsealed only 15 minutes ago?"

"Are you a member of La Cosa Nostra?" *Give me a break.*

These and other questions were being fired at me before I had a chance to answer any of them. I knew it was coming, but I couldn't believe that it happened literally within minutes of the Bellavia verdict.

I thought about those bastards in Philadelphia waiting out our jury deliberation. Here it was March 10, 1992. The indictments were filed months ago and sealed until 15 minutes ago. They wanted to make sure no one else would retain me.

Naturally, I hadn't seen either indictment up to this point, so I couldn't answer any of the questions. The reporters knew more than I did. I would have to wait until I returned to Philadelphia to analyze the situation and prepare for the battle of my life.

That night, Bruce Cutler did not complain anymore about his contempt charge. I did not feel very much like eating dinner. He and Anita Rivkin-Carouthers sat by as I proceeded to get stinking drunk at the lobby bar of the Ritz-Carlton Hotel.

The judge in Chicago later "buried" the defendants. "Roofed them," as Frank Sindone used to say. She sentenced them to outrageously long prison terms of between 18 and 62 years. The judge based her sentences on the murder counts despite the fact that the jury acquitted them of one murder and hung on the other. This was permissible at the time. The remaining charges were insignificant by comparison. No small wonder we have a serious prison overcrowding problem in this country.

A recent opinion from the U.S. Supreme Court (*Apprendi v. New Jersey*) prohibiting such actions may very well aid these defendants and many others in obtaining relief from what amounts to lifelong prison sentences. Back then I asked a few of my colleagues, "How the fuck can any judge overrule a jury's acquittal by sentencing a person to extra time because the judge thinks there was enough evidence?" Some of the lawyers, not including Bruce, looked at me like I was from Mars. No, just Philadelphia.

PART FOUR

"The shifts of fortune test
the reliability of friends."

Cicero

CHAPTER THIRTY-TWO

▼

Unofficial Consigliere

Reliable Ed Harrell was standing next to his black and maroon Oldsmobile Tornado as I walked out of the terminal of the Philadelphia International Airport. I could see in his right hand two separately stapled documents. He gave them to me as I slid into the front seat of the car.

These were the dreaded indictments, one charging me with RICO violations and the other with failure to pay income taxes. I tried to read them during the 15-minute drive to my office.

I looked at the top of the first page of both indictments to see if the names of the assigned judges were listed. I observed the initials "J.G." stamped prominently in the upper left-hand corner of the RICO indictment. After only a few seconds, I realized that those were the initials of Judge James Giles.

My mind flashed back to the Ciancaglini trial many years earlier when Chickie Warrington was overheard on tape telling his buddies not to worry about the FBI raid of their crap game the night before. I could never forget the tape replay of his words, "Bobby Simone will take care of it," and Judge Giles' icy stare when he heard those words.

I remembered the note-passing incident in the same trial and the good judge looking at me and saying, "So what?" when I asked to see the ex parte communication.

Then I thought about how Judge Giles reversed my $1,150,000 Golden Nugget verdict. It was artfully timed to occur just before the jury was to decide my guilt or innocence in the tax case. *Was I going to play against a stacked deck again?*

I glanced at the tax indictment and saw the initials "S.D." I couldn't immediately attach a name to the initials. Later I learned that they stood for Judge Stewart Dalzell, a recent judicial appointment.

Ed dropped me at the office and said, "We'll talk tomorrow." I waved goodbye and went into the empty office to read the indictments in depth.

The RICO indictment was 32 pages long. It contained six counts charging crimes carrying a potential combined sentence of 100 years. A forfeiture count was added wherein the government sought a verdict against me in the amount of $243,000. Apparently, they thought they could get blood from a stone.

Since I hadn't the vaguest idea of what the actual charges were, I studied the document very carefully. I was as interested in who might be testifying against me as I was in the specific allegations. Reading an indictment sometimes provides that information.

Count one charged "conspiracy to commit racketeering" and count two charged "racketeering." The illegal enterprise was alleged to be "La Cosa Nostra, the LCN, the Philadelphia LCN, the Mafia, the mob, 'this thing of ours,' the Bruno family, and the Scarfo family." All the alleged high-ranking members of the Scarfo family were identified: "the boss, underboss, consigliere, and the capos [captains]."

Of particular interest was the statement setting forth that "Robert F. Simone acted as an advisor and unofficial consigliere to Nicodemo Scarfo, the boss of the enterprise since 1981." "Unofficial consigliere" was a new term in mob parlance, not unlike "almost made." I was the "Tom Hagen" of the Philly mob, according to this absurd document.

Now I fully understood the headlines in the *Philadelphia Inquirer* and *Daily News*: "Robert 'Bobby' Simone Charged with Being Mob's 'Unofficial Consigliere.'"

The indictment went on for many pages, describing most of the illegal conduct the government had successfully proved in Nicky's RICO trial back in 1988. It included a couple of murders of which, the government alleged, I had prior knowledge.

I then read the heart of the indictment where the specific crimes I had supposedly committed were listed. The government needed to prove that I was associated with the "enterprise" and that I was guilty of at least two separate crimes on behalf of the "Scarfo family." The specific crimes were referred to as racketeering acts. Six of them were charged.

In addition there were two alleged incidents of "collection of unlawful debt" included in the racketeering charge. The RICO law provided that if the government was able to prove either of the charges of "collection of unlawful debt," then that would be sufficient to establish a RICO violation in lieu of two specific crimes or of racketeering acts. Clear as mud, right? Imagine, if you can, a defendant trying to get a jury of average, ordinary people to understand that kind of legal "gobbledygook," but that is the RICO law.

The income tax indictment accused me of failing to pay my taxes in full. Again there was no allegation of filing fraudulent returns. Here the prosecutors merely charged that from 1984 through 1989 I accumulated tax liabilities of approximately $160,000. Of course, the indictment failed to mention the amounts I paid in taxes for those years—over $120,000.

I said to myself, "How the hell do they expect me to stay current with my taxes and other bills? Every time I start to get back on my feet financially, they come at me with another case. Then I just about have to give up my practice and all income ceases while I defend myself."

Both indictments named and charged a co-defendant. In the tax case, my accountant of many years, Irv Reiss, was accused of aiding me in the evasion of payment of income taxes. In the RICO indictment, another friend of many years, Anthony DiSalvo, was charged with conspiring with me in two unlawful debt counts. Now they were trying to make me a loan-shark. This was quite ironic since just about everyone in town knew I was a big borrower rather than a lender or collector.

I appeared for a bail hearing and was permitted to sign my own bail in both cases after I surrendered my passport to the clerk's office. I was granted permission to travel anywhere within the United States since I had a few clients and pending cases outside of Pennsylvania.

A rather large group of Philadelphia's best criminal lawyers arranged a meeting in one of their conference rooms. It seemed that most of these people thought I was being persecuted, rather than prosecuted, because of who I represented and the fact that I fought so hard for the rights of my clients. They knew that they could be next.

Just before we met, Ed Jacobs agreed to act as my co-counsel in the RICO case, and Bob Madden would again share representation with me in the tax case.

Approximately 20 lawyers attended the meeting to discuss strategy and make a decision as to which case should go to trial first. We also needed to talk about pretrial motions and who would help prepare them. The informal meeting was called to order, and the first item put on the agenda by several of the lawyers was, "What are you going to do about Judge Giles? Are you going to file a motion to have him recused or disqualified?"

We kicked this subject around for 15 minutes. Half of the group thought such a motion should be filed. The other half said they believed I probably had the worst possible judge for this trial but that I would be unsuccessful if I filed for Giles' removal.

I decided after the discussion not to file any removal motion. Sink or swim, Judge Giles was going to sit in the RICO case, the more crucial of the two. There was no sense alienating him with a motion that was doomed. We also decided to go with the more serious RICO case first.

In only a couple of weeks I received several pretrial motions for filing on my behalf from various lawyers. Ed Jacobs and I prepared several others. We filed the motions and waited for discovery. When the large package of discovery documents arrived we had a pretty good idea of what I was facing.

Bob Madden was able to put the IRS case on hold. Judge Dalzell was a gentleman and extremely understanding. He appreciated my problems and chose not to make things any tougher for me. He postponed his trial until three months after completion of the RICO case. As a result, I would be able to concentrate on the most difficult and important case of my career.

The government recruited no less than eight criminals to testify against me. Of course, they had Caramandi and DelGiorno, but now there was also Philip Leonetti. In addition, they dug up Dave Kurzband and promised Bobby Rego the street if he would join the parade. John Pastorella, the first to wear a wire on Caramandi, was also ready to do his share. Vince Ponzio, another former client, and a fellow named James Santonastasi, whom I had never seen in my life—both full-fledged drug dealers—were now ready to turn over a new leaf, walk the straight and narrow, and do their part for the protection of society by blaming me for their crimes.

I read most of the witnesses' statements and other discovery materials as quickly as possible. The facts that I knew about the Rouse case from representing Lee Beloff and Nicky were embellished with new assertions. Leonetti corroborated Caramandi and DelGiorno by saying that I was to get 10 percent of the proceeds of the attempted extortion. He added that he, his uncle, and I had a conversation in my office when his uncle offered me the 10 percent. He said in his statement that I was glad to help and accept "my end." No such conversation ever occurred. If my office had been wired as I thought, I would have had no problem disproving Leonetti's allegations. No such luck.

The discovery material included a tape and transcript which purported to feature a conversation I had with Scarfo and Caramandi in which the Rouse extortion was discussed while the plot was unfolding. The tape was nearly inaudible. The transcript was the figment of Caramandi's, or an FBI agent's, imagination—possibly both.

The tape and transcript were phony. If not, why weren't they used against Scarfo or Beloff and Rego in the earlier trials? They would have been admissible, if the tape was audible, as statements of co-conspirators.

Ed Jacobs and I concluded that I was going to have to prove my innocence, rather than rely on the so-called presumption of innocence, at least so far as the Rouse extortion was concerned.

The second specific criminal charge alluded to a loan Tony DiSalvo made to Leonard Pelullo. The loan was for $200,000. Months after the loan was made, Pelullo was nowhere to be found. He was always "out of town" or "too busy" to talk to DiSalvo.

The discovery material indicated that Leonard Pelullo borrowed a couple of million dollars from a few banks to renovate several hotels he had purchased in the South Beach area of Miami Beach. Just about the entire neighborhood was done over in the art deco style. There were scores of new restaurants, shops, and hotels. All were painted in pink and yellow pastels. Tourists flocked into the once-quiet neighborhood and business flourished.

Pelullo himself was charged in another indictment with diverting much of the borrowed bank money for personal use. The government tried to show through written records that he repaid DiSalvo the sum of $120,000 out of the bank funds.

According to my "buddy" Leonetti, I asked Philip and his uncle to help collect the original debt. In his statements to the FBI agents and in testimony before the grand jury, Leonetti stated that he and Scarfo knew Leonard Pelullo and his brothers. "Actually, they were friends," he said.

Leonetti further said that he made a deal with DiSalvo to "split down the middle, fifty-fifty" anything he and Scarfo would be able to collect. He also claimed that Scarfo arbitrated the debt down from $200,000 to $120,000. He added, "I gave Robert Simone $10,000 of our end of the money."

The government claimed that this amounted to extortion, because Nicky was the boss and Leonetti the underboss of La Cosa Nostra in the Philadelphia–Atlantic City area. The indictment alleged that Pelullo felt threatened and that was the reason he paid off the settlement figure on the debt.

The third racketeering act alleged that along with Bobby Rego, I shook down two drug dealers. One of them, Robert Wrubel, a former client, denied that this occurred. The other, James Santonastasi, corroborated Rego and gave a statement saying that he spoke to me in my office and I told him to "Do what Rego says and pay." This accusation would rise or fall on the testimony of Rego and the drug dealer.

Next on the list was the alleged extortion to collect a $25,000 debt owed to DiSalvo by Vincent Ponzio. I knew Ponzio to be a builder in the Atlantic City area. Once when he was arrested at the Philadelphia airport for being found in possession of a large cache of illegal drugs, he retained me to represent him.

On one occasion he came to my office to pay me part of my fee. While there he gave me an envelope to give to Tony DiSalvo. I knew that Tony had advanced Ponzio his needed bail money and I figured he was merely repaying that obligation. The discovery material revealed that Ponzio had worn a wire during several attorney-client conversations with me. I thought to myself, *Isn't that nice? I am forbidden to divulge the contents of any conversation I have with my client, but he can wear a wire and broadcast the full conversation to the FBI and any jury that might be called to listen.*

The fifth racketeering act in the indictment charged me with collecting $30,000 from James DeBattista, whom everyone knew as "Jimmy Milan." He was the owner and operator of a popular Italian restaurant in Center City called Jimmy's Milan.

I learned that FBI agents and federal prosecutors threatened Jimmy with prosecution if he didn't corroborate what Leonetti and DelGiorno told them about my extorting money from him. To Jimmy's credit, he refused to lie about me despite being scared stiff.

The last allegation of crime was that I attempted to extort $100,000 from Joe Kanefsky. The indictment alleged that his alias was "Midnight." I knew him as "Joe Kane." Twenty years or so before, I had represented Joe before the Pennsylvania Crime Commission. Later I helped him with a problem his wife had as a favor. He was by then well over 70, and he and I were friends. Caramandi and DelGiorno made up this totally absurd accusation, or should I say, blatant lie. Kane called me when he read about it in the paper and offered to testify on my behalf.

My major concern, after digesting all the material, was that I was supposed to have extorted drug dealers for part of their profits by using Scarfo's name. I was embarrassed, humiliated, and outraged by those accusations. I didn't like taking legal fees from drug dealers, even though they are entitled to have the best defense possible, just like anyone else accused of a crime. I was worried that people who respected me might change their opinion just because of the nature of these charges.

Another item of interest in the indictment, although not listed as a crime, was a statement Leonetti gave to his interrogators concerning Raymond and George Martorano. Philip was now claiming that a few years after I was warned by state law enforcement people that I was going to be killed by someone on behalf of the Martoranos I was again threatened by them. If this was true, I didn't know about it.

Leonetti went on to tell FBI agents and the grand jury that I spoke with him and his uncle about the plot to kill my son and me. He added that Nicky told me, "Don't worry about it. As soon as he gets out of jail, he's dead."

It was obvious that the government intended to put on so much evidence about the alleged violent nature of Nicky Scarfo, his nephew, and the rest of his "family" that the jurors couldn't help but be prejudiced against me. I was, after all, their lawyer and friend. This was to be a trial of guilt by association.

One of the pretrial motions was to strike certain portions of the indictment that would, if granted, prevent the introduction of certain prejudicial evidence into the trial. Our claim was that the prejudice outweighed the relevancy of the evidence. After a hearing, Judge Giles decided to allow most of it in. Not much of a surprise.

Another pretrial motion was one to exclude the inaudible tape as evidence. After a full hearing, with Judge Giles listening to the tape, he surprised everyone by ruling the tape "inaudible" and ordered it out as evidence. Maybe, I thought, everyone had misjudged Giles' ability to be fair.

Guess what? Two months later he reversed himself and ruled the tape admissible—this after the government filed a motion for reconsideration. The prosecution claimed they had the tape enhanced, thereby making it audible.

At the second hearing, Giles again listened to the "enhanced" tape. It seems that only the prosecutors and Judge Giles could now hear and understand the garbled words. Although 20 or so people I had listen to this so-called enhanced tape agreed with me, it was no different from the original.

There was something wrong here. Why wasn't this tape used in previous trials? Why was it excluded as evidence for being inaudible and then, without any noticeable difference in the quality or its admissibility, readmitted?

Maybe it had something to do with the fact that the government brought in a special prosecutor from Washington, D.C., for this case. William Lynch was a white-haired, red-faced, short, chunky Irishman. He looked like Santa Claus without a beard. He wasn't giving anything away for Christmas, however.

One of his cases in federal court in California had just been dismissed for prosecutorial misconduct on his part. He concealed favorable evidence from the court and the defense lawyers. Then he lied about it. That's the kind of lawyer they needed to prosecute me—innocent-looking but treacherous.

I had little or no time to do much but prepare for the battle of my life. I managed to handle a few short trials just to make sure I wasn't put out on the street to starve. I had to eat and sleep, and it takes money to do so. By taking care of my needs, I devoted less time to my major priority. I was really in a bad position, but my health was good and my hopes were high.

Even before the trial started, it was obvious that the government had achieved one of its goals. I was unable to take on any new cases. Several lawyers called me, asking if I was available to represent their civil clients in criminal trials. Many people accused of crimes came in directly, asking me to represent them in their trials. I had to decline. This was nothing new to me. I had experienced this several times in the last decade. For all intents and purposes, I was out of business again.

But just a few weeks before my trial was to begin, I started a jury trial I knew was going to take less than one week in state court. I had to eat and it served as a warm-up for me. My client, a druggist, was accused of shooting a drug dealer who had been trying to extort prescription drugs from him. He was acquitted of attempted murder and conspiracy. Convincing a jury that my client was innocent gave me a positive feeling, especially knowing that the next jury would decide my own fate.

My trial was listed for early November 1992. Jury selection was to be the first order of business. The real question was, Could I get a fair, impartial jury, one that was not down on lawyers. Many consider criminal lawyers to be second-class citizens. Nicky Scarfo's lawyer probably rated alien status.

This time I would not have the benefit of Jake Kossman's genius and know-how. My dear friend, constant dinner companion, and legal mentor passed away and is now, I am sure, with his soulmate, Angelo Bruno. Several years ago an article in *Philadelphia* magazine mentioned Jake and me, referring to us as the last two "mouthpieces" in the area. It was an honor to have been mentioned in the same breath as Jake. I imagine his passing made me "The Last Mouthpiece."

▼

CHAPTER THIRTY-THREE

Health and
Freedom

Tom Carroll, an experienced and able criminal lawyer, represented Tony DiSalvo, who was also charged with RICO violations and use of extortionate means in collecting debts from Pelullo and Ponzio. Tony and I were to be tried together but most of the charges, evidence, and witnesses were directed at me.

Approximately 150 jurors were given lengthy questionnaires to complete before the questioning of the jury panel started. Many of the questions dealt with the jurors' knowledge of the reputation of Nicodemo Scarfo and me as his lawyer. How did they feel about lawyers in general? They were asked if they had any opinion about the case and whether they could follow the law, especially on the presumption of innocence and reasonable doubt.

There were many questions that required the jurors to note their education, job, and family history. They were even asked to list hobbies and favorite movies and TV shows. We could only hope that they would be honest with their answers.

The jurors completed their written questionnaire forms, and then Judge Giles spoke to them on the record for a few minutes. His talk set the tone for the trial. First he told them that both defendants were presumed innocent and didn't have to prove anything. Then he erroneously stated, "This case involves a claim by the United States Government against two persons, and the claim that each of those persons was a member of organized crime and did certain things as alleged in the indictment."

Neither DiSalvo nor I was, in fact, charged with being "a member of organized crime." To make matters worse for us, Judge Giles then said, "This case claims that each defendant was a member of La Cosa Nostra or the Mafia." Again, Judge Giles misstated the indictment and the facts. A jury would be inclined to think, *If the judge said it, then it must be true.*

Since the indictment set forth a history of the Scarfo crime family and many of the violent crimes attributed to the organization, both Tony and I were tarred with the same brush. This had to prejudice the jury against both of us.

The first juror selected was a young, attractive Italian-American housewife. All of us sitting at the defense table were pleased that she was chosen. Unfortunately for us, the woman called someone at the courthouse that evening to report there was something she forgot to reveal when she was being questioned by the judge and the lawyers.

She reported to the courtroom the next day and testified that years ago her brother had been hassled by FBI agents who sought to prove he was involved in an illegal gambling business. He moved from the area where he lived because of the harassment he suffered at the hands of the FBI.

A short time later, while he was driving his car, he got lost and became so upset about being late for work that he was involved in an accident. He died as a result of injuries he sustained. The juror testified that she could not help but feel animosity toward the FBI. She was stricken for cause—a great loss to the defense.

One of the early jurors accepted was an engineer who worked at a nuclear plant in central Pennsylvania, approximately 50 miles from the courthouse. Ed Jacobs, Tom Carroll, and I were at first concerned about whether he could be fair to the defense. His answers on the written questionnaire contained the statement "I was a witness for the prosecution in a murder trial."

The juror also stated unequivocally that he believed in the presumption of innocence, and further that the government had the burden of proof beyond a reasonable doubt. His oral answers in open court more than satisfied all of us at the defense table that he could be fair and open-minded. And really that is all we were entitled to and all we wanted out of a juror.

Jim Burgund, my jury expert, was not with us when we picked this jury. I did have a jury composite he prepared with general pluses and minuses listed. Engineers were on the minus side. More importantly, I now know that Jim would have recommended we strike the gentleman for writing that he was a witness for the prosecution.

Jim always said, but somehow I had forgotten, that what a person writes in his questionnaire is more likely to be telling than what he verbally says in front of others. The truth of the matter is that I fell asleep at the switch when I accepted this juror.

By week's end we had a jury of twelve plus four alternates. Opening speeches would take place on Monday, the start of the second week of trial.

William Lynch gave his opening address first. He repeated the specific charges against DiSalvo and me. But he went further. He recited most of the crimes committed by members of the Scarfo family over the past decade, even though neither Tony nor I had anything to do with them. Lynch told the jurors that I became "very close" to both Scarfo and Leonetti after the Falcone murder trial in 1980. He added that Scarfo asked me if I would accept a membership in La Cosa Nostra. This fact, he said, would come from the lips of Philip Leonetti.

Lynch closed by saying the evidence would prove that I was more than just Scarfo's lawyer. He said that I advised Nicky and his group on how to violate the law without getting caught.

I stood before a jury for the third time to make my opening address in a case where I was both counsel and the accused. I doubt anyone else had ever done that, surely not three times.

I started by explaining to the jurors that when I referred to myself I would use the third person since the judge prohibited me from using the word "I" when speaking to the jury and when questioning witnesses. In the past, Judges Katz and Rodriguez were not so inclined. I knew I would have to be careful. Judge Giles seemed to think that I would have an unfair advantage by saying "I" instead of "Mr. Simone" when questioning witnesses or speaking to the jury. Can you imagine having an advantage over the federal government in a criminal trial?

I told the jury that Nicodemo Scarfo and all other members of La Cosa Nostra were not on trial. I added that during the last decade, Scarfo and the others were arrested, indicted, and tried for many crimes. "The government fought hard to see that justice was done. And Robert Simone, Scarfo's lawyer, did the same. You will find from the evidence that he fought the government tooth and nail."

I pointed out that the government had lost several of these trials and that the losses irked the government. I went on to say that when the defendants lost, some of them who are witnesses in this case blamed Mr. Simone and they sought to get even with him.

"This is not a mob lawyer case," I insisted. The jury listened attentively as I explained that I was a criminal lawyer who represented people in all walks of life, not strictly mobsters and organized crime defendants. They were told how I spent a great deal of time with all my clients, eating with them and visiting their offices. This was a 24-hour-a-day job.

I tried to prepare the jurors for some of the evidence that I knew would be forthcoming: the Kurzband tapes and all the photographs of me with Nick Scarfo, Philip Leonetti, and the others. I even alluded to the inaudible tape, and I added that the judge would instruct them that the transcript of that tape is not evidence. Next I made reference to the witnesses who would testify against me, their criminal records, and the fact that they had lied before. I referred to the sweet deals they made with the government. "You are going to hear them say almost in unison, almost as if it were rehearsed, you are going to hear them say, 'I'm sorry. I didn't mean to do that. I killed twelve people. I killed ten people. I made widows. I made fatherless children. But I'm sorry.'"

I felt strongly that the outcome of this case would depend largely on the credibility of the government's witnesses. I kept hammering away at them. I tried to set the tone for the trial.

I looked in the eyes of the jurors and said, "They are all going to say, 'Now I am a good citizen. I have turned over a new leaf. I am a patriot. I am a law-abiding citizen.' Let me remind you of the words of Dr. Samuel Johnson, who said, 'patriotism is the last refuge of a scoundrel,' and these witnesses will be proven to be scoundrels."

I thanked the jury for their attention and for not prejudging me. I ended by saying, "If you follow the court's instructions on how to judge the credibility of the government's witnesses, both Mr. DiSalvo and Mr. Simone will not only get the fair trial they are entitled to, but they will also get the acquittals they are entitled to."

Tom Carroll reserved his opening speech until after the government rested. The court took a ten-minute break and Lynch then told us that his first witness would be Philip Leonetti. Word that Philip was going to testify right after the break spread like wildfire throughout the courthouse. By the time court reconvened, there wasn't an empty seat, and this trial was taking place in one of the largest courtrooms in the building.

A tan, handsome, and fit Philip walked into the room, surrounded by two United States Marshals and two FBI agents for his protection, as if I were going to have someone do him some physical harm. He put his right hand on the Bible, and he swore to tell the truth, but he failed to look at me.

I couldn't help but stare at him. Approximately three years had passed since I last saw him. There was a sadness in his dark eyes that made me feel he wasn't comfortable doing what he was about to do.

Lynch started out by asking Philip if he was found guilty of the RICO charges a few years back. Philip acknowledged this and confirmed that he had committed those crimes. His RICO conviction included four murders, numerous extortions, and being involved in illegal gambling and loansharking activities. Leonetti also stated that he pled guilty to two additional murders in state court in Pennsylvania. I am sure Lynch asked him about his convictions to diffuse the effect they would have if elicited on cross-examination.

Philip went on to testify calmly, coolly, and quietly about his life in La Cosa Nostra from the time he was in his teens to when he recently "saw the light." He told the interested jurors about meeting me in 1978 when his uncle hired me to represent him in the Pepe Leva murder case.

He told the jurors all he remembered about the Falcone murder trial and my actions as the lead counsel. He also admitted that he shot Vincent Falcone—for the first time, I might add.

To add some drama to Philip's testimony, Lynch had him describe his "making ceremony." That, of course, is the ritual that all members of La Cosa

Nostra are supposed to go through before being declared a full-fledged Mafioso.

His description went something like this: "I was brought into a room and asked if I knew why I was there. I answered, 'No.' Then I was asked if I knew everyone present. I answered, 'Yes.' Next I was asked if I liked everyone there. Again I said, 'Yes.' I was shown a gun and a knife and I was asked if I would use them to help 'my friends.' Again I said, 'Yes.' My uncle asked for my shooting finger, which he pricked with the knife. He placed a piece of tissue paper in my cuffed hand. He set the paper on fire and said, 'This paper is a picture of a saint. May I burn like a saint if I betray my friends.'

"My uncle then asked me to kiss him on both cheeks, which I did. He spoke a few words in Italian that I didn't understand. Then all the others gathered around me and hugged me and kissed me on the cheek. My uncle announced that I was now a member of the La Cosa Nostra family."

Lynch then asked, "Were you given any rules to abide by?"

"Yes," Philip answered. "We can't fool around with drugs. We can't use bombs to kill anybody. No counterfeit money, and we're not allowed to sell arms to foreign countries."

"Anything else?" Lynch asked.

"We can't talk to law enforcement officers, and we must live by 'Omerta.'"

"What happens if you break the rules?" Lynch asked.

Philip gave him a one-word answer, "Death."

It seemed to me that my "friend" had broken most of the rules, and he was very much alive.

Lynch led him through some more background information including, "Did your uncle try to recruit Robert Simone as a member?"

"Yes."

"Was any position in the family discussed?"

"Yes. Consigliere."

"Did Mr. Simone accept?"

"No, he did not."

"Was Mr. Simone's membership ever discussed again?"

"Yes. A couple of years later, Mr. Simone mentioned it, but again he said, 'No.'" This statement made no sense.

Lynch certainly tried to show that I was a member of the family, and I guess he came as close as he could without "making" me himself.

While this was going on, I thought, *Could anyone imagine that I would even consider joining a mob with the likes of Caramandi, DelGiorno, Yogi Merlino, Gene Milano, and even Philip as ranking members?* I looked at Judge Giles, and then at the jury, and I didn't need to have anyone answer the question.

Leonetti told the jury that I acted as his uncle's go-between by carrying messages back and forth while Nicky was incarcerated in La Tuna. He testified that he helped me with Dave Kurzband's junket business. He also said that he and his uncle spent New Year's Eve 1984 in Miami at the Jockey

Club with Tony DiSalvo and me. He added that I formed the corporation, Casablanca South, for his uncle, which was used to generate legitimate income for Nicky Scarfo. Nicky leased space in his house in Fort Lauderdale and also chartered the boat on occasion. All this evidence failed to establish a crime on my part, but it had to prejudice me with the jury. They had to wonder just how close I was with Nicodemo Scarfo.

When Leonetti testified about the Rouse extortion, he more or less repeated the testimony of DelGiorno and Caramandi that he heard in the prior Rouse trial when Nicky was convicted. He did, however, add that he and Nicky talked to me in my office when I supposedly agreed to accept 10 percent of the million they were going to get from Rouse. He conveniently forgot about the time I rushed to Atlantic City to tell Nick and him what I learned from The Crow and how I warned them to stop him if they could.

Leonetti answered Lynch's questions about the Pelullo loan by saying that I set up a meeting between him and DiSalvo and that he helped collect the $120,000 settlement on the loan. To his credit he admitted, even on direct examination, that he never threatened any of the Pelullo brothers and, more importantly, that neither Tony nor I asked him to do so.

Lynch went back in time and asked Philip about his RICO conviction again. "What was your sentence in the RICO case?"

Leonetti answered, "Forty-five years."

"After you started to cooperate with the authorities, what happened to that sentence?"

Philip answered softly, "I filed a motion to reduce the sentence, and Judge Van Antwerpen reduced it to six and a half years."

"Are you still in prison?"

"No. I was released several months ago."

Can you imagine the government causing the release of a man who murdered so many people so he would testify against some others and me? Well, you better believe it. It happens all the time.

His direct examination concluded when, over strong objections, he was allowed to testify that I spoke to him and his uncle while they were in jail about my concern for the safety of my son and myself. He said I feared Raymond Martorano was out to kill us both. Then he said, "My uncle said, 'Don't worry. When and if Raymond gets out, I already arranged for Patty Specks to kill him.'" Specks was a North Jersey mobster that I never met.

The jury had to infer that I was asking Nicky to kill Martorano. The judge, at sidebar, reached that same conclusion and yet ruled the evidence admissible.

Bill Lynch cleverly concluded his direct examination of his most crucial witness just as the court day was to end. When court was adjourned, Ed Jacobs and I went to The Saloon for a few drinks and dinner. Neither of us was worried about my not being ready the next morning for the all-important cross-examination of Philip Leonetti. Jacobs gave me his thoughts on how to cross Philip.

Ed Harrell picked Kim and me up at my apartment as he did every morning of the trial. My son, Scott, did not attend court only because he was, by this time, living and working in Las Vegas. Jennifer came whenever she was able to get time off from work. My brothers, Ron and Joe, appeared just about every day. Tony DiSalvo's brothers and three children were constantly in attendance as well.

Finally, it was my turn to cross-examine. I thought, *Let me first see what Philip is willing to give me before I go after him hard.* I knew he hurt me, but something told me he was holding back. I had read all his statements, and as harsh as his testimony was, I knew from his statements that it could have been worse.

I couldn't help but notice that once or twice while Philip was on direct examination, he hesitated before answering. On those occasions, his head tilted forward and his eyes seemed to blink. He raised his right hand as if he were about to catch or dry a tear. I was positive he had to stop himself from crying. Others I spoke to after court said they believed Philip appeared to be close to tears while he was testifying.

I walked to the podium and placed several papers in front of me on the top shelf for use during cross. I looked at Philip, and for the first time, Philip looked directly at me. In all the years I had known him and all the times I had been with him, I never saw him look so sad. This was no act, I'm sure. He didn't want to hurt me, but he felt he had to save himself. The government had made him "an offer he couldn't refuse."

I asked him, "When you were first brought to me by your uncle when you were charged with shooting Pepe Leva to death, did you tell me you shot him?"

"No, I didn't."

"Would you agree that you were cleared of that murder charge as a result of my advice and representation?"

"Yes, and I was innocent."

I wanted the jurors, most of whom probably had a low opinion of lawyers in general, to know that I didn't help free a guilty man.

Next I asked him about the Falcone murder. "Mr. Leonetti, you, Lawrence Merlino, and Nicky Scarfo were charged with killing Vincent Falcone, weren't you?"

He answered, "Yes," calmly.

"You have already told the jurors that you did in fact shoot and kill Vincent Falcone. Is that correct?"

"Yes. I was guilty."

"I acted as lead counsel in that trial, and you, Merlino, and your uncle were found not guilty in the trial in 1980. Is that correct?" I asked.

"Yes, we were found not guilty," he said with a straight face. The jurors now knew that I did help free a murderer. I needed to soften that blow.

"Did you ever tell me . . . Robert Simone, that you were guilty of killing Falcone?"

"No. My uncle always denied that we were guilty and so did I."

"When you were arrested and indicted for extortion along with the mayor of Atlantic City, who did you initially retain to represent you?"

"I hired Robert Simone," he answered, referring to me in the third person as was required by Judge Giles.

"Why did you want Mr. Simone as your lawyer in that case?"

"Because you're a good lawyer."

"You didn't want Simone as your lawyer because I was a mob guy?"

He answered, "No," and he volunteered, "You're not a mob guy."

"What was that?" I asked to make sure the jury heard his previous answer.

He answered louder this time. "I said you're not a mob guy."

He said he had confided in me, trusted me, and agreed that I never lied to him. I felt that he was going to be honest with regard to many of his answers, so I questioned him softly, not so much to impeach him, but more to rehabilitate myself in the eyes of the jury.

He told the jurors that he was really not guilty of conspiracy to commit extortion in the drug case and that through my efforts he was acquitted. I got him to agree that the reason I let George Martorano plead guilty in his extortion case was because he was in fact guilty.

I was trying to show the jurors that as a criminal lawyer I represented men who were innocent despite their reputation and also that when I represented a guilty defendant and I knew about the client's guilt, I let him plead guilty.

I asked him about the Sal Testa murder trial and got him to say that he told me he was innocent of those charges. He admitted he lied to me about that. He also told the jurors that he told me that Caramandi and DelGiorno were lying on the witness stand about his involvement.

I asked him if he and his uncle made a substantial amount of money from their illegal activities over the past several years. He answered affirmatively. Then I asked, if I needed money from him or his uncle, couldn't I have gotten it by merely asking? Of course, I made it clear that would be for the legal work I was doing. He agreed that I could have gotten hundreds of thousands of dollars from both him and his uncle.

Here I was trying to show the jury that I didn't need to participate in any illegal conduct with Philip or Nicky in order to earn money. I got him to admit that I had many other clients whom he often saw whenever he came to my office. That was to show that I was not just a "mob lawyer."

I showed Philip numerous photographs depicting him and me standing outside his office, relaxing on a boat, walking into a restaurant, and sunbathing on a beach. He said that we were not then engaged in conversations concerning illegal matters. For this I was grateful—after all, he could have said anything the government wished. He was not a Caramandi or a DelGiorno.

When I asked him about his trip to St. Barts, he told the jury that he came to see me as a friend. His trip had nothing to do with "family business." He said he was depressed and upset about the argument he had with his uncle.

Looking back now, it is easy for me to see that even if Philip denied my complicity in many of the criminal affairs of the enterprise, I still had a serious problem because I was in his company so frequently, and we were so close as "friends." Put simply, it was guilt by association.

At one point I asked, "As a result of Mr. Simone's representation, and we've gone over some of the things that he did on your behalf, you know now and you knew then, that these people," I pointed to the prosecution table, "the government, became very angry at the successes he was having on your behalf."

He answered, "Yes," before I finished the question. Lynch objected, and Judge Giles sustained the objection.

I countered, "He knew of his own knowledge." Judge Giles sustained Lynch's motion to strike the testimony.

"Well, just a minute . . . when I rule, respect it," Judge Giles warned. "The objection is sustained."

I refused to give up on this point. Judge Rodriguez had allowed me to use the government's vendetta against me as a defense a few years ago, so I assumed that it was still a legal and viable defense now. I asked Leonetti, "Whether you remember their names or not, didn't law enforcement people tell you on occasions, 'We're going to get Bobby Simone'?"

Philip answered, "I don't know, Bob." How nice it would have been if I had located his letter to me in which he stated that he knew I hadn't done anything illegal and that the government was out to get me because I had beaten them in court so often.

"Did you have any knowledge . . ." My question was interrupted not by an objection from the prosecutor, but by Judge Giles.

He said in a rather angry and loud tone, "Well, just a minute, just a minute. Come to sidebar."

Lynch and I went to sidebar accompanied by Carroll and Ed Jacobs. Out of range of the jury, Judge Giles said, "A grand jury has returned an indictment against you . . . not law enforcement officers." There was that same cold stare I had seen before. "Proceed." That meant the sidebar conference was over.

I couldn't believe what I just heard from the judge. He must have been living and working in a dream world. Just about everyone associated with the criminal justice system knows that a federal grand jury is merely a tool of law enforcement people who bring their accusations there for a stamp of approval.

I thought, *Is he out to get me again, or is he merely naive?* Either way I was in a lot of trouble. There was no choice but for me to move to another subject.

I was also able to clean up the allegations that I delivered messages to and from Scarfo while he was in La Tuna prison. Leonetti admitted that there was nothing illegal about the subject matter I discussed with his uncle.

There was a tremendous amount of material really having nothing to do with the specific charges against me, but I knew I had to deal with this evidence to shake the prejudicial effect it might have upon me with the jurors.

Bobby Rego was going to testify that he gave me the sum of $5,000 while he, Philip, and I were in a restaurant. He also told FBI agents that he saw me hand it to Leonetti. However, when I asked Philip if this occurred, he said, "No, it didn't."

Philip also denied that he ever threatened Jimmy Milan in an effort to help me collect a legal fee. That statement would contradict DelGiorno's later testimony on this charge.

Before going into the Pelullo loan transaction and the Rouse extortion in which I knew Philip would inculpate me, I asked some other questions about his life of crime.

Particularly, I asked him if he was guilty of murders in addition to the ones he pled guilty to and he said, "Yes." He admitted to being criminally involved in another four murders. I finally got him to admit his complicity in a dozen murders.

Then I asked about his deal again. "How much time in prison have you done?"

He answered, "Five years, five months, and five days."

"Are you still in prison?" This was a question Lynch asked earlier, but I wanted the jurors to remember the fact that Philip was free despite his violent criminal career.

"No, I was released several months ago," he answered.

Philip then told the jurors that he was given no additional time in New Jersey and Pennsylvania as a result of his guilty pleas in the state courts. But the biggest surprise was when he testified that he was not on probation or parole under the federal or state agencies.

I asked Mr. Leonetti, "You are free as a bird, aren't you?"

"Yes," he answered with a smile.

Well, I guess that's justice for you. Free a guy who commits over a dozen murders, a hundred extortions, and who knows how many other crimes in order to take Bobby Simone's law license, earning capacity, freedom, and reputation away from him.

On cross-examination with regard to the Pelullo debt collection, Leonetti stuck to his story that he and his uncle helped collect money for DiSalvo after I asked him to do so. He said he never threatened Pelullo. I thought that statement would save Tony and me on this count. Leonetti would not alter his testimony that he gave me part of the money collected as a "commission."

I tried to get him to say that the money he gave me was part payment on legal fees from him and/or his uncle, but Leonetti refused to budge. "You never charged us legal fees." That, of course, was a lie and absurd. For some reason I believed then, as I still do, that Philip lied about the fees I was paid only to help me — at least in his own mind. Of course, it had the opposite effect. The jurors had to think, *Why would Simone not charge them fees unless he was one of them?*

When it came down to the Rouse extortion, Philip would not explain to the jury why he, his uncle, and I would even talk about the plot to extort from Rouse while we were in my office, which we all feared might be bugged. I questioned him on this.

Q. Didn't you, your uncle, and even I worry about electronic surveillance?
A. Yes. We were always concerned about that.
Q. Isn't it a fact we never wanted to, nor did we ever, discuss anything illegal in my office for the same reason. Isn't that so?
A. Yes.
Q. Well, how can you explain the conversation you say occurred in my office when your uncle supposedly offered me 10 percent of the Rouse extortion money?
A. I can't explain it.

I knew Philip would not now change his testimony about the conversation, but I felt good that he answered my questions as he did.

The last thing I went into on cross was the Martorano incident, where I supposedly told Philip and Nicky that I feared Martorano was going to kill me and my son. Philip again refused to budge, even though I showed him an FBI 302 statement he made in which he said that Nicky was going to have Raymond Martorano killed, not because of me, but because Nicky felt Raymond was trying to steal the Culinary Workers Union Local 54 from him.

Lynch had a few questions on re-direct. As it turned out, his most important question went like this:

"You said you never threatened Pelullo. Did you have to threaten him?"

"Objection, objection," Tom Carroll and I called out at the same time.

"Overruled."

"No," Philip answered.

"Why not?" Lynch asked.

My objection to this question was also overruled. Philip answered, "Because he knew my uncle was the boss and I was the underboss. He knew about the organization."

Lynch was also permitted, over objection, to ask Leonetti if the Pelullo brothers knew of the violent reputation of the "Scarfo organization." Naturally, Philip responded, "Yes."

Before Lynch finished his re-direct, he got Philip, again over my objection, to testify that "he liked me" and that he did not want to testify against me, but he was compelled to do so because of his plea agreement.

Shortly after Philip left the witness stand, court was adjourned for the day. It was difficult for Ed Jacobs and me to say just how much his testimony hurt me and how effective the cross-examination had been. The next morning's *Philadelphia Inquirer* carried a story written by popular columnist Steve Lopez in which he stated that Philip Leonetti's testimony was not worthy of belief. Lopez went further in his article and said that it didn't make any sense to free a murderer to put Robert Simone in jail. Then he added that even if I was guilty, which he didn't believe me to be, I should be exonerated. Other press reports also read favorably. We couldn't be sure how the jury was reacting, but we were happy with the reaction from the press.

There were to be many more witnesses testifying for the government, but none of them as crucial as Philip Leonetti.

David Kurzband and FBI agent Ron Morretti repeated their testimony as presented in my earlier case in Camden. I cross-examined Kurzband, and I noticed that this time he just didn't give a damn. He agreed with everything I suggested in my questions.

The same tapes were played, and Ed Jacobs did a fine job of keeping Morretti from hurting me. This segment of the trial merely proved that I was close to Nicky Scarfo and Philip Leonetti. By now, this was not even an issue in the trial.

The government paraded all their fact witnesses before the jury in the Rouse part of the case. It was the same old song and dance. None of these people could say I was involved in the extortion.

They followed with their two professional witnesses, Caramandi and DelGiorno. I agreed to let Jacobs take these witnesses on cross. As always, he did a great job. Their stories were inconsistent, and Ed pointed that out to the jurors.

He destroyed their credibility on the counts involving the alleged extortions of Joe Kane and Jimmy Milan. There wasn't much he could do, however, with the inaudible tape on which Caramandi insisted that the conversation was about "Rouse." But the worst thing for us was that the witness, the prosecutor, and the jury had a typewritten transcript of the conversations while The Crow testified. The tape did not contain the words in the transcript, but it was impossible to convince the jury that the FBI agents and Caramandi, the preparers of the transcript, were lying about what they heard on the tape.

As the case was winding down, several United States District Court judges, who sat in the very court where I was being tried, approached me in the courthouse lobby at different times, and they all wished me well with the outcome of the trial. One or two told me how absurd this all was—to put me on trial based on the nature of the evidence the government had. Unfortunately for me, none of these fair-minded gentlemen was presiding at my trial.

Bobby Rego took the stand, and he enjoyed his role as a government informant. I was able to destroy his credibility mostly by asking him simple questions. "How many people did you shake down for bribes when you worked for Councilman Beloff?" I asked.

"Many," he said. He could not lie since I was armed with his statements admitting to scores of his extortions and bribes. I thought he was a weasel, and I felt sure the jury thought the same. I showed him his testimony in his own trial on the Rouse matter, and he had to admit that he committed perjury when he testified under oath.

At least three FBI agents, who had conducted a surveillance of a Center City restaurant at the time an important meeting of co-conspirators was going on, testified that they observed Caramandi, Beloff, and Rego at the meeting. Both The Crow and Rego testified that I was there. However, on cross, I elicited from the agents that none of them saw me enter or leave the restaurant. How could they? I was not there. Caramandi and Rego both lied. I thought to myself, *I have been trying to clear myself of these extortion charges for over five years, and now, unbelievably, the FBI did it for me.*

Ed Jacobs and I walked into the courtroom one morning, and there, standing by the witness box, we saw three well-dressed men. We both knew two of them to be FBI agents. I asked Ed, "Who is that other agent? Do you know his name? Have you seen him before?"

He shook his head and said he didn't know the gentleman either. When we asked Bill Lynch we were told the man was not an agent. He was James Santonastasi, the drug dealer who was to testify that he gave $5,000 to Bobby Rego to give to me. That, he would say, was done to permit him to stay in the drug business or suffer harm from the "Scarfo mob." I almost laughed. Here was a man I had never laid eyes on saying that I suggested he pay Rego what he demanded. Another criminal buying his way out of jail in exchange for perjured testimony against me.

The government called its seventh informant to the witness stand to testify against Tony DiSalvo and me. Vince Ponzio was a client of mine back in the early 1980s. Little did I know that just about every time he visited me to talk about his case, he wore a wire to record the conversations.

While he was on direct examination, Ponzio testified that he borrowed money from DiSalvo on two occasions. Once he took a loan of $100,000 that he repaid along with interest of 3 percent a week. He acknowledged that I had nothing to do with the whole transaction. Then he testified that later he borrowed $25,000 from Tony that he was still paying off when he was arrested for dealing in cocaine and illegal pills.

I arranged bail for Ponzio and represented him in two separate cases, one in federal court and the other in state court. He came to my office to discuss his case and pay me part of my fee. When he handed me several thousand dollars in cash, he said, "Four thousand is for you to be deducted off what I owe on my fee." He then said, "The other four thousand is for Tony. I don't really know what I owe him. Could you check it out for me and see if you can get me a break on the interest?"

Believe it or not, this was the basis for my being charged with collection of an unlawful debt.

On cross-examination, I asked Ponzio if I was his lawyer at the time. "Yes," he answered.

I then asked him if he was asking me, as recorded on tape, to act on his behalf and pay a debt for him. Again he answered, "Yes."

When I asked him if I had anything to do with arranging the loan with Tony or setting the terms, including interest, he honestly answered, "No."

On further cross, he testified that I did not know, as far as he was concerned, that he was borrowing money from DiSalvo except for the fact that I knew Tony loaned him money to post for bail in his case.

At the end of his testimony, Ponzio told the jurors that I was merely acting as his lawyer when the FBI asked him to approach me, wearing a wire to try and entrap me into committing a crime. He said he did not want to do this, but since he was in serious trouble for dealing drugs and the FBI offered him an easy and sure way out of his problems, he consented.

Vince Ponzio, I am happy to say, told the whole truth. I believe he did so because he was already safely out of his trouble and also because he never really wanted to act as an informer in the beginning.

The government rested its case, and Tom Carroll and I argued to dismiss some of the counts against Tony and me. Judge Giles granted acquittals in all of Ponzio's predicate acts included in the RICO counts. He also dismissed the charge of collection of unlawful debts as to both the Ponzio and Pelullo loans.

These four acquittals resulted in the dismissal of the RICO counts against DiSalvo. He only had the Pelullo loan extortion counts remaining, one for the act and the other for conspiracy.

As far as my case was concerned, the RICO counts were still intact. Five of the six racketeering acts outlined previously remained. In addition, I still faced the two Pelullo counts and the two Rouse counts.

Both Tony and I called numerous character and reputation evidence witnesses to the stand. Tony's lawyer then rested, but I had another witness.

I was deeply concerned about the tape recording that was played earlier to the jury when Caramandi testified that the conversation related to the Rouse extortion. The tape was in fact recorded while John Pastorella, Caramandi's construction company partner, was working as an informant. I found a 302 FBI report in which Pastorella told his control agent that the conversation dealt with another subject—two guys from upstate, not Beloff and Rego as Caramandi said.

Pastorella, a convicted drug dealer, was the only one of eight criminals seeking leniency who was not called as a government witness for fear he might aid my defense. I called him as my witness.

I asked Pastorella if he was the person wearing the wire when my conversation with Scarfo and Caramandi took place. He admitted to that fact. He further admitted that what he told the FBI agent, as stated in the 302 report, was the truth.

The trial was now in its third week. One week was spent picking a jury, and two weeks of testimony flew by quickly. Four local television stations featured the trial's events four times a day. Several local newspapers ran front-page stories daily.

Usually, I was referred to as "mob lawyer Bobby Simone." I must say, however, that in many instances, the content of the articles was favorable to the defense. Several articles and reports seemed to indicate that most of the government's witnesses were unworthy of belief. I recall several reporters, who had covered the trial every day, encouraging me by saying they didn't feel the government had proved anything. Be that as it may, it was time for closing arguments, and I needed to decide who would make the summation on my behalf—Ed Jacobs or me.

Had I testified as a witness, I probably would have gone with Ed. He was more than competent, and I knew I could rely on him. One of the primary reasons I chose to speak to the jurors myself was that I knew how much was at stake, and I felt that I would be placing too much of a burden on Ed. My freedom and license to practice law were on the line.

Bill Lynch spoke to the jurors first. Before Lynch started his summation, I asked Judge Giles for a sidebar conference. I needed to object to the use of a blown-up copy of the transcript of the inaudible tape, which Lynch intended to exploit as a guide while he spoke to the jury.

I objected on the grounds that the transcript was not evidence under the law. The tape was the evidence, and the jury should determine what words were spoken by listening to it. After a lengthy and heated argument, Judge Giles denied my objection and permitted the use of the blown-up transcript.

Caramandi had given his recollection of the conversation when he testified. I had no objection to the use of a blown-up transcript of his notes of testimony on this point. I worried that the jurors might feel the transcript was a correct interpretation of what the government and The Crow said was spoken at the time on tape.

Lynch played the cards Judge Giles dealt him to the hilt. He made the tape and the transcript the centerpiece of his case. He argued that the evidence against me with regard to the Rouse extortion came from my own lips, not just the informants. "Look at the transcript of the conversation. Simone was discussing the Rouse extortion."

He discussed the five racketeering acts that were the basis of the RICO violations. The sixth, which alleged that Tony DiSalvo and I had used extortion to collect money from Vince Ponzio, had been dismissed by the judge.

Then Lynch argued that the evidence he presented proved that DiSalvo was guilty of extortion and conspiracy to extort money from Leonard Pelullo along with me. He based his argument on the testimony of Philip Leonetti.

After he disposed of the Pelullo portion of the case, he went after me. He outlined the evidence in the other four racketeering acts—those involving Willard Rouse, Jimmy Milan, Joseph Kanefsky, and James Santonastasi.

Lynch then played his ace, my close association with Nicky Scarfo and Philip Leonetti. As he recounted all of the violent acts committed by them, he kept showing the jury photographs of me with Nicky and Philip as well as many of the other members of the "Scarfo family." Again, he implied that I was guilty by association.

The most potent prejudicial evidence was the conversation I had with Nicky and Philip when Nicky allegedly said he was going to kill Raymond Martorano for me. That was a tough nut to crack. It would take a strong, independent, and fair-minded jury to disregard this argument. I could only wait and hope that I might be able to convince the jury that a lawyer who represents criminals should not be judged guilty for doing his job.

Lynch took the entire morning session, and he still was not finished. He reminded the jurors of all the murders and dead bodies found lying on the streets of Philadelphia over the past dozen years. It seemed that Nicodemo Scarfo was on trial, not me.

After Lynch finished, Tom Carroll made his closing argument. All he had to worry about were the facts surrounding the Pelullo loan transactions. He argued that there were no threats and no extortion. He claimed that according to the evidence, DiSalvo was a victim rather than a criminal. He pointed out that Leonetti had testified that the Scarfo family did take tribute in the form of money from his client. DiSalvo couldn't collect his money from Pelullo unless he went through Scarfo and Leonetti because of Pelullo's close relationship with them. He left most of the credibility argument to me, but he did point out that Leonetti was testifying in return for his freedom and was likely to say anything to save himself.

Since Lynch was going to get the last crack at the jury, I asked to begin speaking the next morning so that both our final arguments would be made on the same day. Judge Giles granted my request.

The large, paneled courtroom was packed with spectators the morning of my final summation. My daughter Kim, who hadn't missed a session, my two brothers, Jennifer, and about a dozen friends sat together in one section. Sitting nearby were Tony DiSalvo's three children, two brothers, and several friends.

On the other side of the center aisle sat scores of FBI and IRS agents and at least a dozen Assistant United States Attorneys. It reminded me of a wedding.

Slowly I walked to the stand before the jury box. I uttered my first words. "Mr. Lynch has told you about all the violent shootings and the many bodies left on the streets of Philadelphia. What he did not say was that his witnesses were responsible for most of this violence. Not only did his now-reformed witnesses kill all these people, they got away with it as well. All they had to do was come into this courtroom and tell lies about me."

I showed the jury the letters that were introduced into evidence, which confirmed that the government spent $1,400,000 for gifts and living expenses on behalf of the witnesses. I reminded the jurors that despite all the crimes these people committed, they were all out on the streets, released from long prison terms. "Is there any doubt they will violate the law again?" I asked.

I quoted Clarence Darrow, perhaps the greatest American criminal lawyer, who said, "I would rather die than live in a country where even the lowest citizens could be imprisoned on the testimony of convicted criminals and lowlifes like you have seen in this courtroom."

Next, I had to address the specific crimes that were the basis of the RICO and conspiracy counts. I asked, "Since when is collecting a legal fee a crime in this country?" I reminded the jurors that there was no evidence of any threats or extortion on anyone's part with regard to Jimmy "Milan" DeBattista paying me any money. I pointed to the witness box and said, "You don't see Jimmy Milan come into this courtroom and testify that these things happened.

"The accusation about attempting to extort $100,000 from Joseph Kanefsky comes from the mouths of Caramandi and DelGiorno. Mr. Kanefsky did not appear." I argued that they could not and should not find guilt on this charge. "There isn't any credible evidence.

"The racketeering act which alleged I extorted and collected $5,000 from Santonastasi and Wrubel must fail. Rego says I did, Leonetti says I didn't, and Mr. Wrubel doesn't say anything." I then asked the jurors, "Could it be that Bobby Rego took $5,000 from Santonastasi and kept it for himself after he told him he was giving the money to Simone?"

I wanted to cover these charges, because it was so important to me that I be cleared of taking money from drug dealers so that they could continue their illicit business. A loss in any of these counts would have destroyed my reputation.

Next, I discussed the evidence in the Rouse extortion. Several witnesses, including Caramandi, DelGiorno, Rego, and Leonetti, testified that I was supposedly to get 10 percent of the $1 million they were attempting to take from Rouse. I reminded the jurors that Caramandi and DelGiorno had said this early on and that Rego and Leonetti had heard that testimony several times in court. I asked the jury to consider how easy it was for Rego and Leonetti to model their testimony in the same fashion. I reminded the jurors how the FBI agents had contradicted Caramandi and Rego, who said that I attended an important meeting at a Center City restaurant. I pointed out that when Ed Jacobs cross-examined Caramandi and DelGiorno, he showed that at one meeting when they referred to "Bobby," they meant Rego, not Simone.

I begged the jurors to play the tape that we claimed was inaudible. "Listen to it in the jury room without the transcript, and see if you won't agree with me that the words are so garbled that you cannot say that the topic of this conversation was the Rouse extortion. Remember," I said, "that John Pastorella, who wore the wire that night, reported to the FBI that 'we were talking about two guys upstate—not Beloff and Rego,' as the prosecutor would have you believe.

"Philip Leonetti first tells you he and his uncle would never talk about legal strategy or about any illegal activities in my office, and then Leonetti says we had this conversation about Rouse. He then states, 'I can't explain it.' I submit he lied to you."

The last specific charge to be covered was the Pelullo loan transaction. I argued that none of the Pelullo brothers came into court to testify that they felt intimidated or threatened when Leonetti and Scarfo asked for the money. "As a matter of fact," I told the jurors, "the evidence shows that DiSalvo only went to Leonetti—through me—when he couldn't reach Leonard Pelullo, who was ducking him."

I continued, "Leonetti claimed that he did a service for Pelullo as well as DiSalvo. He arbitrated the figure down from $200,000 to $120,000." And finally,

I reminded the jury that Leonetti did not pressure any of the Pelullos to pay the money immediately. "They took over a year to pay the reduced sum."

I could tell the jury was paying close attention to me and the words I was speaking. Every once in a while I said something that made them laugh or at least smile. I referred to Philip's testimony that on two occasions, "My uncle asked Mr. Simone to become a member of La Cosa Nostra." I said, "In the words of Groucho Marx, 'I wouldn't want to join any club that would have me as a member.'" I referred to David Kurzband as "Jabba the Hut" and the "consummate con man."

The spectators laughed out loud, and the jurors smiled from ear to ear. But at this point, Judge Giles intervened and said, "This is not the Apollo Theatre!" I couldn't tell if he was reprimanding the audience or me. The jury could very well have interpreted the judge's remarks as directed at me.

After a short break, I returned to the podium in front of the jury. I mentioned each of the informants by name and recited many of their crimes. "In each instance, the government has made a deal with the devil to convict a lawyer who would not stop fighting for the rights of his clients."

A few months earlier, I had read a great book about the French Revolution, entitled *Citizen*. I told the jury what happened to the lawyer, Malsherbes, who dared to represent the unpopular King Louis XVI. It seemed that no attorney would get involved with Louis until the ill-fated Malsherbes took his case.

The French lawyer was able to slow the process and put off the inevitable end for well over a year. Soon after Louis was separated from his royal head, the revolutionaries went after his wife, Marie Antoinette. Again, no lawyer but Malsherbes dared to represent such an unpopular client. She met the same fate as her husband.

The bloodthirsty mob, looking for more victims, decided that Malsherbes was as good a target as any other. Based on the perjured testimony of informants, he, too, was convicted by the Assembly and forced to walk the steps to the guillotine platform. "How dare he represent these criminals" was all the excuse needed. I could only hope the jury could see the similarity between his case and mine.

I argued, as I had in the past, that freeing criminals in exchange for their testimony "rewarded rather than punished criminal behavior." I added that this kind of law enforcement tactic "promoted rather than deterred crime." I asked the jurors to consider some criminal learning about an informant who killed many people and then saying, "I might as well continue killing people. If I get caught, I can always testify against someone the government wants more than me."

"Ladies and gentlemen of the jury, you have heard from the evidence that I won many cases against the government and oftentimes they," pointing to the prosecutor's table, "would get angry with me. And you have heard that there were many instances when my clients were convicted. In those instances, my clients would become resentful. And now we have the government and some of my clients getting together to get even with me. I was in a position where I couldn't win."

I thanked the jurors for their attention over the past three hours and walked over to my table. I poured a glass of water into a cup and walked back to face the jury. I raised my cup in a toast-like manner and said, "Health and freedom. Your health and my freedom."

I walked back to my chair, exhausted. Ed Jacobs leaned over and whispered to me, "Perfect!"

That night Ed Jacobs and his girlfriend joined Jennifer and me for a relaxing dinner at The Saloon. We were not celebrating, but we were glad that our job was over. All that remained was the instructions on the law by the judge and then the deliberations. It would all be over soon, I thought. But it wasn't.

Judge Giles instructed the jury on the law. No easy task in a RICO case. He recited the elements of all the various crimes that were either charged or referred to in the indictment. He explained to the jurors that in order to convict me of RICO and/or conspiracy to commit RICO, the jurors must be satisfied beyond a reasonable doubt that the government proved the existence of an illegal enterprise and that I had committed at least two of the remaining racketeering acts listed in this indictment.

Counts one and two charged the RICO violations. Counts three and four charged me with the Rouse extortion and conspiracy to extort from Rouse. Counts five and six charged both Tony DiSalvo and me with extortion and conspiracy to extort from Pelullo.

Judge Giles instructed the jurors that DiSalvo and I could be convicted even if no explicit threat was proved. "All the government needs to prove is an implicit threat made to one of the Pelullo brothers."

The jurors were told that the tape was evidence, but the transcript of the tape was not. I hoped the jurors would be able to follow that instruction, especially since Lynch was allowed to argue to the jury while he displayed the blown-up chart of the transcript in question.

After hearing approximately two hours of legal mumbo jumbo, the twelve jurors who would decide my fate filed out of the jury box and into the jury room. By now there were only two remaining alternate jurors, and they were discharged from further service.

A general rule of thumb, which cannot be relied upon, is that for every day of testimony the jury will deliberate for one hour. In this trial the actual testimony took less than ten days. I was hoping for a quick verdict. After all, if the witnesses were not to be believed, the jury would not have to concern itself with all the complicated legal instructions and the rather complex elements of the crimes set forth in the indictment and the judge's instruction.

Judge Giles ruled that the jurors would be allowed to go home at night rather than remain sequestered during the deliberations. It was the first week of December 1992. Christmas was on the horizon.

CHAPTER THIRTY-FOUR

▼

Guilt by Association

The jury deliberated my fate and that of Anthony DiSalvo for nine days over a 13-day period. During this time they heard the testimony of Philip Leonetti and the drug dealer Santonastasi for the second time. A few days after Leonetti's encore and a few days before the drug dealer's testimony was repeated, the jury sent a note to the judge which read: "We have reached a stalemate. Several of the jurors refuse to believe the criminals who testified or the FBI agents who interviewed them. What should we do?"

What an encouraging question, we all thought. The jurors, or at least some of them, called the witnesses "criminals" and they even had doubts about the credibility of the FBI agents. On the down side, DiSalvo, Tom Carroll, Ed Jacobs, and I noticed that the foreman who signed the note was none other than Richard Emory, the engineer about whom we all had strong reservations.

Judge Giles instructed the jury to continue to deliberate, adding, "You have a duty to review all of the evidence in the case." Was that like telling the jury they should consider the evidence, no matter the source or despite credibility problems? I did not think so at the time, but now I can see that a juror might believe that is what the judge meant.

During the jury's deliberation several more United States District Court judges stopped me in the lobby and wished me well. They expressed their opinions: "You will win" or "You might get a hung jury and they will never try you again." Each thought I was getting a "raw deal," being indicted and tried on the words of the lowest criminals.

It was apparent, however, that Judge Giles was not of the same mindset. He saw nothing wrong with the way the system was working. I can well imagine there were others who felt as he did, but it seemed to me that they were in the minority.

Waiting for a jury verdict was always the toughest part of my job, but this time the ordeal was almost unbearable. Then came the customary knock on the door to announce that the jury had reached a verdict.

My daughter, both of my brothers, and a few other relatives of mine hurried into the courtroom to hear the verdict. Jennifer arrived as they were about to close the front door and seal the courtroom. The crowd was large, as it had always been whenever something of importance was going on.

Despite the fact that I felt that Ed Jacobs and I had tried the case as well as possible, I expected an unfavorable verdict. I knew I had won tougher cases over the years, but each jury and judge react differently to the evidence and personalities involved.

The foreman rose and answered the clerk by reading from the verdict form. "As to the defendant Robert Simone, guilty on count one, conspiracy to commit racketeering. Count two, guilty of racketeering. On the racketeering acts in counts one and two, number one, extortion — not proven. Conspiracy to extort — proven [Rouse]. Number two, extortion and conspiracy — proven [Pelullo]. Number three, extortion — not proven [Rego, Wrubel, and Santonastasi]. Number four, extortion — not proven [Kanefsky]. Number five, extortion and threats — not proven [DeBattista-Milan]."

The foreman also announced, "Count three, extortion — not guilty [Rouse]. Count four, conspiracy to extort — guilty [Rouse]. Count five, use of extortion to collect debt — guilty [Pelullo]. Count six, conspiracy — guilty [Pelullo]." DiSalvo was also found guilty of counts five and six.

My friends, relatives, and Jennifer were more upset than I was. At least it appeared that way as we huddled with Tony and his family in our little room just outside the courtroom. We had spent 13 grueling days in this attorney's room speculating about the verdict and which jurors might be on our side.

The prosecutors were so happy about the guilty verdicts that they moved to dismiss the forfeiture count against me. There was no way they were going to let that jury hear another argument from the defense.

Judge Giles permitted Tony and me to remain free on bail pending post-trial motions and sentencing. When I finally left the courthouse, a large throng of reporters surrounded me for my impressions of the verdict. I spoke to the newspaper and television people as I always did after either a big win or loss.

I told them I did not do anything wrong, and I would definitely appeal the verdict. I repeated my oft-stated claim that because I represent unpopular defendants and fought for their rights, "Law enforcement authorities had conducted a vendetta against me."

I looked into the television cameras and spoke into the microphones that were thrust into my face. "They sent three guys up to my office wired up, and none of them could get me to commit a crime. Unfortunately for me, when Leonetti was in my office, he was not wearing a wire. If he had been, the jury and the world would know that he lied on the witness stand."

I ended my comments by saying how tough it is for a defendant to prove he is not guilty. "The presumption of innocence sometimes is disregarded by jurors and the public at large."

Immediately after the interrogation by the press, Ed Jacobs, Kim, Jennifer, Luther Fleck, and I went to Bookbinder's, which was only about six blocks from the courthouse. Of course, I needed a drink, and we all needed to eat lunch, having deprived ourselves of eating decently for the almost two weeks it took the jury to burn me.

Fleck was one of my older clients who for years came to court to observe many of my trials. Often he gave me suggestions on what I might stress in my closing argument. He offered to pay the rather large lunch check that included several drinks, a couple of bottles of Meursault, and the expensive seafood we ordered. But he got lucky. Jon Taxin, the youngest of the Taxins who helped manage the establishment, picked up the check himself. It struck me as funny: I had been dining at Bookbinder's for over 30 years, and I had to get convicted of serious crimes before any of the managers or owners signed my check. It was the first of many kind gestures that would come my way while I fought my appeal.

Jennifer, Kim, and I walked back to my apartment at Independence Place, arriving at about 5:00 p.m., just in time for all the television reports.

The verdict was the lead story on all four local networks. The next morning's newspapers would report the verdict and some impressions on the trial's outcome on the front page. Several jurors spoke to the press, and we learned quite a bit about what provoked the jurors to convict me of the serious charges.

One woman juror was quoted as saying, "Simone is a mob lawyer." Another woman said, "The word mob is intimidating, and when Simone lifted his paper cup and toasted, 'Your health and my freedom,' some of us took that as a threat." *Give me a break!*

One male juror gave several statements and interviews to the press. Some of his remarks follow:

> I still believe Mr. Simone is not guilty. I only voted guilty because I felt Simone would have a better chance on appeal. Several jurors violated the judge's instructions and discussed the case before the deliberations started. I can't sleep at night—I have considered suicide. The witnesses against Simone were killers and perjurers, how

can the other jurors believe them? Several jurors read the newspapers and watched television accounts of the trial. Some of the jurors felt threatened because of the violence and the fact that this was a mob trial.

For over a week, the news reported several instances of potential jury misconduct—predeliberation discussions and reading or watching extraneous reports on the trial. I kept busy gathering as much material as possible for use as exhibits in a motion to have Judge Giles interview the jurors individually to determine if anything improper occurred with the jury, and if so, whether or not it was substantial enough to warrant a new trial.

I was so busy tracking and compiling this information that I had little or no time to think of the consequences of my guilty verdict. There were several pending cases I had to dispose of, and they took the balance of my working hours. There was one client I continued to represent who was charged with serious drug violations in Charlotte, North Carolina. The man knew of my problems, but despite them he very much wanted me to continue representing him. He had read about Noah Robinson's trial in nearby Greenville and was hoping for at least a similar result.

A few nights after the guilty verdict I was in The Palm restaurant with Jennifer and a few friends. Mayor Ed Rendell came walking in, surrounded by a few official-looking gentlemen. I had known Mayor Rendell for many years, dating back to when he was a proficient prosecutor. This was before he won elections for District Attorney and Mayor of Philadelphia.

Rendell spotted me standing at the bar, waiting for a table. Of course, I had a martini in my hand. Without any hesitation the popular mayor walked over to me, offered his verbal condolences, and then in front of the large gathering he gave me a big hug. I shall never forget how good that made me feel. The highest-ranking politician and city official was not afraid to show the public how he felt about the verdict and me.

This was no holiday to celebrate, party, or vacation, so I remained in Philadelphia for the first time in 20 years. I was still determined to fight like hell to overturn the conviction that I and many members of the press and public thought was so unfair.

I filed a motion asking Judge Giles to interview the jurors to determine if they had read and considered extraneous material during the trial. I also alleged that the jurors had discussed the case before they reached the deliberation phase. Judge Giles granted the motion, and the jurors were summoned to the courthouse in March 1993, approximately three months after their verdict.

The juror who told the press that the panel members read the media reports failed to repeat this statement during the inquiry. He did, however, say that one of the alternates told him after the trial that he heard a juror tell other jurors just after the opening addresses that "This is going to be a guilty verdict." He also said the alternate told him that some juror remarked,

"You don't get yourself in this situation unless you are guilty." The same juror said to other jurors, "Be careful or Simone will get his men after you."

In other words, this particular juror decided I was guilty before he heard any evidence, and he inferred that merely because I was indicted and facing trial, I must be guilty.

When the alternate was questioned, he said that generally the jurors felt I was guilty before deliberations, but he wasn't specific about what words he heard uttered. Judge Giles refused to question him as to whether or not he told the concerned juror the specific statements he heard. The judge also would not let me ask any questions.

Other jurors said they listened to part of the television news reports, but they said they weren't influenced. All of the jurors, except one, appeared in chambers to answer the judge's questions. The defense attorneys were forbidden to interrogate the jurors. Coincidentally, the one juror who did not appear was the juror who allegedly made the statements about believing I was guilty before hearing any evidence. The inquiry turned out to be a sham.

Judge Giles denied my motion for a new trial, and in so doing, wrote a short opinion stating that he didn't believe the missing juror made the statements attributed to him. I thought that was quite bizarre since that juror wasn't even questioned, but after what I had been through, anything was possible.

Judge Giles again ruled that the questionable tape was audible and the use of the blown-up transcript was proper. He also decided that my conduct and DiSalvo's did constitute a crime, even though Leonetti made no explicit threats when he helped collect the debt for DiSalvo.

Shortly after the guilty verdict, I received a call from Lisa DePaulo, a features writer for *Philadelphia* magazine. She wanted to interview me for an article she was going to write. I knew she would write the story with or without my cooperation, so I consented to be interviewed.

Ms. DePaulo wined and dined me for over a week. I was in the mood to drink dry martinis, eat the best food in town, and sip my favorite wines. She took me to Morton's of Chicago, Le Bec-Fin, and a few other top Philadelphia restaurants, all this on her magazine's credit card.

The article, titled "Bobby Simone's Last 1,000 Martinis," hit the news-stands on the first day of May 1993. My sentencing date was scheduled for May fifth. Lisa had sent me a copy of the article a few days before.

The article quoted me after three or four martinis: "Tomorrow morning, that fucking broad [Joan Leiby, the officer assigned to write my presentence report] from probation is coming to my apartment to talk to me . . . to look in my closet . . . to look at my clothes to see if I really live there. Nobody went to Philip Leonetti's apartment to check him out." I was complaining about how people like me were treated compared to the real criminals.

The problem I created for myself was that the probation officer who was doing my presentence report would make a recommendation to the judge who was about to sentence me. Joan Leiby was actually very pleasant and very fair throughout the presentencing period. I read her report the day before the sentencing, and it did not appear to have been inspired in any way by the animosity she might have had for me.

When I saw Ms. Leiby in the hallway outside the courtroom, I walked over to her, concealing my embarrassment, and handed her a small envelope containing a note I had written to her the night before.

Dear Ms. Leiby,

I am truly sorry for the remarks that appeared in the *Philadelphia Magazine* article. When I said those things, I did not believe my words would be published. I really feel that you have been truly professional and extremely fair in all our dealings. I apologize and thank you for everything.

Respectfully yours,
Bob Simone

P.S. Would you believe that F_____ B_____ really published that?

RFS

A few minutes after she read my note, Ms. Leiby came over and smiled, shook my hand, and wished me luck. She also said that many of her friends and co-workers told her that I meant she had "broad experience." Classy woman.

Now it was time for Judge James Giles to sentence Tony DiSalvo and me. I knew that I would not receive the maximum sentence of 100 years, but I had no idea what the good judge might do.

Again, the courtroom on the eighth floor of the United States Courthouse was packed. Judge Giles asked me if I had anything to say before he pronounced sentence. I stood at the podium and said, "Your Honor, there are those who say that I crossed the line and went on the other side. Let me say that whatever one believes about that, I would prefer to be on this side of the line." I made an imaginary line with my left arm, separating me from the prosecutor's table.

"I would rather be here than on the other side with the prosecutor, the FBI, Philip Leonetti, Caramandi and Rego . . . and the others." I meant every word and I still feel the same. As Tom Cruise said in the movie *Risky Business,* "Sometimes you just got to make a stand and say fuck it!"

The judge surprised me by saying some rather nice things about me, about how I appeared in his courtroom protecting the rights of many defendants in the past and how well I conducted myself representing others and, most recently, myself. To prove that talk is cheap he then sentenced me to 48 months in prison.

To show the world that I was the one they were all after, he then sentenced Tony DiSalvo to a year and a day. That meant six to eight months of confinement. I now knew that I was running out of time as a trial lawyer, even though the judge continued my bail pending appeal.

I appealed to the Third Circuit Court of Appeals and anxiously awaited the decision. In the meantime, Judge Stewart Dalzell postponed my criminal income tax trial. He stated at one conference, "It seems apparent to me that Mr. Simone is going to win his appeal, so we will wait for that decision before proceeding."

After I finished writing a rather lengthy brief for my appeal, there was hardly any legal work or business for me to handle. I spent my time completing my few pending cases. I played golf with my dear friend, Vincent Pileggi, who always beat me in our two-dollar Nassau bet. On the weekends, Jennifer and I often played. She usually won. Just about every night we dined out — La Veranda, Mona Lisa, Bookbinder's, Morton's, Ruth's Chris, Jimmy's Milan, downstairs at Le Bec-Fin, Pasta Blitz, Susanna Foo's, Felicia's, D'Angelos, and The Saloon. Kim let me run up thousands of dollars on one of her credit cards to finance my year and a half in limbo. I knew that in the near future I would be eating tasteless prison food.

I learned, after the fact, that the United States Attorney's Office had obtained a court order to intercept and read all legal correspondence between Nicky and me while I continued to represent him in his appeals and pending the New Jersey case. This started before I was even indicted. Oscar Goodman, my lawyer friend from Vegas, made inquiries on my behalf and he learned that the Feds found no evidence of criminality in the hundreds of pieces of correspondence between Scarfo and me. It appears that the law protecting the attorney/client privilege was not applicable to Nicodemo Scarfo and his lawyer, Robert Simone.

During this time I traveled to Charlotte, North Carolina, for the drug conspiracy trial. The Assistant United States Attorney filed a motion to disqualify me from representing the defendant because of my conviction, even though my appeal was still pending. United States District Court Judge Graham Mullen denied the government's motion, and the trial proceeded.

There were at least ten co-defendants who decided, after being granted immunity, to testify against my client, a resident of Charlotte. I did my usual number on all these highly rewarded and perjurious witnesses, and I had the assistance of my friend from Chicago, Anita Rivkin-Carouthers, as co-counsel. There was, however, quite a bit of corroborating evidence, and after a two-week trial, my client and the others were convicted of most of the charges.

Before the jurors returned to give their verdict, Judge Mullen called all the lawyers back to his chambers. He said to the four local defense lawyers, "I hope you people learned something from Mr. Simone. He knows how to fight the government. You should do the same things." Looking at me, he said, "It was a pleasure to have you in my courtroom." *Why wasn't he my trial judge?*

He shook my hand, and I said to myself, "You have no idea how dearly that costs me." I must admit that I appreciated the compliment, especially coming from a stranger who happened to be a federal judge and quite a gentleman.

▼ ▼ ▼

Prior to my appeal being decided, Chief Judge Robert N. C. Nix of the Supreme Court of Pennsylvania filed an order temporarily suspending me from practicing law in the state courts. The United States District Court refused to issue a similar order. I was still licensed to practice in the federal courthouse, but there was very little work and few new clients. Again, I just couldn't make the necessary commitment to any client's cause that involved either a long or complicated matter.

My appeal was taking longer than the usual 30 to 60 days from the date of argument. I can't say which was tougher on me—the two weeks waiting for the jury verdict or the three and a half months sitting idly by, waiting for the Third Circuit to either grant or deny me a new trial.

One day when I called the office as I normally did for my messages, B.J. answered the phone and broke the news to me. "Bob, I hate to tell you the bad news . . . they ruled against you. They denied the appeal."

Her voice was calm but sad. I told her not to worry about anything, but I knew she was hoping and praying for a different result. She had worked harder on this appeal—typing, correcting, and fastening the papers—than she had for any of my clients. She knew my days of freedom were limited, and at the same time she must have known that she would have to find another job—soon.

The opinion was filed on August 31, 1994, only a few days before Labor Day. I walked to the clerk's office where I picked up a copy to read. I didn't want to wait over a four-day weekend.

The three appellate judges joined in an opinion denying the appeals for a new trial for both Tony DiSalvo and me. The written decision started out with these damning words: "We examine the defendant's affiliation with the hierarchy of the Philadelphia La Cosa Nostra . . . members of the Scarfo Family and their nefarious affairs are not strangers to this court."

The court was obviously referring to several earlier appeals that it heard on behalf of Nicodemo Scarfo and a larger group of his cronies. Again, guilt by association—the new American way.

Before the appellate judges considered the evidence relating to Rouse or Pelullo, they made up their minds. That was evident when I read the beginning portion of the opinion where the judges recounted how I begged Nicky to spare George Botsaris' life, asked him to intercede on my behalf against Raymond Martorano, and represented Nicky and Philip without fee.

All three of these premises were false, but there was no way of knowing whether the jury bought the story since I was not charged with that conduct and there was no verdict to say I did these things. As a matter of fact, none of them is a crime. The appellate court put their stamp of approval on the lies and the verdict.

At one point the judges stated, "Because of the closeness of the call, we will describe the supporting evidence and relevant case law with particularity." Were they kidding when they said this was a "close call" and then they ruled against me? One must wonder, when a person has his freedom, license to practice law, ability to earn a living, and reputation on the line, why and how those most important things could be taken away in a "close call" decision based on a finding of facts never submitted to a jury.

I had asked the panel members to listen to the inaudible tape—they never said whether they did or not. There is no question in my mind that if they had taken a couple of minutes to do so, they would have agreed that the conversation was completely inaudible. As far as the use of the blown-up transcript was concerned, the court said that Judge Giles did not abuse his discretion in allowing it. That, of course, meant that Judge Giles could have denied use of it if he wanted to be fair—really fair, that is.

The judges also said that Judge Giles did not abuse his discretion when he held that the jurors did not violate their oaths to listen to the entire case and decide the case only on the evidence. I had a difficult time accepting that statement when they added, "even if a juror stated, 'you better be careful or Simone will get his men after you' . . . since that was said as a joke." Some joke! Unfortunately, the joke was on me—as if this case were some laughing matter.

They concluded that the same juror who made that nasty "joke" did not make the statement that "This is going to be a guilty verdict" right after the opening addresses. Judge Giles had reached the same conclusion, even though he didn't think it was necessary to question that juror. Again, the appeals court ruled that there was "no abuse of discretion."

I filed a motion for the entire court to rehear the appeal. One of the judges of the court voted in my favor. The game was over—the joke was complete. I had very little time left to accomplish quite a bit.

▼ ▼ ▼

Without much trouble, I was able to work out a plea agreement on my tax indictment. Naturally, it made no difference—guilty or not guilty. The prosecutor and the IRS agreed to concurrent time for me. That means any sentence would run at the same time as the four-year sentence I had received in the RICO case.

There was just no sense in fighting this case, even though I was innocent of any criminal wrongdoing and even though it would have been extremely tough for me to lose if the case went to trial. The bottom line was that Judge Dalzell sentenced me to 15 months, concurrent.

I almost laughed at my sentencing hearing on the tax case. The prosecutor told Judge Dalzell that the citizens and the government could have used the money I owed the IRS for many good causes. I guess she meant that they could have given this money to some other informants to get them to come into a courtroom and lie so they could win more convictions.

I thought it ridiculous that the government was making a big deal out of my owing the IRS about $160,000, especially after paying Caramandi, DelGiorno, and Leonetti over $1,400,000.

I even said to the sentencing judge, "These people told me several times over the years that I was going to be killed by some of my own clients. I never imagined I would live so long that it would be necessary to pay these taxes."

Of course, the fact that the government knocked me out of business every couple of years was not considered a valid defense. Their murderers and perjurers were treated more fairly than I was. For that matter, they received better treatment than any average citizen can hope for.

CHAPTER THIRTY-FIVE

▼

Five Hundred
New Clients

After so many wins against the government, I found myself convicted of serious charges—sentencing complete, appeals exhausted, my surrender date drawing near. It was a waiting game of sorts, though I kept my spirits up and took my remaining cases as far as time would allow. There were loose ends to be tied up, some difficult good-byes to be said, and the ordeal of crowding my life into cardboard boxes. My mind wandered as I finished packing up my entire office, including the thick files, each filled with memories—all the victories and those occasional defeats that hurt so much.

Both of my sentencing judges signed an order recommending that I serve my time in Nellis Federal Prison Camp on the United States Air Force Base in Las Vegas, Nevada. Scott and Kim lived there and they would be able to visit me frequently—good therapy for all of us.

As the plane lifted I looked down at the familiar Philadelphia skyline for the last time in a great while. I saw the statue of William Penn perched atop City Hall, the site of many of my courtroom wins. City Hall, once the tallest building in the City of Brotherly Love, was dwarfed by the new skyscrapers popping up around it. These were the product of Mayor Wilson Goode's order allowing buildings to exceed the age-old height restriction—no building higher than City Hall. The tallest of these newer edifices were developed by Willard Rouse.

My destination was Las Vegas, where I'd been many times before, under much happier circumstances. Put on the map by Bugsy Siegel and his buddies and financed by Jimmy Hoffa's Teamsters Health and Welfare Fund, Vegas had been rejuvenated by the financial wizardry of Michael Milken, together with the imagination and foresight of Steve Wynn and other giants in the casino industry.

It was just before noon on November 24, 1994, when my son and daughter drove me to the prison camp on the grounds of Nellis Air Force Base. Kim had moved to Vegas shortly after my conviction to be near Scott and to get away from all the notoriety. The temperature was around 50 degrees, much warmer than in Philadelphia. On the horizon I could see the hulking hotel-casinos sitting on the strip and off to the right in downtown Las Vegas, a tempting site that I would have to behold for my entire stay at Nellis.

We hugged and kissed, but there were no tears. Jennifer and I had said our farewells the night before at McCarren Airport. She was going home after we spent my last week of freedom together at the nearby Rio Hotel. I walked to the front door of the administration building carrying a duffel bag stuffed with two jogging suits, two pairs of sneakers, several pairs of white jockey shorts and T-shirts, sweat socks, a tennis racket, two cans of balls, and two cartons of Merit 100s. Believe it or not, those were the items they told me I was allowed to bring when I called the institution for instructions. I brought the tennis stuff with me, even though I rarely played the game. The Federal Bureau of Prisons changed the rules sometime after I arrived to prevent new inmates from bringing anything with them. Now all items must be purchased at the facility's commissary.

I watched my kids drive away down the road toward Las Vegas. I noticed for the first time that there were no gates or fences separating the institution from the free world. I entered the building and was ordered into a small, windowless room. The door was locked and I stood there for the better part of an hour. There was no furniture in the room. Next a uniformed guard came in and told me to strip and to open my palms and my mouth. Then he told me to lift my scrotum, turn around, and spread my cheeks. Now that's a job with a strange view of life. I passed the inspection—no contraband was found.

I was given a pair of shorts, a sleeveless khaki jumpsuit, and a pair of blue sneakers with no laces, all of which I quickly put on my very cold body. It was the end of November and even Vegas gets cold in the late afternoon, all the more so when there's no crap table in sight. The guard ushered me into the office. I sat across a desk from an attractive blonde, a caseworker who proceeded to interview me. "So how do you think your family will get along while you're in here?"

"I am sure my two children will be fine. They live in Las Vegas, and will be able to visit me often."

"Come on, Simone, I'm not talking about that family. You know what I mean." She added, "Do you know a man named Joe Esposito from Philly, New York maybe?"

"Is he a lawyer?" I asked.

"No. He's a wiseguy," she said with a straight face.

Another wannabe. I did not attempt to answer that one. I could see she had a copy of my presentence report sitting on her desk. So I was saddled with the tag "O.C." —short for "Organized Crime." Another piece of baggage I had to carry with me.

The intake interview complete, I was given the items I brought with me along with a pillow, two sheets, a toothbrush, a small bar of soap, and several other miscellaneous articles. Everything was stuffed into a pillowcase. By now it was quite heavy, so I picked it up with both hands and swung it over one shoulder. I was directed out of the building and told to walk down the cement path leading to Unit 203, one of the two buildings that housed half of the 500 or so inmates.

As I approached the housing unit, which looked like military barracks, I saw a group of about 25 guys milling around, smoking, and talking in a small courtyard. One of the men started to walk toward me as I reached the area. The pillowcase dropped off my shoulder and was about to hit the ground when he grabbed it.

Grinning, he said, "You're Simone, the mouthpiece from Philadelphia?"

I couldn't help but stare at this guy's chest and biceps, bulging through his khaki, short-sleeved shirt.

"Yes," I said. "I'm Simone. But I'm no longer a lawyer."

He smiled again. "There are a lot of guys here that hope you are." For the first time I looked closely at his tanned face. He was quite good-looking with dark eyes and hair.

With little effort he picked up my pillowcase and said, "Follow me inside. What's your room number? What bunk do you have? I was told to look for you when you got here, you know, keep an eye out for you. Sort of take care of you, make sure you got no problems."

I thought about asking him who told him to watch over me, but decided against it. As he ushered me inside the building and up the stairs to the second floor, he remarked, "J.C. from New York got out of here a couple of weeks ago. He got the word from some of his guys that you were on your way. It's my ass if anything happens to you."

I had no idea who J.C. was, but I wasn't going to tell him that. As the new guy in this alien world, having no idea what to expect, I welcomed the help.

"My name is Wayne. I'm from Vegas. I'll be here for about another year." We entered a small room, about 12 by 20 feet, with three double-tiered bunk beds.

Wayne threw my pillowcase on one of the top bunks. "I gotta get you a better mattress. You need a Cadillac. See how dirty and thin this one is?"

It was only about four inches thick. He left the room without saying anything else. In a few minutes he came back with another inmate. They were carrying a comparatively new mattress, about 18 inches thick. "Here's a

Cadillac. We took it from this rat's bed." Wayne and the other guy grabbed my dirty, thin mattress and left the room with it.

A few seconds later they were back, making my bed for me. Wayne introduced me to his friend and said, "We just did two good things. First, we got you, a stand-up guy, a Cadillac. Second, we gave that rat bastard down the hall what he deserved."

"Justice at last," I said. They both laughed and so did I.

At dinnertime Wayne walked with me over to the dining area. There was a long line of guys—all sizes, colors, and shapes—waiting for the uniformed guard to give them the okay to enter the building.

After standing in line for about 15 minutes a short, thin, African American man in civilian clothes walked over to me and said, "You're Robert Simone, the lawyer from Philadelphia, aren't you?"

I looked at Wayne and he introduced me to Mr. Lee, the education supervisor at Nellis. Lee smiled and said, "I was just transferred from Fairton in New Jersey. I used to see you on television every day. And now I am going to see you in person every day." He laughed openly, and the inmates who heard his words just shrugged.

Some joke, I thought as I entered the dining hall. It was nothing like I imagined. There were regular wooden tables, comfortable captain's chairs and, amazingly enough, a large aquarium in the middle of the room filled with the most colorful tropical fish I'd seen since St. Barts.

The food was served cafeteria-style and was surprisingly better than I'd anticipated. Scattered among the inmates in line were several members of the U.S. Air Force. We ate the same food as the enlisted men—not gourmet but hardly what you would consider prison food either.

Wayne introduced me to at least a dozen guys. They all shook my hand, wishing me well and offering me toiletries, shaving items, and clothing. I learned later that this was standard conduct when new inmates arrived, except when the new inmate is a known informant.

That first night after dinner, Wayne walked me down to Unit 201 and introduced me to many other guys. Several were from Nevada, California, Hawaii, Utah, and Arizona. Quite a few came from Buffalo and some were from as far away as Guam. There were even a couple of Native Americans from the Northwest. I was the only one from Philadelphia and I did not know a soul before I arrived. Wayne and the others helped make me feel welcome and comfortable under the circumstances.

We walked back to our unit and went downstairs to the recreation area where I saw at least three card games in progress, a couple of guys playing pool, and scores of inmates watching television in two separate designated areas.

Wayne seemed to enjoy introducing me to most of the inmates. "This is Mayor Joe, from New Jersey. Say hello to Jeff, a city councilman from Washington State. There are two lawyers from California sitting over there. The one in the corner is a doctor."

The mayor asked me if I played poker. As soon as I said yes, he told me to play his next hand since he had to go to the john. I sat down and by the time he came back, I was holding no less than a royal flush. The first time in my life I get a royal and I have to be in prison. To make matters worse, it wasn't even mine. After I won the hand, the mayor asked me to play a few more hands for him. He probably thought I was very lucky, but in a matter of minutes I lost everything that I had won and more. Story of my life. He quickly reclaimed his seat.

Soon it was time to go to our rooms for the ten o'clock count. The daily counts took place at 4:30 a.m., 4:00 p.m., 10:00 p.m., 12:00 midnight, and 2:00 a.m. I met my five roommates just before the count. They all seemed to be decent guys. Wayne's room was around the hall, also on the second floor. He asked me if I wanted to move into his room. He said he could arrange it the next day. I was beginning to feel that Wayne was sticking too close to me, so I declined. I did not want the others to think I needed a babysitter or a body-guard.

Lights went out in our room right after the count. I learned that I could leave the room as long as I stayed in the building or the courtyard right outside, and was back for the next count. I smoked a couple of cigarettes and thought about my new situation, my first day of incarceration behind me. I returned to my room and climbed into my upper bunk. Later I was told that most of the men over 50 get a lower bunk. I was glad to hear that. Soon after I was given a lower.

I put my head on my small, hard pillow and stared at the ceiling only inches away. Before I was even put on trial I had a premonition that some day I would end up in prison. My thoughts traveled back to all those prisons I had visited over the years. Every time I'd finish with a client in prison, I was relieved to walk out, the slam of the metal gate behind me loud as a jackham-mer. *I got out this time,* I remember thinking each time I left, wondering what happens when you have to stay.

How do you prepare yourself for a stretch in the joint? Well, I read loads of books about prisons and the people they put there believing—no, know-ing—that I would someday spend more than the usual visiting time for a lawyer. I read *Papillon, The Willie Sutton Story*, and Nien Chen's *Life and Death in Shanghai.* Later I read Solzhenitsyn's *The Gulag Archipelago* and *The Count of Monte Cristo.* These books and others were about the power of the human spirit over the often inhumane prison system, a story older than I had imagined. While Nellis was a far cry from Shanghai or a Soviet gulag, I identified with these books somehow. The injustice I had experienced was the same, and while I was not beaten or interrogated nightly, I had lost my freedom, my practice, and my home.

Just before my eyes closed that first night, I told myself I was going to make a positive out of this negative. I decided I was going to gain from this experience, learn from it, and no matter what, be a better man when it was all over.

It took nearly a week to go through the process of learning everything about the institution, including all the rules, and believe me, there were plenty of them. My first job in prison was in the regular library. Larry Lee, the education supervisor, gave me the opportunity to be near all the great books and have my own desk as well. Soon my desk was surrounded by dozens of inmates, each of them hoping I'd review their cases to see if I could find a basis for a successful appeal. The word was out throughout the institution—We have a real criminal lawyer here, one who knows his shit.

The other two lawyers doing time at Nellis worked in the prison's law library. Their prior experience was in civil as opposed to criminal law. They were bright and hard-working and had several wins between them. But by accepting a job in the law library they were compelled to handle the cases of all inmates who came to them, whether or not there was any merit to their claims. As I'm sure you can imagine, sob stories aside, more often than not the cases were losers, bulletproof on appeal.

I tried to accommodate as many inmates as possible. It seemed as though the entire population at Nellis felt they did not belong in prison. I reviewed scores of criminal files, but agreed to take on a case only when I thought I could actually help someone obtain relief in court. I did not allow myself to give anyone false hopes. I was brutally frank with those whom I believed had no chance of winning. If, after reading an inmate's legal file, I felt he had decent grounds for an appeal, I would prepare his motion for new trial or sentence. I would mark the spot where the inmate was to sign "pro se," meaning he was acting as his own lawyer. After all, having lost my license, I could not very well sign as the attorney on the case.

They had taken my law license and my freedom, but they could never take away my knowledge, talent, experience, ability, and desire to fight for justice. Just when they thought they were rid of me, they sent me to a place where there were 500 guys waiting for someone like me to appear.

It took about a month until I was able to get myself into some sort of routine. I tried to develop a healthy balance between my growing stack of legal work and getting myself into top physical shape by reading, recreation, visits, and writing. The legal work consisted of reviewing scores of files and then determining if there was a valid legal basis to file a 2255 motion. That is a federal habeas corpus petition designed to correct errors made by judges, prosecutors, and defense attorneys who screwed up their cases. When it is alleged to be the defense lawyer's error, they call it "ineffective assistance of counsel." In addition to reading the files and preparing the motions, I wrote legal briefs to support the inmate's position. The law library at Nellis was adequate for these purposes.

About half of the inmates worked on the prison grounds in the main library, the law library, the warehouse, the business and records office, or with the landscaping, construction, or maintenance crews. The other half worked at the Air Force Base, less than five miles away. They were driven by bus every morning at 6:00 a.m. and returned to the camp at 1:30 p.m. Initially,

I preferred to stay at the camp, so the library job was perfect. I usually worked between 7:00 a.m. and 3:00 p.m. Normally, I was able to finish my duties at the library in less than an hour. Then I concentrated on the legal work. The library was in the same building as the law library and in an adjoining room that made it simple for me to do the necessary research.

Since there was plenty of downtime, I concentrated on getting myself into shape. I learned that those inmates who kept themselves busy were able to handle the confinement better than the rest. So I walked and jogged about five miles a day, every day. I was out on the half-mile cinder track between 5:00 and 6:00 a.m. Funny, I remember thinking, the only track I would have anything to do with before had thoroughbreds on it. Each morning as I circled the track, I was taken by the beauty of the mountains surrounding the camp and the adjoining air base. The peaks were covered with snow from December to April. During the rest of the year the foothills of the mountains turned various shades of brown and rust, breaking the flat sprawl of the barren desert. But there is no place like home, and I thought often of the lack of greenery in Nevada, how infinitely more beautiful it was in Fairmount Park and on Kelly Drive in Philadelphia.

Every morning I marveled at the sight and booming sound of the jet fighters flying overhead in perfect formation. The sound intensified as the fighters were joined in the usually blue sky by the larger bombers. Our private air shows lasted all day, every day, compliments of the United States Air Force. At night the glimmering lights from the strip and downtown Las Vegas were brighter than the stars. Only the moon was more glowing and then only when it hung low and full. In the winter months the weather was mild during the day but cold at night. Rarely was there snow except up in the mountains. Summers, on the other hand, were incredibly hot, but even when the temperature reached 120 degrees there was dryness in the air and little or no humidity.

In addition to the daily track time I managed to hit the weight pile about three times a week. A couple of the heavies helped me create a suitable workout. Let us not forget that I was over 60 at the time. In a few months I felt healthier, stronger, and younger than I had in years.

Recreation for me consisted partially of playing cards once or twice a week, usually poker. I guess I was hooked that first night when I caught the royal flush. Here I was 3,000 miles away from home within eyeshot of Las Vegas, playing poker in a high-stakes game. Gambling for money was forbidden, but there were always the means to avoid detection. If you want to know how, you're just going to have to get convicted and do a stretch in the joint. The government really knows how to help a guy who might have a gambling problem. When I mentioned this around the card table the only retort was, "Shut up and deal!"

Once in a while they showed a current, decent movie in the theater recently built by the inmates. I will never forget the way they cheered loudly, whistling and clapping, while rooting for "the bad guys" against the cops. When the movie *Heat* was shown, the inmates were delirious during the gun battle scenes, applauding as the thieves shot their way to freedom with all that cash. Robert DeNiro was hailed as the gang's leader, but poor Al Pacino, playing a cop, lost most of the points he had earned when he played the role of Michael Corleone. We were a tough audience. It reminded me of how upset Nicky Scarfo became after he learned that Pacino was cast as Serpico.

One night as the movie started, a copyright warning flashed on the screen saying the FBI would prosecute anyone convicted of violating the criminal statute. For some unknown reason I yelled, "Fuck the FBI." With that just about all of the other 250 moviegoers chanted, "Fuck the FBI, fuck the FBI." This went on for about ten minutes. The theater rocked that night. Everyone including the guard on duty laughed before we settled down and watched and cheered as Kevin Spacey, in an Academy Award–winning performance, made sure Kaiser Sosa got away with it in *The Usual Suspects*. Just think, Nicky Scarfo's boat and a movie with the same name.

Besides the occasional movie, weekend card games, morning trips around the track, visits to the weight room, and several hours a day doing my thing as a jailhouse lawyer, I managed to read a couple of hours a night before going to sleep. I read most of the contemporary popular authors and many of the classics, some for the second time. Looking back now I wonder why I did not read as much when I was a free man. I have the same thought about all the physical training I stepped up at Nellis.

Soon I found myself considering the evils of smoking two packs of cigarettes a day. What good was all this self-improvement doing me while I was poisoning myself with each drag I took? Cold turkey was the only way to go. I did it. For six weeks I tossed and turned in my small bed, agonizing with severe stomach pains, the result of tobacco withdrawal. I promised myself I would never have to go through that again. To this day I have kept that promise. I cannot take any credit for giving up alcohol. It goes without saying there's no booze for the residents of federal penal institutions, no happy hour hosted by the warden. No matter, the news of my first win was soon to arrive in the afternoon mail, and believe me, that was intoxicating enough. Well, almost.

One of my fellow inmates, a resident of Boulder City, just outside of Vegas, was sentenced to 30 months in prison and ordered to forfeit the sum of $89,000 to our government. This was the result of a guilty plea entered before the United States District Court in Las Vegas. When I reviewed his legal file, I noticed that the written judgment and commitment order listed both the 30-month period of incarceration and the forfeiture order in the amount of $89,000. However, when I read the stenographer's notes of the sentencing hearing, I was surprised to observe that the judge failed to verbally order forfeiture at the time of sentencing.

I argued in the motion and brief that the fact that the judge subsequently added the forfeiture order to the written judgment did not cure his error in failing to verbally order it when the defendant was present in court. My fellow inmate and three other lawyers who examined his file overlooked this problem with the sentence. Fortunately for him, I caught the error and the Ninth Circuit Court of Appeals agreed with me, vacating and striking the forfeiture order. In so doing the appellate court stated, "The only sentence that is legally cognizable is the actual oral pronouncement in the presence of the defendant." The court added it was too late to bring the defendant back to court to verbally impose the forfeiture order.

I was thrilled that one of us just saved the substantial sum of $89,000. But to tell the truth, I felt even better knowing that I was now a little closer to getting even with those bastards in the Justice Department. In a matter of a few hours the good news traveled throughout the prison. The next day more than the usual number of new "clients" approached me with their thick legal files in hand. I was looking forward to the action.

Within weeks of my first win as a jailhouse lawyer, I helped another inmate by getting eleven months knocked off his sentence. That may not sound like a big deal, but when someone is locked up in prison looking forward to freedom, even eleven days is a hell of a long time.

In this case, rather than file a formal motion and brief, I wrote a letter to the sentencing judge, and then had the inmate sign it. This inmate, covered with more tattoos than Dennis Rodman, was initially arrested by local authorities in southern California and charged with possession of a gun. Later the Feds charged him with illegal possession of the same gun by a convicted felon.

The state court judge had sentenced him to three years in prison. Shortly thereafter he was given a consecutive five-year sentence in federal court. After reviewing the man's paperwork, I searched the law books and found a case very much on point. In an earlier decision the United States Court of Appeals for the Ninth Circuit held that someone who is being sentenced in federal court should be given some credit for state time when some of the same conduct is involved in both crimes. In this case the possession element was included in both the state and federal crimes.

When we mailed the letter to the federal judge we enclosed a copy of the decision. The judge, to his credit, acknowledged that he had failed to give the defendant the credit to which he was entitled. Within days of reading my letter and the case, the judge had the inmate brought back to court for resentencing to a term eleven months shorter than before.

For the next couple of weeks I did not have to bother with shopping at the commissary. Canned foods, pretzels, fruit, ice cream, salsa, chips, and whatever other goodies were on sale mysteriously appeared on my bunk. A grateful, smiling man also gave me a tight hug and whispered the address of the best tattoo parlor in San Diego as he departed from Nellis almost a year earlier than he anticipated.

Six months or so into my sentence I switched jobs. I moved to the Officers Club on the base, where I helped set tables for lunch and banquets. The guys who worked at the club ate the same food as America's best pilots. It was pretty good, but I still missed the fine food served in Philadelphia's great restaurants—probably not as healthy, but certainly tastier. By then I had filed several motions attacking the validity of convictions of some of my fellow inmates. The courts were taking their time in moving these cases along. Prosecutors usually ignored the motions unless and until a judge ordered them to file an answer. Sometimes it took many, many months to get a favorable decision. These delays often kept prisoners in jail when they really were entitled to their freedom.

I recall waiting months for judges to act after I filed motions in a couple of cases that involved a change and lowering of the federal sentencing guidelines. The lowering of the guidelines in these cases sometimes required the immediate release of inmates. The good news was that they were out earlier than their original sentence mandated; the bad news was that these men had been illegally held for months. Who knows how long they might have been incarcerated had it not been for my actions and those of the other former lawyers (now inmates) who kept after the authorities.

I changed jobs again, returning to the camp where I could get back to my regular routine: walking, exercising, reading, writing, researching law, and doing whatever was necessary to perform my job or fake it as best I could.

During these times I often wondered how Nicky Scarfo was doing in the super-max prison, locked up 23 hours a day. How Lillian Reis was making out with her beloved Junior locked away in some faraway federal joint. I thought about my other clients and how they were doing without me. Who was taking care of them? At least I did not need to worry about my kids. I could speak to them on the phone every day and they visited me twice a month. They were doing just fine.

Scott and Kim visited as often as they were allowed. While I was on "vacation" my daughter met, fell in love with, and married a U.S. Air Force sergeant who was stationed at Nellis Air Force Base. Soon after my homecoming, they made me a proud grandfather for the first time. Adam Ikehara, my grandson, makes it all worthwhile. Talk about turning a negative into a positive.

I received several visits from friends. Gigi Bulgarino, a native Philadelphian and former roofer, came to see me on just about every other weekend. He had been living in Vegas for many years. Vince Pileggi surprised me about half a dozen times, stopping at Las Vegas on his way to Palm Springs, his winter home. We spent many hours talking and laughing about the good times we had drinking, betting horses, and playing golf. He broke up when I told him I had this problem—"fast women and slow horses."

Jennifer flew out to see the blackjack tables and me at least four times. It was nice to look at and talk to a beautiful woman. I'll never take that for granted again. Howard Landa, a former standout high school and college basketball player from Philadelphia, shocked me with his visit. I hadn't seen him in over 30 years. He had just been fired as head coach of UNLV's troubled basketball team despite the fact that he was the only one of three coaches to have a winning record the season after Jerry Tarkanian left. Harry Gratz and Dave Levy, both good friends, also made the long trip a couple of times just to say hello. Those few friends who went out of their way to visit me will always be appreciated and never forgotten.

In December 1995, the United States Supreme Court decided an important case relating to criminal law and the legal definition of "use" of a firearm during commission of a drug offense. There were scores of inmates confined in Nellis as a result of having been convicted of drug crimes. Many of these were caught with various amounts of marijuana or cocaine and a firearm that happened to be stashed in the same closet or car trunk as the drugs. Under the law before this new Supreme Court decision, judges were required to give a consecutive sentence for use of a firearm while committing a drug offense. Several guys at Nellis were doing extra time as a result of this.

I obtained a copy of the new case and studied every word of it. When I was confident that I totally understood the decision and its ramifications, I started to review files of inmates who might be able to take advantage of the ruling. Before the decision, "use" of a firearm included mere possession of a gun if found close to the drugs. The Supreme Court now said that close proximity to drugs alone is insufficient to show the gun was "used." The Court went on to say there must be proof that the gun was actively employed by being brandished, displayed, bartered, used to strike, or fired. The decision let stand the proposition that one carrying a gun would still be criminally liable. The Supreme Court's action was small consolation for the inequities of the recent and ridiculously severe federal sentencing guidelines.

I prepared motions to vacate convictions in three cases where inmates had completed their sentences except for the time they were doing for violating the law against use of a firearm while involved in a drug crime, usually possession of a controlled substance. Two of the men were looking at doing a few more years in prison. The third guy had approximately one year left to do. In each case I not only quoted the new law in my motion and brief, I asked the judges to issue an order releasing the defendant "forthwith." I was thrilled when in a matter of less than 48 hours the paperwork came ordering the immediate release of two of the inmates. One of these was a roommate, good-looking Steve from L.A. He was released so fast we did not have time to give him the standard going-home party. I was pleased to note that the judge ordered that Steve be released "forthwith."

I did not give up on my third guy. After I finished my sentence, while working in a Philadelphia law office, I hounded the Texas judge for three weeks until he reluctantly signed an order releasing him. In each of these cases the inmate had already served more time than the crime justified.

A young man in his early twenties approached me one evening in the law library and asked me to read his paperwork. I took his file and told him to get back to me in a few days. After all, neither of us was going anywhere.

I learned that this kid started serving a 36-month sentence for mail fraud about six months before. He pled guilty. All ten of his co-defendants, who were also co-conspirators, received much lighter sentences, ranging from 6 to 18 months, despite the fact that they went to trial before a jury that convicted them.

I investigated further and obtained all the paperwork on the co-defendants' cases. It seemed that their lawyers filed a motion to reduce the amount of financial loss attributed to their clients. They convinced the court that the amount of the fraudulent loss was substantially less than the prosecutor claimed. The young man's lawyer neglected to speak to other counsel or check with the clerk's office to learn that there had been a motion and a favorable ruling. Had he done so the sentence of his client would have only been about a year rather than three. Within two months the motion and brief I prepared helped this lad gain his freedom and cut approximately two years off his sentence.

There were so many inmates serving excessive sentences at Nellis that I could not help but wonder how many other poor souls there were in all the other prisons throughout the country. I do not know who is more responsible, the incompetent defense lawyer or the overzealous prosecutor. There are just not enough qualified and dedicated criminal lawyers. To make matters worse, the government keeps going after guys like Bruce Cutler, Oscar Goodman, and me just to make it easier for them to deny justice.

I will never forget the incident when I wrote a letter to a prosecutor to help an inmate reduce his restitution by way of settlement. After the government accepted the offer, the inmate thanked me and asked, "Bobby, what's your favorite dessert?"

I answered, "Lemon meringue pie."

That night when I opened my locker I found a large, luscious, whole pie, which my roommates and I shared along with a few laughs. It was a few days before my release, so the timing could not have been better. It always amazed me how bringing in contraband was child's play for some of the seasoned drug smugglers in our midst. Whole turkeys would suddenly appear, and once even a barbecued pig, complete with an apple stuffed in its mouth. Equally amazing were the sometimes laughable lapses in security. I remember the time we were watching a fight on television, Tyson slugging his way to the top at one of the Vegas hotel-casinos. How we howled when the camera panned to show some of our fellow inmates cheering away in the audience.

When I left Nellis, some of the guys wished me well, and others asked my advice about their cases. I could not say no; you see, it's in my blood. I walked out the same door that I first entered 26 months earlier, but I was a lot healthier and wiser. I could not conceal my broad grin as I thought about how many times I was able to help others in the same boat seek and obtain a little justice. I now looked forward to freedom and to continuing the never-ending struggle.

Four months after my release to a halfway house, I was expelled, like some grammar school student, for a minor infraction and sent directly to jail. I was not allowed to pass go and pick up the usual two hundred. Anyone else having dinner instead of watching the compulsory movie would lose one of his passes for an evening or at most a weekend. They sent me to Fairton

Federal Correctional Institute. And if that was not enough, I was placed into "the hole" where I would still be if it were not for attorney Hope Lefeber and Judge Stewart Dalzell. The inspiration I drew from the books I had read helped me endure a most horrible and unexpected experience, living in solitary confinement, where I remained incommunicado for about a week.

The judge responded to the petition Hope filed on my behalf and prevented the prison officials from retaliating against me for obtaining a court order prohibiting the Federal Bureau of Prisons from shipping me back out west by bus. Thanks to Hope and Judge Dalzell, I was released from solitary confinement where I was deprived of my blood pressure medication, fresh air and sunshine, showers, exercise, and phone calls. Judge James Giles had ignored my handwritten pleas for relief.

On August 1, 1997, I was released from prison after serving the maximum time inside, the last two months upstate in Minersville Prison Camp. My life had come full circle. I was back in Schuylkill County, the scene of my first big win. Funny how all the local hacks and inmates remembered Lillian Reis, the case, and me. When Lillian and I beat the *Saturday Evening Post* years ago, the large verdict was the reason the magazine fired their law firm, Pepper & Hamilton—coincidentally, Judge Giles' former employer.

I was free but on probation under the supervision of both Judge Giles and Judge Dalzell. I filed for permission to travel to New Jersey to perform some of the duties relating to my job as a paralegal and to visit Jennifer. I also asked if I might be exempted from reporting a list of clients of my employer, Chuck Peruto, Jr., who had criminal records. Judge Dalzell granted my requests. Judge Giles said, "Denied. If Mr. Simone can't comply with his conditions of probation, he should get another job." He added, "He may obtain permission to travel to New Jersey only if he has to visit a sick relative." No matter, I lost the job and the girl, although Chuck did go out of his way to get me started with a job, an office, and a car.

Presently I am planning to apply for restoration of my license to practice law. Now that my probation has been terminated, there are no restraints on the filing of the necessary moving papers. Should my application for reinstatement be denied, I will continue to work as a legal consultant on criminal cases, some of them high-profile with stakes to match. And so the fight continues, even if for now I am only an understudy, working behind the scenes, helping where I can. If my application is granted, I will return to the courtroom the way a hungry fish returns to water, and you can bet I will be swimming against the current.

EPILOGUE

A "potato chip gangster" by the name of John Veasey admitted to government agents that he shot and killed Michael Ciancaglini and wounded Joey Merlino. Veasey struck an easy deal with the federal prosecutors. No surprise that they accepted him with open arms. Naturally, he claimed that John Stanfa, the rumored successor of Nicodemo Scarfo, had ordered the hit.

Veasey had to know before he pulled the trigger that if he got caught, he could readily make a deal for a light sentence. The likes of Caramandi, DelGiorno, Gravano, and Leonetti showed him the way. Today's criminals have little or no fear that they will suffer severe punishment if they commit a serious crime. They will either get away with it, or if caught, buy their way out of prison by testifying against one of the government's prime targets. I had been preaching this for years, but my words often fell on deaf ears.

Within the last year or so the boss of the Philadelphia mob joined the ranks of the Philadelphia Rat Society. Ralph Natale is a former union leader and president of the Culinary Workers Union in South Jersey. Knowing Ralph, I suspect he is now organizing a large group of stool pigeons from the East Coast with the intention of forming a national union and collecting millions in dues. At the same time he manages to duck a life sentence for several murders.

On the other hand, Philip Leonetti is enjoying himself cruising on a small yacht somewhere in the tropics. Why not? He's got his uncle's fortune and if that's not enough he can always tap Uncle Sam, who is more than willing to give him your hard-earned tax dollars. When Leonetti was interviewed on *Prime Time Live* in the mid-nineties, he showed absolutely no remorse. He thought his murders were acceptable since he killed only "bad people." He likened his conduct to that of a soldier fighting for his country "in Saudi Arabia, Vietnam, or Bosnia." To make matters worse, FBI agents said on the same broadcast that they felt "bad," because they couldn't deliver everything they promised to Leonetti, such as phony documents to help him conceal his true identity. The FBI now admits that one of its agents physically aided Philip Leonetti's mother in carrying the safe out of the Scarfo compound when her son went into the Witness Protection Program. I have reason to believe there was in excess of a million dollars in the safe. The FBI claims they never opened and looked in the safe since they did not have probable cause to do so. Give me a break!

Nicholas "The Crow" Caramandi and Tommy DelGiorno are living in separate cities somewhere in the United States. The two of them and Leonetti go by assumed names. All this at the expense of American taxpayers. How would you like to have any one of them as your next-door neighbor? Maybe you already do. Imagine how those unsuspecting citizens in Arizona felt when they learned that the neighbor who was selling their kids the designer drug Ecstasy was none other than 19-time slayer Sammy "The Bull" Gravano.

Angelo Bruno, Philip and Sal Testa, Frank Sindone, Chickie Narducci, John McCullough, Saul Kane, and many of my other former clients are dead. Nicodemo Scarfo, Chuckie Merlino, Joseph Ciancaglini, Faffy Iannarella, Sal Scafidi, Ralph Staino, the Narducci brothers, Noah Robinson, Bobby Bellavia, and several others are buried in prisons. The reputations of all these men for loyalty and honesty remain intact. "So what?" one might say. Well, compared to the rats, informers, snitches, and stool pigeons, the men who refused to turn on their friends can at the very least get a good night's sleep. And if they were sent to prison, then they didn't get to sell drugs to neighborhood children like Gravano or kill people like the two Boston informants written about in *Black Mass*.

I believe that the responsibility for the inequities and injustices that occur does not lie solely with the informants. The fault must be shared with the agents who offer the deals, the prosecutors who deliver the packages, the juries who buy the lies, and finally the judges who by releasing the real criminals, sanction these outrageous deals. While this situation continues to worsen there is hope that the tide can be turned, that the battle can be won. Whether it is from the sidelines or the courtroom, from the corner or the center of the ring, or just by my written or spoken words, rest assured I will be part of the fight.

PARTIAL LIST OF SUPPORTING PLAYERS

▼

Honorable Marvin Aspen. Federal court judge in Chicago. Presided over El Rukns–Noah Robinson case. Wrote scholarly opinion on severance and later reversed convictions, citing prosecutorial misconduct.

Honorable Louis C. Bechtle. Former Chief Judge of the U.S. District Court for the Eastern District of Pennsylvania in Philadelphia. Presided over many trials when Simone represented defendants, including the Silvio Iannuccio case.

Diane Beloff. Leland's wife. Co-defendant with husband in vote fraud case. Pleaded guilty to misdemeanor charge. Subsequently graduated from University of Pennsylvania's Wharton School. Now owns an upscale women's clothing store, Toby Lerner.

Honorable Emanuel Beloff. State court judge. Lee Beloff's father. Dismissed perjury charges.

Leland Beloff. Politician, former Democratic ward leader, state representative, and Philadelphia City Councilman. Refused government's offer of prison release in exchange for testimony against Simone. Sentenced to ten years in Rouse case and concurrent time in vote fraud case. Now owns and operates a nursing home.

John Berkery. Former neighbor and friend who was charged and convicted of Pottsville burglary but was later cleared.

Jerry Blavat. Radio personality and disc jockey. Owner of Memories nightclub in Margate, New Jersey. Friend of alleged organized crime figures and well-known entertainers.

Jeffrey Blitz. Atlantic City prosecutor in the Falcone murder case.

Stanley Branche. Former president of Chester branch of NAACP. Close friend and drinking buddy. Also worked as investigator and often testified on behalf of Simone.

Sidney Brooks. Arsonist, burglar, and scam artist. Testified against Simone and others for leniency.

Honorable Stanley Brotman. Federal court judge in Camden, New Jersey. Presided over Scarfo's gun case and several trials in which the jury acquitted Simone's clients. Told U.S. prosecutors to stop harassing Simone.

Angelo Bruno. The "Godfather" of the Philadelphia–South Jersey area for over 20 years. Often referred to as "The Docile Don." Murdered in front of his house.

Eugene "Gigi" Bulgarino. Lived in Las Vegas for many years. Visited Simone every other weekend at Nellis Federal Prison Camp for over two years.

Antonio "Tony Bananas" Caponigro. Reputed to be responsible for planning and ordering the Angelo Bruno hit. His body was found in the Bronx, New York. He was beaten and shot and $20 bills were stuffed in his rectum.

Nicholas "The Crow" Caramandi. Killer, drug dealer, and thief. Testified against Scarfo and later Simone in exchange for freedom and several hundred thousand dollars.

Rita Carr. Second wife. Met in 1975 in Miami, Florida, married in 1980. Constant traveling companion to Caribbean and other locations. Divorce finalized in 1994.

Barbara Christie. Assistant District Attorney who tried the Sal Testa and John McCullough murder cases.

Joseph "Chickie" Ciancaglini. Close friend and associate of Frank Sindone. Frequent traveling companion on Vegas trips. Convicted in two separate RICO trials.

William Couples. FBI agent who took part in Simone's perjury trial and handled informant David Kurzband.

Bruce Cutler, Esq. Friend. Attorney for John Gotti. Co-counsel in Chicago RICO trial.

Frank "Flowers" D'Alfonso. Friend and associate of Angelo Bruno. Ran gambling junkets to London. Shot and killed close to his home.

Honorable Stewart Dalzell. Federal court judge. Presided over second tax case. Ordered concurrent sentence after guilty plea.

James "Jimmy Milan" DeBattista. Owned and managed the popular Jimmy's Milan restaurant. Refused to cooperate with government against Simone despite intense pressure to do so.

Anthony "Spike" DeGregorio. Friend of Ralph Staino, Nicholas Caramandi, and Frank Narducci, Sr. Later caretaker of Scarfo's Florida residence.

Thomas DelGiorno. Killer, major bookmaker, and loan shark. Testified against Scarfo and later Simone in exchange for freedom and several hundred thousand dollars.

Tyrone DeNittis. Former musician and entertainment manager. Associate of Harry Riccobene and Nick Scarfo.

Anthony DiSalvo. Co-defendant in RICO case. Longtime friend, drinking and traveling buddy.

Felix "Skinny Razor" DiTullio. Friend and associate of Angelo Bruno. Loved golf and owned the Friendly Lounge in South Philly.

Larry Feinstein. Office manager/investigator. Key defense witness in first tax trial.

Joel Friedman. Headed the United States Justice Department's Philadelphia Strike Force.

Honorable John P. Fullam. Federal court judge. Trial judge in Rouse case. Sentenced Beloff, Rego, and Scarfo to prison terms. Refused government's request to disqualify Simone.

Barbara "B.J." Futty. Second and last loyal secretary. Frequently testified as defense witness on Simone's behalf.

Honorable John Geary. Former Chief Judge of the U.S. District Court of New Jersey. Presided over many trials when juries acquitted. Came to courtroom to hear jury acquit Simone.

Honorable James T. Giles. Federal court judge. Reversed Simone's jury verdict of $1.15 million against Golden Nugget at precisely the wrong time. Presided at RICO trial and sentenced Simone to four years in prison.

Gary Glazer. Former Assistant U.S. Attorney who prosecuted and lost Simone's first criminal tax case.

Oscar Goodman, Esq. Friend. Represented Lee Beloff and Philip Leonetti. Mayor of Las Vegas.

Joseph and Salvatore "Wayne" Grande. Brothers convicted in RICO prosecution. Wayne became an informant in an unrelated drug case while in prison.

Charles "Joey" Grant. Assistant District Attorney who tried the first D'Alfonso murder case.

Barry Gross. One of two Assistant U.S. Attorneys at the Scarfo drug trial.

Honorable John Hannum III. Federal court judge. Sat on Luther Fleck case and sentenced George Martorano to life without parole. Testified as character witness in tax case.

Edward Harrell. Former captain in Philadelphia Police Department. Investigator and reliable expert witness.

Frank "Faffy" Iannarella. Friend and associate of Scarfo. Acquitted in two murder trials and a major drug prosecution, but convicted and sentenced to prison for RICO violations.

Charles "Charlie White" Iannece. Friend of Ciancaglini. Acquitted in murder and drug trials but convicted and sentenced to prison for RICO violations.

Kelly "Ike" Ikehara. Married Kimberly Simone while in the U.S. Air Force.

Kimberly Simone Ikehara. Daughter. Now married to retired member of U.S. Air Force whom she met at Nellis Air Force Base, site of Nellis Federal Prison Camp. Mother of one child, Adam. Living in Las Vegas.

Carl "Pappy" Ippolito. Avoided prison in New Jersey for contempt as a result of winning his appeal. Subsequently, RICO charges were dismissed due to mental infirmities.

Edwin Jacobs, Esq. Friend. Co-counsel in RICO trial. Represented Philip Leonetti and Chuckie Merlino.

William Jahoda. Chicago bookmaker who became a wire-wearing federal informant and testified against others in exchange for leniency.

Jennifer. Met soon after the breakup of second marriage. Former friend and companion for many years, and a frequent visitor during Simone's incarceration.

Saul Kane. Friend from high school days. Moved to Atlantic City and opened a popular bar. Befriended Nick Scarfo and Philip Leonetti. Died in prison rather than cooperate.

Honorable Marvin Katz. Federal court judge. Presided in tax case acquittal.

Maximillian J. Klinger, Esq. Preceptor and first employer.

Jacob "Jake" Kossman, Esq. Friend and mentor. Represented his dear friend, Angelo Bruno.

David Kurzband. Con man and convicted scam artist. Wore a wire and testified against Simone.

Stephen LaCheen, Esq. Friend. Co-counsel in perjury trial. Represented Joseph Pungitore.

Hope Lefeber, Esq. Friend. Co-counsel in Scarfo RICO trial. Represented Simone at sentencing.

Philip Leonetti. Scarfo's nephew. Involved in at least a dozen murders. He claimed to be a good friend of Simone before testifying against him. Testified against many others, including John Gotti and Vincent "The Chin" Gigante in New York.

Michael Levy. One of two Assistant U.S. Attorneys at the Scarfo drug trial.

Michael Leyden. FBI agent who worked on Simone's RICO case, and often interrogated Leonetti.

Joseph Ligambi. Acquitted in the D'Alfonso murder trial, but served approximately eight years since he had been denied bail.

William Lynch. Former Assistant U.S. Attorney who prosecuted Simone and DiSalvo.

Robert Madden, Esq. Friend. Aided in defense of tax indictments. Represented Frank "Faffy" Iannarella.

James Maher. FBI agent who worked on many reputed organized crime cases.

Bill "Wally" Malone. Newspaper reporter for the *Philadelphia Daily News*. First met in Pottsville when he covered the Lillian Reis case.

Terri Marinari. Assistant U.S. Attorney who prosecuted Simone in the second tax case.

George "Cowboy" Martorano. Raymond's son. Serving a life sentence after his guilty plea in a drug case heard by Judge John Hannum.

Raymond "Long John" Martorano. Onetime associate of Angelo Bruno in the cigarette and vending machine business. Later a friend and associate of Philip Testa and Nick Scarfo. Won appeal after serving many years, reversing his conviction for the murder of John McCullough. Blames Simone for his son's life sentence. According to law enforcement sources, he wanted to have Simone killed.

John McCullough. Longtime friend, client, and drinking pal. Boss of the powerful roofers union. Tough as nails but earned the love and respect of his membership and friends due to his intense loyalty. Shot and killed in front of his wife.

Salvatore "Chuckie" Merlino. Longtime friend and associate of Scarfo and Philip Testa. Lawrence Merlino's older brother and Joey Merlino's father. Acquitted in two murder trials and a major drug prosecution, but convicted and sentenced to prison for RICO violations.

Marianne Micoli. First longtime, loyal secretary. Refused to testify falsely for government in tax trial.

Eugene "Gino" Milano. Flipped on the eve of the first D'Alfonso case and testified against Scarfo and others.

Honorable William Miller. New Jersey state court judge. Sat on Falcone murder trial.

Cecil B. Moore, Esq. President of Philadelphia branch of NAACP and criminal lawyer. Close friend and co-counsel in Altemose trial and several other cases.

Ronald Morretti. FBI agent who worked undercover investigating Simone.

Frank "Chickie" Narducci. Friend and associate of Bruno, Testa, and Scarfo. Operated card games and loved to gamble in Las Vegas. Shot and killed in back of his house on the way home from court.

Frank Jr. and Philip Narducci. Brothers convicted in RICO prosecution. Philip was cleared by a jury in the Frank D'Alfonso murder trial.

Honorable Thomas N. O'Neill. Federal court judge. Sat on drug importation case when jury acquitted Scarfo and four others. Presided when the Beloffs pleaded guilty to vote fraud charges.

Dolores "Cookie" Pagano. Former barber, married to Vincent Albert "Al Pajamas."

Vincent Albert "Al Pajamas" Pagano. Restaurant and bar owner. Longtime companion and husband of Dolores "Cookie." Convicted as an associate of John Stanfa in RICO case.

Lynn Panagakos. Attorney who assisted Lynch in prosecuting Simone and DiSalvo.

John Pastorella. Convicted drug dealer. Wore a wire when speaking with Caramandi. Witness in Scarfo RICO case.

Stuart Peim. Former Assistant U.S. Attorney who prosecuted and lost Simone's perjury trial.

Charles Peruto, Jr., Esq. Retained Simone as paralegal upon prison release.

Charles Peruto, Sr., Esq. Co-counsel in Altemose trial. One of many character witnesses.

Joseph Petrellis. Superior forensic photographer and expert witness.

Louis Pichini. Federal prosecutor in many of Simone's clients' trials.

Vincent Pileggi. Former beautician and restaurant owner. Golf and drinking buddy. Made several trips to Las Vegas to visit Simone in prison.

Vincent Ponzio. Builder and convicted drug dealer. After wearing a wire and making incriminating statements, he recanted and told the truth, clearing Simone and DiSalvo of loansharking and extortion counts.

Joseph and Anthony Pungitore. Brothers convicted in RICO prosecution. Friends and associates of Scarfo and Sal Testa.

Bobby Rego. Beloff's legislative aide. Drug dealer and shakedown artist. Testified against Simone.

Edward Reif, Esq. Friend, former partner, and often co-counsel.

Lillian Reis. Former chorus girl who was arrested for allegedly masterminding the "Pottsville heist" soon after she purchased a Philadelphia nightclub. The only defendant who did not go to prison. She was finally exonerated.

Harry "Little Harry," "Hunchback Harry" Riccobene. Longtime associate of alleged organized crime figures. Successfully fought off attempts on his life only to die in prison.

Mario "Sonny" Riccobene. Testified against his brother, "Little Harry." Shot and killed after leaving the Witness Protection Program.

Anita Rivkin-Carouthers, Esq. Friend. Co-counsel in Noah Robinson case in Chicago.

Noah Robinson. Chicago businessman tried for murder in South Carolina. Half-brother of Jesse Jackson.

Honorable Joseph Rodriguez. Federal court judge in Camden, New Jersey. Presided at perjury trial when jury acquitted.

Honorable Albert Sabo. State court judge. Presided at Salvatore Testa murder trial.

Joseph Salerno. Key witness in the Falcone murder case.

Joseph Santaguida, Esq. Friend and co-counsel in several "mob" trials.

James Santonastasi. Convicted drug dealer. Testified against Simone.

Salvatore "Torry" Scafidi. Acquitted of a murder charge despite eyewitness testimony, but later convicted in RICO trial.

Nicodemo Scarfo. According to the press, the FBI, and local police agencies, he became "Boss" of the Bruno family upon Testa's death. The subject of constant law enforcement surveillance and widespread prejudicial news reports which made it difficult, if not impossible, to receive a fair trial. Despite this he was acquitted in three major jury trials. Imprisoned for RICO violations, he refuses to give up hope of someday winning his freedom.

Sylvan Scolnick. Seven-hundred-pound master criminal. Testified against Simone and others for leniency.

Angelina Simone. Mother, raised three sons. Married in 1929, widowed in 1965, then spent most of her remaining years in Hallandale, Florida.

Arlene Feingold Simone. First wife and mother of two children. Divorced, lives in Miami.

Joseph F. Simone. Father, emigrated from Calabria, Italy. World War I veteran. Owned and operated restaurants and nightclubs.

Joseph T. Simone. Oldest brother. Now the family patriarch and a successful businessman.

Ronald C. Simone. Youngest of three brothers. Former Temple University quarterback.

Scott Simone. Son. Used to work in father's law office. Often traveled with him to see clients. Now in sales.

Frank Sindone. Acquitted twice of loansharking charges. Owned a steak shop and a restaurant, but his first passion was shooting craps in Las Vegas. Shot in the back of the head, his body was found in a trash bag in South Philly.

Arlen Specter. Former District Attorney of Philadelphia, now U.S. Senator.

Richard Sprague. Former leading trial lawyer in the Philadelphia District Attorney's office.

Ralph Staino, Jr. Longtime companion, later married to Lillian Reis. Charged and convicted of Pottsville burglary but subsequently cleared after serving time in prison. Acquitted of counterfeiting.

Bobby Stone. Owned and operated a jewelry store. Close friend to Frank Sindone and Nicky Scarfo. Loved to drink and gamble, often did so with Simone.

Philip Testa. Close friend and associate of Angelo Bruno. Anointed by the press and FBI to succeed Bruno. Killed by an explosive device at his front door.

Salvatore Testa. Philip Testa's son. Friend and associate of Scarfo. Shot and killed, his body was dumped on a roadside in New Jersey.

Steve Vento, Sr. Convicted drug dealer who unsuccessfully attempted to escape from prison to avenge his son's shooting. Testified against Scarfo and others.

Nicholas "Nick the Blade" Virgilio. Friend and neighbor of Scarfo in Atlantic City. Died in prison after having been convicted of RICO violations.

INDEX